THE EYES OF THE DESERT RATS

British Long Range Reconnaissance Operations in the North African Desert 1940–43

David Syrett

Foreword by David M. Glantz

Helion & Company Ltd

Helion & Company Limited
Unit 8 Amherst Business Centre
Budbrooke Road
Warwick
CV34 5WE
England
Tel. 01926 499619
Email: info@helion.co.uk
Website: www.helion.co.uk
X (formerly Twitter): @Helionbooks
Facebook: @HelionBooks
Visit our blog at https://helionbooks.wordpress.com/

Published by Helion & Company 2014. New edition published 2024. Reprinted in paperback 2026
Designed and typeset by Aspect Book Design (www.aspectbookdesign.com)
Cover designed by Paul Hewitt, Battlefield Design (www.battlefield-design.co.uk)
Text © Elena Frangakis-Syrett 2014, 2024
Images © as individually credited
Maps © Helion & Company Limited 2014. Maps designed by Paul Hewitt, Battlefield Design (http://www.battlefield-design.co.uk/)

ISBN 978-1-806721-31-3

British Library Cataloguing-in-Publication Data.
A catalogue record for this book is available from the British Library.

For details of other military history titles published by Helion & Company Limited, contact the above address, or visit our website: http://www.helion.co.uk

We always welcome receiving book proposals from prospective authors.

Contents

List of Maps

List of Photographs

Foreword

As relevant as it is today, this book was conceived in 1981, at a time when only the most perceptive observers could even imagine the mosaic of near constant warfare tormenting the Middle Eastern region today. David Syrett, whose past writings primarily addressed topics in British naval history, was then serving a year-long stint as John F. Morrison Professor of Military History at the Combat Studies Institute (CSI), an institute which served as the history department of the U.S. Army Command and General Staff College at Fort Leavenworth, Kansas. As the director of CSI's Research Committee, it was my responsibility to consult with the Morrison Professor to ensure he or she could contribute a written study to CSI's burgeoning publishing program on military historical topics of relevance to the U.S. Army. Normally, substantive studies produced by Morrison professors and other CSI faculty members were published as formal Leavenworth Papers or less formal CSI Research Surveys.

When David and I discussed appropriate topics for his research, he suggested desert warfare primarily because he believed, correctly as it turned out, that the Soviet invasion of Afghanistan, which had taken place about two years before, coupled with periodic Arab-Israeli wars, would likely ignite wider conflicts throughout the entire Middle East, in fact, in an emerging zone of instability stretching from the plains of western China to the Maghreb region of North Africa. How prescient David was! Ultimately, he refined his topic to include a detailed study of the operations by British Army Long Range Reconnaissance patrols in the vast hinterlands of North Africa during the first three years of World War II. Syrett, displaying uncommon tenacity combined with his well-honed research skills, attacked the topic with his usual vigor, travelling far and wide in search of materials on British Army desert operations. His research took him to the archives in London and Washington and to far-flung cites where soldiers practiced their desert operations. Evidencing his tenacity, his search for an elusive sun-compass used by soldiers to navigate desert wastes actually unearthed what was probably the last example of this instrument, somewhere in the deserts of Utah.

Ultimately, after a full year of research, David produced a long and substantive, if not definitive, study of desert operations. However, as luck would have it, he gave birth to his over 250-page manuscript at a time when its length, coupled with fiscal constraints, prevented its publication. I, being a historical pack-rat and appreciating the manuscript's value, kept a copy in my cellar in the hope it would see the light of day sometime in the future. At long last, years after David prepared his study and well after my retirement from the Army and David's untimely death that hoped-for moment finally materialized. Resolved to complete David's unfinished work, his widow, Elena, who had heard rumors about David's unfinished manuscript, approached me in an attempt to learn whether or not it still existed. It did and the rest is history.

Elena, without altering the format, contents, or conclusions of David's manuscript, has painstakingly edited and polished it into its present form. In addition to being a superb study of this oft-neglected aspect of British Army operations in North Africa, this study provides fresh insights into the nature of desert warfare, past, present, and future. While describing the obvious, it also reveals the peculiarities of this warfare often lost to modern armies. In short, the study is a virtual primer, useful to commanders and soldiers alike, as they ponder just how to operate, survive, and achieve victory in the most inhospitable circumstances of terrain and weather. At long last, this book can find its rightful place in the classroom of military courses and colleges and in the hands of those interested in the intricacies, complexities, and problems of military operations in desert regions. Most important, David's book, as was intended years ago at the time of its conception, can also save lives. For these reasons alone, its relevance is assured.

David M. Glantz
Carlisle, PA, 2013

Editorial Comments and Acknowledgements

As mentioned in the Foreword, this monograph was first conceived by my late husband whilst he was John F. Morrison Professor of Military History, at the U.S. Army Command and General Staff College at Fort Leavenworth, Kansas, in 1981-82. He continued working on it subsequently through to 1990 with periodic visits to the National Archives (previously known as the Public Record Office) at Kew, London. Following his unexpected and untimely death, in October 2004, it is my sad but necessary duty to take this monograph through its final stages of publication. This task would never have been possible without the invaluable help and advice of Colonel (Retired) David M. Glantz. I would further like to take here the opportunity to thank him for honoring my late husband's work by writing a Foreword to the publication. Furthermore, I would like to thank the staff of the Rosenthal Library of Queens College, City University of New York and, in particular, Mr. Manuel Sanudo and Ms Marianne Conti Stein for their assistance and diligence in helping me with my bibliographical queries. I would equally like to express my thanks to Ms Alice Chan of the Office of the Dean of Social Sciences of Queens College, City University of New York. Finally, I would like to thank Mr. Duncan Rogers of Helion for publishing the book and for all his kind cooperation and assistance.

Elena Frangakis-Syrett
New York, July 2013

Preface

This is the story of a small number of men from the British Empire and Commonwealth who explored and fought in the wilds of the deserts of Egypt, and Libya during the years 1917–1943. When this study was begun, it was envisioned as a thesis on the techniques employed by the men of the Long Range Desert Group to live in, travel across, and fight in the Western Desert during the North African campaign of 1940-43. But what began as a study of the techniques of a particular type of desert warfare soon evolved into a work of much greater scope and complexity.

It was quickly discovered that most of the methods the Long Range Desert Group used to exist and travel within the vast wastes of the Western Desert were first thought up by the Light Car Patrols during the Senussi campaign in World War I and then at the end of the war were forgotten. During the 1920's and 1930's, a small number of British soldiers and colonial civil servants in Egypt rediscovered the techniques of the Light Car Patrols for desert travel by motor vehicle and used them to explore unmapped regions of the deserts of western Egypt and the Sudan. When war broke out between Britain and Italy in 1940, three of these pre-war desert explorers—Ralph Bagnold, W.B. Kennedy Shaw, and P.A. Clayton—formed the Long Range Desert Group to undertake reconnaissance missions deep into the deserts of Egypt and Libya in order to forestall any Italian activities in southeastern Libya and southwestern Egypt. The capture of Kufra by the Free French and the operations of the Long Range Desert Group quickly forced the Italians out of southern Cyrenaica.

It was seen by various British headquarters that the Long Range Desert Group had the ability to penetrate with relative ease the deserts of Egypt and Libya. With the removal of the Italian threat in southwestern Libya, British commanders were confronted with the problem of how best to employ the Long Range Desert Group. Should the unit be used for long-range reconnaissance or for raiding behind enemy lines, or a combination of both? There was also some question about whether the Long Range Desert Group should be employed in conjunction with the main British Forces in Egypt and Libya fighting along the coast of the Mediterranean or as an independent unit operating alone at great distances from the main battlefields of North Africa. The problem of how best to use the Long Range Desert Group became even more difficult when the Special Air Service, a unit specializing in raiding, attached itself to the Long Range Desert Group.

When studying the operations of the Long Range Desert Group in the Western Desert, one is confronted with all the problems of command and control that small specialized elite units can present in the midst of a great war. The student of the operations of the Long Range Desert Group and the Special Air Service during the North African campaign of 1940-43 must understand the problems of policy, strategy, and tactics that the existence of these two elite reconnaissance and raiding units posed for the command structure. Which headquarters, for instance, should control units of this type—theater, army, corps, or some special headquarters outside of the regular chain of command? And how is a policy formed which reconciles the conflicting requirements of a raiding and reconnaissance unit? The British command in the Western Desert never satisfactorily answered these basic questions and many others, too. Nothing that one could call a theory or philosophy of irregular warfare ever emerged from higher headquarters concerning the operations of the Long Range Desert Group and the Special Air Service during the 1940-43 campaign in North Africa.

The tactics and techniques of the Long Range Desert Group and the Special Air Service are nevertheless of great interest to the student of military affairs. During the North African campaign, the Long Range Desert Group conducted almost every type of ground reconnaissance mission possible in desert warfare. Huge areas of the desert were explored and mapped, and the patrols of the Long Range Desert Group undertook topographical reconnaissance missions which required crossing hundreds, and in some cases thousands, of miles of desert. The Long Range Desert Group also conducted numerous reconnaissance operations to determine the strength and location of enemy forces. The men of the Long Range Desert Group became very skilled in the art of "road watching," that is, hiding for long periods of time near a road or track thought to be used by the enemy and making a detailed record of everything that passed up and down it. Probably never in the whole history of mechanized warfare has a unit become as skilled as the Long Range Desert Group in reconnaissance operations.

The Long Range Desert Group and the Special Air Service were in some respects very British organizations. Both were *ad hoc* units. Instead of being thought up, planned for, and organized by a staff, they were conceived and sold to General Headquarters, Middle East by two men—Major R.A. Bagnold and Lieutenant David Stirling. Both units were recruited for the most part through the "old boy" network and their commanders at times used personal connections to get men and equipment and to win support for their operations. The Long Range Desert Group was especially British in its organization by class and nationality. There was a guards patrol formed by members of the Coldstream and Scots Guards, a yeomanry patrol made up by members of British yeomanry cavalry regiments, and there were New Zealand patrols, as well as patrols made up of Rhodesians and men drawn from various British infantry regiments, and finally Indian patrols made up of men belonging to the Indian Army. The Special Air Service was formed along different lines. It was a hodgepodge of British, Free French, Commonwealth, and Jewish Palestinian soldiers. Despite its cosmopolitan makeup, however, the Special Air Service, especially when Stirling and Mayne were about, tended to treat some operations as British public school pranks with live ammunition.

The history of the Long Range Desert Group and the Special Air Service form an encyclopedia of raids, ambushes, and the like conducted behind enemy lines. These two units mined roads, and shot up enemy aircraft on the ground. One raid made by the Long Range Desert Group, in conjunction with the Free French, required travelling over four thousand miles of desert. The Special Air Service attacked enemy installations of all types, sometimes using units no larger than three or four men and once storming an airfield with as many as eighteen armed jeeps. Using every conceivable method, the Long Range Desert Group and the Special Air Service attacked the enemy again and again in his rear areas. A less resolute commander than Rommel probably could not have withstood the pounding that the Long Range Desert Group and the Special Air Service gave to the German and Italian rear areas during the North African campaign.

The Long Range Desert Group and the Special Air Service are extremely difficult to write about because they were not ordinary units, nor were they made up of ordinary men. These two units were elite because as a matter of course their members did extraordinary things. These were men for whom the heroic was commonplace, and their story might better be told by an ancient writer of epics than a modern day historian.

A Note on Place Names

There is a great deal of confusion about the spelling and usage of place names in the Western Desert. No two authorities agree on the spelling, or at times even on the names, of various towns and oases in Libya and Egypt. In 1982, for example, the National Geographic Society lists on a map four different names for the same place: Barce, Al Maj, Barca, and Barqa.[1] There is confusion even among the British who served in the Long Range Desert Group about the spelling of place names in Libya. David Lloyd Owen uses the name Giarobub;[2] while W.B. Kennedy Shaw calls the same place Jaghbub.[3] The British official history of the Second World War calls this oasis Jerabub,[4] and *Funk & Wagnalls Hammond World Atlas* covers itself by citing the place as "Jarabub (Jaghbub)."[5] Then there is the question of whether to use "Tobruk,"[6] "Tobruck,"[7] or "Tubruq."[8] These examples can be increased a hundredfold. The policy followed in this study was to attempt to use the place names and their spelling which the author, rightly or wrongly, concluded were used by the majority of the British Empire and Commonwealth forces during the 1940-43 campaign in the Western Desert. Inevitably, there will be a number of Arabists, Libyan nationalists, and veterans of the fighting in North Africa who will take exception to the author's usage and spelling of certain names.

---

1   The Historic Mediterranean, 800 B.C. to A.D. 1500, Cartographic Division, National Geographic Society, Dec. 1982.

2   David Lloyd Owen, *Providence Their Guide* (London: Harrap, 1980), p. 42.

3   W.B. Kennedy Shaw, *Long Range Desert Group* (London: Collins, 1945), p. 252.

4   I.S.O. Playfair, *Mediterranean and Middle East* (London: HMSC, 1956), vol. II, map II.

5   *Funk & Wagnalls Hammond World Atlas* (New York: Funk & Wagnalls, 1875), p. 38.

6   Lloyd Owen, *Providence*, p. 238.

7   TNA, CAB/44/151, f. 215.

8   The Historic Mediterranean.

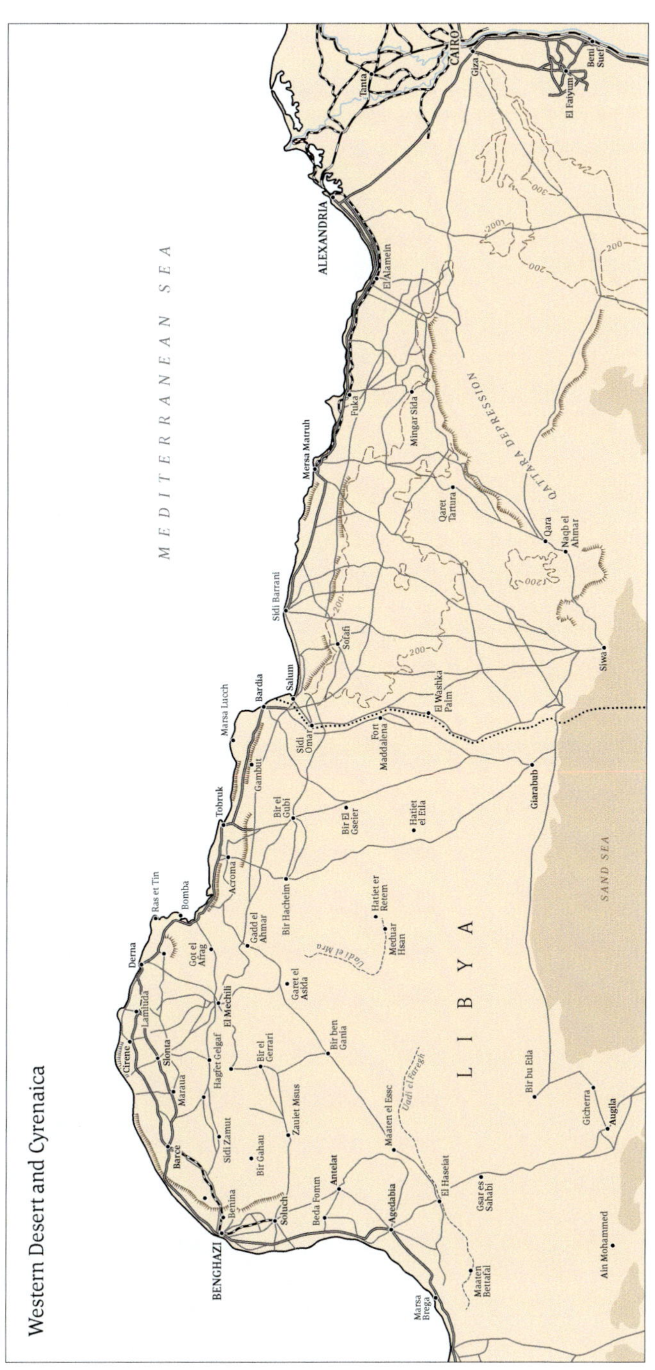

Map A. North-east Africa (TNA, CAB 44/151).

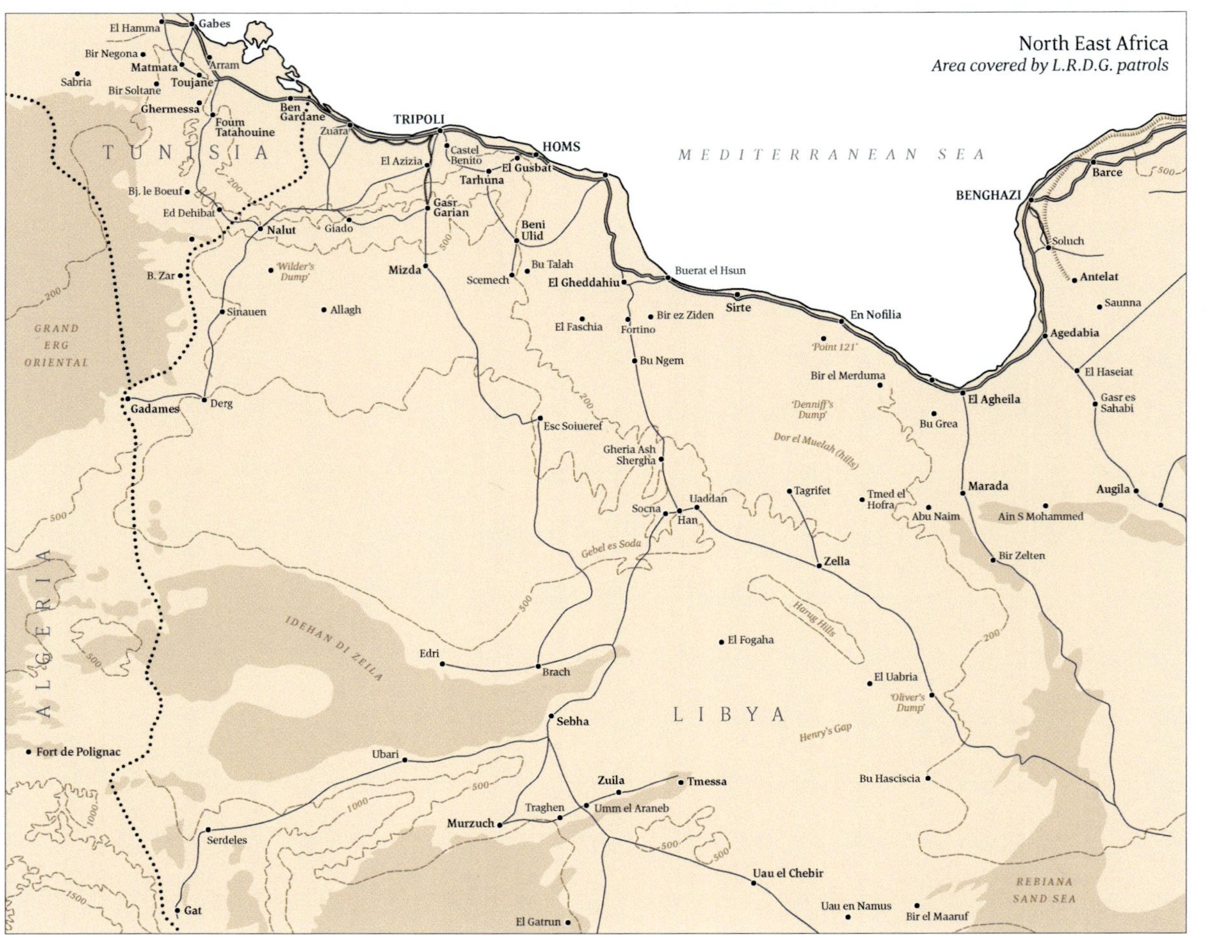

Map B. Western Desert and Cyrenaica (TNA, CAB 44/151).

1

The Western Desert

"The Desert: It's Different"
—S.L.A. Marshall, 1970

The great deserts of Egypt and Libya were called the Western Desert by the men of the British Empire and Commonwealth Forces who fought along the African coast of the Mediterranean Sea during the Second World War. The battles of the Second World War for control of North Africa were fought along the northern edge of the Western Desert, and at no time did large Axis or Allied forces venture more than sixty to a hundred miles south of the Mediterranean Sea. The average soldier never penetrated the depths of the great deserts of North Africa.

The Egyptian and Libyan Deserts are immense. The east side of the Egyptian Desert begins at the edge of the Nile River Valley and its western side merges with the Libyan Desert, which covers all of Libya and merges in the west with the Sahara Desert, the western limit of which is the Atlantic Ocean. The northern border of the Western Desert is the Mediterranean, and the desert runs for hundreds of miles southward into the Sudan and the Chad and almost as far south as equatorial Africa. The Western Desert is roughly the same size as the Indian subcontinent, and this vast expanse of desert is one of the harshest terrains in the world.

The Western Desert is arid but has a great variety of topography. There are mountains, hills, canyons, wadis, and areas peppered with sandstone, limestone, and volcanic rocks. Great and small salt marshes and brackish mud holes are also found in the Western Desert along with quicksand, rocky escarpments, and a few oases. There are also the great sand seas, which were long thought to be impassable in vehicles. W.B. Kennedy Shaw wrote of them:

There is nothing like these sand seas anywhere else in the world. Take an area the size of Ireland and cover it with sand. Go on pouring sand on it till it is two, three, four hundred feet deep. Then with a giant's rake score the sand into ridges and valleys running north-north-west and south-south-east, and with the ridges, at their highest, five hundred feet from trough to crest.

Late in the evening when the sands cool quickly and the dunes throw long shadows the Sand Sea is one of the most lovely things in the world; no words can properly describe the beauty of those sweeping curves of sand. At a summer midday when the sun beats down all its shapes to one flat glare of sand and the sand drift blows off the dune crests like the snow-plume off Everest, it is as good an imitation of Hell as one could devise.[1]

In marked contrast to the great sand seas, there are areas in the Western Desert which are so flat and firm that wheeled vehicles can be driven for hundreds of miles without having to change course. While varied in nature, the terrain of the Western Desert is some of the most difficult to cross in the entire world.

The climate of the Western Desert matches the terrain for harshness. During the day temperatures are hot—sometimes as high as 132 Fahrenheit; but at night especially during the winter, temperatures drop quickly and it can be very cold. The whole region is swept by hot, dry winds that often cause sand storms of such violence that all activity and movement is impossible. There are also sudden rain storms that can burn the desert into a bog and in a matter of minutes can transform wadis and canyons into flooded rushing rivers of water, mud, and rock which can carry away men and the largest of vehicles. In the Western Desert terrain and climate conspire to make the region one of the most difficult in the world for men to live and survive in. It is not an overstatement to say that one wrong move in the wilds of the Western Desert can cost a person his life.

In the desert there is eternal sand and dust. Everything is affected by sand and dust. It gets into food, clothing, and eyes, mouth, nose, ears, and hair. It wrecks machines, jams equipment, renders electronic components useless, and causes stoppages in weapons. Moving vehicles are followed by long tails of dust, and helicopter pilots are blinded by the dust and sand thrown up by the motors of their aircraft. In a sand storm so much sand is blown around with such force that

---

1   W.B. Kennedy Shaw, *Long Range Desert Group: The Story of its Work in Libya, 1940-1945* (London: Collins, 1945), p. 37.

sometimes paint is blasted off the windward side of a vehicle. Everywhere in the desert man has to contend with the problems caused by dust and sand.

Before the First World War almost nothing was known by Europeans, Egyptians, and most Libyans about the geography of the great deserts of Egypt and Libya. "To most Egyptians," even in 1982, "the desert remains a mystery. Few are familiar with its place names. Fewer still venture into it."[2] Except for a few desert Arabs, names such as Kufra and Uweinat were unknown to most people and shrouded with mystery to those few people who were familiar with them. Even Siwa, which is only several score of miles from the Mediterranean coast, was almost unknown until the First World War. During the nineteenth and early twentieth centuries the deserts west of the Nile were a blank on the map of Africa.

During the First World War, owing to military needs, some knowledge was gained of the geography of the Western Desert. Then in the 1920's and 1930's more knowledge of the deep desert was obtained by a handful of explorers; and during the Second World War, again because of military necessity, additional regions of deserts of Egypt and Libya were mapped. But it was not until the discovery of oil in the Libyan Desert and the use by the United States of pictures taken from satellites for mapmaking that the world gained detailed information about the geography of the interior of Egypt and Libya. Even nowadays, however, it is extremely difficult to obtain detailed large-scale maps of various sections of southern Libya. It was in the depths of the mostly unmapped and vast Egyptian and Libyan Deserts, with their harsh terrain and climate, that the Long Range Desert Group conducted military operations during the Second World War.

---

2   Farouk El-Baz, "Egypt's Desert of Promise," *National Geographic* 161 (Feb, 1982), p. 198.

2

The Great Unexplored Desert, Mechanization, and the Initials F.R.G.S. After Your Name

"As other people collect their poems and finally re-publish them, I have collected my travels."
"Travels among the ruins of desert kingdoms and the crocks and querns of prehistoric tribes; beyond them among creeping dunes, petrified forests and sand seas, beyond the last bone of man or of mouse; in places where nothing exists, no sprouting grass blade nor worm of decay; where perhaps in certain spots, nothing ever did exist; – travels shared, companions changing but ideas preserved; and over all a sense of what travel is, how it can be done with little pomp, little money, much love of it and very much preparation."
—*Major R.A. Bagnold, F.R.G.S.*

The historical roots of the Long Range Desert Group reach back to Egypt during the First World War and to an era when motor-driven vehicles were replacing camels and horses as a means of transport. It was during the Anglo-Senussi War of 1915-18 that most of the technology and methods of long-range travel across the desert by motor vehicles were first developed. The Light Car Patrols used during the Senussi War were the direct forerunners of the Long Range Desert Group.

In November 1915 the Senussi Arabs of Cyrenaica, aided and abetted by a number of Turkish officers, attacked British and Egyptian posts in the Western Desert of Egypt and captured the city of Salum on the coast. To counter these attacks, the British, in the middle of a great European war, mounted a nineteenth-century style punitive campaign, employing several thousand troops, in the Western

Desert. The British counter-attack smashed the military power of the Senussi in several months of fighting along the Mediterranean coast of western Egypt.[1]

The British campaign ended on 4 March 1916. On this day, as British cavalry entered Salum, the Duke of Westminster's Armoured Car Squadron was ordered to advance past Salum and to overtake and destroy the main body of the Senussi and their Ottoman Turkish advisers. The desert west of Salum is hard and flat and the heavy Rolls-Royce armored cars could at times move at speeds as high as 40 miles per hour. Soon after the British armored cars had passed Bir Wair, they encountered hundreds of armed Arabs fleeing westward mounted on camels and horses. The British armored cars drove on without firing a shot at the armed Arabs, for their objective was the Senussi main body and their Ottoman advisers. Undoubtedly, the Senussi leaders felt safe from attack, having put a day's march by horse and camel between themselves and the British; but twenty-five miles west of Salum the main body of the enemy was spotted by the British about a mile south of the main track. The Duke of Westminster's Armoured Car Squadron immediately charged the enemy. In the mad rush that followed, those few Turks who did not flee with the Senussi and attempted to resist were killed or wounded by the machine-guns mounted in the British armored cars. The chase lasted for another ten miles with the British armored cars gunning down fleeing Senussi mounted on camels and horses as they overtook them.[2] After being defeated by the British forces in northwest Egypt and then chased, overtaken, and shot up by the Duke of Westminster's Armoured Car Squadron, what remained of the Senussi forces melted into the deep desert.

The Senussi, although defeated in open battle in the Western Desert, still posed a military threat to Egypt. Based on oases such as Siwa, Farafra, Dakhla, Bahariya, and Kharga in the Western Desert, the Senussi could mount raids against the Nile Valley. The main defense in western Egypt from Senussi attack was the Imperial Camel Corps, which was established in 1915 with men drawn mostly from Australian units along with some men from the New Zealand forces and from British yeomanry and territorial units.[3] It was the task of the Imperial Camel Corps to patrol the Western Desert and to protect the Nile Valley from groups of raiding Senussi. The employment of troops mounted on camels in desert warfare

---

1   E.E. Evans-Pritchard, *The Senussi of Cyrenaica* (Oxford: The Clarendon Press, 1954), pp. 127-128.

2   S.C. Rolls, *Steel Chariots in the Desert* (London: Jonathan Cape, 1937).

3   See Geoffry Inchald, *Imperial Camel Corps* (London: Johnson, 1970).

has a long history;[4] but because of the great distance between British bases along the Nile River, the Imperial Camel Corps introduced patrols using American-made Ford cars in place of camels. These car-borne patrols were known as Light Car patrols. While the range of a camel-mounted patrol was measured in tens of miles, patrols using Fords covered hundreds of miles of desert. The Light Car Patrols were so effective that the Senussis were not only completely cut off from the Nile Valley but also each oasis in the Western Desert of Egypt was isolated from the others. The Light Car Patrols' duties were arduous: heat, flies and endless miles of desert to cross, always with the chance of mechanical failure resulting in either a very hot and long walk, if one were lucky, or death.[5] In 1917 the British military authorities in Egypt put an end to the Senussi War using Light Car Patrols, armored cars, the Imperial Camel Corps, and other British forces to seize control of and to occupy oases in the Western Desert used as bases by the Senussi.[6] After the end of the Senussi War, however, and even after Armistice Day, the Light Car patrols continued to operate in the Western Desert.

The officers and men of the Light Car Patrols in the Western Desert were the first to develop the techniques of long-range travel in the deep desert by motor vehicle. On 25 January 1917 Dr. John Ball, who worked for the Survey of Egypt and was himself a notable desert explorer, wrote a handbook for Light Car Patrol officers doing surveying work in the Western Desert. In this document, which is based in part upon information supplied by several officers of the Light Car Patrols, Ball explains most of the techniques later used by explorers in the 1920's and 1930's to penetrate the Western Desert by motor vehicle, techniques that would also be used by the Long Range Desert Group in the years 1940-43.

Ball's handbook begins with a discussion of the advantages and disadvantages of using motor vehicles in the desert as opposed to camels, the traditional method of desert travel. Well up into the 1930's, desert travelers engaged in violent arguments over the pros and cons of camel and motor transport in the desert. Even among Europeans, the belief that animal transport in the desert was better than the motor vehicle died very slowly. Orde Wingate, a radical on almost everything, in 1933 used camels in a one-man expedition into the Western Desert in search of the lost oasis of Zerzura;[7] and as late as the spring of 1940 the British shipped a whole

---

4   George MacMunn and Cyril Falls, *History of the Great War: Military Operations in Egypt and Palestine* (London: HMSO, 1928), p. 138.

5   For a first hand account of the operations of the Light Car Patrols, see Royal Geographical Society Manuscripts, C.H. Williams, "Light Car Patrols in the Libyan Desert." (1918).

6   MacMunn and Falls, *History of the Great War*, pp. 139-145.

7   Orde Wingate, "In Search of Zerzura," *The Geographical Journal* 83 (April, 1934), pp. 281-307.

division of horsed cavalry to the Middle East.[8] Ball's position on the question of the relative value of camels as opposed to motor vehicles as a means of desert transport is slightly in favor camels. He argues that while camels are a lot slower than motor vehicles, they can cross terrain which is impassable in wheeled vehicles. Also, more men are required when traveling by motor vehicle because at least six to eight men are needed to push a vehicle out when it becomes stuck in soft ground. The need for these extra men, their food, and kit reduces the amount of cargo that can be carried by each vehicle. Further drawbacks are that some of these men have to be skilled mechanics capable of repairing broken down vehicles and finally that the range of motor vehicles in the desert is limited by the amount of fuel they can carry. As for camels, Ball wrote that one does not have to carry much camel food, and men who know how to handle camels are easy to find in the Middle East and do not cost much to hire.

> An explorer who makes use of camels ... can load up with all necessary provisions and kit and say farewell to civilization for months at a stretch; and he is not worried in his work by a perpetual fear that the state of his supplies may render a return impossible if he delays for a day at a place in order to carry out some observations which may be necessary to make certain of his position.[9]

However, Ball was a realist and knew that because of their speed motor vehicles would not be replaced by camels in the military, where speed is often everything. Ball thus discusses the subject of the "Management of Motor-Cars on Desert Patrols" in some detail. He thought that American-made Ford vehicles were the best for work in the desert because they were the least liable to break down while crossing rough terrain. To be fit for use in the desert, however, the Ford had to be modified by removing all unnecessary parts, such as cabs. Also, to avoid water loss when radiators boiled over, each vehicle had to be fitted with a condenser. Ball explains that this could easily be done by running a metal tube from the radiator outlet to a two-gallon tin can mounted on the running board of the vehicle. The two-gallon can would be half filled with water and the tube would extend under the surface of the water in the can, however, the whole system had to be airtight in order to work. When the radiator boiled over, the steam would be forced out of

---

8   I.S.O. Playfair, *The Mediterranean and Middle East* (London: HMSO, 1954), Vol. 1, p. 104.

9   Royal Geographical Society, John Ball, "Desert Reconnaissance by Motor-Car: Primarily a Handbook for Patrol-Officers in West Egypt," 25 Jan. 1917, pp. 2-4.

the radiator into the can, where it would be condensed. The vacuum created in the radiator would then draw the condensed water in the can back into the radiator. Ball calculated that under average conditions a Ford fitted with a condenser would lose only two gallons of water per hundred miles. In order to cool the engine, during the day, the metal hood had to be removed from each vehicle and then replaced at night. During the winter months, before replacing the hood, the engine and battery had to be covered with a blanket to prevent them from getting wet from dew. Ball gives his recommendation concerning the best size for a motor-car patrol; each patrol should consist of two Ford cars carrying three people and two light Ford trucks, each able to carry 850 pounds including the driver, for a total of four vehicles and eight men in each patrol. As for the skills required for desert driving, Ball says that these can only be gained by experience. He does, however, give the following advice concerning soft or upward sloping ground:

> It should be taken at full speed on the high gear as far as possible, only putting in the low gear when the speed slackens considerably, and returning to high gear as soon as sufficient acceleration has been obtained. Stopping anywhere but on hard and slightly elevated ground should be avoided; and getting into the ruts of a preceding car is dangerous if the ground is at all soft. A car will frequently go without difficulty on virgin ground, but will stick if the same ground has been ploughed up by other cars.[10]

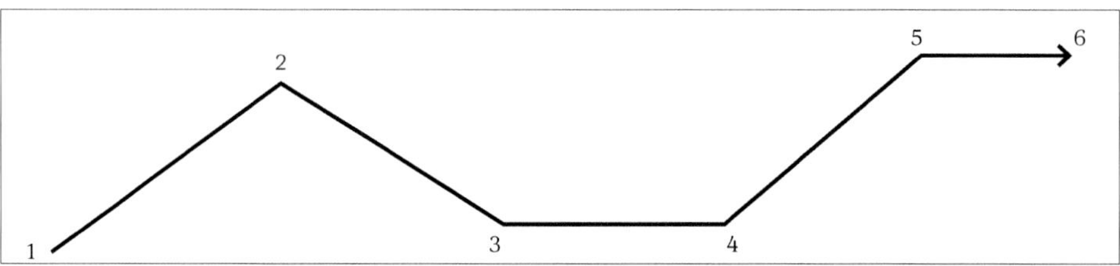

On the subject of desert navigation, Ball goes into considerable detail on what he calls "Traversing," which is dead reckoning navigation when there is no object on which to take a bearing. A "traverse" is a continuous series of straight line courses, beginning at a known position, with each leg of the course being measured for distance. If the measurements of the direction of each bearing and the length of each leg of the course are correctly plotted, then at the end of the entire movement

10   *Ibid*, pp. 5-7.

a person can figure out his new position relative to the known starting point. The ability to do this kind of navigation depends greatly on the skill of the navigator and can be gained only through experience. It also depends on the accuracy of one's compass and the odometer on the vehicle.

Since nothing is perfect machined, it is necessary to find the average error in a vehicle's odometer by driving three or four times over a measured course on average desert ground. Once the average error of a vehicle's odometer is known, this figure is then used to calculate the true distance a vehicle has travelled over each leg of a course or traverse. This is extremely important: for, as Ball points out, if 935 meters on the odometer equals a true distance of 1,000 meters, then after a run of 100 miles, if not compensated for, there would be an error of 7 miles.[11] A navigator had also to watch out for false distance being put on the odometer by wheels spinning in the sand and the like.

On the subject of compasses, Ball further points out that "An error of a single degree in the bearing of a line will displace the further end of the line by nearly two percent...."[12] If one is using an ordinary prismatic compass, a bearing should be taken at least ten yards in front of the vehicle in order to avoid the magnetic disturbance caused by the vehicle and its load; and to ensure greater accuracy a compass mounted on a tripod should be used instead of a hand-held one. Moreover, the bearing should be taken more than once and by two different people.

Ball further explained how to use the primitive sun compass that was invented by a Lieutenant Williams of the Light Car Patrols. This sun compass consisted of a horizontal light colored piece of sheet iron fixed to the dashboard of a vehicle; and mounted vertically in the middle of this sheet iron plate there was a metal needle about three inches high. Attached to the base of the needle was a piece of sheet similar in shape to a compass needle, which could be rotated about the axis of the vertical needle.

The use of the dial is to enable a straight course to be steered towards a distant point, even when that point is invisible over a great part of the course. At starting, a bearing is taken to the distant point and the car is started in the required direction. Immediately after starting, the needle is moved till the shadow of the style cast by the sun falls on it; and during the remainder of the run the car is steered so as to keep the shadow on the needle.[13]

---

11   *Ibid*, pp. 8-12.
12   *Ibid*, p. 12.
13   *Ibid*, p. 13.

The obvious weakness of this primitive type of sun compass was that there was no way to systematically adjust the sun compass as the sun moved across the sky;[14] however, this problem was overcome very quickly as more sophisticated types of sun compasses came into use.

Ball covers such problems as obtaining the longitude and latitude of a position and how to correct compass variations. He says that in order to find the latitude, that is, how far north or south of the equator a position is to within half a mile, and true bearings within one twentieth of a degree, all that is required is to know how to find the North Star or the Southern Cross and how to take a sight on one of these stars with a theodolite, which is an instrument for measuring horizontal and vertical angles. Then, by applying some very simple math to the problem, it is possible to arrive at the correct position. To find the variation of a compass, one should compare the bearing given by the compass needle to the bearing of the North Star or the Southern Cross at their meridian passage. The difference between the two bearings is in fact the difference between true north and magnetic north. On the subject of longitude—namely, how far east or west a position is from the Greenwich meridian—Ball explains how to find the longitude of a place if one can see a landmark with a known longitude. However, Ball begs off the problem of finding the longitude of a position not within sight of a mark with a known longitude, by saying, "arrangements may be made for selected patrol—officers to obtain special instruction...."[15] The reason for this is that finding a longitude involves such things as radio time fixes or chronometers, tables, and the like.

From Ball's "Desert Reconnaissance by Motor-Car" it is very clear that as early as the beginning of 1917 the officers of the Light Car Patrols had discovered the basic techniques that were later to be employed by explorers and the Long Range Desert Group to penetrate by motor vehicle far into the Western Desert. In fact, the only major piece of equipment not known to the Light Car Patrols was a sand channel. In the months after the end of the First World War, however, the Light Car Patrols slowly were disbanded, and it would be up to others to refine the methods of desert travel by motor vehicle developed by the British in response to the problems of the Senussi War.

When Captain Ralph Alger Bagnold, Royal Corps of Signals, arrived in Cairo for the first time in October 1925, there was nothing in his background to indicate that he would become one of the great desert explorers of the twentieth century. Bagnold had been educated at the Royal Military College, Woolwich, and

14   *Ibid*, pp. 12-14.
15   *Ibid*, pp. 34-46.

Cambridge University. Commissioned in the Royal Engineers in 1915, Bagnold served on the Western Front during the First World War, in Ireland during the "Troubles," and in 1920 transferred to the Royal Corps of Signals. The Royal Engineers, Signals, and Tanks had a common officers' mess at the British base of Abbassia, just outside Cairo. The 3rd Armoured Car Company represented the Royal Tank Corps at Abbassia and among the officers of the unit were several who had served with the Duke of Westminster's Armoured Car Squadron in the Western Desert during the First World War. One of these officers, who had served with the Duke of Westminster, was Lieutenant A.J. Bather. Bather had been stationed with a section of armored cars for a year at Salum which had served as a base for the Light Car patrols and armored cars during the Senussi War. After the Senussi had been driven out of Salum, the city reverted back to its old status as the starting point for the old caravan routes to the oases of Siwa, Jarabub, and Kufra in the unknown desert to the south. Salum was also where Hassanein Bey began his famous trip across the desert from the Mediterranean to the Sudan.[16] While at Salum, Bather alone of all the officers who served in the Western Desert fell in love with it.

When Bather was transferred to Cairo in 1924, he brought to the mess at Abbassia his attraction to the desert. Bather knew little more about the Light Car Patrols' techniques of desert travel than that their first rule was never to go anywhere off the beaten track with less than two vehicles; for if one vehicle broke down beyond repair, there was always a second one to get the party out of the desert. Bather knew nothing about condensers and sun compasses. The few cars that the officers at the Abbassia mess owned were cheap English-made ones and which were unsuitable for desert work, but Bather owned a Ford car, which he modified for desert use. Lieutenant V.C. Holland, Royal Corps of Signals, soon fell under Bather's influence and was bitten by the desert bug. Holland bought a Ford car and had it modified for desert travel too. At Christmas time, in 1924, Bather and Holland spent a week driving around the desert, near Patridge's Dunes, and both officers had a great deal of fun. Both before and during this trip, Bather taught Holland some of the methods and techniques used by the Light Car Patrols for desert travel. Soon after this trip, however, Bather lost interest in the desert; and he returned to Britain in the winter of 1925.

When Bagnold arrived at the officers' mess at Abbassia, he soon discovered that Holland shared his interest in ancient Egypt, which naturally led to trips to the

---

16   Ahmed Hassanein Bey, "Through Kufra to Darfur," *The Geographical Journal* 64/4 (Oct, 1924), pp. 273-291.

pyramids and then to other ruins not usually seen by tourists. Within a very short time, Bagnold had fallen in love with desert travel, and he too, bought a Ford car and modified it for desert use. He and Holland, accompanied by a few other officers from the mess at Abbassia, began to take longer and longer trips in the desert, on both sides of the Nile Valley, in search of more ruins and other interesting sights, such as the abandoned railroad stations of the disused Cairo-Suez Railroad. At other times Bagnold and Holland simply played with their two Fords to see what kind of ground they could go over. Both men looked on this as "a new game"; but as their desert driving skills increased, they discovered that the Ford cars could go over just about any type of country except soft sand. It was not long before Bagnold and Holland exhausted their interest in trips around Cairo and the Nile Valley.[17]

In 1926 Bagnold and Holland undertook their first really long trip, going from Cairo across the Sinai Peninsula and Transjordan and then back to Cairo. For this trip, Bagnold and Holland made very careful and complete plans as well as preparations. Food, fuel, spare car parts, extra tyres, and the like were obtained ahead; for both men were working on the principle that an expedition had to have the means to return, after reaching, or almost reaching its objective, by the same way that it had come. This was because there was always the possibility that an expedition might get within a few miles of its objective only to find the way blocked by impassable sand or a flooded region; therefore, it must have the means to return by the same route it had come without being resupplied.

In March 1926 Bagnold and Holland, with three other officers—one of whom had a large Harley Davidson motorcycle—from the mess at Abbassia, left Cairo in two Fords to cross the Sinai to Palestine. The first day was spent getting across the Suez Canal and finding the line of stone cairns which marked the track to Mitla Pass. Locating the ferry to cross the canal and convincing a local policeman that they had the correct permits to enter the Sinai delayed them considerably, and it was not until dark that they found the cairns. The next day, some miles east of the canal, the party was confronted with a belt of sand drifts, which had to be crossed.

It got very hot. The ground rose steadily mile after mile, and our engines boiled. The sand was now everywhere, in yellow undulating cushions with only a few streaks of grey ground left exposed. The sand all looked the same; but sometimes it was hard like the floor below while at others one could see where the tracks of previous cars had ploughed in deep. The only way to

---

17   Ralph A. Bagnold, *Libyan Sands: Travels in a Dead World* (London: Hodder and Stoughton, 1942), pp. 11-24.

take that sort was to fly at it with open throttle, gripping the steering wheel with all one's might. The car seemed bewitched, squirming and wriggling sideways quite out of control. Often a car would arrive at the far side of one of these drifts broadside on; often we could not hold the steering wheel at all, and the front wheels would lock round, pulling the car up dead in a cloud of sand.[18]

Hour after hour, under the desert sun, the five men drove, pushed, and dug out the two Fords as they moved at a slow rate across the sand towards the base of the mountains where the Mitla Pass is located. In the early afternoon, with the help of some Bedouin, the party managed to get the two Fords onto a track strewn with large rocks. Bagnold wrote of this part of the trip:

All that afternoon we bumped and wriggled up a valley, over rocks, in and out of steep-sided watercourses, rising gently for twenty-five miles till at last the head of the Mitla Pass was reached, and we looked out eastwards over the central plateau of Sinai. I never dreamed that cars could twist and bend to such an extent. Sometimes it seemed as if the front and back axles were at right angles to one another.[19]

After reaching the top of the Mitla Pass, the rest of the trip was easy. Bagnold, Holland, and the others drove to Jerusalem on a disused military road constructed by the Ottomans during the First World War. They then proceeded to the Dead Sea, across the Allenby Bridge to Amman in Transjordan, and on to the ruins of Jerash, and then back to Cairo. This trip had covered over a thousand miles, had taken ten days, and had cost only four or five pounds a head, exclusive of the cost of buying the two Fords.[20] From this first trip across the Sinai, Bagnold and Holland learned a number of lessons. One of them one that motorcycles were useless because they were unsuited for crossing very rocky ground, and did not carry enough to pay their way. Another was that the size of the party had to be increased to six in order to have enough men to push a car caught in the sand; however, this would mean that a third Ford car would have to be found. Finally, they decided that some methods had to be devised for crossing deep sand and traveling along very rocky tracks.

---

18   Bagnold, *Libyan Sands*, pp. 27-28.
19   *Ibid*, pp. 28-29.
20   *Ibid*, pp. 25-30.

Bagnold and Holland managed to recruit Lieutenant E. Bader of the Sappers into their ranks. Bader in turn bought a Ford car, too, which was then modified for desert travel. As a means of crossing sand drifts, Bagnold and Holland obtained some twenty yard-long rolls of "rabbit wire," or chicken wire. These were to be unrolled in front of a vehicle in soft sand to give it traction. After several unsuccessful attempts to make portable metal ramps to be laid like bridges when crossing rocky regions, such as the track leading up to the Mitla Pass, Bader discovered in one of the used iron shops in Cairo some "strong rolled-steel troughing designed in the war for roofing dogouts."[21] The second crossing of the Sinai was so much easier than the first, however, that the lengths of steel troughing were never used and were brought back to Abbassia, where they sat in the mess garage for three years until it was discovered that they made very good sand channels.

On 26 December 1926, Bagnold, Holland, Bader, and three other officers crossed the Suez Canal in three Ford cars and headed eastward into the Sinai. When the expedition reached the sand drifts, it was found that

The wire netting saved a great deal of pushing and digging in the sand beyond, though it was by no means an ideal method of progress, and was very slow. Each time a car got stuck, the two lengths of wire were unlashed from the top of the car that happened to be carrying them, unrolled and laid out side by side in front of the front wheels. With everyone pushing behind, the car was moved bit by bit with the back wheels spinning in the sand, till at last it was far enough forward for the back wheels to catch on the rear edge of the wire. There was then something for them to pull against, for the wire was held firmly down by the weight of the front wheels; and if the front wheels had not by that time skidded sideways off the wire, the car would usually take charge and run along the wire, gathering speed as it went. That was what was supposed to happen. Often, in practice, though, since the wire was springy and as it had to be carried tightly rolled up on the cars, it would jump up after it was laid out, just at the critical moment when a car was about to reach it, and roll itself up again. After a car had been over it, and when we wanted to roll it up, it was of course much distorted and very difficult to roll.[22]

---

21   *Ibid*, p. 36.
22   *Ibid*, pp. 37-38.

With the assistance of the wire netting, the expedition was able to get through the belt of sand in the approaches to the Mitla Pass in only three hours and arrived at Nekhl by noon, having traveled in a half day a distance that took more than two days during the first crossing of the Sinai. After leaving Nekhl, the expedition drove due east across the Sinai plateau to the cliffs west of Aqaba. The six British officers found a very narrow road leading down the two thousand foot high cliffs. This road had been built at the beginning of the 19th century by the Khedive Muhammad Ali and his son Ibrahim to enable them to march their army to Arabia. Since then, the road had been unused and forgotten; however, even with a gradient of 1 in 3 and a precipice on one side, the party was able to move the cars down this road cut into the side of the cliff and then they easily reached Aqaba. After leaving Aqaba, the expedition went north along the track to Maan. The terrain was difficult and Holland's car, being the oldest and most battered, broke down on several occasions, and at other times one or the other of the cars had to be pushed out of sand using the wire netting. Nevertheless, the six British officers and their Fords reached Maan in one day. The next day they set off to take a look at the ruins at Petra and then drove on to Amman. At Amman the cars needed to be repaired. There were mercifully only a few regularly recurring mechanical problems with the Ford cars, such as broken main springs and worn out brake bands. After the Fords were repaired, the expedition returned to Cairo by the same route taken on the first trip and reached the base at Abbassia ten days after having left it.[23]

During 1927, Bagnold made two more trips into the Sinai. In April 1927, Bagnold, Holland, Bader, and three other officers crossed the Suez Canal and instead of heading east across the Sinai turned south along the western shore of the peninsula. Armed with a map and an old guide book, which Holland had found somewhere in Cairo, the expedition drove down the west side of Sinai to the southern tip of the peninsula and then back to Cairo. Following this expedition, during the 1927 Christmas leave, Bagnold, Holland, and Guy Prendergast, a Royal Tank Corps officer and a future commander of the Long Range Desert Group, made a last trip across the Sinai into Palestine and then back to Cairo. Of the two trips, it was the expedition to the southern end of the Sinai Peninsula which was the most significant; for it was the first time that the group did something that no one else had ever done before. They drove to the southern end of the Sinai Peninsula by motor vehicle. The success of the trip to the tip of the Sinai Peninsula produced in Bagnold and some of the others a real desire to open up other new desert routes for travel by motor vehicle. Also, the trip to the southern Sinai required a different

---

23   *Ibid*, pp. 31-54.

type of planning than those across the Sinai into Palestine and Transjordan. In the Sinai, unlike Palestine and Transjordan, there was no place to obtain fuel for the cars and, therefore, they had to plan to carry enough of everything with them to complete the trip without being resupplied. This requirement forced Bagnold, Holland, and Bader to take another look at their capacity for desert travel by Ford car. They now had some idea of what the Fords could do, and thus could calculate the consumption of fuel in terms of miles and types of terrain to be crossed and figure out how far they could go without refueling. They came to the conclusion that, except for water, the Ford cars could carry enough fuel, food, spare parts, and the like to be able to run for a thousand miles or ten days. If the cars could go for a thousand miles, or for ten days, then why not attempt something in the Western Desert, such as reaching Siwa Oasis by a new route directly across the desert, south of the Qattara Depression, from Cairo? [24]

Before attempting to reach Siwa overland directly across the desert from Cairo, Bagnold's group had, nevertheless, to solve several problems. In 1927 Bagnold, Holland, Bader, and Prendergast were fairly young men and in some respects comparatively new to Egypt. They apparently did not know Ball, nor had they read his paper "Desert Reconnaissance by Motor-Car," and their knowledge of the techniques employed by the Light Car Patrols was limited to what Holland had learned from Bather in 1924. During the trip down the western side of the Sinai Peninsula in April, the Fords' radiators had repeatedly boiled over and as much as two gallons of water per car per day was lost. In the Sinai this did not make much difference because water could be found about every thirty or so miles, but in the Western Desert there was no sure source of water for hundreds of miles. Bagnold and Bader, after several attempts, solved the problem of radiators boiling over by reinventing the type of condensers which were used by the Light Car Patrols and described by Ball in his 1917 memorandum. In fact, the Bagnold-Bader condenser system was better than the ones that had been used by the Light Car Patrols because it did not lose any water.

Bagnold later admitted that the possibility of getting lost made him somewhat "afraid" of the Western Desert. The Sinai, Palestine, and Transjordan might have harsh terrain, but they also had places in them which were known, such as Mount Sinai and the Mitla Pass, whereas most of the Western Desert was a blank on the map and consisted of mile after mile of the same seemingly unchanging topography. Moreover, the Light Car Patrols' methods of navigating by dead reckoning with a sun compass had been forgotten. Bagnold had experimented with

---

24   *Ibid,* pp. 55-63.

a regular prismatic compass and had found that it was not much use for navigating a motor vehicle across the desert. In September 1927 Bagnold, while returning from setting up an advanced dump of water and fuel some one hundred and twenty miles out in the Western Desert from Cairo, discovered that he could navigate by the stars and he concluded that if one could navigate by the stars, then why not by the sun. In the event, Bagnold designed a sun compass which, as was the case with the condenser, was a better design than the one that had been used by the Light Car Patrols; for it could be adjusted systematically as the sun crossed the sky.[25] By the end of September, Bagnold had had a sun compass made and had successfully tested the instrument. In so doing, he found that,

> To steer a course, all that is necessary is to keep the sharp black shadow of the needle on the required figure on the dial, which, if silvered or painted white, shows up even if the sunlight is partly obscured by thin cloud.[26]

On the first day of the expedition from Cairo to Siwa, Bagnold, Bader, Prendergast, and three other officers had reached a point a hundred miles west of the Nile, where they made camp for the night. After having made four trips across and into the Sinai, the process of making camp for the night had become a routine. Bagnold, Bader, and Prendergast, who were the drivers, checked out the cars and made any repairs required; while Captain V.F. Craig, M.C., of the Royal Engineers, who was in charge of provisions, decided what the evening meal would be. According to Bagnold, Craig "had a special sense of food" learned while serving in Siberia during Koltchak's War.[27] Water was rationed and used only for drinking and cooking. They drank mostly tea, except at midday when each man was issued a pint of water mixed with lime juice. Both water and fuel were stored in two gallon tin cans bolted along the running boards of each car. Additional fuel was carried in four gallon tins crated up in wooded cases. About one case of fuel was used per car per hundred miles, so by the end of the day there were several empty fuel cans and their crates available. The tin cans were used as tables and seats and then abandoned, and the wooden crates were broken up and used as firewood. Although they still carried around a gasoline stove, the cooking was done on a stove made out of a four gallon fuel can with the top cut off and a hole made at the bottom on one side for stoking the fire with bits of packing crates. It was found that the

---

25   *Ibid*, pp. 64-71.
26   *Ibid*, p. 71.
27   *Ibid*, pp. 74-75.

wood from one crate was more than enough fuel to do all the required cooking for the group. After a meal, each man cleaned his plate and other utensils with sand.

On the second day, twenty miles off their camp the night before, the expedition sighted the southern limit of the Ramak Dune Range, which was one hundred and twenty miles west of Cairo. This showed that Bagnold, who was doing the navigation with a sun compass, was only two miles off his dead reckoning position. One hundred and fifty miles were traveled on the second day as the expedition skirted the southern limits of the Ramak Dune Range. It was the first time that Bagnold had seen a sand sea, and probably it was here that he first became interested in the movement of sand. On the third day the six British officers passed the oasis town of Qara and pushed on for another seventy miles to Siwa. Only half a day was spent at Siwa; the next afternoon the group headed for the border of Libya, which was reached in two days, and then turned north for the coast and Salum. From Salum the six officers returned to Cairo by way of the coast road.[28]

At the beginning of 1928, Bagnold thought that his days of traveling through the deserts of the Near East were over, for he had been ordered to India. Bagnold had his belongings all packed and was ready to board a troop ship for India when, without warning, he was visited by N.D. Simpson of the Cotton Research Board. The government of Egypt had received a report that in the region of Bir Terfawi and Shebb, in Egypt, about three hundred miles southwest of Aswan, a swarm of locusts had been sighted, which could possibly descend on the Nile Valley. Nobody in Cairo had any idea what the terrain was like three hundred miles southwest of Aswan, nor did anyone know if there was enough vegetation there to support a swarm of locusts. Consequently, the government of Egypt ordered Simpson to organize, in four days' time, an expedition to that region to find out about the reported locusts. Simpson consulted personnel in the Survey of Egypt about the problem of finding the places where the locusts were reported to be. The Survey had no one available for such a job, but suggested that Simpson request from the British authorities for Bagnold to be made available to act as navigator. Bagnold, as he said, "naturally[…]jumped at the chance."[29]

In a mad rush, Simpson managed in only four days to obtain all the necessary equipment, kit, supplies, food, and maps from the government of Egypt. He also arranged for everything to be sent by train to Oasis Junction on the Nile. It was thought at the time that only six-wheeled trucks would be able to cross the sandy desert southwest of Kharga. The Renault Company had three demonstration six-

---

28   *Ibid*, pp. 72-87.
29   *Ibid*, p. 89.

wheeled trucks in Cairo, and Simpson bought them and all the necessary spare parts. The manager of the Renault Company in Cairo, M. Leblanc, said he would go on the expedition with two of his mechanics, if he could bring along his cook too! This was agreed to, but it was discovered that the Renaults could not be sent by train to Oasis Junction in time; however, the Renault Company agreed to drive the trucks three hundred and fifty miles over Egyptian country roads to Oasis Junction.

At 0400 on 18 January 1928, Bagnold and the other members of the expedition got off the Luxor Express at Oasis Junction, which got its name because it is where the narrow gage railway from Kharga Oasis meets the main north-south railway line in the Nile Valley. At daylight the three Renaults and all the equipment and supplies for the expedition were loaded onto the train to Kharga Oasis, and soon the narrow train was moving across the Nile Valley into the desert; fourteen hours later it had arrived at Kharga. The next day the group, consisting of Simpson, a botanist; F. Shaw and Mistakowi Effendi, entomologists; M. Leblanc with two mechanics, who also acted as drivers, and one cook; Flying Officer Thomas, R.A.F.; and Bagnold, who departed from Kharga. On the first day the expedition headed south-southwest for one hundred and fifty miles through a desert of sand and rocks. There was no sign of life of any type. While the northern part of the Western Desert was a blank space on the map, this desert was not even on the map. In fact, Bagnold had never seen a map of this part of Egypt until several days before he left Cairo, when he had met for the first time with Ball, –who was one of the few people who had ever been in this part of Egypt –, to learn what he could about the region. The following day the rocks disappeared, and

> Only a boundless sand-sheet remained, whose tiny ripples glided by without any perceptible vibration of the car. As the surface warmed up, a mirage, hovering in the distance, approached to within less than half a mile, began to surround us on every side like a vast sheet of steaming water. We were flies crawling across the upper surface of an almost submerged ball revolving slowly in a rough pool. During all the midday hours there was no land in sight, not even a horizon, for the mirage curled up into the sky—nothing but the sun and the blue disc above, and the sandy disc below, the two separated by a close wall of dazzling shimmer.[30]

---

30   *Ibid*, pp. 96-97.

That afternoon the expedition reached Bir Terfawi, a hollow with a waterhole and a few date palms sheltered by a group of tamarisk. The palms had been attacked by locusts, which had apparently recently flown away. Although the expedition had arrived too late at Bir Terfawi to catch and kill the locusts, this did not seem to trouble the naturalists; for, in Bagnold's words, "No one had botanised or bug-hunted before between Kharga and the Sudan frontier."[31] The next morning it rained, probably for the first time in scores of years. In the afternoon the expedition searched the region for miles around looking for locusts without success, and then headed southeast for Shebb, which was reached without difficulty. After a day or so of looking around Shebb and the surrounding desert, it was decided that there was not enough vegetation there to support a swarm of locusts and that they probably were headed for the Sudan. It was decided, therefore, to return directly to Kharga along the great slave traders' route, which was clearly marked all the way to Kharga with the bones of camels. When the expedition arrived at Kharga, Bagnold left it and went to India by way of Baghdad.[32]

The officers from the British base at Abbassia were not the only ones exploring the deserts of Egypt and the Sudan in the 1920's; there were others who would later play an important role in the formation and operations of the Long Range Desert Group. Around the time Bagnold was acting as navigator for the Egyptian government expedition in search of the disappearing locust swarm, W.B. Kennedy Shaw and Douglas Newbold, of the Sudan Forest and Civil Services respectively, made a thousand-mile-long expedition by camel into the unknown deserts of the western Sudan. Both Kennedy Shaw and Newbold would become well-known desert explorers and would later join Bagnold on one or more of his expeditions. Kennedy Shaw, the younger of the two, was educated at Oxford and was a botanist, who would later become an archeologist; throughout the North African campaign he served as the intelligence officer of the Long Range Desert Group. There was also Patrick Andrew Clayton, who was educated at the University of London, served as a gunner in the First World War, and from 1920 to 1938 was the inspector of Desert Surveys, Egypt. Clayton spent years driving around the Western Desert in Ford cars conducting surveys for the Egyptian government, and he influenced and advised Bagnold and others on techniques of desert travel.[33] When Italy declared war on Britain, Clayton helped form the Long Range Desert

---

31   *Ibid*, p. 99.

32   *Ibid*, pp. 88-107.

33   G.W. Murray, *Dare me to the Desert* (London: George Allen Unwin Ltd, 1967), pp. 127, 156, 159, 165, 175, 178, 179, 182, 183.

Group and served as a patrol commander until he was wounded and captured in 1941, during the first Allied attack on the oasis of Kufra.[34] By the late 1920's, Bagnold, Prendergast, Kennedy Shaw, and Clayton, the four men who would later organize and command the Long Range Desert Group during the North African campaign, had already gained considerable experience and expertise in desert travel by motor vehicle. During the 1930's, Bagnold would emerge as the acknowledged leader of the explorers of the Western Desert.

When Bagnold went to India in 1928 he thought he had left Egypt behind forever and was to start a new chapter in his life. But in the wilds of Waziristan on the Northwest Frontier, Bagnold found himself back among rocks, sand, and camels. It was a country similar to Egypt in some respects, but with a difference—anywhere he was permitted to go was populated, mapped, and known and, unlike Egypt, it was impossible to drive off into an unexplored desert. In the Western Desert there were still huge areas which were unmapped and unexplored. The more Bagnold thought about the experience that he and the other officers from Abbassia had gained in desert travel by car, the more he believed that this experience should be put to use exploring the Western Desert. There was a problem of logistics, however, for neither Bagnold nor his friends had the money to have dumps of fuel and water sent out beforehand. Such dumps were necessary because without pre-positioned dumps of fuel the Ford cars had only a range of about a thousand or so miles. At about the same time as Bagnold arrived in India, however, the first of a new type of Ford 30 cwt truck also appeared in the country. Bagnold inspected this vehicle and thought that, when loaded, it could get between twelve and fourteen miles to the gallon in the Western Desert. The use of two trucks of this type would increase the range of an expedition mounted from Cairo into the Western Desert to over two thousand miles. There were still other problems in organizing an expedition that had to be solved, such as, for instance, arranging for the officers in Egypt to get leave at the same time as Bagnold during the winter months. Moreover, an expedition of this nature was difficult to arrange and orchestrate by letter between two such distant places as Egypt and India.

In April of 1929, Imperial Airways began commercial service between Egypt and India. Bagnold flew to Egypt and was the second passenger to make the flight. In Cairo, "with the welcome help from influential quarters, Pharaoh's heart was so far softened," according to Bagnold, "that he let his people go—for a month!"[35]

---

34   After his capture in 1941, Clayton was awarded the DSO for his work with the Long Range Desert Group; and the Royal Geographical Society awarded him with its Founders Medal in recognition of the importance of his work in mapping the Western Desert.

35   Murray, *Dare Me*, p. 114.

While in Egypt, Bagnold and the other members of the party planned the expedition. Craig, as usual, would take care of provisions. Bagnold and Prendergast would each buy a 30 cwt Ford truck, and Captain R.G.L. Giblin, Royal Corps of Signals, would use his own Ford car. With the addition of two other officers, the expedition would consist of three vehicles and six men. They decided at this time to explore the eastern edge of the Great Sand Sea, which begins west of the Oases of Ain Dalla, Bir Aub Mungar, and Dakhla. Their objective was to see if there was any kind of passage through the sand sea to the Libyan Desert. There was no thought at this time of trying to cross the sea itself, with its huge dunes of sand. When most of the details had been worked out, Bagnold flew back to India.

When Bagnold returned to India, he bought at Rawalpindi a Ford 30 cwt truck without a body and had one made out of wood to his specifications. At the end of September, 1929, Bagnold and two other officers headed westward into Iran and drove to Cairo in Bagnold's new truck, arriving there at the end of October. This trip cost the three officers thirty-seven pounds each for food and fuel, much less than any other method of getting from India to Egypt, except perhaps by camel. The expedition to the edge of the Great Sand Sea was to be conducted more as a scientific expedition or for exploration than one for sightseeing or the pleasures of desert driving. Bagnold "was nervous of relying entirely on a dead-reckoning compass course to tell [...] where amongst the dunes [...] for by dead-reckoning alone one can never recover from an error once made."[36] The ability to know their true location was also necessary if the expedition was going to be one of exploration, too, for they could not use dead reckoning as a means of placing newly-discovered terrain features on the map. So all necessary equipment—a shortwave radio, a theodolite, and the tables required to find the latitude and longitude of a position by means of a star shot or fix—had to be obtained. The radio was put into a padded box mounted on the running board of Giblin's car. At the suggestion of Clayton, Giblin constructed a pair of "rope ladders made up with bamboo rungs lashed to light cords of stranded wire, for laying in front of his car in soft sand, in place of our usual rolls of wire netting."[37] And at the last minute, Prendergast decided to take along the two steel channels that Bader had bought in 1926 for crossing rocky areas but which had never been used.

When the expedition left Cairo, it was found that the loaded 30 cwt Ford trucks were not very good in the desert. In areas where Giblin's Ford car could move at will, the loaded trucks would get stuck. It was the two steel channels that made it

---

36   *Ibid*, p. 121.
37   *Ibid*, p. 122.

possible for the expedition to continue; for they proved to be the best means to get a vehicle stuck in the sand moving again. Every time a truck got stuck,

> ...the mode of operation was as follows. With our hands or with shovels sloping grooves were dug out between the front wheels and the back, reaching down to the lowest point of the back tyres sunk in the ground. In these grooves the channels were laid with their rearmost ends almost underneath the tyres. Then, when the clutch was let in, the back wheels at once began to grip firmly on the steel, on which they rolled forward easily up the slope. By the time the front ends of the channels were reached, the lorry had attained sufficient momentum to carry it on for some distance beyond. The great thing was to keep the speed up once it started moving.
>
> The whole procedure soon became a drill. Three would push behind while the remaining two waited one on each side to seize the half-buried channels as they emerged behind the struggling lorry, lift them up and run with them to overtake it as it went forward, and then throw them down in position just in front of the back wheels again, so that the lorry got a second forward impulse from them.[38]

At the rate of about sixty or seventy miles a day, the expedition proceeded westward across the desert towards the Great Sand Sea. But the continual running of the trucks in low gear ate up fuel at a far faster rate than expected, and the overheating of the truck engines caused a loss of water. A side trip of about one hundred miles north had to be made to get more water from Moghara Well. After this, the going became easier because the loads of the two trucks were now lighter, owing to the expenditure of gasoline, and also because the ground was firmer. Each day the expedition ran on a dead reckoning sun compass course. Each night the latitude and longitude of the expedition were obtained by taking a star shot. Bagnold's skill as a desert navigator had become so good that the dead reckoning position was rarely more than a mile off the position obtained by a star shot. The fixing of the expedition's position each night was very important because it gave Bagnold the ability to plot, on blank places on the map, the various terrain features they passed each day.

After what must have seemed like an endless journey across the Egyptian Desert, the expedition reached the edge of the Great Sand Sea. The desert they had

---

38   *Ibid*, pp. 123-124.

traveled over was flat, and the huge sand dunes of the Great Sand Sea seemed to rise up out of the ground like mountains. When they reached the base of the first dune, the six British officers climbed to the top of it on foot and saw ridge after ridge of sand dunes. Each dune appeared, however, to have a definite beginning and end to it, and there were gaps of hard surface desert between each dune. By running south for ten miles, the expedition was able to pass between two dunes, then a gap was found in the second row of dunes and passed through, but very quickly the expedition found itself stopped by a hundred foot high dune. Bagnold knew there were only two choices: turn back or attempt to drive right up the side of the sand dune. Bagnold decided to try the latter:

I increased speed to forty miles an hour, feeling like a small boy on a horse about to take his first big fence…. Suddenly the light doubled in strength as if more suns had been switched on. A huge glaring wall of yellow shot up high into the sky a yard in front of us. The lorry tipped violently backwards— and we rose as in a lift smoothly without vibration. We floated up and up on a yellow cloud. All the accustomed car movements had ceased; only the speedometer told us we were still moving fast. It was incredible. Instead of sticking deep in loose sand at the bottom as instinct and experience both foretold, we were now near the top a hundred feet above the ground. Then the skyline receded disclosing a smooth blank surface of some sort, nearly level. The glare was intense; one could distinguish nothing, but from the slow rolling movements of the lorry we must have been going over a series of gentle undulations.

I cut off the engine and let the car come to rest gently to wait for the others. The sand was covered with little ripples that had flown by too fast to be seen while the car was on the move. Our wheel tracks behind were barely half an inch deep; they trailed out behind cleanly like a pair of railway lines. Yet the sand was quite soft; I ran my fingers through it easily, and there was no surface crust to support the wheels. It was just the special way the grains were packed.

I remembered when for the first time a chance remark of Clayton's while describing his boundary commission trip two years previously, about running along the tops of some dunes instead of between them because it was easier.

Not understanding what he meant and thinking I had heard him wrong I had dismissed it without a thought.[39]

When the other vehicles had joined Bagnold on the top of the sand dune, the six British officers found that they were on top of a type of sand dune they had never seen before. It was almost flat and had no collapsing edges. The top of the dune was about half a mile wide, and the length formed a huge whaleback of sand which ran on and on as far as they could see. It was then found that one could drive very fast on top of a dune of this type, but there were also areas of soft sand into which one could sink a six foot rod without effort. "These 'liquid' pools were seldom more than a dozen yards wide, and often if one was driving fast enough the momentum would carry one through them...."[40] Prendergast discovered that if the pressure in his truck's tyres was reduced from ninety pounds to fifteen pounds, the performance of the vehicle was greatly improved. On the first day, either by going around the dunes or over the tops of the whale-backed dunes, the expedition had penetrated fifteen miles into the Great Sand Sea. Each mile was difficult going, but with every hour spent in the sand sea the skill of the drivers increased. On the third day, however, the expedition had to turn back because fuel and time were running short.

Getting out of the sand sea was comparatively easy because the wind had not destroyed their tracks, and the expedition very quickly reached the oasis of Ain Dalla. The group wanted to return to Cairo by way of the oases of Dakhla and Kharga, but after leaving Ain Dalla the transmission on Prendergast's truck broke down beyond repair. There were now two choices: continue on the planned route with two vehicles; or drive directly to Cairo, pick up a new transmission, return with it, repair Prendergast's truck, and then return to Cairo with all three vehicles. In the end it was decided to repair the truck, for to abandon it was looked upon the group as an act similar to abandoning one's wounded on the battlefield. Several things were learned from this expedition: the Great Sand Sea could indeed be crossed; however they had been caught short by the desert when it came to spare parts and the rate of consumption of fuel and water.[41]

By the third week in December, 1929, Bagnold was back on the Northwest Frontier of India; however, he was already thinking about mounting another

---

39   *Ibid*, pp. 128-129.

40   *Ibid*, p. 131.

41   Bagnold, *Libyan Sands*, pp. 112-138. See also, R.A. Bagnold, "Journeys in the Libyan Desert 1929 and 1930," *The Geographical Journal* 78 (July-Dec, 1931), pp. 13-19, 522-535.

expedition into the Great Sand Sea. Because of the policy of the military authorities on granting leave, however, only Bagnold and Prendergast could obtain leave for an expedition in 1930. Bagnold started a correspondence with Holland, who was in England, with the idea of having Holland find three people besides himself who were interested in and able to undertake an expedition into the Great Sand Sea. Bagnold was in fact taking part in putting down a rebellion on the Northwest Frontier, while he planned, by means of a three-way correspondence between England, Egypt, and the Northwest Frontier of India, an expedition into and across the Great Sand Sea of Egypt.[42]

During the summer of 1930, Holland enlisted Kennedy Shaw, who in turn brought on board Newbold, his companion during a 1927 camel trip in the desert of the Sudan. The sixth member was an officer of the Royal Corps of Signals who was stationed with Holland at Colchester. As the letters and cables passed back and forth between England, Egypt, and India, an ambitious but seemingly well-thought out scheme was put together. In the course of these preparations, Bagnold arranged to have five hundred gallons of fuel transported to Ain Dalla, and Kennedy Shaw had a smaller amount of fuel transported to Selima Oasis. The plan was to head west from Ain Dalla, cross the Great Sand Sea, then head south to Uweinat, then eastwards to Selima, and return to Cairo heading north by way of Asyut. The distance to be covered in the first stages of the trip was so great that it was decided to return to Ain Dalla to pick up more fuel and, after crossing the Great Sand Sea, to establish a third dump west of it.

Although Craig could not join the expedition because the army would not grant him leave, he organized all the provisions for the expedition. Prendergast obtained three Ford cars. He took off most of their bodies—hoods, mudguards, bumpers, cabs, and the like—to lighten the cars and also to make it easier to get at various parts of the vehicles to make repairs. All the stores and fuel were packed in boxes of the same shape and size. The new car bodies, which were made out of wood, were designed by Prendergast to hold an exact number of these boxes by length and breadth so that all the fuel and stores could be fitted tightly into the cars and would not jump around and break.

On 13 October 1930 the expedition left Cairo for Ain Dalla, and several days later, running west, reached the edge of the Great Sand Sea. When he saw the first large whaleback type of dune, Bagnold, as he later said,

---

42   Bagnold, *Libyan Sands*, pp. 139-141.

… went straight for it, keeping an interested eye on Newbold, who was by my side as navigator noting the compass bearings of our course and the mileage readings. I was sure he didn't really believe in this business of crossing dunes; it was against all the ideas of his sixteen years' service in Egypt and the Sudan. Everyone knew that cars were no good in soft sand. But the same performance as last year was repeated exactly. We arrived at the top and felt the same sensation of ballooning over the surface without apparent motion. "How did you know that was going to happen?" he asked in astonishment, and I could only answer, "because it happened on another dune sixty miles away last year."[43]

For several days the three cars moved across the Great Sand Sea heading west, either by going over the tops of whaleback dunes or around the ends of other dunes. They then headed south, mostly running along the sides of dunes, to Ammonite Hill, where the third dump was going to be established. Leaving Ammonite Hill and traveling north, they reached Ain Dalla in one day. After spending a day at Ain Dalla, the expedition, loaded with fuel, returned in one day's run to Ammonite Hill. The reason why the group could run back and forth between Ain Dalla and Ammonite Hill with such speed was that the dunes generally run in a northeast-southwest direction, and Ammonite Hill is almost directly south-southwest of Ain Dalla. On 24 October the expedition headed in a generally southerly direction through the Great Sand Sea towards the two large mountains where the borders of Libya, Egypt, and the Sudan meet. One of these mountains, Uweinat, is six thousand feet high—a huge block of sandstone rising out of the desert; and fifteen miles south of Uweinat there is a five thousand foot tall granite mountain known as Kissu, which also rises sheer out of the desert. After some very difficult going, the expedition got clear of the sand dunes and arrived at Uweinat on the last day of October, 1930.

The following day the expedition left Uweinat and traveled eastward towards Burg el Tuyur and Selima Oasis. A few miles east of Uweinat, however, Bagnold's car broke down, and it was discovered that two teeth had broken off a wheel in the transmission. Since they did not have the replacement part and there were no known sand dunes between Uweinat and Halfa, they thought it might be possible to tow the broken car. But Prendergast and Bagnold could not disconnect the back wheels from the axle. What was needed was a heavy sledge hammer, which they did not have, to force the wheels, which were jammed, off their cones. It was finally

---

43   *Ibid*, p. 148.

decided that the car would have to be abandoned, because with the rear wheels unable to turn, it would only be a question of time before the towing car stripped its transmission. Everything possible was taken off Bagnold's vehicle and put on board the two remaining cars, and they continued on to Selima Oasis by way of Burg el Tuyur.

From Uweinat to Burg el Tuyur, which is a rock eight feet high, is a distance of two hundred miles across the desert; finding Burg el Tuyur was, indeed, a triumph of dead reckoning desert navigation for Newbold, who did the navigation on this leg of the expedition. Desert navigation, according to Bagnold,

> is by no means as easy as its counterpart at sea, where a course is decided upon and kept according to a chart comfortably laid out on a table. On land it is very different.
>
> The driver steers wherever he can pick a way, dodging about to avoid rocks big enough to strike the belly of the car, making continual deviations around hills and other obstacles, keeping only a causal eye on the compass to maintain his general direction. The navigator must therefore be alert for every moment of the day's run, trying to read and keep a record of the compass bearing as it flicks about, and noting the mileage at each reading so that he may plot out the zigzag course afterwards from his notes. His work is made still more difficult because the jolting is often so great that he cannot write at all, being entirely occupied in holding on, and must save up a string of figures in his head for the first smooth patch of ground.
>
> There is no room to open out his map, and probably far too much wind to do so, for the driver just at the wrong moment wants the wind-screen open because the sun is shining on it and he can't see: so the map must be kept folded, bound to a small board with elastic bands cut from an old inner tube. He holds this and his notebook and his pencil in his hands ready for use, but at an instant's notice he must dispose of them all and leap from the car to save it by a timely push from sticking in some soft place. At every halt he starts work with a protractor, plotting out the course on the map from his almost illegible notes, while the rest of the party cluster round anxious to know where they have got to.[44]

---

44   *Ibid*, pp. 175-176.

After dark that night, 2 November, the expedition camped at a point which Newbold said was four miles short of Burg el Tuyur. The next morning Newbold and Kennedy Shaw climbed the nearest sand dune with a pair of field glasses and discovered that they were five miles east of Burg el Tuyur. In a two hundred mile run across unknown desert on a dead reckoning course, Newbold was just one mile off his plotted dead reckoning position!

From Burg el Tuyur the expedition proceeded to Halfa on the Nile by way of Selima Oasis. At Halfa two days were spent going over notes and charts sorting out various geographical and other problems. At Halfa, Newbold left the expedition to return to his position in the Sudan Civil Service. Additional fuel and provisions were picked up and the group, now consisting of two cars and five men, left Halfa and continued the one thousand mile trip back to Cairo by way of Kharga and Asyut. They arrived in the Egyptian capital on 15 November 1930. The expedition had traveled over 3,100 miles of the Western Desert at an average distance per day of 138 miles. They had proved not only that it was possible to cross the Great Sand Sea but also to travel through it by motor vehicle. But the desert had struck back by forcing the abandonment of Bagnold's car for the want of a single spare part and the lack of a heavy sledge hammer.[45]

In January of 1931 Clayton and Kennedy Shaw found themselves caught up in the aftermath of the Italian subjugation of the Senussi. The Italians, using aircraft, armored cars, and troops carried by both camels and trucks, had put an end to the Senussi rebellion in Libya by capturing Kufra and driving the Senussi at the oasis into the desert.[46] The Italian attack came so quickly that the Senussi at Kufra had no time to make preparations for an organized retreat from Kufra and were left with a choice of three harsh escape routes. The Senussi could flee across the sand sea to Egypt, which was a waterless strip of three hundred and sixty miles; they could go two hundred miles southeast to Uweinat, where there was water but nothing for them or their camels to eat; or they could head southwest to Sarra and French territory, which was a journey with water but without grazing of about five hundred miles. A few Senussi headed southwest towards French territory, but the majority, which Kennedy Shaw says numbered about five hundred, headed for Uweinat. Some of the stronger among this group then left Uweinat and went off eastward into the desert in hopes of reaching the Nile. Those Senussi who remained at Uweinat had water but nothing to eat.

---

45   *Ibid*, pp. 142-180. Bagnold, "Journeys in the Libyan Desert," pp. 19-39, 522-535.
46   Evans-Pritchard, *The Senussi*, pp. 185-190.

Clayton arrived at Uweinat after having run a five hundred mile triangulation survey from the Nile to find a number of Senussi dying from lack of food. Before reaching Uweinat, Clayton had no knowledge of the Italian attack on Kufra, but he had met Bagnold's expedition when they were at Halfa. Clayton was told of the location of Bagnold's abandoned car and of a hidden cache of fuel. Before leaving Halfa, Clayton received from Cairo the necessary spare parts and tools to fix Bagnold's abandoned car. After a lot of work, Clayton managed to get Bagnold's car in working order and sent it off with ten of the weakest Senussi to Halfa. Clayton sent the others off down a marked track to Dakhla, the nearest place in Egypt where there was water and food; and then he scouted around Uweinat, as long as his fuel permitted, looking for additional Senussi wandering around in the desert. Those that Clayton did come across were sent down the track to Dakhla.[47]

Kennedy Shaw was at Dakhla when the Senussi from Uweinat began arriving at that oasis, and he sent an account of the event to England which appeared as a letter to the editor in the London *Times*. The first to appear at Dakhla were three Senussi who staggered into a police post more dead than alive after walking for twenty-one days across the desert. As soon as the authorities at Dakhla realized what was happening, they organized search parties and sent them into the western and southern approaches of the oasis to look for more Senussi. In the end, about three hundred Senussi reached Dakhla.[48] Because of their hatred of the Italians, the Senussi would later aid the British in Cyrenaica during the Second World War.

In addition to his military duties, Bagnold spent the year of 1931 in England, preparing for another expedition into the Western Desert, writing, and studying. In July of 1931 Bagnold gave a paper to the Royal Geographical Society on his 1929 and 1930 expeditions into the Great Sand Sea of Egypt. In December 1931, he and several other members of the two expeditions gave a series of papers at the Royal Geographical Society on the technical aspects of the two trips. All of these papers were published in the Society's *Geographical Journal*.[49] Bagnold's desert explorations had already been drawn to the attention of the public by the press,[50] but having a paper published by the Royal Geographical Society in the *Geographical Journal* was something very different from one's exploits appearing in the press.

---

47   Bagnold, *Libyan Sands*, pp. 200-201.

48   *London Times*, 25 May 1931.

49   See notes above numbers 41, 45.

50   *London Times*, 3 July 1928, 3 Jan. 1931.

It is almost impossible to understand British exploration of Asia and Africa in the second half of the nineteenth century and the first decades of the twentieth century without knowing the role of the Royal Geographical Society in these events. By publishing Bagnold's papers, the Royal Geographical Society brought a degree of prestige to these trips into the Western Desert. Being backed by the Royal Geographical Society opened doors that otherwise would be closed. The leadership of the Society was made of Peers of the Realm, Members of the House of Commons, and a number of high-ranking military and navy officers. Working through the "old boys" network, there was no telling what the governing officers and council of the Royal Geographical Society could get a government department, such as the War Office, to do. Leave with pay, the use of government equipment, military transport, and the like are examples of what could be forthcoming. When the great nineteenth century British explorers of Africa—Sir Richard Burton, Captain John Hanning Speke, and Dr. David Livingston—first told of their adventures it was to such meetings of the Royal Geographical Society; and their accounts were always reported in the press. This virtually assured the Royal Geographical Society's prestige not only with "official" London but also with the public at large. As the Royal Geographical Society's prestige grew, in the course of the nineteenth century, it attracted a growing membership of British navy, military, and colonial civil service officers, the very people who manned the outposts of empire. By the twentieth century, the Royal Geographical Society had become an important force in the exploration of remote regions at the outer edges of the British Empire, and many military, naval, and colonial civil service officers could write after their names the initials F.R.G.S., Fellow of the Royal Geographical Society. A smaller number of officers also used the Society's journal as a means of publishing accounts of their travels in remote regions of the world; for an article in the *Geographical Journal* conferred, in the eyes of the officer corps, just as much prestige as an article in a service journal, such as the *Journal of the Royal United Service Institution*. And to be awarded the Royal Geographical Society's Founder's, Patron's, or Gold Medal was a very high honor indeed. In 1931, when the Royal Geographical Society published Bagnold's article on his exploration of the Great Sand Sea of Egypt, it was in essence the "establishment" saying that his work in the desert was important and should be continued.[51]

---

51   For an account of the role of the Royal Geographical Society in the exploration of the Egyptian Desert in the first decades of the 20th century, see John Gordon, Jr., "Special Forces for Desert Warfare: British Improvisation, 1915-1943" (unpublished Duke University, Ph. D. dissertation, 1974), pp. 74-97.

In the autumn of 1932 Bagnold undertook a six thousand mile expedition through the Western Desert in Egypt, Libya, the Sudan, and the Chad. This expedition was different from Bagnold's previous trips into the desert and not only because it covered considerably more distance; it was more important because it had the backing of the Royal Geographical Society. Not only did the Society lend the group a number of instruments but also it, along with the University of Chicago's Oriental Institute, paid half of the cost of the expedition. This grant of money enabled Bagnold to set up a large dump of fuel at Selima Oasis. The War Office equally granted leave to five officers to take part in the expedition, which would consist of four Ford cars and eight men. The members of the expedition were: Bagnold; Craig, who was the chief navigator and as usual in charge of provisions; Kennedy Shaw, whose task was to find the longitude and latitude of the expedition each night; Lieutenant O.R. Paterson of the Royal Corps of Signals, who would assist Kennedy Shaw; and Prendergast, who, assisted by Lieutenant R.N. Harding-Newman of the Royal Tank Corps, was in charge of obtaining, modifying, and loading the four Ford cars. The other two members of the expedition were Major J.E.H. Boustead, M.C., Sudan Camel Corps, and Dr. K.S. Sandford of Oxford University.

On 27 September 1932 the expedition left Cairo and headed south across the desert towards Kharga. Just before dark on the first day, an R.A.F. transport aircraft from Cairo landed in the desert near the expedition's campsite. The R.A.F. was attempting to see if they could follow the car tracks of the expedition from the air. It was found to be "a terribly difficult feat…to follow a winding car track from the air. The thin marks are faint and very hard to see in the glare, wriggling from side to side, at one moment away to a flank almost out of sight, darting in suddenly underneath the machine, dodging the next moment round a tiny hill with hard ground where the tracks are lost."[52] One of the tasks of the expedition was to mark possible spots in the desert where aircraft could land. This was done by driving the cars over the sight in such a way that the tyre tracks formed a huge figure eight in the surface of the desert.

The expedition left Kharga on the morning of 2 October, and shortly after leaving the oasis, they were flown over it by an R.A.F. transport aircraft, which was trying to gage whether or not it was possible to follow the track left by the cars. The expedition arrived at Kissu, the mountain near Uweinat, on 5 October. Here they left much of their equipment, believing that it would be safe to do so because there was no water at the place, and then drove over to Uweinat. Fearing there might be

---

52   *Ibid*, p. 216.

bandits at Uweinat, they approached with great care and with loaded army rifles in hand, but found no one. Part of the expedition remained at Kissu and explored Uweinat while three cars and four men made two trips back and forth to Selima Oasis, a distance of two hundred miles each way, to pick up nine hundred and sixty gallons of fuel and transport it back to Kissu. The fuel had been brought to Selima Oasis by the Shell Oil Company, using camels from Halfa on the Nile. It took three days to make the round trip from Kissu to Selima Oasis, and while the first trip was being made an R.A.F. transport aircraft landed in the desert near Kissu. The pilot had tried to follow the expedition's track, but had soon lost them and had to steer for the Kissu-Uweinat area by conventional methods of navigation.

While exploring Uweinat on 8 October, Craig, Kennedy Shaw, Sandford, and Prendergast discovered an Italian patrol had just arrived at Uweinat in trucks with thirty local troops commanded by Major Rolle, the military governor of Kufra. The next day two Italian military aircraft landed there with Colonel Lordi, who was the head of the Italian Air Force in Libya. The British were "much amused"; for here in the middle of nowhere officers of the British and Italian armed forces met on territory claimed by each group's nation as their own. Fortunately, neither group brought up the 'delicate' question of ownership. While at Kissu, Bagnold and Kennedy Shaw did something that they had always wanted to do: they climbed to the top of Uweinat!

On 13 October the British left Kissu, with each of the four cars carrying one hundred gallons of fuel, and headed west into Libya. When the Italians learned of their intention of entering Libya, there was some talk of flying to meet the British at their destination, Sarra Wells. The Italians obviously wanted to keep an eye on the British expedition, for when they arrived at Sarra Wells on 15 October, they found an Italian patrol from Kufra waiting for them. Sarra Wells is nothing but a very deep well dug by the Senussi; so the British expedition continued on the next day traveling west towards the Tibesti mountains in the Chad. Before reaching these mountains, however, the ground became so difficult that the course was changed to the south-southeast towards Tekro in the Chad. With the arrival of the expedition at Tekro, "the Libyan Desert had been crossed for the first time east and west."[53] From Tekro the British party returned by a direct course to Kissu, which they reached on 22 October.

The expedition departed from Kissu on 23 October with each car loaded with enough fuel for fourteen to fifteen hundred miles, food for three weeks and water for eighteen days. The expedition headed south through the desert along the

---

53   *Ibid*, p. 235.

western border of the Sudan. At the Mourdi Depression and again further south at Madi Guroguro, the party approached the eastern border of the Chad, seeking information about a small band of local outlaws they had been told to watch for. However, no-one was found and the expedition proceeded south out of the desert, arriving, on 3 November, at El Fasher in the Sudan, which is located just a little over thirteen degrees north of the equator. The party remained at El Fasher for four days before heading north towards the desert and Egypt. On 19 November, the expedition arrived at Halfa, on the Nile River, and then traveled to Cairo by way of Dakhla and Bahariya Oasis, arriving at the Egyptian capital on 29 November. The 1932 expedition had covered more than six thousand miles of mostly unexplored and unmapped desert in only sixty days.[54]

After the 1932 expedition Bagnold and Craig were posted to China; and in 1933 the Royal Geographical Society published two papers on the trip. While in China Bagnold wrote an account of all his desert trips, from the first ones across the Sinai through the 1932 expedition. This book, entitled *Libyan Sands: Travels in a Dead World*, was first published in 1935. And in that same year the Royal Geographical Society awarded Bagnold its greatest award—the Founder's Medal. It was in China that Bagnold began his investigations into the movement of sand; in 1941 he published the results of his studies in *The Physics of Blown Sand and Desert Dunes*.

In the meantime, in 1935, Kennedy Shaw led an expedition into the Western Desert of Egypt and the Sudan. Accompanying him on the expedition were Colonel and Mrs. G.A. Strutt, Harding-Newman, R.E. McEuen, and M.H. Mason. With the exception of Kennedy Shaw and Harding-Newman, most of the people on the expedition were not familiar with the wilds of the Western Desert. Three Ford pick-up trucks were used instead of the usual Ford cars. The Royal Geographical Society supported the expedition with a small grant and with the loan of some instruments. On 14 January the expedition departed from Cairo, followed the Nile to Asyut, and then went out into the desert, stopping at Kharga and Dakhla Oasis, and then onto Gilf Kebir, which is located some miles north-northeast of Uweinat. After exploring Gilf Kebir, the party traveled on to Selima Oasis, where they picked up additional fuel that had been brought there by camel from Halfa. After three days at Selima Oasis, they went west; and at a point about seventy miles southwest of Kissu, the expedition headed south on a course east of the one followed in 1932 by Bagnold's expedition.

---

54   Bagnold, *Libyan Sands*, pp. 208-276; R.A. Bagnold, "A Further Journey through the Libyan Desert," *The Geographical Journal* 82 (Aug.- Sept, 1933), pp. 103-129, 211-235.

The trip continued without incident until they reached the north side of Wadi Hawar, about three hundred miles from El Fasher. Here Colonel Strutt fell off the running board of a moving Ford pickup truck, broke two ribs, and pierced one of his lungs. On the second morning after the accident, Kennedy Shaw decided that Strutt had to be taken to El Fasher for medical treatment. When the expedition reached Kutum two days later, Kennedy Shaw thought that Strutt had to be moved faster than was possible by motor vehicle. Leaving Strutt and the rest of the party at Kutum, Kennedy Shaw and McEuen drove all night to reach El Fasher the next morning. Prendergast, who was stationed at El Fasher with the Western Arab Corps and who was a pilot of considerable skill, flew through a sand storm to Kutum and back to fetch Strutt. For a time it seemed that Strutt's condition was improving, but there were later complications, and on 6 March he was flown by the R.A.F. to Khartoum, where he died on 25 March.

The expedition remained for several days at El Fasher, and then on 17 February Kennedy Shaw, Mason, McEuen, and Harding-Newman left to return to Wadi Hawar. The group left Wadi Hawar on 25 February and traveled to Jebel Tageru, Abu Safyan, and back to El Fasher. They then went north to Egypt. After obtaining fuel, water, and food at Selima Oasis, the expedition went up the west side of Gilf Kebir and crossed the Great Sand Sea; and on 9 April they reached Cairo by way of the coast road. They had traveled six thousand three hundred miles, roughly half of which was through unexplored regions.[55]

In 1938 Bagnold, who had returned from China, led another expedition to Gilf Kebir and Uweinat. This expedition was jointly supported by the Egyptian Exploration Society and the Royal Geographical Society and was to conduct archeological digs at both Gilf Kebir and Uweinat, study cave paintings, explore and survey the Gilf Kebir, while Bagnold was also to study the movement of wind blown sand. The expedition was formed near Luxor on the Nile and departed on 5 February 1938. The group achieved all it had set out to accomplish and the trip was generally uneventful. It was to be Bagnold's last peacetime scientific trip to the Western Desert. Bagnold returned to England, where on 23 January 1939 he, and other members of the expedition, presented papers on it to the Royal Geographical Society.[56] In February 1939 Bagnold retired from the army with the rank of major in the Royal Corps of Signals.

---

55   W.B. Kennedy Shaw, "An Expedition in the Southern Libyan Desert," *The Geographical Journal* 87/3 (March. 1936), pp. 193-221; Michael H. Mason, *The Paradise of Fools* (London: Hodder and Stoughton, 1936).

56   R.A. Bagnold, "An Expedition to the Gilf Kebir and Uweinat, 1938," *The Geographical Journal* 93/4 (April, 1939), pp. 218-313.

Bagnold and the other explorers of deserts were not the only Britons in the Middle East, during the 1920's and 1930's, who were interested in mechanized travel and transport. In the inter-war years, the British military in the Middle East were also interested in mechanized forces and carried out experiments and operations with them. This interest in mechanized forces did not grow out of the ideas and schemes about tank warfare put forth in Europe by such people as Fuller and Liddell-Hart; rather, it was a direct result of the geographical, political, and military realities of the Middle East. At the end of the First World War, Britain was politically in control of vast areas in the Middle East, much of which was desert, and where there was a need to deploy military forces to carry out what were essentially para-military, or police operations, such as putting down native rebellions and preventing tribal wars.

In the years between the two World Wars, British forces stationed in the Middle East saw a lot of service in the desert. During the 1920's and 1930's in Iraq, for instance, the R.A.F. used aircraft, armored cars, and other types of motor cars mounted with machine-guns to police native tribes in the desert of that country.[57] In 1931 the authorities of the Sudan used a machine-gun battery mounted in Ford vehicles along with R.A.F. aircraft in an attempt to run down and capture or destroy a number of outlaws who had attacked camel caravans in the northwest Sudan.[58] Squadron A of the XII Royal Lancers, which was comprised of ten armored cars and seventeen other vehicles, was sent to Siwa in 1932 by way of Mersa Matruh and Salum. The squadron then returned to Cairo through Mersa Matruh.[59] In 1932, on orders from the War Office in London, a small experimental convoy of four different types of military vehicles was sent on a 5,600 mile trip from Egypt into the Sudan to test the ability of these vehicles to operate in various types of desert terrain. And in the summer of the following year, six different types of vehicles were sent on a 3,557 mile trip from Cairo down into the Sudan and back again to Cairo to test such things as the effect of different types of desert terrain on the vehicles, their cooling systems, and tyres. Both of these experimental convoys were carried out without any major mishaps.[60] In 1933 and 1934, one machine-gun battery, its guns mounted on Ford vehicles, was stationed at Uweinat

---

57   John Bagot Glubb, *The War in the Desert: An R.A.F. Frontier Campaign* (New York: W.W. Norton & Company, 1961).

58   Bimbashi R.L. Scoones, "Ford Cars in the Libyan Desert," *The Royal Tank Corps Journal* 14 (Feb, 1933), pp. 255-258.

59   Thomas I. Dun, *From Cairo to Siwa* (Cairo: privately printed, 1933).

60   H.P. Drayson, "The War Office Experimental Convoy, 1933," *The Royal Engineers Journal* 48 (March, 1934), pp. 60-72.

and another at Merga Oasis, and both of these units were supplied overland by trucks.[61] In 1939 a British officer took a motorized patrol from Alexandria through the Qattara Depression to Siwa.[62] These desert operations and trips are but a very few examples of the many undertaken by the British armed forces during the inter-war years. Despite this experience with desert operations, when war came to the Western Desert in 1940, only Bagnold, Clayton, and a few others, Kennedy Shaw and Prendergast among them, had the knowledge, gained over many years and thousands of miles of desert travel, that would be required to wage mechanized war successfully in the vast wastes of the Western Desert.

---

61   H.P. Drayson, "A Brief Outline of the Supply and Transport Problems Occasioned by the Operations in the North-Western Libyan Desert, 1933-34," *The Army Service Corps Quarterly* 3 (Nov, 1935), pp. 138-145.

62   G. Surtees, "A Thousand Miles of Desert," *Journal of the Royal United Service Institution* 106 (Nov, 1961), pp. 510-516.

3

Forming the Long Range Desert Group and its First Missions

"The Desert has been described as a fortress to him who knows it and a grave to him who does not."
—*British Army Manual, 1979*

In August of 1939, just before the beginning of World War II, Bagnold was recalled to active duty in the army. Bagnold believed, as did many other people, that there was a good possibility that Italy would enter the war on the side of Germany. If Italy came into the war as an ally of the Germans, then there would be fighting in North Africa as the Italians had large military forces in their African colonies of Libya, Eritrea, and Abyssinia. In London, at the suggestion of the Hon. Francis Rodd, who was a banker, desert explorer, and later a major general in the Civil Affairs Administration in the Middle East and East Africa, Bagnold drew up a plan to protect Northern Nigeria from raids by Italian mobile forces from Libya across French territory.[1] Nothing came of this plan, and Bagnold was posted to Kenya, a country he knew nothing about.

On its way to Kenya, the ship on which Bagnold was sailing struck another vessel and had to put into Alexandria for repairs. Bagnold, with time on his hands while the ship was being fixed, went to Cairo to see his friends in that city. While Bagnold was in Cairo, his presence in Egypt came to the attention of Lieutenant General Sir Archibald Wavell, General Officer Commander-in-Chief, Middle East, who had Bagnold's orders changed and got him assigned to the staff of the 7th Armoured Division. Wavell was that rare combination—a soldier intellectual with a grasp of what was in the range of the practical. He also took an interest

---

1   TNA, CAB/44/151, f. 10.

in unorthodox methods of waging war.[2] It was characteristic of Wavell not to let one of the world's leading authorities on the Egyptian Desert slip through his hands. Not knowing the circumstances of Bagnold's arrival in Cairo, the *Egyptian Gazette* "announced the return of Major Bagnold to Egypt, and went on to express gratification at this evidence that the War Office was at last trying to fit square pegs into square holes."[3]

At the suggestion of Bagnold, his commander proposed in November, and again in January of 1940, that a force consisting of small mobile units should be established. It would be the mission of these mobile units to operate deep in the desert collecting information about the enemy's activities in the interior of Libya, attacking Italian communications with such desert outposts as Kufra, locating landing places for British aircraft in the desert, and keeping in contact with the French forces along the southwestern border of Libya.[4] Although for years Wavell had been interested in mechanized guerrilla warfare and the employment of unorthodox forces,[5] no action was taken on Bagnold's proposals because, in an attempt to keep Italy out of the war, it was British policy not to do anything that might be interpreted by the Italians as threatening.[6]

On 10 June 1940, Italy declared war on Great Britain. Bagnold, who was not assigned to Wavell's headquarters in Cairo, thought that the Italians in the southern Libyan Desert could possibly threaten British positions in Africa. What sort of threat the Italians posed was difficult to ascertain, and the problem was compounded by the fact that nobody in Cairo knew anything about the Libyan Desert. When Bagnold arrived at Wavell's headquarters, the only map of Libya there, was one made in 1915 and based on information provided by the nineteenth-century German explorer Friedrich Rohlfs. From his knowledge of the geography of the Libyan Desert, however, Bagnold quickly saw that the Italian threat centered on the oasis of Kufra in southeastern Libya. Using Kufra as a base, the Italians could attack or raid the Upper Nile with air and mechanized ground forces. Or, the Italians could attempt to capture southern Egypt and the northern Sudan by attacks from both southern Libya and Abyssinia. From Kufra the Italians could

---

2   Cf., A.P. Wavell, "The Army and the Prophets," *The Journal of the Royal United Service Institution* 75 (Nov., 1930), pp. 666-675; Wavell, "The Higher Commander," *ibid.*, 81 (Feb, 1936), pp. 15-32.

3   R.A. Bagnold, "Early Days of the Long Range Desert Group", *The Geographical Journal* 105 (Jan. – June, 1945), p. 30.

4   TNA, WO/201/807, ff. 3-4.

5   John Connell, *Wavell: Scholar and Soldier* (New York: Harcourt, Brace & World Inc, 1964), pp. 179-180.

6   I.S.O. Playfair, *The Mediterranean and Middle East* (London: HMSO, 1954), vol. I, pp. 39-40.

also raid the large oases of Egypt and force the British to deploy a large number of troops to protect them. Southern Libya could be used as well to mount an attack southward into the Chad; and long-range aircraft based at Kufra could attack the routes which were used by the British to ferry aircraft across Africa from Nigeria to Khartoum and then to Cairo. In June of 1940, however, the British in Egypt could only guess at what the Italians were doing in southern Libya and there seemed to be no way for them to find out.[7]

Bagnold thought that the only way to find out what the Italians in southern Libya were up to was to go there although he knew that this course of action would present huge problems. Bagnold thought that it would be no problem to set up the necessary dumps of fuel and other stores along the eastern side of the Great Sand Sea, but patrols operating in the Libyan Desert would have to have a range of at least fifteen hundred miles and to carry water and food for several weeks, plus all the tools, arms, spare parts, and radios required for such an undertaking. To do this, Bagnold thought it would require a 30 cwt truck and overloaded by nearly two tons with a crew of three and that a patrol would have to consist of a minimum of ten such trucks. The question was, could a heavily loaded 30 cwt truck be driven in the summer over the dunes of the Great Sand Sea by inexperienced men? And what would happen once the Great Sand Sea had been crossed? Nobody knew what lay behind it, and there were no maps of Libya. There was also the question of Italian military capabilities. It was known that the Italians had special desert-trained mechanized ground and air units, and it was possible that these forces could hunt down and destroy any British party attempting to enter the Libyan Desert. Another problem was that it would be very difficult in a country such as Egypt, where there were many spies, to fit out an expedition in secret. Bagnold later said, "It was a great gamble. But if it could be achieved it would be well worthwhile. For even if we found after all that Italian enterprise did not run to long-distance raids, we might make such raids ourselves."[8]

On 19 June 1940, Bagnold submitted to Wavell's chief of staff a proposal for establishing a unit for long-range desert reconnaissance with the objective of penetrating into the Libyan Desert. On 23 June Wavell sent for Bagnold and ordered that the unit be set up within six weeks and on 10 July the War Office cabled provisional approval for establishing the new reconnaissance unit. The unit was to be under the direction of Wavell's Deputy Director of Military Intelligence,

---

7   Bagnold, "Early Days of the Long Range Desert Group," pp. 30-32.
8   *Ibid*, pp. 32-33.

and Bagnold was given "absolute priority to help [himself] to what equipment there was, with personnel, and with workshop facilities."[9]

In the next few weeks the unit that would become the Long Range Desert Group[10] was formed in a mad, headlong rush. Perhaps only Bagnold could have put the unit together so quickly; for he was one of the few people who knew the army, the deep desert, and how to organize expeditions of the type required into the desert. Of the pre-war desert explorers, only Bagnold and Harding-Newman were in Cairo at the time. Kennedy Shaw was in Jerusalem and Clayton was in the wilds of Tanganyika. Both were sent for by the Deputy Director of Military intelligence, flown to Cairo, and commissioned into the army on the spot. Prendergast, who was in Britain, would later be sent for as well.

Bagnold and Harding-Newman tested every type of 30 cwt American truck that could be found in Cairo and picked a Chevrolet model.[11] The Chevrolet truck they chose was built by General Motors in Canada and had a 1939 Canadian Chevrolet Military Chassis. The vehicle was powered by an 85 horsepower six-cylinder engine and had a 134-inch wheel base.[12] Selecting the right type of truck was just the beginning of the transport problem, for only eleven of the trucks could be found in the hands of commercial dealers in Egypt and another nineteen had to be obtained from the Egyptian army. These thirty trucks were then sent to the British army's ordinance workshops to be remodeled to Bagnold's and Harding-Newman's specifications. The doors, cabs, and windshields of the vehicles were removed, then the bodies were rebuilt and mounts were fitted for Bofors guns, anti-tank rifles, Lewis guns, and sun compasses. Brackets and racks were added for two gallon cans, sand channels, and sand mats. The trucks were also fitted with lockers for tools, spare parts, and the like and clips for carrying rifles, Lewis guns, spare springs, and axles. Housing for radio sets were mounted on the trucks and their radiators were fitted with condensers. The first trucks were ready for use on 30 July, and by 12 August all thirty of the 30 cwt Chevrolet trucks had been converted for long-range desert work. At the same time two five-ton, six-wheel drive Marmon-Herrington trucks were taken over by the army from an oil company to be used to set up dumps of fuel and other stores in the desert. Two 15 cwt Chevrolet pick-up

---

9   *Ibid*, p. 33.

10   At first, the unit was called the Long Range Patrol Unit; however, its name was changed after about six months to the Long Range Desert Group. For the sake of consistency, I have referred to the unit throughout this work as the Long Range Desert Group.

11   Bagnold, "Early Days of the Long Range Desert Group," pp. 33-34; TNA, WO/201/807, f. 7.

12   Chris Ellis, *Military Transport of World War II* (New York: Macmillan Publishing Co., Inc, 1975), pp. 112-113.

trucks were also fitted out, but these vehicles quickly were found to be unsuitable and were later taken out of service.[13]

While the Chevrolet trucks were being modified, Bagnold and Harding-Newman collected the specialized equipment that was required by the unit. The British forces in Egypt in 1940 were very short of equipment of all types, but Bagnold and Harding-Newman got first pick of what little there was. After the Long Range Desert Group had been armed, there remained only three unissued machine-guns in all of Egypt. All the radio sets in Egypt of the type Bagnold wanted went to the Long Range Desert Group. The British army used the Cole sun compass, which Bagnold did not approve of, so the required number of the type that had been designed by Bagnold were obtained from the Egyptian army. At least three theodolites were needed, and the British army had only one. Another was borrowed from the Egyptian Survey, and the third was flown in from Nairobi. Sun and star tables had to be found as well as radio receivers to pick up time signals. Ration tables had to be drawn up and then approved along with tables of organization and equipment.[14] All of these tasks had to be done very quickly and in secret.[15]

Finding the right type of men for the Long Range Desert Group was a problem. Bagnold knew that if the unit was going to be a success he needed men who were tough, self-reliant, and capable of mastering in a few days or weeks all the information about desert travel it had taken Bagnold years to learn. In addition, Bagnold required skilled technicians, radio men, gunners, mechanics, fitters, and navigators. In fact, Bagnold was looking for the very type of men who were most in demand, and commanding officers of other units in Egypt would not want to give up men of this sort for detached duty with a special unit.[16]

In his search for men for the Long Range Desert Group, Bagnold first attempted to obtain Australians from Queensland with a knowledge of the Australian Outback, but the commander of the Australian forces in the Middle East would not release the men because he had orders from his government that all Australian troops were to serve with Australian formations and not be scattered around in various British units.[17] After being turned down by the Australians, the commander of the British forces in Egypt, Lieutenant General Sir Maitland Wilson, requested that the acting commander of the 2nd New Zealand Division supply the men

13   TNA, WO/201/807, f. 7.
14   TNA WO/201/807, f. 11-14.
15   Bagnold, "Early Days of the Long Range Desert Group", pp. 33-34.
16   *Ibid*, p. 34.
17   TNA, WO/201/807, f. 5.

needed by the Long Range Desert Group. Consent was given to this request and some seventy of the best men in the 2nd New Zealand Division volunteered to serve with the Long Range Desert Group. The acting commander of the 2nd New Zealand Division, however, had misunderstood the British request. He thought that his men would be gone only for a short period of time to receive some extra desert training. When Major General Bernard Freyberg, the commander of the 2nd New Zealand Expeditionary Force and the chief representative of the New Zealand government on all matters relating to the war against Germany and Italy, arrived in Egypt he found that a large number of New Zealand troops had been placed on various sorts of detached duty with non-New Zealand units. Freyberg and the New Zealand government both thought that all New Zealanders should fight as a single unit; and the New Zealand commander began forcing the return of all New Zealand soldiers to the 2nd New Zealand Expeditionary Force. But try as he might, Freyberg could not get the New Zealanders back from Long Range Desert Group. In the end, it was agreed that the 2nd New Zealand Expeditionary Force would supply enough men for two fighting patrols and a number of other positions in the Long Range Desert Group until the end of the North African campaign.[18]

The first base of the Long Range Desert Group was at the military complex at Abbassia. The unit was organized into a headquarters section including the commanding officer, Bagnold; the medical officer; quartermaster; adjutant; and intelligence officer, Kennedy Shaw. Two fighting patrols were formed—T and W—each with two officers and twenty-three other ranks. There were as well two other formations in the unit: A Echelon Supply Party, with two subalterns and twenty other ranks; and B Echelon Supply Party, with one subaltern and four other ranks. T and W Patrols and A Echelon were all armed with ten Lewis guns, four Boys anti-tank rifles, and one 37mm Bofors gun in addition to personal arms such as rifles. The transport of the two patrols and A Echelon consisted of ten 30 cwt Chevrolet trucks each; while B Echelon was assigned the two Marmon-Herrington five-ton trucks.[19]

---

18   W.G. Stevens, *Official History of New Zealand in the Second World War, 1939-1945: Problems of the 2nd NZEF* (Wellington: Department of Internal Affairs, 1958), pp. 21, 31; *idem, Documents Relating to New Zealand's Participation in the Second World War, 1939-45* (Wellington: Department of Internal Affairs, 1949), vol. I, pp. 81-83, 184-189, 232-237. See also, Clive Gower-Collins, "Raids, Road Watches, and Reconnaissance. An Analysis of The New Zealand Contribution to the Long Range Desert Group in North Africa, 1940-1943" (unpublished MA Thesis, Massey University, 1999).

19   TNA, CAB/44/151, f. 11.

When the New Zealand members of the unit arrived at Abbassia, they must have wondered what was going on, for their British leaders were decidedly older and, with the exception of Bagnold (Harding-Newman had been reassigned), without much in the way of a military background. Bagnold and Clayton were forty-four years old, and Kennedy Shaw, a lieutenant, was thirty-nine. With the assistance of Lance Corporal C.H.B. Croucher, a New Zealander with a mate's ticket in the merchant service, Kennedy Shaw began to teach a number of New Zealanders the art of dead reckoning navigation and how to take star fixes. Those New Zealanders who were signalers were set the task of mastering the use of number 11 radios and Windom aerials. Others were taught, or learned on their own, how Chevrolet trucks worked.

The first training mission was held near the Qattania Dunes. It began on 5 August and lasted only three days and was undertaken with ten trucks driven by W Patrol, with T Patrol as passengers. On 15 August the whole Long Range Desert Group, including A and B Echelons, had four more days of training that were also used to set up several dumps of fuel in the desert.[20] This was the full extent of the training that was received by the first members of the Long Range Desert Group. Although there is a thirty-three page memorandum on training in the David Lloyd Owen Papers at the Imperial War Museum,[21] General Lloyd Owen has stated that most Long Range Desert Group training in the desert was done on the job.[22]

On 16 July Clayton, who had been commissioned a captain in the army, joined the Long Range Desert Group. Clayton did not get involved with such things as fitting out vehicles or training; instead, he set about trying to find out what was going on in the Libyan Desert. Clayton arranged for an Arab named Manufli, who was in the employment of the Egyptian Survey, to be taken overland, along with a camel, by a motorized patrol of the Egyptian Frontiers Administration to a point just east of Uweinat. Manufli and the camel spent a week reconnoitering Uweinat, and then were picked up by another motorized patrol of the Egyptian Frontiers Administration and taken to Halfa on the Nile. Not much was learned by this expedition, but it must be the first time in history that a camel traveled a thousand miles across the desert in a truck. Another scheme of Clayton's was to find an Arab who had once lived in Kufra, fly him to a point some sixty miles away from

---

20   TNA, WO/201/807, f. 8.
21   Imperial War Museum, David Lloyd Owen's Collection of The Long Range Desert Group Papers, 1/4 Training notes.
22   Lloyd-Owen Interview.

the oasis, and then, after he had reconnoitered Kufra, pick him up by a motorized patrol. The problem was that no Arab was willing to undertake such a mission, not even for money, because of fear of the Italians.

Clayton's third project was reconnaissance of the Jalo-Kufra track. Clayton, along with an Arab employee of the Egyptian Survey and five New Zealanders, departed from Cairo on 7 August in two 15 cwt Chevrolet trucks and reached Siwa the next day by way of Mersa Matruh. At Siwa Clayton was joined by seven trucks of the Egyptian Frontiers Administration which were to carry extra fuel and water. The nine vehicles headed due south across the Great Sand Sea to Two Hills, just east of the Libyan border. The Egyptian Frontiers Administration trucks made a dump of fuel and water at Two Hills and then returned north to Siwa, while Clayton headed west-southwest toward the Jalo-Kufra track. Some miles east of this track, however, Clayton's group discovered an unknown Libyan sand sea which was about sixty miles wide. The party crossed this sand sea and then encountered the eastern side of the Jalo-Kufra track. Not wanting to cross the track and give up the element of surprise in case the Italians were to find the tracks of his vehicles, Clayton sent a patrol on foot westward for five miles. The patrol reported that the Jalo-Kufra track appeared to extent westward indefinitely. It was later discovered that because of the softness of the desert in this region the Italians kept moving their route farther and farther west. Clayton's party then recrossed the two sand seas to Siwa and reached Cairo on 19 August. This reconnaissance provided the valuable geographical information that there was a second sand sea, until then unknown, west of the Great Sand Sea of Egypt. It also showed that the New Zealanders, if led by a person with knowledge of the desert, could cross sand seas in the North African summer.[23]

Eight days after the return of Clayton's party from Libya, the Long Range Desert Group was inspected by Wavell at Abbassia. The unit was now ready to begin operations. From the time it was authorized by Wavell, it had taken about eight weeks only to form the Long Range Desert Group, amass all the necessary equipment and personnel, conduct some training, carry out a preliminary reconnaissance into enemy territory, and set up a number of dumps in the Egyptian Desert.[24]

---

23   TNA, CAB/44/151, f. 13; see also Brendan O'Carroll, *Kiwi Scorpions: The Story of the New Zealanders in the Long Range Desert Group* (Honiton Devon: Token Publishing Inc, 2000), and Brendan O'Carroll, *Barce Raid: The Long Range Desert Group's Great Escapade* (Wellington, N.Z.: Ngaio Press, 2005).

24   TNA, WO/201/807, f. 10.

Before undertaking its first major operation, the Long Range Desert Group formed a third fighting patrol. A Echelon became R Patrol and B Echelon was renamed the Heavy Section. R, T, and W Patrols now each consisted of ten 30 cwt trucks and a 15 cwt truck manned by two officers and twenty-five other ranks. The Heavy Section, which was still equipped with Marmon-Herrington five-ton trucks would have the task of carrying fuel, water, and other supplies from Halfa on the Nile and forming a line of dumps along the eastern edge of the Great Sand Sea and Gilf Kebir, a distance from Halfa of between 350 and 450 miles.[25]

On 4 September operational orders were issued to the Long Range Desert Group. These orders were based on intelligence that the enemy might be preparing an offensive into Southern Egypt from Kufra. It was known that the Italian forces held Jalo and Kufra and that from time to time patrols were sent from Kufra to Uweinat. The mission of the Long Range Desert Group was to set up a number of supply dumps along the Libyan frontier and then to undertake a reconnaissance of the region around Kufra and to raid and destroy any enemy supply dumps found at Uweinat. R, T, and W Patrols were to leave Abbassia the following morning, and the Heavy Section was to move to Halfa by railroad and to begin setting up dumps in the desert as soon as possible.[26]

On the morning of 5 September 1940, W Patrol, under the command of Captain E.C. Mitford of the Royal Tank Regiment—one of the few Englishmen ever to have been to Kufra,[27] left Cairo. Kennedy Shaw went with W Patrol on this operation. For reasons of secrecy, the patrol followed a route that avoided oases and arrived at Ain Dalla on 8 September. At Ain Dalla W Patrol loaded its vehicles with fuel from dumps there, headed west into the Great Sand Sea, and set up a dump near Big Cairn; W Patrol then repeated the process with a second load of fuel. W Patrol also marked the route across the sand sea from Ain Dalla for future use by other patrols.

On 14 September W Patrol left Big Cairn and headed west towards the Libyan border and the sand sea discovered by Clayton in August. Their objective was to determine the extent of Italian activity in central Libya. They crossed the Libyan Sand Sea, and on 16 September found the Italian Landing Ground Number 4 on the Jalo to Kufra air route, then went north to Landing Ground Number 3. At both these airfields some Italian equipment and stores of gasoline were destroyed.

---

25   TNA, CAB/44/151, f. 14.

26   TNA, WO/201/807, f. 24.

27   W.E. Kennedy Shaw, *Long Range Desert Group: The Story of its Work in Libya, 1940–1945* (London: Collins, 1945), p. 171.

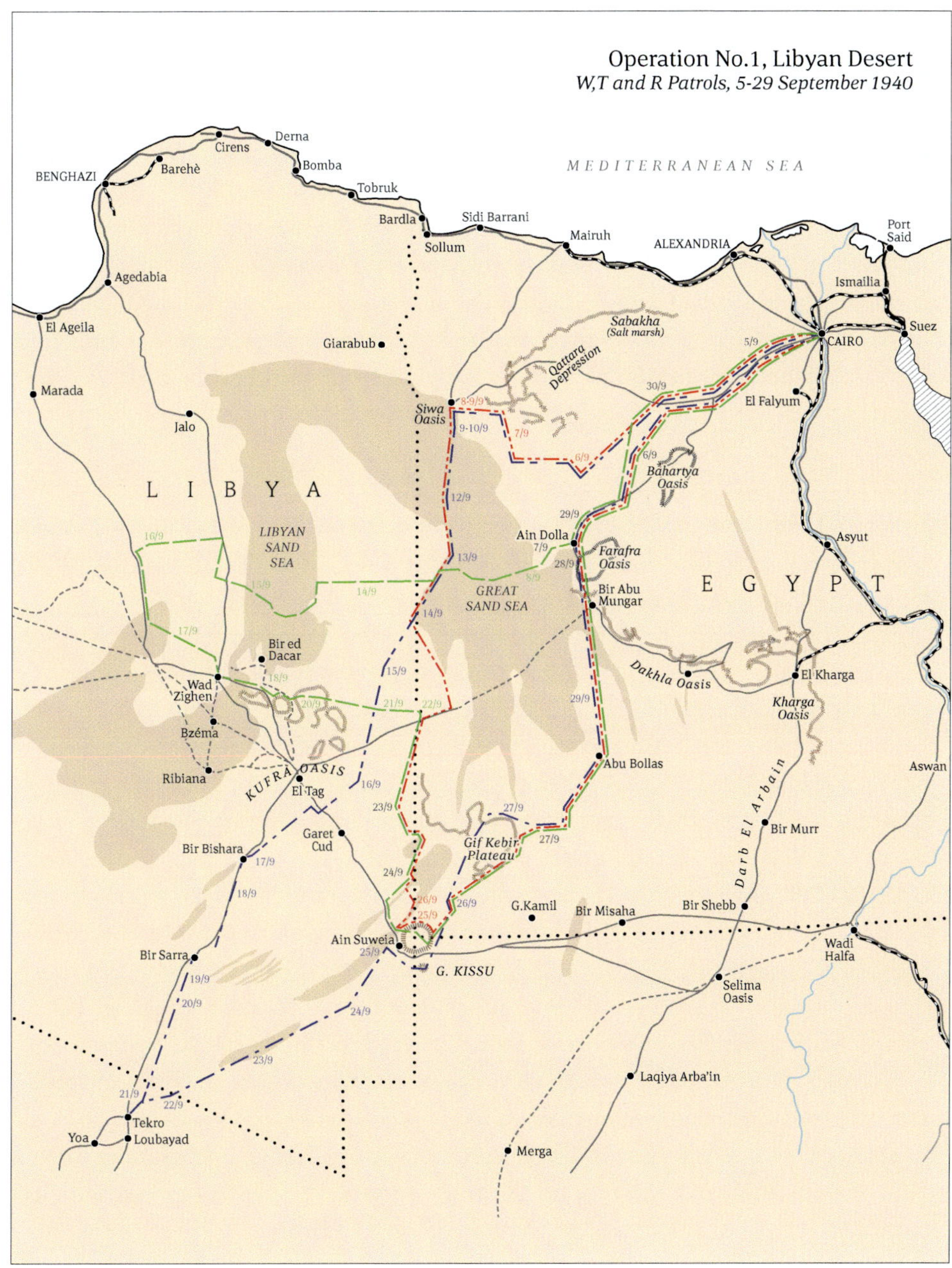

Fig. No. 1. Operation No. 1, Libyan Desert, W, T, and R Patrols, 5-29 Sept. 1940 (TNA, WO 201/807).

W Patrol then headed west to the Marada-Tazerbo track, crossing the Jalo-Kufra track en route. An examination of truck tracks showed that there had not been very much movement up and down the Jalo-Kufra track. When the Marada-Tazerbo track was reached, W Patrol followed it for a time and concluded that only about twenty-five vehicles had ever traveled on it before the arrival of W Patrol. The patrol left the Marada-Tazerbo track and turned southeast towards Bir Harasc and Zighen, which were important because they form a bottleneck through which all traffic bound for Kufra from the north must pass. On 20 September, while on the Jalo-Kufra track, W Patrol met two trucks belonging to the Trucchi Company, a civilian firm that transported military supplies from the coast to Kufra. A few rounds of Lewis gun fire brought the two Italian vehicles to a halt, and they were found to contain two Italian and six Libyan civilians plus two thousand gallons of gasoline, some other stores, and a bag of official mail. After capturing the two trucks W Patrol went to Wadi el Gubba to rendezvous with R Patrol. W Patrol's complete reconnoitering of all the northern approaches to Kufra showed that there was no large-scale movement of Italian forces south to Kufra.[28]

R and T patrols also departed from Cairo on 5 September and headed for Siwa along a route which avoided inhabited areas and arrived at a point a few miles east-southeast of Siwa. From here trucks were sent into Siwa to pick up 820 cases of fuel from a dump there. The trucks left Siwa in an east-southeast direction, giving the impression that the fuel was being taken deeper into Egypt in the direction of Bahariya, when actually it was hidden in a dump just inside the Great Sand Sea. On 11 and 12 September all the food brought from Cairo and half of the fuel that had been brought from Siwa was carried across the sand sea and another dump was made near Two Hills. T Patrol then headed south-southwest into Libya; while R Patrol recrossed the sand sea and picked up the rest of the fuel from Siwa and carried it across the sand sea to the dump near Two Hills, after which R Patrol headed south to rendezvous with W Patrol, at Wadi el Gubba, on 22 September.[29]

When T Patrol left Two Hills, their objective was to check on Italian activity in southeast Libya and the northern Chad. They headed south-southwest across desert never before traveled over to inspect the Kufra-Uweinat track near Gebel Cudi. A close study of the tracks on this route showed that only thirty-six vehicles had traveled over it. T Patrol next went southwest to Bishara Well on the Kufra-Tekro track to see if the Italians were operating in the northern Chad. They found

---

28   *Ibid*, pp. 41-45; TNA, WO/201/807, ff. 16-19.
29   TNA, WO/201/807, ff. 19, 21.

no new tracks on the Kufra-Tekro track, although the patrol went as far into Chad as the outskirts of Tekro.[30]

On 25 September R and W Patrols began an operation to scout the Uweinat region of the Libyan Desert. The two patrols left Wadi el Gubba and headed south to Gebel Babein, where they parted company. W Patrol went southwest to hit the Kufra-Uweinat track northwest of Archenu; and, after examining the track, they circled around to the north of Uweinat and met R Patrol. R Patrol had headed west-southwest from Bebel Babein towards Sarra in order to hit the Kufra-Uweinat track west of the point where W Patrol did. Yet neither patrol saw evidence of much Italian activity west of Uweinat. The reconnoitering done by R, T, and W Patrols south and southeast of Kufra and around Uweinat showed to the British that there was probably a small party of Italians at Uweinat but that the Italians had not sent any patrols southward from Kufra towards the Chad or eastward towards the Sudan from Uweinat. After their reconnaissance was completed, the three patrols returned to Cairo. The vehicles of the Long Range Desert Group had traveled 150,000 truck miles with only minor mechanical problems, and the New Zealanders had quickly learned to live and work in the wilds of the Western Desert.[31]

When the Long Range Desert Group returned to Cairo after its first operation in southern Libya, the British knew that Italian military activity in the southern Libyan Desert was at best very limited. Nothing had been found to indicate that the Italians were up to much in that region. The three Long Range Desert Group patrols had encountered only two trucks, which were captured, and they were overflown by only three enemy aircraft.[32] This lack of Italian activity in the Libyan Desert meant that the Long Range Desert Group could go on the offensive. A small-scale offensive by the Long Range Desert Group would force the Italians to reinforce their garrisons in the Libyan Desert and to place under convoy all men and material being transported in the desert. But before the Long Range Desert Group could go on the offensive, it had to be reorganized. During the first operation it was found to be difficult, owing to the lack of men, to support three separate patrols. The three patrols were retained for the next five months, but for operational purposes they were merged into two patrols. Also, General Headquarters, Middle East decided, while Bagnold was out in the desert, that the Long Range Desert Group should be doubled in size. Under this scheme, the

---

30   TNA, WO/201/807, ff. 19-20.
31   TNA, WO/201/807, ff. 20-21, 26-27, 31.
32   TNA, WO/201/807, ff. 21.

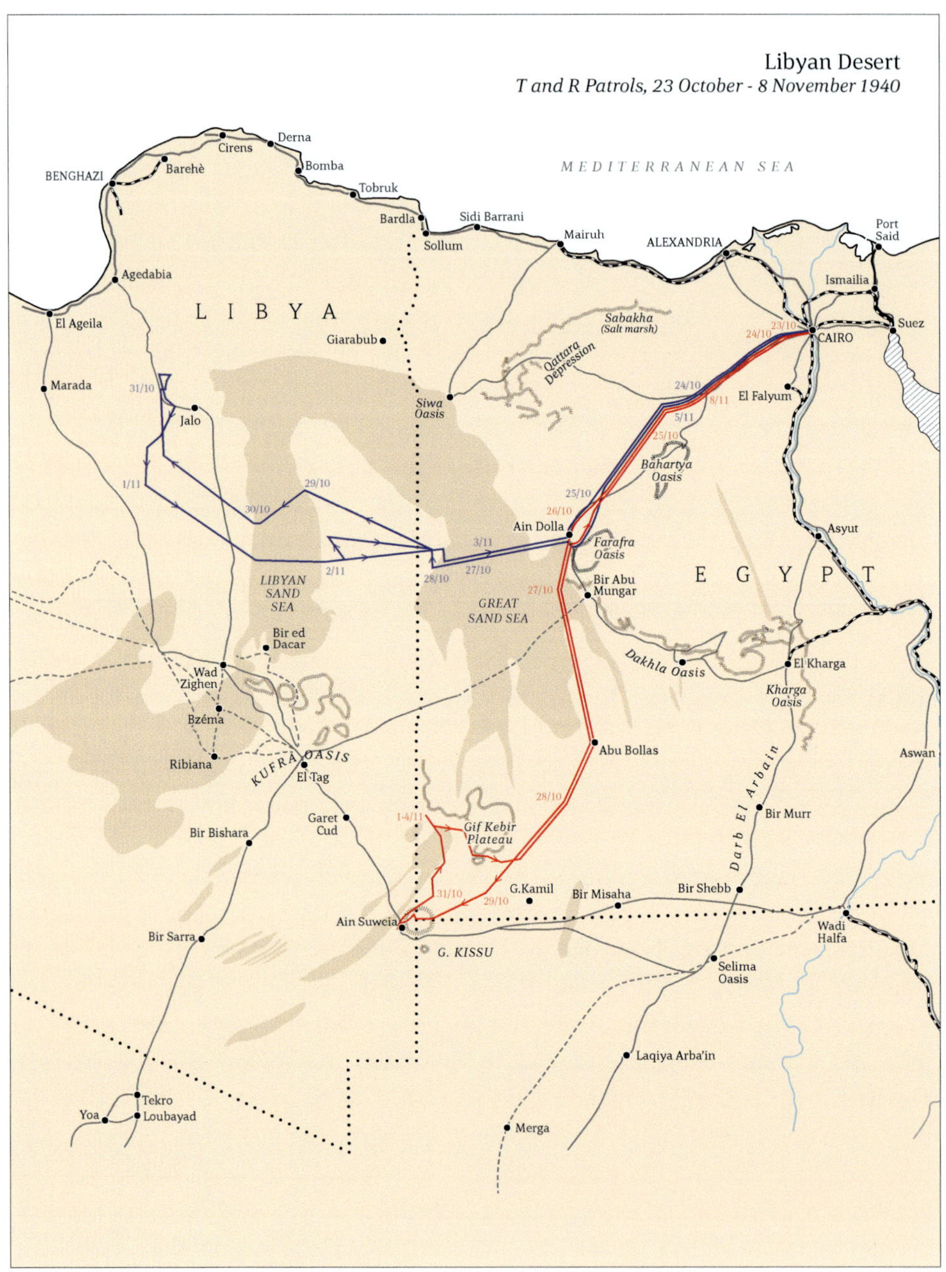

Fig. No. 2. T and R Patrols, 23 Oct.-8 Nov. 1940 (TNA, WO 201/807).

Long Range Desert Group would consist of a headquarters with a radio section, a supply section, and two squadrons of three patrols each, with four troops to each patrol. Although the War Office approved this plan, it could not be put into effect at once owing to a shortage of men and vehicles.[33]

On 23 October T Patrol left Cairo carrying, in addition to the usual fuel and stores, forty-four cases of aviation gasoline. The patrol had two objectives – first, to see if it was possible to land and refuel an aircraft in the desert; and second, to attack the Italians in north-central Libya. T Patrol crossed the Great Sand Sea to Big Cairn, where a dump was made for the aviation fuel and an airfield marked out. Radio contact was made with an R.A.F. Valentia aircraft, which successfully flew into Big Cairn on 28 October. T Patrol left Big Cairn on the morning of 29 October and headed directly for Jalo. They by-passed Jalo and Augila to the south and west and then moved up the Augila-Agedabia track to within a hundred kilometers of Agedabia, where a minefield was laid in the track. On 1 November five more minefields were laid near Augila, and then T Patrol entered Augila and attacked the small fort there. After a few rounds of Bofors and machine-gun fire, the garrison of the fort retreated to a nearby native village. One Libyan soldier, two machine-guns, and four rifles were captured. After leaving Augila, T Patrol traveled along the northern edge of the Libyan Sand Sea, which they mapped before returning to Cairo on 7 November.[34]

On 24 October, the day after T Patrol had departed for northern Libya, R Patrol left Cairo for southeastern Libya. The main objective of both patrols was to demonstrate to the Italians that the British could strike simultaneously at northern and southern Libya. When R Patrol reached Gilf Kebir, one troop under the command of Lieutenant C.A. Holliman was sent to the Wadi el Gubba region to attempt to recover the two Italian trucks that had been captured by W Patrol in September. Kennedy Shaw was sent with another troop to Uweinat to make a detailed reconnaissance of the Italian post at Ain Zwaya; however owing to the fact that they were given so little time for this mission, Kennedy Shaw's men could not climb to high ground and look down on the Italians at Ain Zwaya. By conducting a patrol around the base of Uweinat, nevertheless it was established that there were about thirty Italians and five trucks at Ain Zwaya. While Kennedy Shaw's troop was at Uweinat, the rest of R Patrol found a dump of over seven hundred small bombs, which they destroyed. This dump was located west of Uweinat. Later that same day they found an airfield with one aircraft and one hundred and sixty

---

33   TNA, CAB/44/151, ff. 19-20.
34   TNA, WO/201/807, ff. 33, 41, 44, 50.

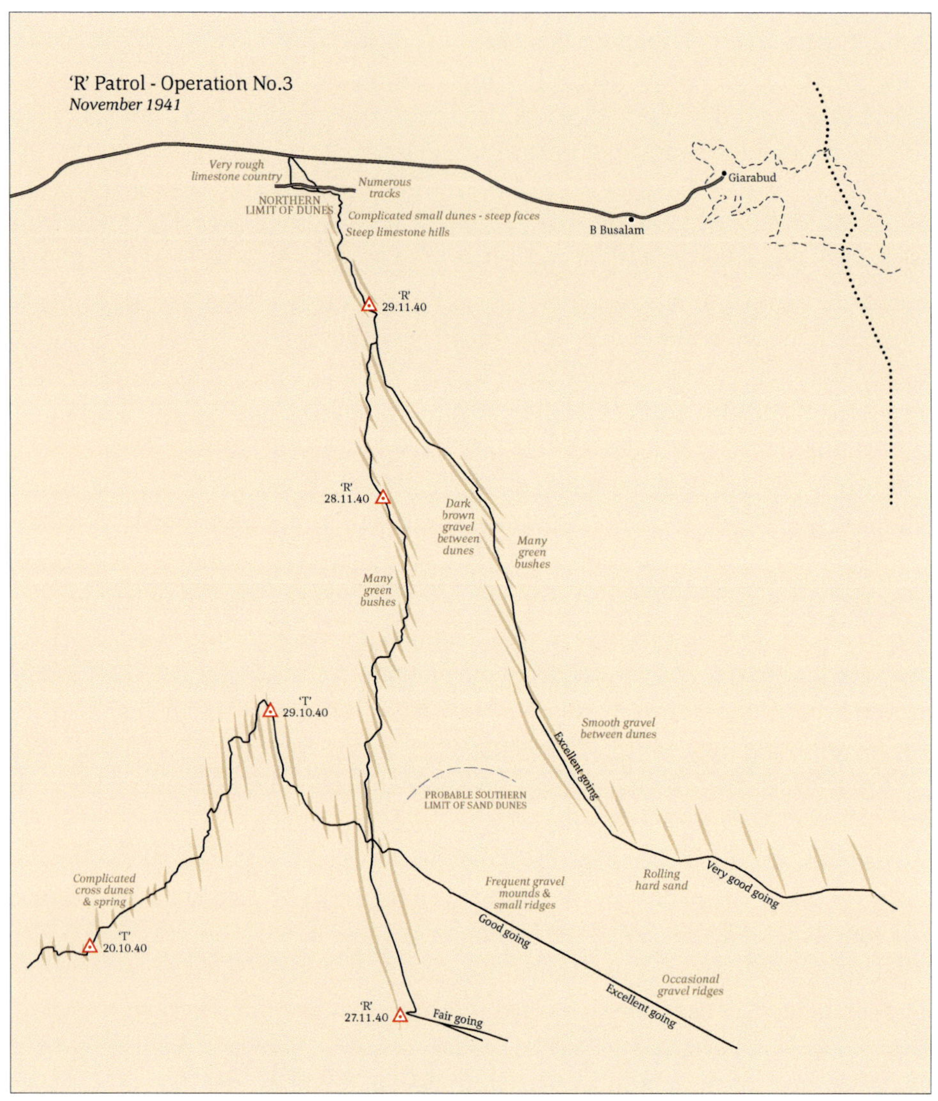

Fig. No. 3. R Patrol, Nov. 1940 (TNA, WO 201/807).

44-gallon drums of gasoline; they set both the gasoline and the aircraft afire. After planting mines in the Archenu-Uweinat track, they were joined by Kennedy Shaw's troop, and soon after R Patrol was subjected to an hour-long ineffectual attack by three Italian aircraft. R Patrol also carried out a successful experiment with landing an R.A.F. Valentia in the desert before heading back to Cairo, which they reached on 8 November.[35] R Patrol's next operation took place at the end of November when it was sent to Ain Dalla and then across the Great Sand Sea and the Libyan Sand Sea to reconnoiter the Jalo-Jarabub track, which was found to be unused by either motor vehicles or camels. R Patrol then made an uneventful trip back to Cairo.

While R Patrol was in northern Libya, W Patrol, with an extra Bofors gun, left Cairo for Uweinat with orders "to take advantage of any opportunities of worrying the enemy."[36] When W Patrol reached Gilf Kebir on 29 November, it split into two groups. One group, under the command of Lieutenant J.H. Sutherland, was to proceed by way of Peter and Paul Hills to a point east of Uweinat; while the rest of the patrol, under the command of Mitford, would make a wide swing to the east in order to give the appearance that the whole patrol had approached from the Nile Valley. However, Sutherland's group was seen and attacked by an enemy reconnaissance aircraft, which attempted to dive on the trucks. In the face of fire from Bofors and Lewis guns, however, it pulled up and broke off the engagement. Shortly after Mitford's and Sutherland's groups met east of Uweinat and began their run around the south of the mountain, W Patrol was attacked by four enemy aircraft. The attack lasted about sixty minutes. The aircraft began their attack from about a thousand feet, but the massed small-arms fire from W Patrol forced them up to five thousand feet and rendered the attack ineffectual, although over three hundred very small bombs were dropped on the patrol.

After the Italian aircraft left, W Patrol went west and found a hiding place in some large rocks west of Ain Dua, where they remained for most of the daylight hours of 30 November to give the enemy the impression that "the Patrol had sustained casualties and would retire EAST."[37] On 30 November, W Patrol moved to another hiding place southeast of Ain Dua, and early the following morning they approached Ain Dua. The airfield there appeared to be empty, and when the patrol neared Ain Dua itself there seemed to be no sign of life. But when W Patrol stopped about eight hundred yards short of Ain Dua and fired one round from a Bofors gun, enemy troops opened fire on W Patrol with machine guns and rifles from positions behind large rocks and stone walls. Mitford judged the enemy position to be too strong for a frontal attack and sent Sutherland and eight men armed with rifles and Lewis guns to make their way, under covering fire from the rest of the patrol, around the left flank of the enemy position. Sutherland's party

---

35   TNA, WO/201/807, ff. 33, 41-42, 45, 50-51.

36   TNA, WO/201/807, ff. 81.

37   *Ibid.*

forced the enemy to withdraw up the hill behind Ain Dua, and then was recalled when Mitford withdrew the patrol to a hiding place among some rocks east of Ain Dua because he thought that enemy aircraft would appear. Three Italian aircraft did overfly the patrol, but didn't see it hidden among the rocks. After the Italian aircraft left, Mitford decided to attack Ain Dua a second time. There was an off chance casualties could be inflicted on the enemy but, more important, Mitford believed that, "the action would show that a Patrol could remain in close proximity to the enemy without being sighted by aircraft. This might make them feel uncertain in the future and would make them use up valuable petrol in fruitless patrolling."[38]

Under covering fire of a Bofors gun and several Lewis guns, W Patrol attacked both flanks of the Italian position with grenades, rifles, and Lewis guns. The enemy was in an extremely strong position and, after inflicting an unknown number of casualties on the Italians, W Patrol withdrew out into the desert. They "assembled in view of AIN DUA and retired due SOUTH making very clear tracks," but once out of sight of Ain Dua, the patrol turned east.[39] The next morning, 2 December, W Patrol started back to Cairo by way of Kharga and reached Cairo on 6 December.[40]

The Long Range Desert Group moved out of Abbassia into barracks at the Citadel on 4 December. The following day the character of the Long Range Desert Group changed; it was no longer a unit made up of New Zealanders and middle-aged British desert explorers, for soldiers drawn from the Coldstream and Scots Guards had, in the meantime, arrived to join them. On 26 November General Headquarters, Middle East had ordered that a Long Range Desert Group patrol consisting of Coldstream and Scots Guards be established. The guardsmen chosen for the patrol were to be high caliber volunteers "carefully selected not only for efficiency in their particular jobs but also for their initiative and readiness to overcome difficulties."[41] With the arrival of the guardsmen, the Long Range Desert Group was again reorganized. W Patrol was disbanded, and the men from W Patrol were used to increase the strength of R and T Patrols. The guardsmen formed G Patrol and took over the equipment and vehicles of W Patrol.[42] Captain M.D.D. Crichton-Stuart of the Scots Guards was to command G Patrol. According to Crichton-Stuart, the commander of the 2nd Battalion Scots Guards picked him

---

38   TNA, WO/201/807. f. 82.

39   *Ibid.*

40   TNA, WO/201/807, ff. 77-78, 81-32; R.L. Kay, *Long Range Desert Group in Libya, 1940–41* (Wellington: Department of Internal Affairs, 1949), pp. 6-7.

41   TNA, WO/201/807, f. 38.

42   TNA, WO/201/808, f. 3.

for the job partly because he was not "indispensable, and partly because I had gained for myself a quite spurious reputation as a desert expert."[43]

When the Guardsmen arrived at the Citadel, they were thrown into a most unmilitary situation for members of the Brigade of Guards. The guardsmen were regular soldiers, and it is axiomatic to members of the Brigade of Guards that "the basis of all discipline is the barrack square."[44] The New Zealanders and their British leaders in the Long Range Desert Group, with a few exceptions, were not regular soldiers; and at the time of the arrival of the guardsmen at the Citadel, the Long Range Desert Group was perhaps the most unmilitary unit in the entire British army. In time, the guardsmen would learn that they would have to rely, as did all the other members of the Long Range Desert Group, on self-discipline of a much more demanding nature than that of the barrack square.

When Crichton-Stuart reported for duty with the Long Range Desert Group, he was informed that he had ten days to prepare "for an operation of not less than forty days,"[45] and that in that time his men would have to learn how to use a number of out-of-date weapons and to maintain and drive 30 cwt American Chevrolet trucks in the desert. Crichton-Stuart was then turned over to Clayton for further guidance and was "a little surprised to meet a grey-haired Englishman in a rather disheveled fore-and-aft cap with a General Service badge—'Crosse & Blackwell', he called it."[46] At one point Crichton-Stuart "ventured to ask rather shyly: What do we take with us?" Clayton replied, "Ask Shorty."[47] Shorty turned out to be the quartermaster of the Long Range Desert Group and he issued G Patrol with over twenty tons of stores and equipment plus machine-guns, a Bofors gun, and ammunition. All of this, along with personal weapons and kits, had to be loaded into ten 30 cwt trucks and one 15 cwt truck. Crichton-Stuart managed to get prepared in ten days' time, but he was still wondering days later when he was in the middle of the Libyan Desert if members of the Brigade of Guards were the right type of soldiers to be assigned to such an unorthodox unit as the Long Range Desert Group. Contrary to everything the men of G Patrol had been taught in years of service, the other members of the Long Range Desert Group did not even attempt to wear proper uniforms, never came to attention for anybody, and would not salute. But Crichton-Stuart discovered that they did their job extremely well.[48]

---

43   Michael Crichton-Stuart, *G Patrol* (London: William Kimber, 1958), p. 24.

44   *Ibid*, p. 23.

45   *Ibid*, p. 28.

46   *Ibid*, p. 28.

47   *Ibid*, p. 29.

48   *Ibid*, pp. 21-31.

The expedition "of not less than forty days" for which Crichton-Stuart was told to prepare had been under consideration for weeks.[49] It was to be a raid into Fezzan in southwest Libya by the Long Range Desert Group and Free French forces. On 21 June the French Government was forced to sign an armistice with the Germans and a pro-German French government was set up at Vichy, while in London an unknown French general named Charles de Gaulle proclaimed over the radio that the French would continue to fight. On 26 August Felix Eboué, Governor of the Chad, announced his support and that of the Chad to de Gaulle's Free French movement. Eboué was the only governor of a major French colony to come over to the Allied side in the first months after the collapse of France in 1940; and at the beginning of 1941 de Gaulle sent Colonel Phillippe Leclerc to take command of the French forces in the Chad.[50] The British in the Middle East were overjoyed when Eboué and the Chad rallied to the side of the Allies and they wanted to help the Free French but the vast reaches of the Libyan Desert stood between the Chad and British forces in Egypt and the Sudan.

Bagnold saw that the Long Range Desert Group working in conjunction with the Free French forces in the Chad might be able to obtain an objective of some worth. There were, however, many problems, such as the great distances involved and the confused state of French politics in their North African colonies. There was also the possibility that the Italians might be able to mount raids, using mobile forces, across French West Africa into northern Nigeria from bases in Fezzan. In a memorandum dated 14 October 1940, Bagnold stated that these problems might be avoided with the introduction of a small British mobile force, such as a Long Range Desert Group patrol, into the Chad to operate with the Free French forces there.[51]

On 8 November Bagnold flew to Fort Lamy in the Chad for two days of talks with the Free French military. While at Fort Lamy, Bagnold discussed a number of subjects with the Free French, for instance, liaison and communications between General Headquarters, Middle East; Free French Headquarters, Chad; and British

---

49   *Ibid*, p. 28.

50   Samuel Decalo, *Historical Dictionary of the Chad* (Metuchen, N.J.: Scarecrow Press, 1977), pp. 114, 175.

51   TNA, WO/201/807, ff. 66-68.

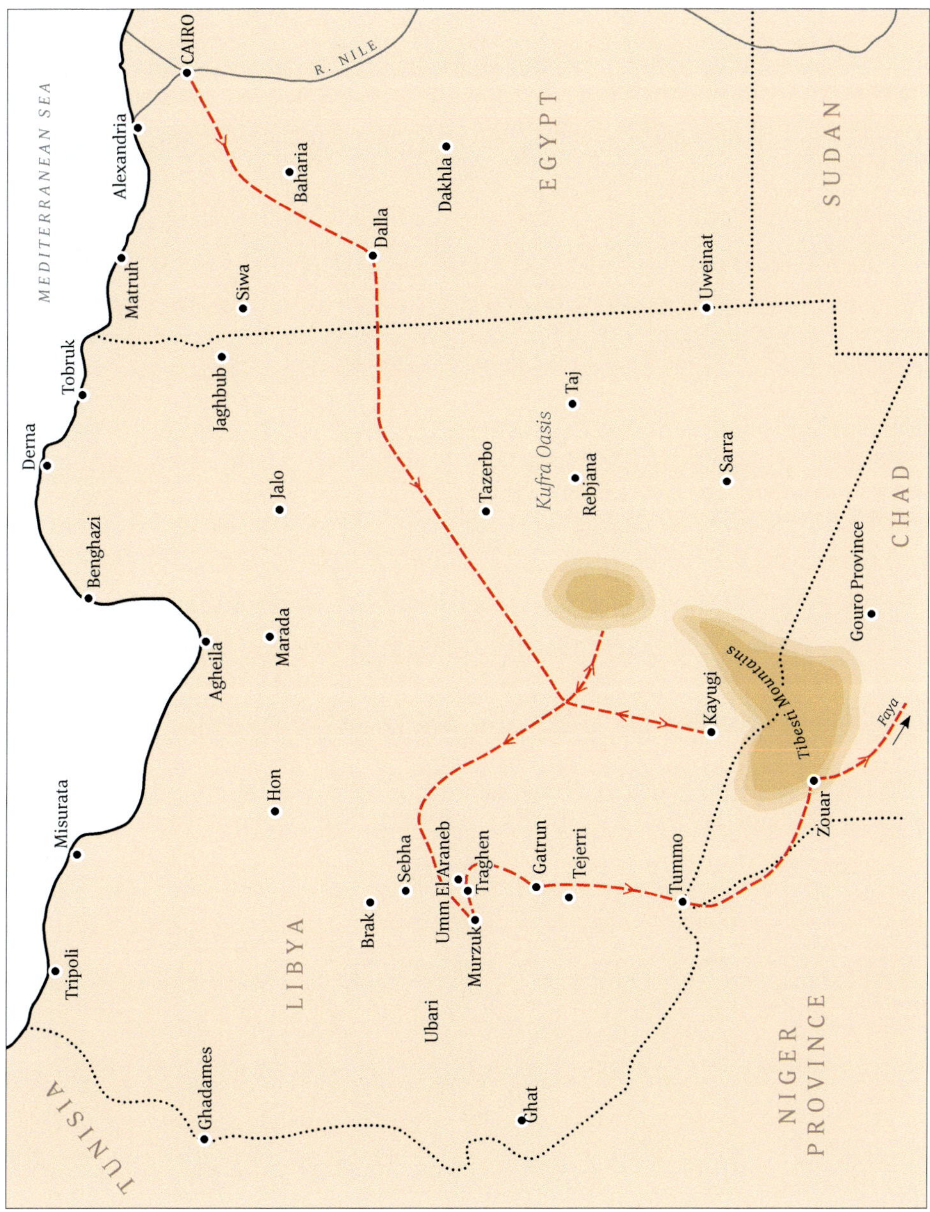

Fig. No. 4. First Fezzan Operation, Map Sketch of Route, 27 Dec. 1940-16 Jan. 1941 (TNA, WO 201/808).

Fig. No.5. First Fezzan Operation, Map Sketch of Route, G and T Patrols, 27 Dec. 1940- 9 Feb. 1941 (TNA, WO 201/807).

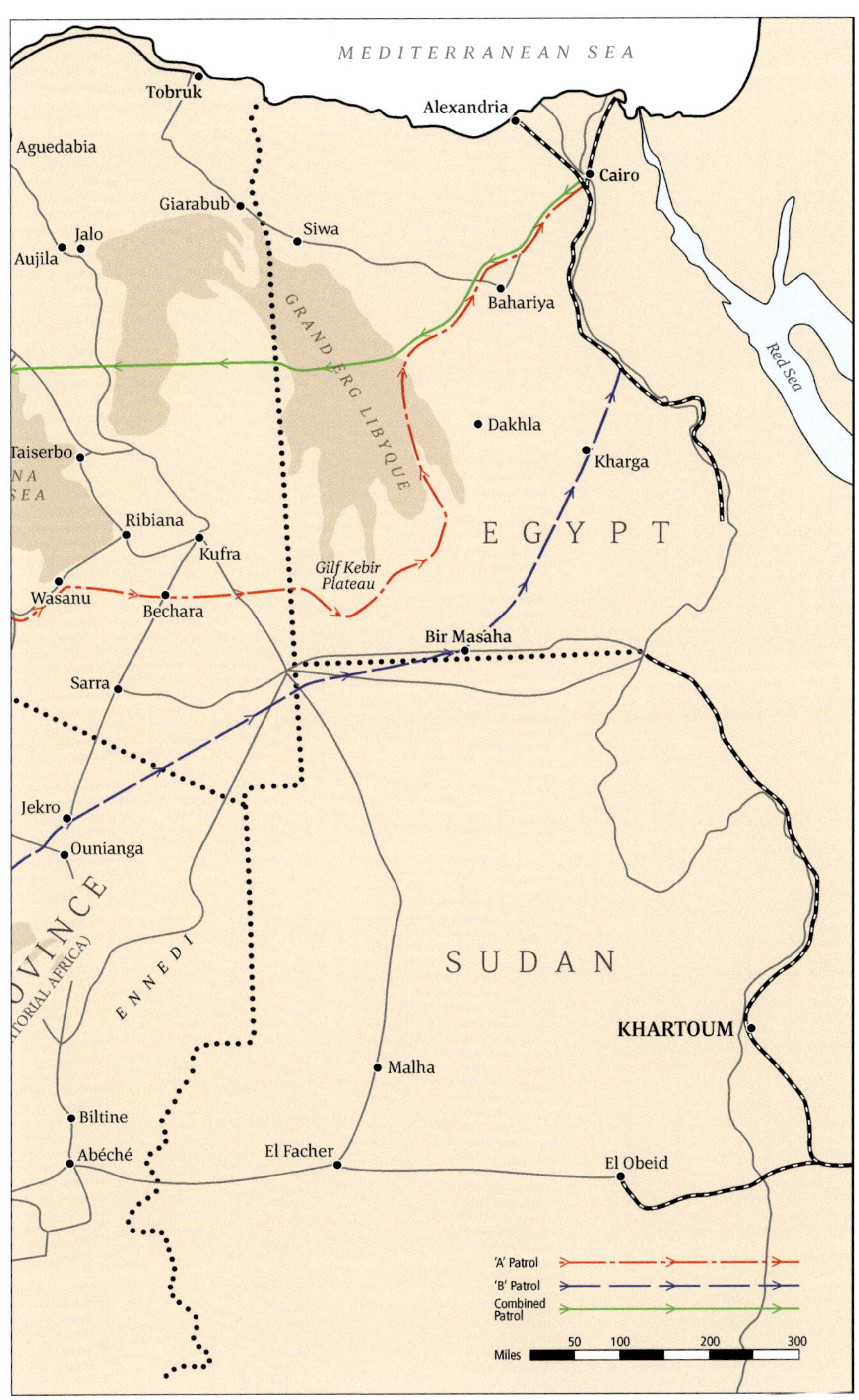

MEDITERRANEAN SEA
Tobruk
Alexandria
Aguedabia
Cairo
Giarabub
Jalo
Siwa
Aujila
Bahariya
GRAND ERG LIBYQUE
Red Sea
Dakhla
Taiserbo
Kharga
NA
SEA
EGYPT
Ribiana
Kufra
Gilf Kebir
Plateau
Wasanu
Bechara
Bir Masaha
Sarra
Jekro
Ounianga
PROVINCE
(EQUATORIAL AFRICA)
ENNEDI
SUDAN
KHARTOUM
Malha
Biltine
Abéché
El Facher
El Obeid
'A' Patrol
'B' Patrol
Combined
Patrol
50   100   200   300
Miles

West Africa. But, above all, what emerged from these discussions was that the Chad believed that

> Immediate steps should be taken to implement their recent change of politics by military action against the Italians to whom they have declared themselves hostile. They feel it is becoming urgent to do something to justify themselves in the eyes of their own people, of the troops and of the native population.[52]

Therefore, a plan was drawn up to attack the Italians as soon as possible. It was decided that a unit of the *Tibesti Groupe Nomade* should rendezvous with two Long Range Desert Group patrols in southern Libya and that the two patrols, accompanied by some Free French troops, should raid the Italians in Fezzan. This plan was quickly agreed to and the details settled by Bagnold and Lieutenant Colonel J. d'Ornano, the second in command of the Free French forces in the Chad. It would give the Free French the opportunity they sought to attack the Italians, whilst at the same time enabling the Long Range Desert Group to carry the war into southwest Libya.[53]

On 16 October a draft of the orders for the raid into Fezzan was drawn up.[54] Several days later the full orders for the raid were issued. G and T Patrols, Kennedy Shaw, a medical officer, and the former Arab guerrilla leader Abd el Gelil Seif el Nasr comprised the Long Range Desert Group's force in the raid into southwestern Libya. Clayton commanded the force and Crichton-Stuart was second in command.[55] During the afternoon of Boxing Day 1940, G and T Patrols—twenty-three vehicles and seventy-six men—left the Citadel in Cairo for Fezzan. The force passed Ain Dalla, crossed the Great Sand Sea, the Libyan Sand Sea, the Jalo-Kufra track, an arm of the Rebiana Sand Sea, and for nine days headed southwest or west across the Libyan Desert for eleven hundred miles to latitude 24° 22' N and longitude 18° 00', known only as "Point A." In the course of the trip from Cairo to Point A, the two patrols saw only three native camel herders and managed to elude being seen by the Italians. On 5 January 1941, Clayton left Point A with four trucks and headed south to Kayugi to meet the Free French; and Kennedy Shaw went off to the southeast with three trucks to attempt to find a route over Terenghi

---

52   TNA, WO/201/807, f. 70.
53   TNA, WO/201/807, ff. 69-73.
54   TNA, WO/201/807, ff. 74-75.
55   TNA, WO/201/808, ff 47-48.

Pass northeast of the Tibesti Mountains. On 7 January Clayton returned with his trucks loaded with gasoline, bringing with him Lieutenant Colonel d'Ornano, two other French officers, two French sergeants, and five native troops. That afternoon Kennedy Shaw also returned to Point A. There was an international council of war held at Point A that night, attended by the representatives of England, France, Libya, New Zealand, and Scotland. The council decided to head for Murzuk, the capital of Fezzan, and attack it.

On the morning of 8 January, G and T Patrols, carrying the Free French as passengers, headed northwest towards a point north of Murzuk on the Hon-Murzuk tract. They camped on the night of 10 January thirty miles north of Murzuk, and the next morning they set up a roadblock on the Hon-Murzuk tract to prevent anyone from entering Murzuk from the north. The main force then proceeded south along the track to a ridge about five miles to the north of Murzuk which overlooked the fort. After Clayton and Kennedy Shaw took a closer look at Murzuk, a quick meal was eaten. Clayton then issued the orders for the attack. The force would move down the road into Murzuk in a column with T Patrol in the van. Half of T Patrol would attack and destroy the airfield, while G Patrol and the remainder of T Patrol would "contain" the fort.

As the column moved down the road toward Murzuk, they captured the local postmaster with his bicycle; and when they neared Murzuk the locals, thinking they were Italian, gave the Long Range Desert Group column the fascist salute. As the British vehicles approached the fort, they saw a number of Italian troops standing around in front of it. Three hundred yards short of the fort those vehicles of T Patrol whose target was the airfield turned off the main street and, without warning, began firing at Italians as they headed for the airfield. The rest of the column opened fire on the Italians in front of the fort while deploying in a semi-circle east to west of the building. After being taken completely by surprise, the Italians in the fort quickly regained their wits and, although the fort was under fire from rifles, machine-guns, and a 37mm Bofors gun, the Italians within it began to return the fire. The commander of the section of T Patrol at the fort, Sergeant C.D. Hewson, was killed while deploying his men. A car drove into the middle of this firefight carrying the Italian commander of the fort. As it pulled up in front of the main gate of the fort, one shot of G Patrol's Bofors gun demolished it. Meanwhile, at the western end of the British position Lieutenant M.C. Gibbs of the Coldstream Guards worked his way with two 2-inch mortars to within three or four hundred yards of the fort and began lobbing shells into it, setting fire to the main tower. By now the fight at the fort was a standoff. With only small arms, two small mortars, and a 37mm Bofors gun, the British could not breach the walls of the fort and whilst the Italians could not escape from the fort, they could beat off any attack mounted by the Long Range Desert Group.

In the meantime, the section of T Patrol sent to attack the airfield overran it before the Italians knew what was happening. But as Clayton's truck turned the corner going around the hanger, it ran into a machine-gun post and was riddled with bullets. D'Ornano was killed before Clayton could throw the truck into reverse. When T Patrol opened up with their Bofors gun on the hanger and the machine-gun post, about twenty Italian and Libyan troops in and around the hanger surrendered to the New Zealanders. Ghiblis reconnaissance aircraft, munitions, gasoline, and other equipment were found in the hanger and at various points around the airfield. Clayton and the New Zealanders, using gasoline, set everything of value at the airfield on fire and then fired a white flare as the signal to withdraw. At the fort the battle, still a standoff, continued because the white flare fired by Clayton was obscured by the smoke of battle and the onset of a sand storm. It was not until about 1600 that Crichton-Stuart's men, under cover of the sand storm, withdrew from the fort. The Italians, unable to see anything, continued for some time firing machine-guns and rifles into the blowing sand.

When T and G Patrols reached the point just off the Hon-Murzuk track where the attack had been planned that morning, they stopped to bury Lieutenant Colonel d'Ornano of the Free French forces and Sergeant C.D. Hewson of the 2nd New Zealand Expeditionary Force. One guardsman was badly wounded in the leg and several other men of the Long Range Desert Group were slightly wounded. Jacques Massu, a Free French officer who would later make a name for himself in Indo-China and Algeria, was shot through the calf of the leg but did not report the wound—he cauterized it himself with a lighted cigarette. That evening G and T Patrols and the Free French camped about twelve miles east of Murzuk.[56]

The following morning G and T Patrols ran east, and thirty miles from Murzuk they entered the village of Traghen, which surrendered without a shot being fired. The local police station was searched and all military stores found were destroyed. Leaving Traghen, the two patrols headed for Ummel Araneb, about twenty miles farther east. When G and T patrols approached the fort at Ummel Araneb, they were met by machine-gun fire. Knowing that the fort had a radio and that there were Italian air bases at Hon and Sebha, and having no weapon that would knock a hole in the stone wall of the fort, Clayton decided that the force should

---

56   TNA, WO/201/808, ff. 56-57; M. Crichton-Stuart, "The Story of a Long Range Desert Patrol," *The Army Quarterly* 47/1 (Oct, 1943), pp. 70-77; Kay, *Long Range Desert Group in Libya*, pp. 7-25; Bagnold, "Early Days of the Long Range Desert Group," p. 38; Kennedy Shaw, *Long Range Desert Group*, pp. 60-62.

proceed south towards the Free French base at Zouar in the foothills of the Tibesti Mountains. They reached Zouar on 21 January.[57]

When Bagnold learned in Cairo that the raid on Murzuk had taken place as planned, he resolved to fly to the Chad to plan the next operation with the Free French. At Faya, Bagnold met Leclerc for the first time. To Bagnold, the French colonel was "a most striking figure, combining determination and resource with great charm."[58] Leclerc wanted to attack and capture Kufra because he believed that the Free French needed a big victory. But Leclerc needed the Long Range Desert Group to help with the navigation.[59] After the meeting with Leclerc, Bagnold flew to Zouar in a Free French aircraft on 20 January. The next day he, Kennedy Shaw, and the guardsman who was badly wounded in the leg at Murzuk flew back to Faya. At Faya Bagnold and Leclerc agreed that G and T Patrols would be placed under Leclerc's command and would act as the advanced guard of the Free French attack on Kufra.[60] When the details of the plan were worked out, Bagnold, Kennedy Shaw, and the wounded guardsman left Faya by air for Egypt.

G and T Patrols departed from Zouar on 21 January and, after encountering very difficult going for most of the way, arrived at Faya on 24 January. With G and T Patrols as an advanced guard, Leclerc intended to march on Kufra across three hundred and fifty miles of desert with a force of some three hundred and fifty to four hundred Senegalese troops, a few automatic weapons, two 75mm guns, a number of Bedford trucks, and all the other trucks that could be found in the Chad. The operation was a gamble because of the fact that the Free French did not have enough fuel to get back to Faya if the operation failed. Moreover, Leclerc intended to attack and overpower, with his small force, thirteen to fourteen hundred Italian troops armed with automatic weapons defending a fortress. It was a "desperate venture," but Leclerc and his men were bound and determined to strike the first Free French blow against the enemy.

The Free French forces left Faya on 26 January and headed towards Oumianga Kebir, a hundred and twenty-five miles to the north. On 27 January, after picking up fuel, and rations, G and T Patrols started north after the Free French column.

---

57   M. Crichton-Stuart, "The Story of a Long Range Desert Patrol," *The Army Quarterly* 47/1 (Oct, 1943), pp. 78-80 and M. Crichton-Stuart, "The Story of a Long Range Desert Patrol," *The Army Quarterly* 47/2 (Jan, 1944), pp. 197-199.

58   Bagnold, "Early Days of the Long Range Desert Group", p. 39.

59   *Ibid.*

60   Kennedy Shaw, *Long Range Desert Group*, pp. 67-69. See also, Jean-Noël Vincent, "Koufra, 23 décembre 1940-1 mai 1941", *Revue historique des armées*, I (1982), p. 4 and Roger Ceccaldi, "Koufra. Souvenirs de l'Artilleur", *Revue historique des armées*, II (1983), pp. 41-49.

One of G Patrol's trucks broke down beyond repair and had to be abandoned. The next day at Oumianga Kebir, G and T Patrols caught up with the Free French, who had had several delays owing to mechanical problems and vehicles becoming stuck in the sand. Clayton and T Patrol left Oumianga Kebir on 29 January and arrived the next day at Sarra, where they found that the deep well had been destroyed. The destruction of the well at Sarra should have warned Clayton that the Italians were aware of the threat from the Chad.

On 30 January G Patrol departed from Oumianga Kebir. By the morning of 31 January they were about twenty-five miles north of Sarra, when they saw T Patrol, less four trucks and Clayton, unexpectedly approaching from the north. Clayton and T Patrol had left Sarra on 31 January and that same day had reached Eishara, where they discovered that the Italians also had destroyed the well. T Patrol continued going north to Gebel Sherif, where at 1130 the patrol was sighted by an Italian aircraft. T Patrol took cover among some rocks, but the aircraft reappeared at 1340; and forty minutes later T Patrol was attacked by an Italian Auto Saharan unit. The Auto Saharan units were the Italian counterpart of the Long Range Desert Group and were armed with 20mm cannon and machine guns. The fire from the Italians was heavy and accurate. Three of T Patrol's trucks were destroyed, and Corporal F.R. Beech and the captive postmaster of Murzuk were killed. Clayton and the remaining trucks withdrew and circled around the Auto Saharan unit; and, just as they were preparing to counterattack from the south, T Patrol was attacked by three enemy aircraft with bombs and machine-gun fire. As the patrol was withdrawing south, Clayton's vehicle was damaged by gunfire. Clayton was wounded and he and two New Zealanders were captured. The remaining vehicles of T Patrol continued withdrawing south until they met G Patrol north of Sarra.[61]

G Patrol and the remainder of T Patrol raced south to warn Leclerc of the Italian ambush at Gebel Sherif. Clayton's last instructions were that if anything happened to him, the Free French must be warned not to continue the operation. In the late afternoon the two patrols reached Leclerc's headquarters. Lieutenant L.B. Ballantyne, now the commanding officer of T Patrol, told Leclerc of the ambush at Gebel Sherif. After the New Zealander finished speaking, the Free French colonel looked at a map and asked the British and New Zealand officers what was known about Italian activity at Uweinat. When this question had been

---

61   TNA, WO/201/808, f. 59; Kay, *Long Range Desert Group in Libya*, pp. 25-26; Kennedy Shaw, *Long Range Desert Group*, pp. 70-71; Crichton-Stuart, "The Story of a Long Range Desert Patrol," *The Army Quarterly* (Jan, 1944), pp. 202-205. For an Italian account of the action at Gebel Sherif, see Imperial War Museum, David Lloyd Owen's Collection of Long Range Desert Group Papers, 4/5 The Kennedy Shaw Papers, No. 5.

answered, Leclerc told the Long Range Desert Group officers that after consulting with his officers he would inform the commanders of G and T Patrols of his plans. That night Crichton-Stuart read an intelligence report that had been flown in from Cairo that afternoon, which stated that there had been breaches in Free French security and that the Italians had been forewarned of the attack on Kufra. The next afternoon, after being shown the intelligence report from Cairo, Leclerc informed the Long Range Desert Group officers that he would not attack Kufra as originally planned. Instead, advanced units of the Free French force would remain at Sarra and conduct harassing patrols, the main Free French force would be concentrated at Tekro, Uweinat would be occupied, and G and T Patrol were released from further service with expression of "gratitude for their cooperation."[62] At this meeting Crichton-Stuart agreed to take two French vehicles with their crews to Uweinat to carry out a reconnaissance there and at the same time mark the route to Uweinat. The commander to the two patrols also agreed to leave with the Free French forces one of T Patrol's trucks, with its crew of three men commanded by Lance Corporal F. Kendall, to help the Free French with desert navigation.[63]

On 4 February G and T Patrols and the two French vehicles ran east-northeast to Uweinat, where they left the French, and then traveled northeast to Kharga and Asyut on the Nile and arrived in Cairo on 9 February. The two patrols had crossed some 4,500 miles of desert in forty-five days. They had lost four vehicles in action and two more to mechanical breakdown. They thought that two men had been killed and three others captured, and four men were missing in action and believed killed or captured. These figures would later be changed to three dead and three captured. At the time, however, it never occurred to anyone in Cairo that any men had escaped from the ambush of T Patrol, and the four missing men were assumed to be dead or captured.[64]

It was not known until some time later that during the Gebel Sherif ambush, the four missing men had escaped from their vehicle when it caught fire and had hidden in the rocks until the Italians left. Under the leadership of Trooper R.J. Moore, a New Zealander, these four men decided not to give up. Instead, they would walk south until they ran into either a British or Free French patrol or reached a Free French outpost in the Chad. Moore was wounded in the foot, Guardsman Easton was wounded in the throat, and Private A. Tighe of the RAOC

62   TNA, WO/201/808, f. 59.
63   Crichton-Stuart, "The Story of a Long Range Desert Patrol," p. 206.
64   *Ibid.*, pp. 206–210; TNA, WO/201/808, f. 60.

had suffered some kind of internal injury. Guardsman Winchester, a veteran of Dunkirk, was the only one of the four who was uninjured.

Under the leadership of Moore, the four began walking south. They had less than two gallons of water and nothing else. On the third day of walking the four men found a two-pound pot of plum jam, which they ate. On the fourth day, Tighe began to falter; and on the fifth day the other three had to leave him to follow as best he could. They put his share of the water into a bottle they found without realizing that the previous contents of the bottle would make the water undrinkable. On the sixth day Moore, Easton, and Winchester managed to reach, in a sand storm, a hut at Sarra. They found no food, but they did find some motor oil, which they bathed their feet in and used to make a fire for the night. At this point, they had walked through the desert for one hundred and thirty miles. The next day the three continued walking south. Meanwhile, Tighe managed to reach the hut at Sarra and to make a fire to keep warm that night, which probably saved his life. On the ninth day Easton fell behind. Later that day a Free French aircraft flew over Moore and Winchester and dropped some food, which the two men could not find, and a bottle of lemonade, but the cork came out of the bottle on impact leaving only about an inch of lemonade in the bottle. Moore continued south and Winchester, who was now in a state of delirium, struggled along behind.

On 8 February a Free French patrol returning from a reconnaissance of Kufra went to the sight of the ambush at Gebel Sherif and buried Corporal F.R. Beech with full military honors and also the dead postmaster of Murzuk. The next night this patrol found Tighe near death in the hut at Sarra, but the British soldier managed to tell them that there were three other men ahead of him walking south. On 10 February a search party found Easton about fifty-five miles south of Sarra, but he died that night. Winchester was located twelve miles further south. And Moore was found two hundred and ten miles south of Gebel Sherif "plodding on with swinging arms. Perfectly clear headed and apparently normal he waved to them without stopping, as if to an acquaintance during a walking race."[65] Thus ended the first of many epic walks through the desert by the men of the Long Range Desert Group. Trooper Moore was awarded the DCM for his leadership after the ambush at Gebel Sherif.

When the Western Desert Force drove the Italian army out of Northern Cyrenaica in January of 1941, the Italian border garrisons fell back to the oasis of Jarabub. The British wanted to capture Jarabub; so, an R Patrol was placed under the command of the General Officer Commanding British forces in Egypt. Under the command of Captain D.G. Steel, R Patrol left Cairo on 1 January 1941 and

---

65   TNA, WO/201/808, ff.61-63, 72-73A.

passed through Ain Dalla, crossed the Great and Libyan Sand Seas, and reached the Jarabub-Jalo track. It was the task of R Patrol to block this track and to see that no supplies reached Jarabub from Jalo; however, Jarabub was being supplied from the air and the oasis could not be forced to surrender by a land blockade. R Patrol continued this operation on the Jarabub-Jalo track until 2 March, when it was relieved by T Patrol. Finally, an Australian force brought down from the north stormed Jarabub, and on 26 March T Patrol returned to Cairo.[66]

In the first six months of its operations, the Long Range Desert Group had shown that it could operate almost anywhere in the Western Desert. The patrols of the Long Range Desert Group had been as far west as Murzuk in Fezzan, as far south as Faya in the Chad, and as far north as the Agedabia-Augila track. Also, except for the ambush of T Patrol at Gebel Sherif, the unit had suffered almost no casualties at the hands of the enemy. The patrols of the Long Range Desert Group had shown that there was no Italian threat to the British in the southern Libyan Desert. And, although the operations of the Long Range Desert Group were carried out by a mere handful of men, they forced the Italians to escort supply convoys to their posts in the interior of Libya and to keep reinforcing those posts. To the Italians it appeared that the Long Range Desert Group came from nowhere and could go anywhere. Their ability to conduct operations hundreds of miles into Libya threatened the whole interior of Libya at a time when the Italian empire in East Africa was being attacked from all sides, their invasion of Greece was failing, and their army in Libya was being crushed by British Commonwealth forces along the coast of the Mediterranean. But in February of 1941 the first units of the *Deutsches Afrika Korps* began to arrive in Tripolitania and a new war was about to begin in the North African Desert. In this new war in the Western Desert, would the British commanders know what role to assign to the finely tuned instrument known as the Long Range Desert Group?

---

66   TNA, CAB/44/151, f. 39.

4

Frustration

"Passive misuse and active misuse."
—*Captain Michael Crichton-Stuart, Commander G Patrol*

At the beginning of 1941 the Long Range Desert Group was enlarged and reorganized. S and Y Patrols were added to the Group. S Patrol was manned by Rhodesians and men from the Northumberland Fusiliers and the Argyll and Sutherland Highlanders; Y Patrol was made up of men belonging to the Yeomanry cavalry regiments in the 1st Cavalry Division in Palestine. The Long Range Desert Group was divided into A and B Squadrons, H Section, and a headquarters group. A Squadron was made up of G, S, and Y Patrols; while R and T Patrols formed B Squadron. The headquarters unit consisted of Bagnold, who had been promoted to Lieutenant Colonel and was the group commander; Major Guy Prendergast, who had come out from England and was second in command; one officer who acted as adjutant and another who was the quartermaster; an intelligence officer—Kennedy Shaw; and a signals officer, a medical officer, and the administrative officer of the group headquarters. In addition, there were forty-three other ranks, some of whom—radio operators and medical orderlies—were detached to squadrons or patrols. H Section, while still having the task of setting up dumps, was now equipped with a light tank and a 4.5-inch howitzer. The tank and the howitzer were for attacking forts, such as the one at Murzuk, which could not be attacked successfully with lighter weapons; apparently, however, the tank was never used and the howitzer only once.[1]

Men of the type required to fill the ranks of the enlarged Long Range Desert Group by the 1st Cavalry Division to form Y Patrol were found, upon arrival at the Citadel, to be "unsuitable, being ex-cavalry reservists of bad character whom

---

1   TNA, CAB/44/151, ff. 40-41.

their units wanted to get rid of."[2] Bagnold would have none of this old army trick, and most of the "ex-cavalry reservists" were returned forthwith to the 1st Cavalry Division along with a demand that only qualified men be sent to the Long Range Desert Group. Setting up S Patrol took time, for the commanders of the units which were to supply the men for it were reluctant to give up anyone while still engaged in the Battle of Sidi Barrani.[3]

The problem of finding officers of the right type was even more difficult than filling the ranks of the Long Range Desert Group. Bagnold could not find officers with knowledge of the desert that equaled his own or that of Clayton, Prendergast, and Kennedy Shaw except for Harding-Newman, but he was assigned to the 7th Armoured Division which would not permit his reassignment. Bagnold required an adjutant or a staff officer "with the mental ability to keep track of a Unit scattered between CAIRO, TAISERBO, and WADI HALFA, and doing desert journeys of 600 to 1,000 miles as a normal routine."[4] The Long Range Desert Group also needed an officer to command B Squadron but apparently could not find one with the proper qualifications. In the end, the problem of finding qualified officers was solved by making do with those officers who knew the desert and the fact that officers who were new to the desert quickly learned how to live and fight in it. Under the pressure of war, it was found that a good young officer could learn very quickly the skills that during peacetime took years even for Bagnold and Kennedy Shaw to learn. David Lloyd Owen, for example, was selected to command Y Patrol by Bagnold and Prendergast after admitting that he knew nothing about Arabic, the desert, and the workings of motor vehicles, Breda guns, or Lewis guns. When asked by Bagnold, "What do you know?" the future commander of the Long Range Desert Group answered, "Not much, sir...but I am dreadfully keen and sure I can learn."[5] The trick was to select officers who had brains, wanted to learn the skills required to be an officer in the Long Range Desert Group, and would be good leaders.

As the fame of the Long Range Desert Group grew, the number of men wanting to join the unit increased to the point where Captain David Lloyd Owen once had to pick twelve men out of seven hundred volunteers. Years later Lloyd Owen explained the method he used to select men for the Long Range Desert Group:

2   TNA, WO/201/808, f. 3.

3   TNA, WO/201/808, ff. 3-4.

4   TNA, WO/201/220, f. 40A.

5   David Lloyd Owen, *The Desert My Dwelling Place* (London: Cassel and Company, Ltd, 1957), p. 49.

What I used to do, I used to sit with two of my men. I had the patrol sergeant on one side, and a trooper on the other side. And I would say to them, 'Now look here, what we've got to do is look at the sort of chap we would like to live with behind the lines' … and if he is a loudmouth bugger none of us wanted that and if he's a bragging sort of swashbuckling chap, none of us want that. We want the perfectly ordinary guy that we're all going to get on with and that doesn't panic and behaves perfectly naturally and normally and that's what we used to look for...[6]

At the beginning of 1941 the problem of finding suitable vehicles for the Long Range Desert Group was even more pressing than that of manpower. All the Chevrolet 30 cwt trucks and the two Marmon-Herrington trucks of H Section were worn out and were beyond repair because of continual hard usage. In order to find replacements for H Section's Marmon-Herringtons, Bagnold conducted a test in December 1940 on two American ten-ton trucks. One was a ten-ton White truck and the other was a ten-ton Mack truck. Each of these vehicles was loaded with a little under ten tons of fuel at Cairo. Bagnold then had both trucks driven to Ain Dalla. The Mack truck was found to be inferior to the White truck in the desert. Bagnold thought that the White ten-ton truck did fit the specifications for desert work and requested that four of these vehicles be issued to H Section for the purpose of setting up dumps of fuel and stores in the desert. Bagnold also thought that White trucks might be used at times to carry a heavy cannon or a light tank to increase the firepower of the Long Range Desert Group patrol.[7]

The biggest problem of all was to replace the Long Range Desert Group's fleet of 30 cwt Chevrolet trucks. By the beginning of 1941, those Chevrolet trucks that had not been lost in action were falling apart and were in such a state of disrepair that they could not be used for future operations. There were, however, no additional 30 cwt Chevrolet trucks in the Middle East, and it had become War Office policy to "abolish all 30 cwt" trucks within the British army. But 30 cwt trucks were the only type of vehicle that the Long Range Desert Group could use for their patrols into Libya. There were a number of Ford 30 cwt four-wheel drive trucks in Egypt and Bagnold, although he did not like the Ford 30 cwt trucks, was forced to settle for them. By 20 March 1941, the Long Range Desert Group had been issued with seventy Ford 30 cwt trucks with four-wheel drive

<hr>

6   Lloyd Owen Interview.
7   TNA, WO/201/808, ff. 34-55; WO/20/220. f. 12A.

which had been modified for use in the desert.[8] At the same time the Long Range Desert Group was issued ten Italian SPA 30 cwt four-wheel drive trucks which had been captured from the Italian Auto Saharan units.[9] Both the Ford 30 cwt and captured Italian trucks proved to be unsuitable for the use of the Long Range Desert Group when compared to the Chevrolet 30 cwt trucks; and in July of 1941 a "special" order was placed with General Motors to ship to Egypt two hundred 30 cwt Chevrolet trucks for the use of the Long Range Desert Group.[10]

At the end of 1940 the Long Range Desert Group was established. Two New Zealand regimental signalers were assigned to each patrol to conduct radio communications with the group's headquarters. The original signal scheme called for a No. 11 radio transmitter to be mounted on one truck in each patrol or sub unit, and this radio set was powered by two six-volt commercial truck batteries which were recharged by the truck's generator. If the truck with the radio set was motionless for any length of time, the batteries would be kept charged by exchanging them with batteries from other trucks, thus avoiding the need for carrying around the equipment required to recharge batteries. In November of 1940, however, the New Zealand radio operators were replaced by operators from the Royal Corps of Signals. These men were drawn from an elite of signalers formed to serve with special forces, such as the commandos and the Long Range Desert Group. At the same time the Group's signal procedures were studied and then overhauled by Pilot Officer Jacquement of the R.A.F., who was a signals specialist. In December 1940 2nd Lieutenant G.B. Heywood of the Middlesex Yeomanry was assigned to the Long Range Desert Group to be the unit's permanent signals officer. Heywood carried out a number of changes which Jacquement had begun and instituted a number of others.[11]

Radio communications were of the utmost importance to the Long Range Desert Group because its main mission was to gather intelligence and to report it back to British Middle East Headquarters. Radio was also the only means by which the commanding officer of the Long Range Desert Group could control and command various patrols scattered across the Libyan Desert. But radio communications are a two-edged sword. By using radio direction finders, the enemy could locate the position of a patrol making a radio transmission; or by means of traffic analysis, that is, by studying over a period of time the form and patterns of the Long Range

---

8   TNA, WO/201/808, f. 4; WO/20/220, f. 35A.
9   TNA, WO/20/220, f. 19A.
10   TNA, WO/20/220, f. 70A.
11   TNA, WO/20/220, f. 70A.

Desert Group's standard operating procedures. Moreover, radio transmissions could be intercepted by the enemy and then subjected to cryptographic attack with the objective of breaking the codes of the Long Range Desert Group and reading the contents of its radio messages. Heywood and the Long Range Desert Group took a number of steps to prevent the enemy from using direction finders on its radio transmissions and to ensure that traffic analysis and cryptographic attack were nearly impossible. In this the Long Range Desert Group was incredibly successful, for its radio transmissions were tracked by direction finders only once or twice.[12]

The Long Range Desert Group went to great lengths to obtain very highly qualified radio operators. All signal personnel in the Long Range Desert Group were volunteers. Patrol radio operators were picked not for their toughness or skill at soldiering but rather for their intelligence, keenness, self-reliance, and technical skills. Before being assigned to a patrol, a trained Royal Corps of Signals radio operator received three weeks of intensive training by the Signals Troop at the headquarters of the Long Range Desert Group. This was then followed by a month's work in the Signals Troop at headquarters. During this training, a large number of competent radio operators were found to be incapable of mastering the skills required by the Long Range Desert Group and were sent back to their units.

As far as the No. 11 radio used by the patrols in the field was concerned, there were found to be a number of problems with it. To begin with, it had a lower limit of its frequency range as high as 4.2 Mc/s., which meant that even though the sets were designed for short range work, there was always the fear that if a patrol was one hundred and fifty to two hundred miles from headquarters there would be a communications failure because of signal skipping. That is, the ground signal from a No. 11 set could only be picked up at a range of thirty or forty miles but not at a range of one hundred and fifty to two hundred miles because the signal would hit the ionosphere and skip right over the receiver at headquarters. Another weakness of the No. 11 set was that it was a "trans-receiver," which was not suitable for conditions of low signal strength and heavy interference that were common in the desert. To work a No. 11 radio set or to pick up its signals over great distances required radio operators of exceptional skill.

The Long Range Desert Group instituted a number of measures to ensure the security of its radio transmissions. Being a small isolated unit, the Long Range Desert Group could use methods to protect its radio transmissions which regular military formations could not use. To further lessen the risks involved, there was an extremely high standard of security right from the start. Frequencies were changed

---

12   Lloyd Owen Interview.

at least two times a day and no frequency was used more than twice a month. Call signs were changed every time the frequency was changed and never repeated. International commercial procedures were always used instead of military ones and in no way altered. The call signs of known local commercial stations, such as those in Egypt and French Equatorial Africa were used whenever possible. No speech or plain language in any language was ever used. All papers that were used to record signals, or for encoding or decoding, were destroyed immediately after use. The types of ciphers used were designed to fit into commercial formats, depending on the type of transmission to be made. Before being sent to higher headquarters, all coded information received from patrols was rewritten and recorded using a different code and a different type of format. Further, there was extensive use of a one-at-a-time pad codes. At first the Long Range Desert Group attempted to set up transmissions schedules for each patrol, but this did not work because the patrols could not send or receive signals when on the move and only the patrol commander could decide when his patrol could stop moving long enough to send

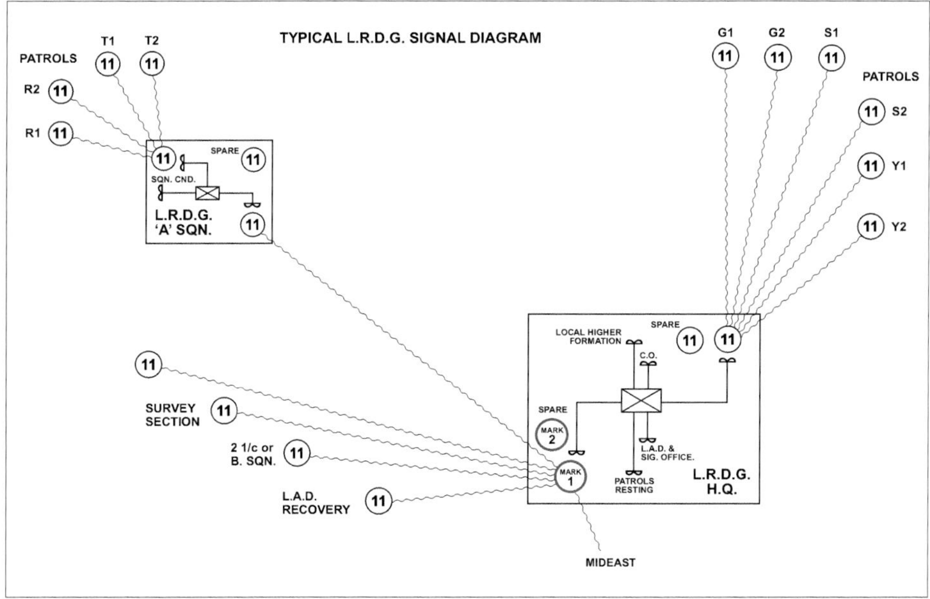

Fig. No 6. Signal Diagram, Appendix A to Prendergast's report on Signals, 5 Dec. 1942 (TNA, WO 201/816).

and receive a radio transmission. So the Long Range Desert Group did not have a fixed schedule for radio transmissions.[13]

The great success of the Long Range Desert Group's communications security was primarily the result of the skill of the unit's radio operators but it also owed much to the utilization of complex codes, following commercial procedures, the constant changes in frequencies and call signs, and the weakness of the signals from the No. 11 radio sets. Axis communications intelligence was very good in North Africa, but it was overworked. The methods used by the Long Range Desert Group time after time forced enemy communications intelligence officers to make a choice between attacking the command frequencies of known British military formations or a very weak commercial signal sent by what appeared to be, for instance, a firm of Tunisian wine merchants. Having limited resources, Axis communications intelligence officers naturally chose to attack high-grade British military transmissions rather than a number of very weak commercial-type transmissions coming from Long Range Desert Group patrols.

While the Long Range Desert Group was being refitted, reorganized, and reinforced at Cairo, the entire course of the war in North Africa was changing. Leclerc's Free French force, navigated by the crew of the Long Range Desert Group truck that had been assigned to Leclerc after the failure of the first attack on Kufra, marched north out of the Chad. Leclerc's troops attacked Kufra and forced its surrender on 1 March 1941. The capture of Kufra was the first victory of the Free French forces;[14] and with Kufra now in Allied hands, all of Libya was open to raids carried out by the Long Range Desert Group. But as the Free French in Southern Libya were gaining their victory at Kufra, men and equipment of the *Deutsches Afrika Korps* began arriving in northern Libya. On 13 March, German and Italian troops occupied Marada and removed the threat of a British invasion of Tripolitania.[15] Within weeks, Axis forces under the command of General Erwin Rommel would drive the British out of all of Cyrenaica, except for the Australian-held port of Tobruk, and back into Egypt.

---

13   *Ibid.*; Imperial War Museum, David Lloyd Owen's collection of The Long Range Desert Group Papers, 1/6 File of papers on the signaling Unit; TNA, CAB/44/151, ff. 217-219.

14   Henry Maule, *Out of the Sand: The Epic Story of General Leclerc and the Fighting Free French* (London: Odhams Books, Ltd, 1966), pp. 98-102. On the cooperation of and support by the R.L.D.G. of operations of Free French Forces, particularly on the taking of Kufra, there are the following two studies: Jean-Noël Vincent, "Koufra: 23 décembre 1940 – 1er mai 1941", *Revue historique des armeés*, I (1982), pp. 4-19; Roger Ceccaldi, "Koufra. Souvenirs de l' Artilleur", *Revue historique des armeés*, II (1983), pp. 40-49.

15   I.S.O. Playfair, *The Mediterranean and Middle East* (London: HMSO, 1956), vol. II, p. 15.

As Rommel's forces poured into North Africa during the spring and early summer of 1941, the commanders of the British forces in the Middle East failed to recognize the value of the Long Range Desert Group for long-range penetration and reconnaissance. Half of the Group was used for garrison duty, and the other half kept in Cyrenaica and used as if they were a squadron of armored cars. B Squadron, H Section, the Signal Troop, and the Headquarters group were sent to Kufra to act as garrison troops. After the Free French captured Kufra, Leclerc made it known to the British that he could commit only very limited forces to garrison Kufra.[16] And with the British conquest of Cyrenaica at the beginning of 1941, the headquarters of the Long Range Desert Group had to be moved forward from Cairo. Some thought had been given to moving the Long Range Desert Group's headquarters westward to El Agheila, but with German forces now operating in East Tripolitania this idea was dropped and Kufra appeared to be the best base for the Long Range Desert Group.[17]

On 7 March Bagnold ordered S Patrol to proceed to Kufra by way of Ain Dalla and Big Cairn. The objectives of this operation were to make contact with the Free French, to enable British political and medical officers to gain first-hand knowledge of Kufra, to set up a radio station at Kufra, to inspect all the dumps of fuel and stores on the route leading to Kufra, and to reconnoiter the northern approaches to Kufra. On 9 March S Patrol departed from Cairo for Kufra. The patrol was accompanied by Bagnold, two political officers, one medical officer, and two radio operators.[18] After crossing the Great Sand Sea, S Patrol arrived at Kufra on 16 March. This was the first operation carried out using the new four-wheel drive 30 cwt Ford trucks. Even with four-wheel drive, the Fords did not handle as well in the desert as the 30 cwt Chevrolet trucks and their four-wheel drive capability caused them to use more fuel than the Chevrolet trucks.

From Kufra Lieutenant J.R. Olivey was sent with two trucks westward into the Rebiana Sand Sea to reconnoiter Rebiana Oasis, while Bagnold went north with six vehicles to scout Tazerbo and Zighen. Meanwhile, Holliman with several other vehicles scouted the northwest approaches to Kufra. When all the parties had returned to Kufra, Holliman, with the bulk of S Patrol, was ordered back to Cairo by way of Gilf Kebir, Uweinat, and Kharga to inspect various dumps of fuel and stores on the way. Bagnold went north with three vehicles along the Kufra-Marada track, which was found to be very good going. They by-passed Msus, where the

---

16   Maule, *Out of the Sand*, p. 102.
17   TNA, WO/201/808, f. 7.
18   TNA, WO/201/808, f. 65.

enemy was known to be, and reached Barce on 22 March. Two days later, Bagnold was back in Cairo,[19] having demonstrated that he had lost none of his skill at rapidly travelling across large expanses of desert.

On 30 March Bagnold took the first steps in setting up the defense of Kufra. He issued orders for R Patrol to leave Cairo on 1 April and proceed to Tazerbo by way of Ain Dalla, Big Cairn and Bir Harash. Upon arrival at Tazerbo, Captain D.G. Steel, the patrol commander, was to send one troop to hide at the edge of the Maabus airfield to observe enemy activity, if any. The remainder of the patrol was to conceal itself along the Kufra-Marada track, while two trucks were sent to Kufra with orders for the commander of the Free French forces at that oasis. Two other trucks were to be sent northwest of Tazerbo to carry out a one hundred and fifty mile reconnaissance. The dispatch of R Patrol to Tazerbo was undertaken to secure Kufra against attack from the North.[20]

On 6 April Bagnold issued orders for S and T Patrols, H Section, and the Headquarters Group to leave Cairo and to garrison Kufra.[21] Upon arrival at Kufra, Bagnold became military governor of the oasis with the mission of holding it against enemy attack. Bagnold had been informed that "No air or ground assistance can be expected,"[22] and he, therefore, arranged the defense of Kufra into outer and inner lines of defense. Any Axis force attacking Kufra would have to pass through the gap between Tazerbo, which is two hundred miles northwest of Kufra, and Zighen, which is one hundred and twenty miles north of Kufra. S Patrol was stationed at Zighen and R Patrol at Tazerbo. The mission of these two units was to patrol the area between Tazerbo and Zighen and to attack any force marching on Kufra as well as to give Kufra timely warning of an impending attack. The inner or close defense of Kufra consisted of the Free French forces garrisoning Fort Taj at the oasis, a platoon mounted in Bedford trucks, and two armed Lysander aircraft, with T Patrol held in reserve.[23]

As Rommel's armored formations swept across northern Cyrenaica in April of 1941, Bagnold and R, S, and T Patrols, the Signal Troops, the Headquarters Group, and H Section defended Kufra from an attack which never came. Kufra was supposed to be garrisoned by the Sudan Defense Force, but until this unit could be pulled out of the East Africa campaign, it was left to the Long Range Desert Group to defend the oasis. The garrisoning of Kufra by the Long Range Desert

---

19   TNA, WO/201/808, f. 7.
20   TNA, WO/201/809, f. 17.
21   TNA, WO/201/809, f. 19.
22   TNA, WO/201/809, f. 30.
23   TNA, WO/201/809, f. 4.

Group was a classic example of the misuse of a highly specialized reconnaissance and raiding unit.

While Bagnold served as the military governor of Kufra, he had, as he said, "a resplendent title like Lord of the Isles," but the job was a dreary one.[24] He had to spend much of his time on problems to do with civilian matters, such as opening trade with the Chad and with the Nile Valley and proclaiming that the Free French franc be accepted as local currency. The military problems confronting Bagnold at Kufra were all the ones which would trouble the commander of an isolated military post hundreds of miles from anywhere. There were also huge logistical problems to be dealt with, for the headquarters in Cairo and Khartoum took some time to learn that there was more to supporting Kufra than simply dumping supplies at Halfa on the Nile. For weeks on end the vehicles of the Long Range Desert Group at Kufra were immobilized owing to a lack of fuel. And Bagnold and the support units of the Long Range Desert Group at Kufra had no way, except by radio, of assisting or controlling patrols at Tazerbo and Zighen, let alone A Squadron which was operating in northern Cyrenaica. It was also found that radio was a less than satisfactory way of dealing with General Headquarters, Middle East at Cairo. In time, these problems were overcome. For example, the Long Range Desert Group obtained two single-engine aircraft made by Western Aircraft Corporation of Ohio and known as WACO's, which Prendergast and a New Zealand sergeant flew. The R.A.F. did not like the Long Range Desert Group having a private air force, but was forced to accept it, albeit with ill grace, because it could not fulfill the needs of the Long Range Desert Group. The WACO's gave the commander and other officers of the Long Range Desert Group the ability to move quickly across vast distances of the Libyan Desert in order to visit the scattered units of the Long Range Desert Group and various headquarters of British formations. As the weeks passed, the authorities at Cairo and Khartoum slowly overcame the supply problems of Kufra. But the longer Bagnold remained at Kufra, the more convinced he became of the need to have someone at British Middle East Headquarters at Cairo who could speak with authority on long-range desert operations. "So in July…" Bagnold "…handed over command of the L.R.D.G. to Prendergast and put on a red hat at G.H.W."[25] Bagnold became a staff officer in Cairo in order to attempt to protect the interests of the Long Range Desert Group and have a say in its employment.

---

24   The actual title was Military Governor of the Oases. R.A. Bagnold, "Early Days of the Long Range Desert Group", *The Geographical Journal*, 105 (Jan. – June, 1945), p. 40.

25   TNA, WO/201/809, ff. 4-9; CAB/44/151, ff. 41-47; Bagnold, "Early Days of the Long Range Desert Group," pp. 39-42.

On 18 July the Sudan Defense Force officially assumed responsibility for the defense of Kufra from the Long Range Desert Group and the Free French. The Free French troops were transported to Tekro in the Chad by British trucks,[26] but the Long Range Desert Group patrols remained based at Kufra in order to undertake a number of reconnaissance operations. Eight days before the Long Range Desert Group's garrison duties at Kufra ended, General Headquarters, Middle East had issued a directive placing the Long Range Desert Group at Kufra under its direct command with orders to carry out a number of reconnaissance missions in North Central Libya designed to gain geographical information and knowledge of enemy movements.[27] The Long Range Desert Group at Kufra had already undertaken several reconnaissance missions—patrols had been sent out in April, May, and June to scout the southern portions of the Kufra, Marada, and Tazerbo tracks. But little sign of enemy activity was seen.[28] After the garrison duty at Kufra had ended, the Long Range Desert Group reconnaissance patrols ventured as far north as the Mediterranean.[29]

At the end of July, T Patrol left Tazerbo and headed towards Bir Zelten on the Kufra-Marada track. Near Bir Zelten the patrol was divided into three groups. One group hid near Bir Zelten while the other two carried out a reconnaissance of the region around El Agheila and the coast road near Sirte. The only enemy movement seen was one aircraft and a few vehicles on the coast road. T Patrol returned to Kufra on 10 August.[30] Six days later S Patrol departed from Kufra and carried out a detailed reconnaissance of the Jalo-Agedabia track. A number of enemy vehicles, aircraft, and some natives were seen, but S Patrol returned to Kufra without incident on 12 September.[31] The reconnaissance missions into northern Libya in the summer of 1941 showed that the Long Range Desert Group, based at Kufra, could penetrate undetected and almost at will the coastal regions behind enemy lines.

One of Bagnold's last acts before giving up command of the Long Range Desert Group and leaving Kufra was to set up a small Survey Section in the Long Range Desert Group. From the time that the first Long Range Desert Group patrol crossed into Libya, the lack of maps had been a problem. The Italian maps

---

26   TNA, WO/201/809, f. 9.

27   TNA, WO/201/809, ff. 38-39.

28   TNA, WO/201/809, ff. 9, 135.

29   TNA, WO/201/809, ff. 43-47; see also, R.L. Kay, *Long Range Desert Group in the Mediterranean* (Wellington: Dept. of Internal Affairs, 1950).

30   TNA, WO/201/809, ff. 48-72.

31   TNA, WO/201/809, ff. 75-95.

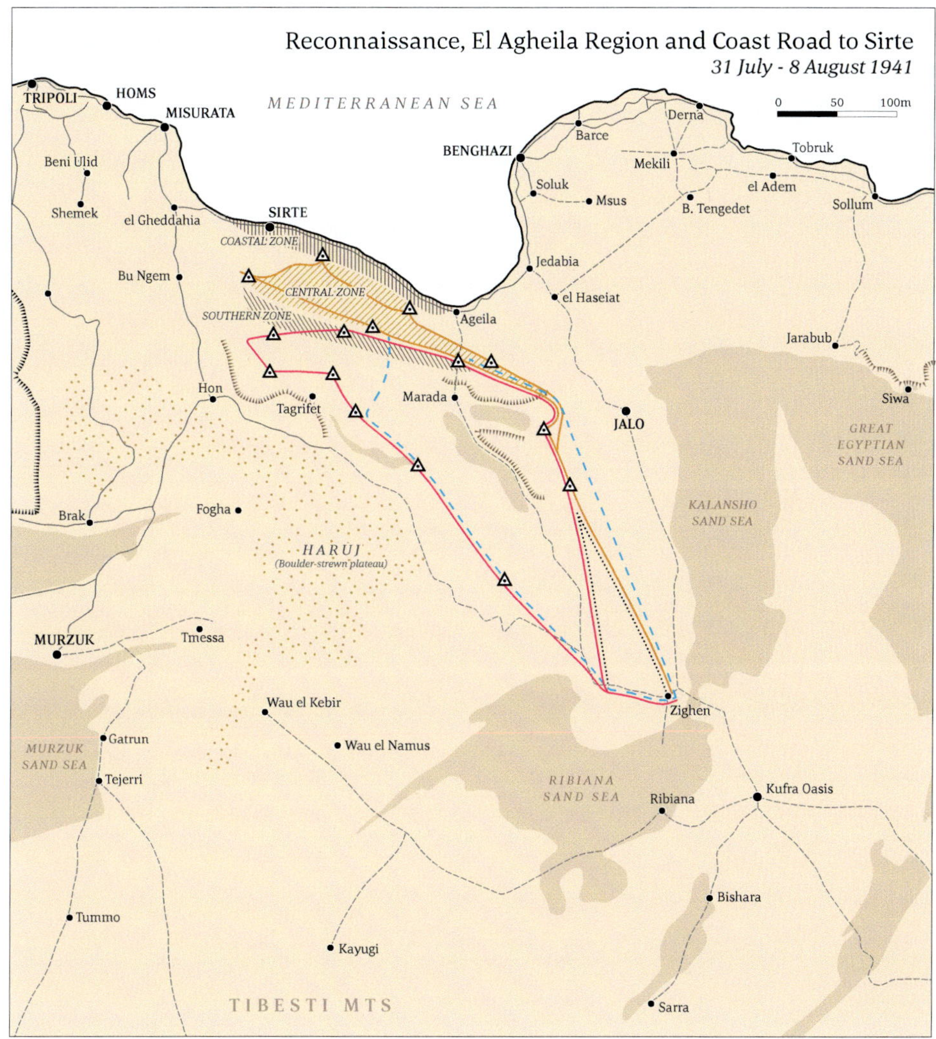

Fig. No 7. Reconnaissance of Agheila region and coast road to Sirte, 31 Jul.-8 Aug. 1941 (TNA, WO/201/809).

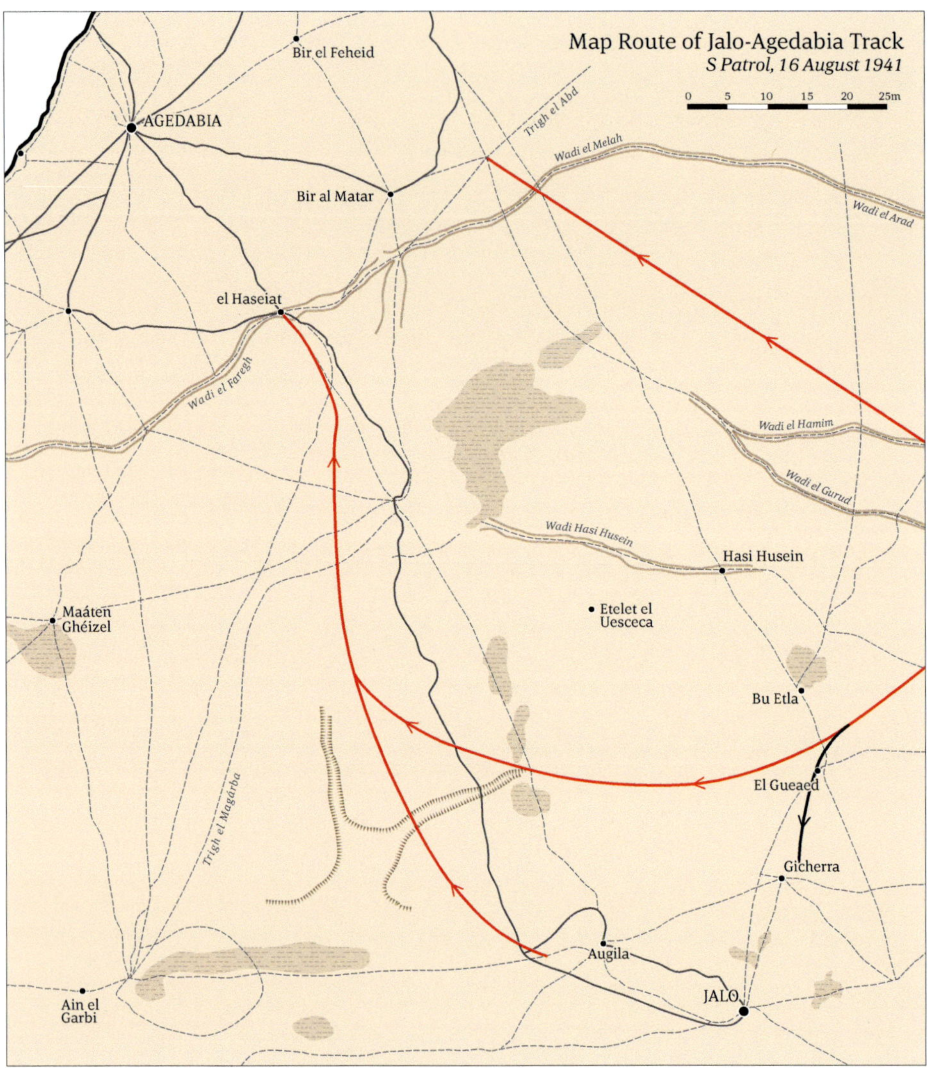

Fig. No 8. Map Route of Jalo-Agedabia track, S Patrol, 16 Aug. 1941 (TNA, WO/ 201/809).

of Libya, except for the 1/100,000 ones covering the coastal region, were useless. There was an Italian 1/1,000,000 map series which covered the whole country and a 1/400,000 map series for about half of Libya;[32] however, both of these series of

---

32   W.B. Kennedy Shaw, "Desert Navigation: Some Experiences of the Long Range Desert Group", *The Geographical Journal* 102, 5/6 (Nov. – Dec, 1943), p. 257.

maps had little to do with reality. Kennedy Shaw had a theory that Italian maps of Libya

> Must…reflect the Italian national character in its aspects of bombast and self-assurance. There was no nonsense about the petty details of topography on these sheets. Many of them were obviously based on air observation (but not on air survey), and after a few flights across the country the cartographer had roughed in a range of mountains here and a sand sea or two there. The mountains were all high as became the dignity of Fascist Italy. Making our way anxiously towards an obviously impassable range of hills, we would find that we had driven over it without feeling the bump. But I have a certain grudging admiration for Captain Marchesi of the Instituto Geografico Militare, the equivalent of our Ordinance Survey, who made the 1/100,000 map of Jalo. Marchesi, I am sure, was a realist. Jalo, he felt, was a one-eyed hole of which no map was really needed. The sand was soft and the day hot, so why worry? Marchesi put his feet up on the mess table, shouted for another drink, and drew his map. It is just possible that the absurd inaccuracies were a deep plot to mislead our attacking forces, but it seems hardly likely that the Italians had thought of that as long ago as 1931.[33]

From the beginning of its operations, the Long Range Desert Group began collecting topographical information about the Libyan Desert. The navigators and commanders of each patrol made detailed reports on, and in some cases drawings of, the terrain across which the patrol had passed. At the end of each patrol, this topographical information was turned over to Kennedy Shaw, who served not only as the Long Range Desert Group's intelligence officer but also as its topographical officer.[34] Kennedy Shaw would then use this topographical information to update the Long Range Desert Group's maps, which were drawn on a scale of 1/400,000 – one of the scales used by the Italians. As a way of collecting topographical material this was a hit or miss method because the information received depended to a great extent on where military needs required a patrol to go. Further, for a long time none of the Long Range Desert Group's topographical information was passed on to the military or civilian cartographers in Cairo. The information was not relayed to Cairo because the army Survey Directorate could not decide whether maps of

---

33   W.B. Kennedy Shaw, *Long Range Desert Group* (London: Collins, 1945), pp. 24-25.
34   Lloyd Owen, *The Desert*, p. 162, TNA, WO/208/51 contains a number of "going reports" or "route reports" in which there are huge amounts of information on the geography of the Libyan Desert.

Libya should be drawn to the scales used by the Italians –1/400,000 or 1/100,000 – or to the scale of 1/500,000, which was the scale of British maps of Egypt. It was not until the spring of 1941 that the Survey Directorate came to the decision that both the Italian 1/400,000 scale and the British 1/500,000 scale could be used. And in June of 1941 Bagnold and the Survey Directorate finally agreed upon a common set of symbols to be used on maps of Libya. It was also agreed at this time that the Survey Directorate would map everything north of latitude 30°, and the Long Range Desert Group everything south of that line;[35] although it was obvious that only the Long Range Desert Group could do any secret mapping north of 30° latitude.

In July of 1941, Lieutenant K.H. Lazarus of the East African Engineers joined the Long Range Desert Group to command the Survey Section. For the rest of 1941 and the first half of 1942, Lazarus spent weeks on end with two or three vehicles mapping the Libyan Desert behind enemy lines. Probably never in the history of warfare has so much mapping been done in an enemy's rear areas as was done by the Long Range Desert Group. The maps made and used by the Long Range Desert Group were so superior that the Germans considered them "a particularly valuable prize when captured."[36] Along with surveys, the Long Range Desert Group also produced a huge flow of topographical information from the patrol reports of commanders and navigators, and this information was sent to the cartographers in Cairo.[37] The Long Range Desert Group's surveying efforts were greatly helped by Captain J.W. Wright, R.E. who while serving with the Sudan Defense Force at Kufra surveyed large areas of the Libyan Desert.[38] The British army in general and the Long Range Desert Group in particular did so much surveying in Libya that Dr. K.S. Sandford, one of Bagnold's pre-war explorer friends, could remark at a meeting of the Royal Geographical Society that the Long Range Desert Group "had brought to a close the military exploration of the Libyan Desert."[39]

---

35   TNA, WO/201/809, f. 14.

36   Alfred Topp, "Desert Warfare: German Experiences in World War II" (Historical Division, United States Army, European Command, 1952) (Fort Leavonworth, KS: Combat Studies Institute, 1991), p. 3.

37   TNA, Cab/44/151, f. 65; Kennedy Shaw, "Desert Navigation", pp. 257-258; Kennedy Shaw, *Long Range Desert Group*, p. 25; Lloyd Owen, *The Desert*, p. 163.

38   J.W. Wright "War-Time Exploration with the Sudan Defense Force in the Libyan Desert, 1941-1943", *The Geographical Journal* 105, 3/4 (March-April, 1945), pp. 99-111.

39   Bagnold, "Early Days of the Long Range Desert Group", p. 45. If one compares British army maps of various dates, it can quickly be seen that during the Second World War knowledge of Libyan topography greatly increased. TNA, Map Room, MR. 761 (3, 6), MHP 1095 (1-3).

While Bagnold and R, S, and T patrols were garrisoning Kufra, the Long Range Desert Group's A Squadron consisting of G and Y Patrols were placed under the orders of Lieutenant General Philip Neame, the Commander of the British forces in Northern Cyrenaica. Neame, who was soon to suffer a crushing defeat and capture by Rommel, did not understand what the Long Range Desert Group was and hence did not know how to deploy the unit. As a result, A Squadron would be caught smack in the middle of Rommel's April 1941 offensive. Apparently, Neame looked upon A Squadron of the Long Range Desert Group as something akin to the King's Dragoon Guards, or as an armored car unit or some kind of light cavalry to be used to protect his southern flank.

On 25 March 1941 A Squadron left Cairo under the command of Mitford with orders from Bagnold to report to Neame's headquarters. On 30 March A Squadron reached Barce where CYRCOM, Neame's headquarters, was located. Mitford reported at once to CYRCOM and the next day received his orders. A Squadron would be headquartered at Jalo. The squadron was to reconnoiter Marada to see whether or not there was an Axis built-up there. It also was to give warning of any enemy movement east from Marada and to scout the area around Marada, Zella, and Tagrifet.

Mitford gave Crichton-Stuart, with five trucks from G Patrol, the task of making a circuit around Marada, whilst the rest of G Patrol, under the command of Lieutenant Martin Gibbs of the Goldstream Guards, was attached to Y Patrol. Crichton-Stuart left Barce early in the morning of 31 March. While heading south the following afternoon, the five truck patrol heard artillery fire near the coast. The next day the patrol crossed the Marada—El Agheila road and that night heard on the B.B.C. news that the enemy had broken through the British positions at Agedabia. Nevertheless, Crichton-Stuart's patrol continued its mission, and after crossing some very difficult ground circled Marada and found no sign of enemy activity. A *ghibli*—a hot, dry wind from the inner desert—was blowing when Crichton-Stuart headed for Augila. He found no sign of the enemy at that oasis, but while camping there that night, 6 April, the patrol heard on B.B.C. news that Benghazi had fallen to the enemy. Crichton-Stuart attempted to reach Mitford by radio but failed, and the next day was spent sorting out supplies. It was found that they had just enough fuel for one truck to reach Jarabub. And in the late afternoon Crichton-Stuart finally made radio contact with Mitford who was at Mechili and surrounded by enemy forces. Mitford suggested to Crichton-Stuart that he attempt to reach Jarabub with one truck. Crichton-Stuart's guardsmen disabled all the vehicles except the truck with the radio on it and buried all stores, equipment, and arms which could not be carried on one truck. On 9 April at 1700

Crichton-Stuart's truck ran out of fuel ten miles from Jarabub. He and two of his men walked into Jarabub, which was still in Allied hands. The next day, 10 April, Mitford and the rest of A Squadron arrived at Jarabub.[40]

A Squadron was not as lucky as Crichton-Stuart's five truck patrol, which had slipped around the southern flank of Rommel's offensive. A squadron found itself in the path of the Axis attack. On 1 April A Squadron had left Barce for Augila. Just east of Msus they sighted a group of six trucks with four or five men in each vehicle. As these trucks approached, A Squadron turned to meet them head on, but the six trucks then turned around and drove off in an easterly direction. A Squadron gave chase, but Captain P.J.D. McCraith's truck ran over an Italian Thermos mine,[41] which exploded wounding McCraith in the left arm and destroying a rear wheel and tyre, but not damaging the rest of the truck. That night A Squadron camped twenty-five miles east of Msus. The next day A Squadron went into Msus and reported to CYRCOM that it had chased six trucks the day before east of Msus. CYRCOM blithely informed Mitford that the six trucks he had sighted were a unit of the Long Range Desert Group, which Mitford knew was impossible. CYRCOM then ordered Mitford to send in situation reports by radio from Msus every half hour, which required that A Squadron remain at Msus all that day. The next day, 3 April, Gibbs took the G Patrol trucks to scout the area north and northeast of Msus. At 1200 word was received at Msus from the R.A.F. that the enemy was advancing on the city from the south. A Squadron deployed south of Msus, the stores were destroyed, and the British forces withdrew from the city. All the British had left Msus when at 1600 five enemy armored cars appeared to the south of the city. A Squadron then withdrew to the east, picking up Gibbs's trucks on the way.

The next day A Squadron moved southeast to the Trigh el Abd, and then on 5 April the squadron went northeast towards Mechili and reached a spot west of there on 7 April. Mechili was being attacked from the south, and Mitford went into the city and was asked by the commander of the British forces to attack the flanks of the enemy force assaulting the city. Mitford divided A Squadron into two groups: one under his command and the other commanded by Gibbs. Mitford's force attacked a field gun forcing it to withdraw and taking one prisoner, while

---

40   TNA, WO/201/809, ff. 108-111, Crichton-Stuart, *G Patrol*, pp. 71-75.

41   An Italian 4AR anti-personnel mine, which is known as a "Thermos mine" because it looks like a Thermos bottle. These mines are extremely sensitive and will explode when subjected to the slightest movement. The Italians scattered hundreds of these mines in the North African desert. TM 20-420, *Handbook on the Italian Military Forces* (Washington, D.C.: War Department, 1943), pp. 286-287.

Gibbs's force attacked a headquarters before being forced by enemy armored vehicles to withdraw to the southwest. The next day A Squadron went into Mechili to get supplies and left one truck with a hole in its radiator to be fixed; Trooper Titch Cave of Y Patrol, the truck's driver, also remained.[42] A Squadron then left Mechili and attacked a group of enemy cars and trucks. In this fight one truck and a German were captured. Next, A Squadron sighted a column of forty odd vehicles heading east and attacked the column, forcing it to withdraw to the west and capturing the first 88mm gun taken by the British in North Africa. That night A Squadron camped on high ground about six miles to the west of Mechili. At 0630 on 8 April the Axis assaulted Mechili from three different directions and captured it. Under the cover of a dust storm, A Squadron escaped from the enemy by heading north and then east and then southeast around Mechili. But while on the southeastern leg of the course, a truck hit a Thermos mine which destroyed the front wheel, tyre, and brake drum. This truck was repaired in sight of an enemy column.

On 9 April A Squadron continued on a southeast course and encountered a force of about forty to fifty enemy vehicles that were halted. The Long Range Desert Group squadron took cover in a depression in the desert but were seen by an enemy aircraft that attacked them with machine-gun, hitting one man in the wrist and a truck's radiator. As A Squadron moved out of the depression and retreated southeast, it attacked the enemy vehicles nearby with gunfire. The truck with the damaged radiator was driven until the engine seized up and was then abandoned. The enemy did not attempt to follow A Squadron southeast into the desert. And on 10 April, after crossing the axis of the enemy's main advance, A Squadron arrived at Jarabub and met Crichton-Stuart's group. The following day A Squadron left for Siwa, carrying with them into exile Jarabub's only prostitute, who had been spreading anti-British propaganda among the Libyan garrison of the oasis.[43]

Rommel's April 1941 offensive drove the British forces out of all of Libya except for the Australian-held port of Tobruk and the oases of Kufra and Jarabub, which were defended by the Long Range Desert Group. When A Squadron arrived

---

42   When Mechili was overrun by the enemy, Trooper Titch was captured and placed in a prison camp near Derna. On 22 April Titch and an Australian named Alfred escaped from the prison camp and made their way on foot eastward along the coast. The two men, living on what food and water friendly Arabs gave them and on what they could take from the enemy, spent thirty-seven days in the desert before reaching Australian lines at Tobruk. TNA, WO/201/809, ff. 102-107.

43   TNA, WO/201/809, ff. 91-101.

at Siwa on 13 April, G and Y patrols had to be reorganized into two combined patrols of six trucks each using men and vehicles from both patrols. One patrol was put under the command of Crichton-Stuart, and the other was commanded by Gibbs. Shortly after A Squadron arrived at Siwa, Prendergast flew into the oasis in a WACO with orders from the headquarters of the Western Desert Force, which had replaced CYRCOM, calling for A Squadron to watch for any enemy movement towards Jarabub and Siwa. On 15 April Crichton-Stuart's patrol left Siwa and arrived at Augila at 1430 on 17 April. The objective of this trip was to recover the four trucks that had been abandoned at this oasis several days before. The British patrol found that the trucks were gone and Augila was in the hands of the enemy. There were also reports that the enemy were using the airfield at Jalo. When the British were sighted by the enemy, Crichton-Stuart's patrol escaped in a northerly direction.

While en route back to Jarabub along the Gardaba track, Crichton-Stuart's patrol received orders to watch for enemy movement eastward around Jarabub and Siwa. Crichton-Stuart placed his patrol just inside the sand sea at a point just off the Gardaba track and settled down to very boring duty. The only thing the men could do to pass the time was to play football in the sand. The patrol experienced a huge sand storm on 20 April and the soldiers had to shelter as best they could in their vehicles. While Crichton-Stuart's patrol was watching the western approaches to Jarabub, Gibbs's patrol was watching the northern approaches, and his men were just as hot and bored as Crichton-Stuart's. Both patrols finally were ordered to go to Siwa by way of Jarabub on 25 April. The British had decided to evacuate the remaining population of Jarabub and A Squadron's trucks were used to carry their household goods to Siwa, which was reached on 26 April.

The two patrols were then sent back to continue watching the western and northern approaches to Jarabub. This time though Gibbs's patrol was assigned the western approaches and Crichton-Stuart's the northern ones. The men of both patrols were bored with this duty; it was hot, and they were beset with flies during the day and mosquitoes during the night. And there was only a limited amount of water. On 6 May an Australian demolition unit arrived at Jarabub with orders to destroy the oasis. The Australians spent two days blowing things to bits, including a huge amount of captured Breda ammunition, and it was only with great difficulty that Crichton-Stuart stopped them from destroying the mosque.

Everybody in A Squadron thought that sitting in the middle of the desert watching for the enemy to approach what was left of Jarabub was a waste of time and that the task could have been carried out by aircraft just as well. This duty was also very dangerous, for beginning on 8 May there was a very bad *khamseen*—a hot, dry wind from the inner desert—which lasted for three days.[44] The *khamseen* proved to be too much for most of Gibbs's patrol, for although the water ration of one gallon per day was maintained, it was not enough to keep their bodies and minds functioning properly. The men suffered heat exhaustion and worse. According to Gibbs,

> The guardsmen couldn't guard, the fitter became unable to fit and the navigator went right off his head and became very violent when asked to navigate. He is a big man and started knocking people about. When he did consent to navigate he was 180° out exactly.[45]

Crichton-Stuart met Gibbs's patrol at Jarabub and sent the whole patrol back to Siwa except for two trucks and their crews, who could still function; Gibbs and several others were so sick that they had to be sent to a hospital in Cairo. Poor Gibbs was put into a mental ward for two weeks' observation. In the bed next to him was a man who thought he had lost three Mobile Bath Units and loudly lamented his loss. It took several months before Gibbs had regained enough strength to leave the hospital and rejoin his regiment.[46]

On 13 May Crichton-Stuart received orders to deploy his patrol in support of a limited offensive in the Salum region with the objective of taking Bardia. During this operation the armored cars of the 11th Hussars were to screen the southern flank of the British army by patrolling westward from Sheferzen on the Egyptian-Libyan border. The task of Crichton-Stuart's patrol was to link up with the 11th Hussars at Sheferzen and patrol on their flank further to the west—a mission for which it was neither trained nor equipped to carry out. Operations of this type should have been undertaken by armored cars and not by thin-skinned 30 cwt trucks of a long-range reconnaissance unit that were loaded up with gasoline and munitions.

On the morning of 14 May Crichton-Stuart's patrol proceeded north towards Sheferzen along the wire fence that marked the Egyptian-Libyan border. At 0800 the Long Range Desert Group saw a number of armored cars and what appeared to be two British tanks at Sheferzen.[47] As the British patrol approached Sheferzen, where it was supposed to link up with the 11th Hussars, the British trucks were

---

44   TNA, WO/201/809, f. 113.

45   Chrichton-Stuart, *G Patrol*, p. 85.

46   TNA, WO/201/809, ff. 112-113; Crichton-Stuart, *G Patrol*, pp. 82-86. The quote is from p. 85.

47   TNA, WO/201/809, f. 113.

fired on by light and heavy machine-guns and a few rounds from one of the tanks. The enemy's aim was not very good and only Crichton-Stuart's truck was hit with about a dozen bullets. The British withdrew quickly to the south, and about half a mile from the enemy and out of sight, the patrol stopped and an attempt was made to change a back tyre on Crichton-Stuart's truck. At this time Guardsman Fraser, who had been hit in the arm two times, was given first aid. Crichton-Stuart ordered four of the five remaining undamaged trucks to go five miles further south and to wait for further orders while he kept the fifth truck with him in order to make a quick getaway if the enemy appeared before his own vehicle was repaired. But before the tyre on Crichton-Stuart's truck could be changed, enemy vehicles were heard approaching. Crichton-Stuart, taking a box with all his maps and papers, jumped with his crew into the undamaged truck and headed south, chased by German armored cars. Crichton-Stuart picked up the four trucks he had sent ahead and the patrol was chased southward at a speed of forty-five miles per hour. For a time the German armored cars were gaining on the British trucks, but the British increased the speed to fifty miles an hour and drew ahead of the Germans. A bullet hit one British truck in a rear wheel, but the crew was picked up by Crichton-Stuart. The chase did not end until the British were some thirty miles south of Sheferzen. When Bagnold learned of the action between Crichton-Stuart's patrol and the German armored cars, he angrily remarked, "This use of unarmored vehicles so close to known enemy armored forces was clearly a mistake which should never have been permitted."[48]

Lieutenant J.R. Easonsmith, of the Royal Tank Regiment, arrived at Siwa during the last days of May and took command of Y Patrol, which was then sent to guard the approaches to Jarabub. After the encounter with the German armored cars, G Patrol had only three of its original trucks and for the most part the patrol remained at Siwa, where a malaria epidemic broke out. A Squadron could easily obtain the drugs required to treat malaria, but the authorities maintained that "Siwa was NOT (they repeated NOT) malarial" and would not provide the necessary means to rid Siwa of *anopheles* mosquitoes.[49] Malaria became such a problem that it was only with great difficulty that men could be found who were medically fit to undertake patrols. Finally, Crichton-Stuart obtained the services of a malariologist who managed to confirm that Siwa was alive with *anopheles* mosquitoes.[50]

---

48   TNA, WO/201/809, ff. 113-114; Crichton-Stuart, *G Patrol*, pp. 86-88.
49   Crichton-Stuart, *G Patrol*, p. 89.
50   *Ibid*, p. 89.

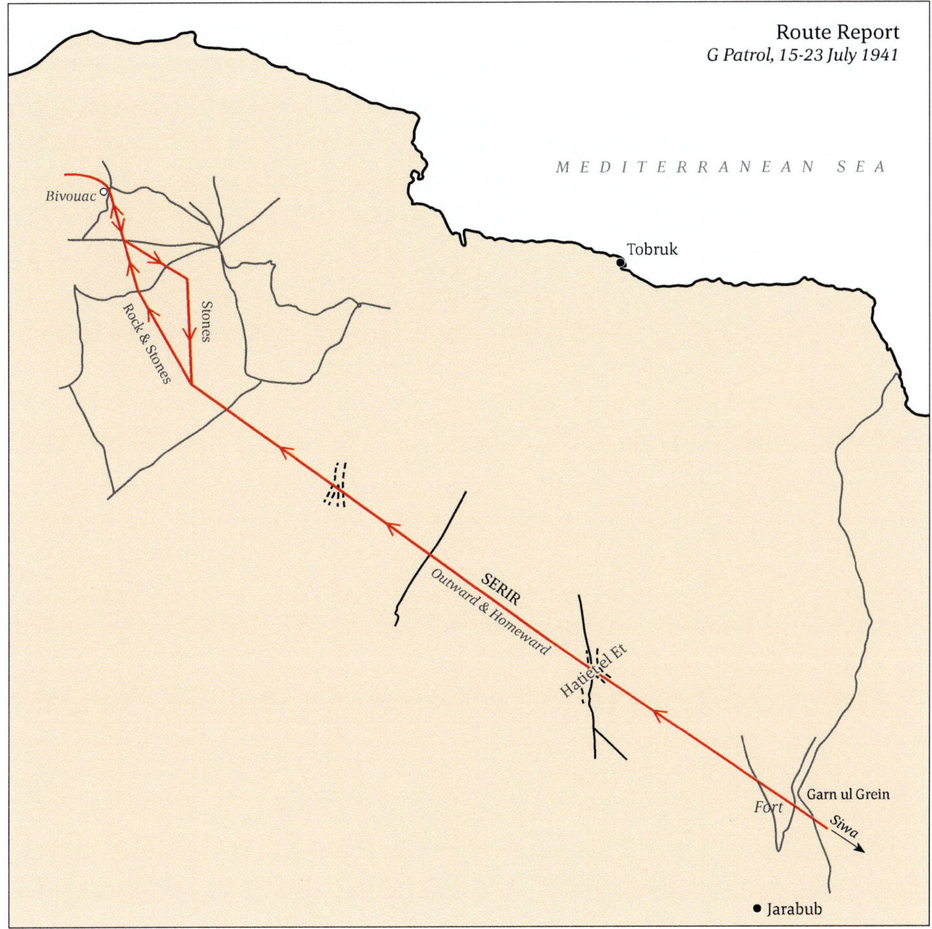

Fig. No 9. Route Report, G Patrol, 15-23 July 1941 (TNA, WO 201/809).

On 6 June McCraith, who had, by now, recovered from the wounds he had received when his truck hit a Thermos mine, arrived at Siwa with additional trucks. Easonsmith was recalled from Jarabub and A Squadron was reorganized into G, H, and Y Patrols consisting of six trucks each. Half of H Patrol was made up of men from G Patrol and the other half of the men came from Y Patrol. And because Mitford was on leave, Crichton-Stuart was in command of A Squadron. Y Patrol was sent to guard the approaches to Jarabub and Crichton-Stuart, being the commander of A Squadron, had to stay at Siwa, and G Patrol carried out tasks such as transporting supplies and making fuel dumps.[51]

On 10 June H Patrol left Siwa with three trucks to take two Arab agents to a point as close to Gambut as possible. The patrol was commanded by Easonsmith, a natural leader and a born soldier who would rise to command the Long Range Desert Group before he was killed in action in 1943 on the island of Leros in the Aegean. After dropping the two Arabs within sight of Gambut, H Patrol proceeded north to a point where the traffic on the coast road between Tobruk and Bardia could be observed. Easonsmith set up an observation post of the side of a valley overlooking the coast road, which was two and a half miles away. Vehicles on the road were clearly visible to Easonsmith, but after a strafing attack by a squadron of Hurricanes, the traffic dropped off. In the valley below H Patrol there were about sixteen large enemy trucks which were dispersed for fear of attack from the air. Easonsmith decided to attack and destroy these enemy vehicles in the valley. The plan was for Easonsmith and his patrol sergeant, J. Dennis, to each pick eight vehicles to attack. When the attack was to begin, the truck with the radio on it would cross the valley and block the track leading to the coast road to prevent any enemy vehicles escaping from the valley.

As the sun was setting, H Patrol went down into the valley and at about four hundred yards range the enemy fired some warning shots followed by some light machine-gun fire. H Patrol returned the fire with .303 Vickers machine-guns with one tracer in every three rounds, which gave the British "a definite scare value, resistance soon stopped."[52] Round after round of .303 bullets were fired into the enemy vehicles. Then Easonsmith and Dennis got out of their trucks and threw grenades into three trucks and shot up six others with .45 caliber submachine-guns. Easonsmith took two prisoners, and when H Patrol left the valley on the track leading to the coast road the truck, which had been sent to block this track, could not be found. Easonsmith then went back down into the valley on foot to look for the missing truck and set fire to three more enemy trucks, for a total of twelve destroyed and four probably destroyed or at least damaged. On the way back to Siwa, the steering arm on Dennis' truck broke and Easonsmith towed the sergeant's truck two hundred and forty miles back to the oasis, which was reached on 13 June. They found that the missing truck with the radio had arrived the day before.[53]

---

51   *Ibid*, p. 90.
52   TNA, WO/201/809, f. 117.
53   *Ibid*.

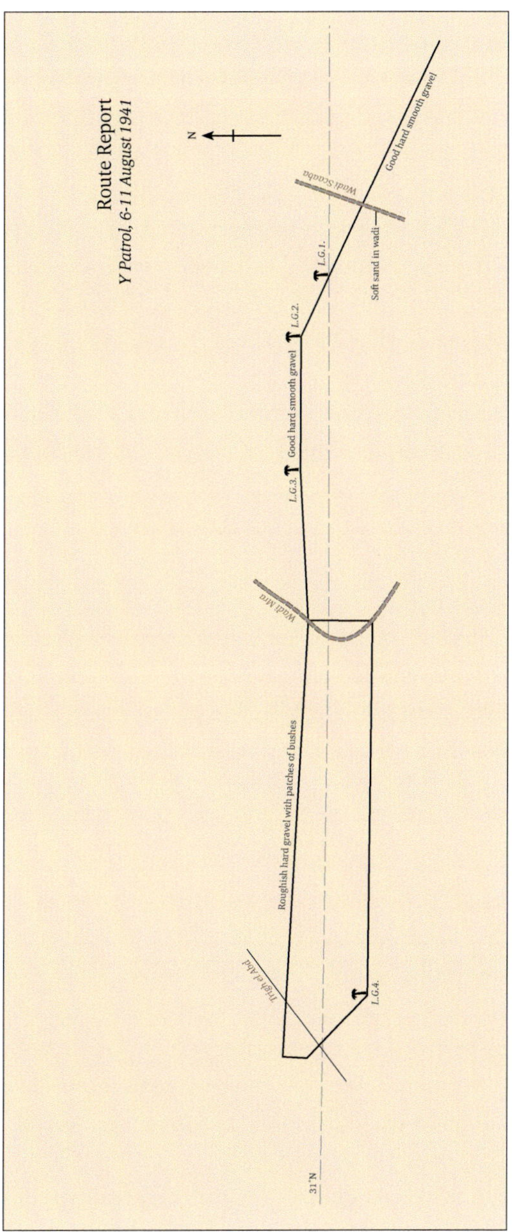

Fig. No 10. Route Report, Y Patrol, 6-11 Aug. 1941 (TNA, WO/201/809).

At 1230 on 15 June Easonsmith left Siwa with two trucks to find a Free French pilot believed to be hiding with some Bedouin at Bir Bidihi, two miles out of Trigh el Abd. The place was supposed to be marked by three Bedouin tents. Easonsmith found the *bir*, or well, but no tents, Bedouins, or any Free French pilot. A search of the region was begun and Easonsmith found a dry well from which emerged a Bedouin who denied all knowledge of the pilot. But then Pilot Officer Pompey, a Free French fighter pilot, clambered out of the well. He had heard Easonsmith talking with the Bedouin and realized he was English. Easonsmith brought Pompey and the Bedouin, who was wanted by the Italians, back to Siwa, which they reached by 1430 on 16 June.[54]

On 19 June Easonsmith left Siwa with three trucks, a British intelligence officer, and two Arabs, who were also intelligence agents. His mission was to leave them at a point in the Jebel Akhdar for two days and then pick them up and return to Siwa. The next day the patrol crossed the Trigh el Abd, but on 21 June the speed of the patrol was reduced to five miles an hour because they had to cross a seventeen mile wide belt of broken stone. On 22 June the three intelligence agents were dropped off and arrangements were made to pick them up in two days.[55] The patrol then headed for Mechili. Easonsmith had orders to see if the enemy had developed an east-west convoy route through Mechili. The patrol made a circuit around Mechili and established that there was no major, west to east, convoy route there. The following day the patrol found an abandoned Bedford truck that appeared to be in good condition. Easonsmith stopped his truck near the Bedford and went up the left side of the vehicle while some of his men went up the right side. Just as Easonsmith was about to look into the cab there was an explosion which set the Bedford on fire, killed Guardsman Hopton, who had opened the right door on the booby-trapped truck, and wounded Trooper Wise. Hopton was buried on the spot and his grave marked with a wooden cross. The patrol then quickly left the region because the burning Bedford was giving away their position. The three intelligence agents, along with two men belonging to the Northumberland Fusiliers, who had been evading the enemy in the Jebel Akhdar for sixteen weeks, were picked up and the patrol returned to Siwa on 26 June.[56]

During July and most of August G, H, and Y Patrols of A Squadron continued to make patrols into Cyrenaica and to put in and bring back agents. On 26 July Crichton-Stuart with G Patrol left Siwa carrying Major David Lair, U.S.A., an

---

54   TNA, WO/201/809, f. 118.
55   TNA, WO/201/809. f. 119.
56   TNA, WO/201/809, ff. 118-119.

American Liaison officer, and went to Jarabub and then on the airfield near Bir el Gsieir where two thousand gallons of gasoline and five hundred gallons of oil were destroyed by punching holes in the sides of the drums that contained them. G Patrol returned to Siwa on 29 July and then left the next day with orders to go up the Egyptian-Libyan border to a point five miles south of Fort Maddalena because there were reports of parties of enemy troops operating in the desert along the border. The mission was completed by noon on 31 July, but Crichton-Stuart came down with malaria in the middle of a *khamseen* and returned to Siwa with a temperature of 106° and was evacuated to Cairo.[57] In August units from A Squadron made patrols looking for possible sites for aircraft landing fields and to put agents into Cyrenaica and to bring them out. On 6 August R Patrol arrived at Siwa from Kufra and T Patrol was assigned to Siwa even though it was in Cairo being refitted.[58] Under the command of Steele, R and T Patrols would become A Squadron while the headquarters unit of the old A Squadron and G and Y Patrols, who had been based at that oasis since April were withdrawn to Cairo because their personnel were badly in need of rest—they had suffered greatly from malaria and what was left of their equipment was in need of replacement or repair.[59]

The withdrawal of G and Y Patrols from Siwa in August of 1941 marked the end of a period of frustration for the Long Range Desert Group. After its first successful patrols into the southern Libyan Desert, the Long Range Desert Group had been misused by the commanders of the British forces in Egypt and the Middle East. The Long Range Desert Group was a specialized unit with the capability of penetrating the Libyan Desert at almost any point to conduct either reconnaissance missions or raids. But in 1941 the Long Range Desert Group had been used to garrison Kufra, protect the approaches to Jarabub, and to operate in conjunction with armored cars and A Squadron had been placed in the path of Rommel's April 1941 offensive in Cyrenaica. The group, squadron, and patrol commanders knew that these tasks were a misuse of the Long Range Desert Group. The problem was that in the middle of a complex and extremely taxing campaign, higher commanders had little time to think about the correct employment of such an odd and specialized unit as the Long Range Desert Group. However, the officers of the Long Range Desert Group saw that the proper role of the group was to carry out long-range reconnaissance of a type which could not be carried out by aircraft, transport intelligence agents to and from almost any point in enemy territory, and, if necessary, to undertake raids hundreds of miles behind

---

57   TNA, WO/201/809, f. 115.
58   TNA, WO/201/809, ff. 121-122, 127.
59   TNA, WO/201/809, ff. 121-122, 127.

enemy lines. Perhaps now that Bagnold was a staff officer at General Headquarters, Middle East, the powers that be might come to have an understanding of how the Long Range Desert Group should be employed.

5

Through *Crusader*

"Very tough, but not pub tough."
—*Colonel Eric Wilson, V.C.*

Between the end of August and the end of October 1941, G, T, and Y Patrols were being refitted at Cairo, leaving only two Long Range Desert Group patrols in the fields. A Squadron, composed only of R Patrol and based at Siwa, operated under the direction of the commanding officer of the West Desert Force. S Patrol, which formed B Squadron, was based at Kufra and was under the direction of General Headquarters, Middle East. The headquarters of the Long Range Desert Group was also at Kufra along with H Section, the Signals Troop, and the Survey Unit.[1] Dividing the Long Range Desert Group between Siwa and Kufra resulted in A Squadron becoming for a time almost a separate unit from the rest of the Long Range Group; but this divided command did not make much difference in the autumn of 1941 because the patrols of the Long Range Desert Group were for the most part engaged in reconnaissance for the British offensive planned for November. R Patrol operated mainly in northern Cyrenaica, while S Patrol operated mostly in northwestern Tripolitania.

Almost all of R Patrol's operations from Siwa were part of the preparations for the forthcoming British offensive, known as *Crusader*, in Egypt and northern Cyrenaica. At the end of August a small patrol under the command of Lance Corporal W.J. Hamilton was sent from Siwa to look for suitable sites for aircraft landing grounds in an area west of Jarabub.[2] This operation was followed by one led by Easonsmith, who had remained at Siwa to command R Patrol instead of

---

1   TNA, WO/201/810, ff. 2, 4.
2   TNA, WO/201/810, ff. 7-8.

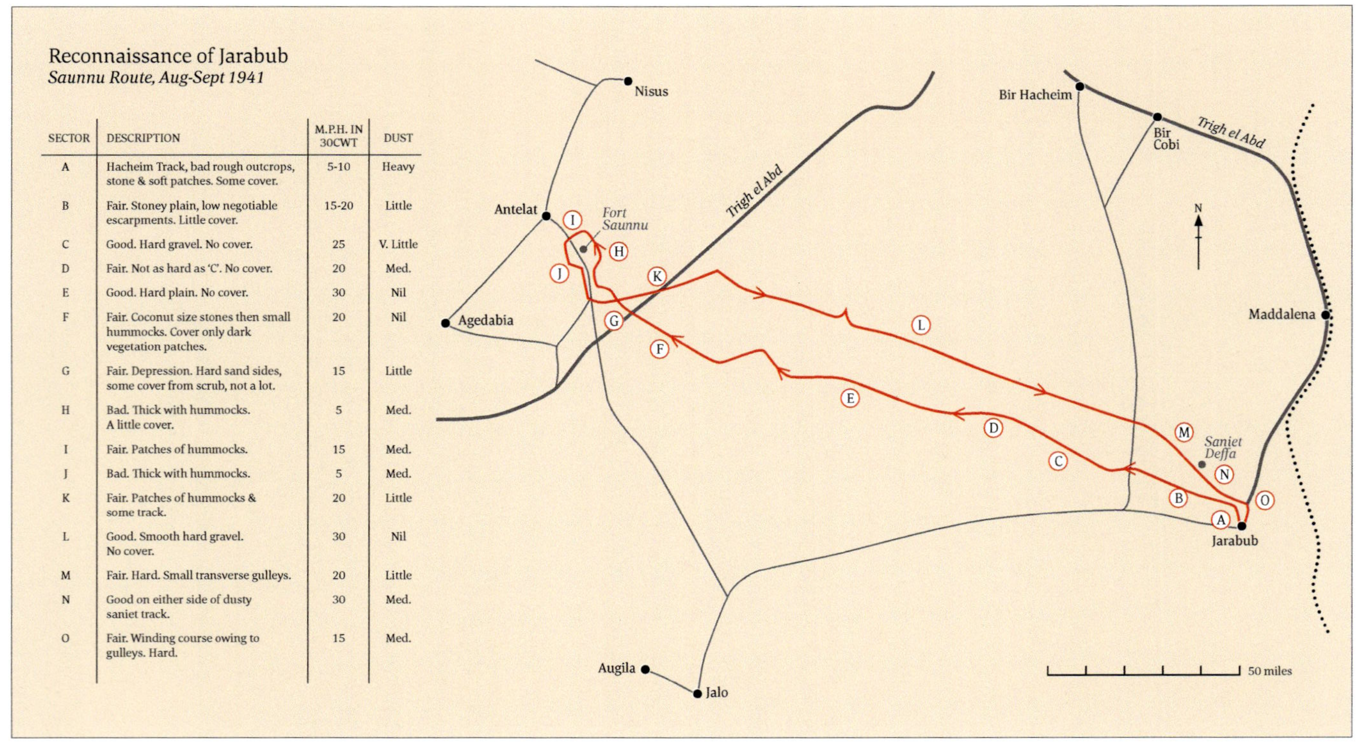

SECTOR	DESCRIPTION	M.P.H. IN 30CWT	DUST
A	Hacheim Track, bad rough outcrops, stone & soft patches. Some cover.	5-10	Heavy
B	Fair. Stoney plain, low negotiable escarpments. Little cover.	15-20	Little
C	Good. Hard gravel. No cover.	25	V. Little
D	Fair. Not as hard as 'C'. No cover.	20	Med.
E	Good. Hard plain. No cover.	30	Nil
F	Fair. Coconut size stones then small hummocks. Cover only dark vegetation patches.	20	Nil
G	Fair. Depression. Hard sand sides, some cover from scrub, not a lot.	15	Little
H	Bad. Thick with hummocks. A little cover.	5	Med.
I	Fair. Patches of hummocks.	15	Med.
J	Bad. Thick with hummocks.	5	Med.
K	Fair. Patches of hummocks & some track.	20	Little
L	Good. Smooth hard gravel. No cover.	30	Nil
M	Fair. Hard. Small transverse gulleys.	20	Little
N	Good on either side of dusty saniet track.	30	Med.
O	Fair. Winding course owing to gulleys. Hard.	15	Med.

Fig. No 11. Reconnaissance of Jarabub-Saunnu Route, Aug.- Sept. 1941 (TNA, WO/201/810).

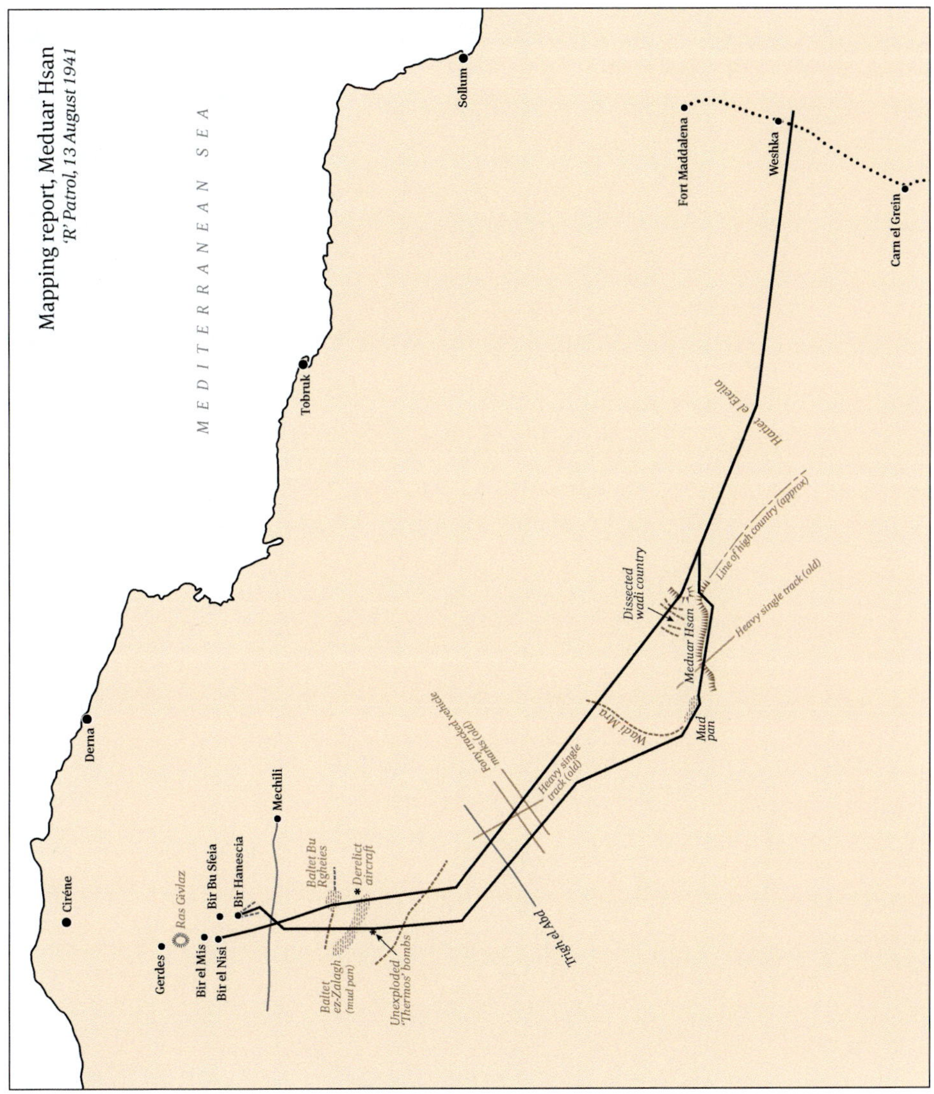

Fig. No 12. Reconnaissance Report, Meduar Hsan, R Patrol, 13 Aug. 1941 (TNA, WO 201/809).

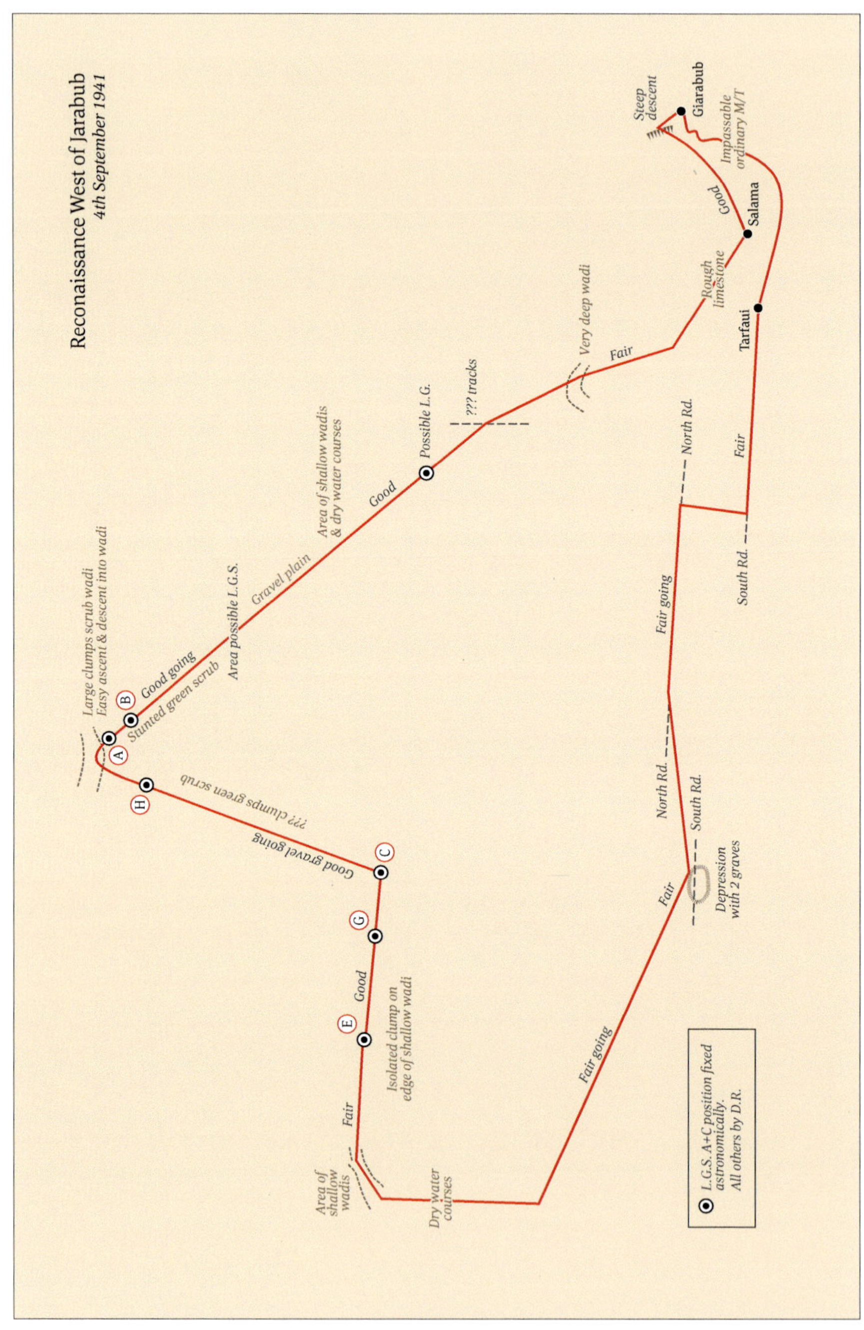

Fig. No 13. Reconnaissance West of Jarabub, 29 August −4 Sept. 1941 (TNA, WO 201/810).

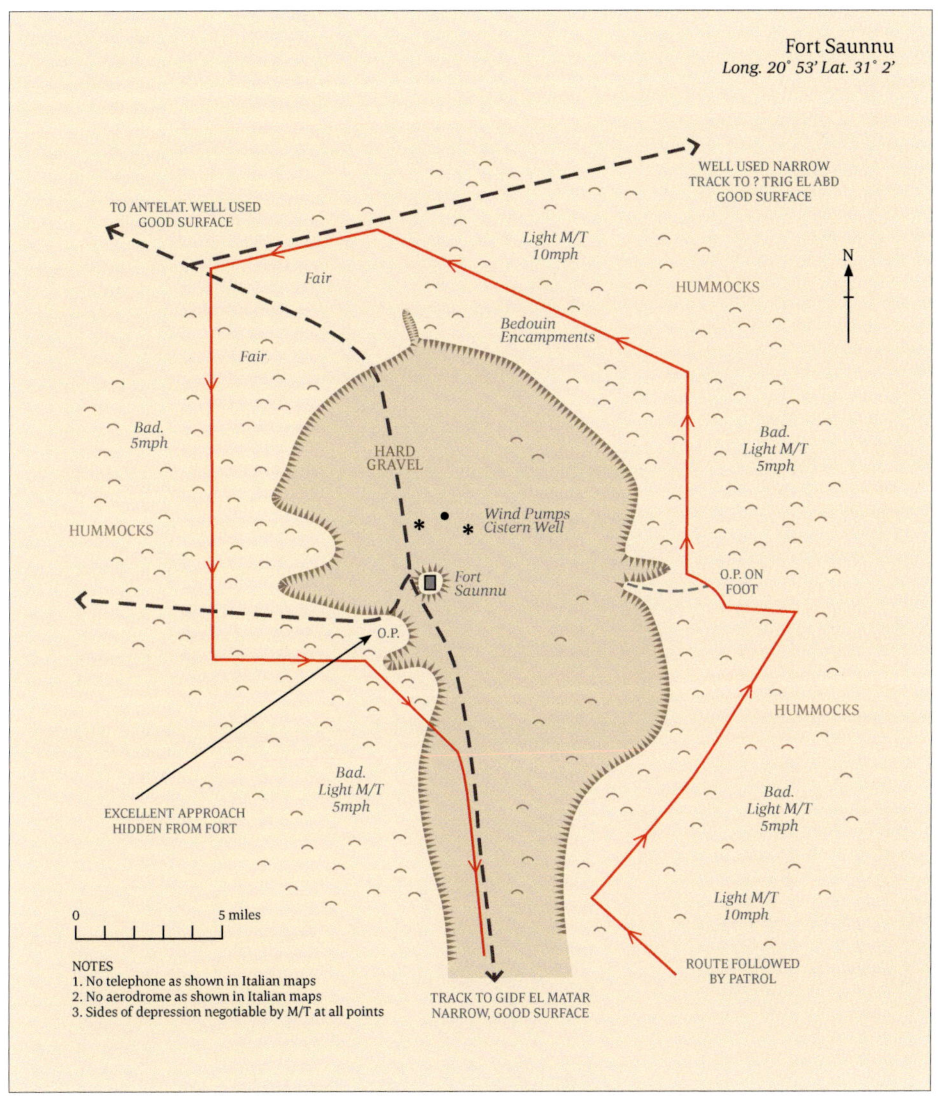

Fig. No 14. Sketch Map of Fort Saunnu, 4 Sept. 1941 (TNA, WO 201/810).

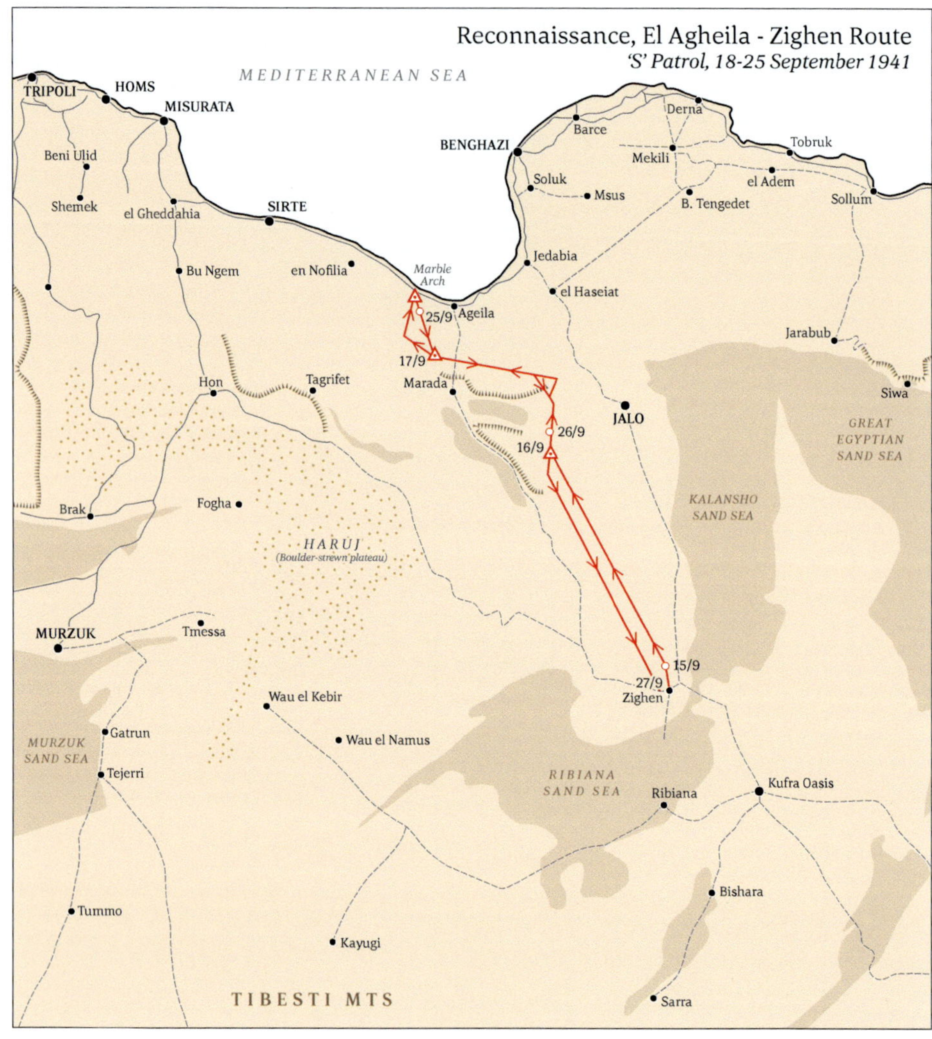

Fig. No 15. Reconnaissance, El Agheila-Zighen Route, S Patrol, 18-25 Sept. 1941 (TNA, WO 201/810).

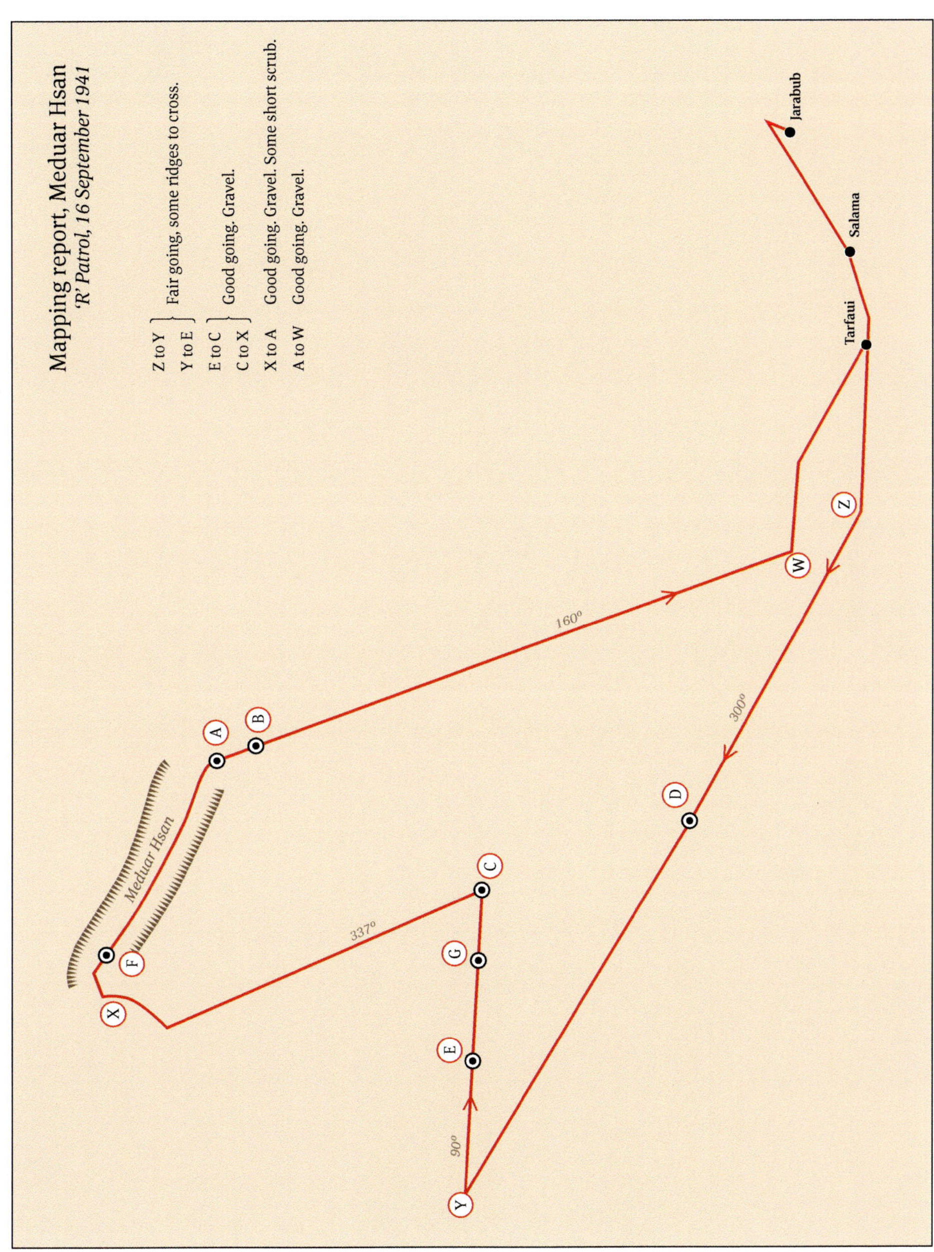

Fig. No 16. Mapping Report, Meduar Hsan, R Patrol, 16 Sept. 1941 (TNA, WO/ 201/810).

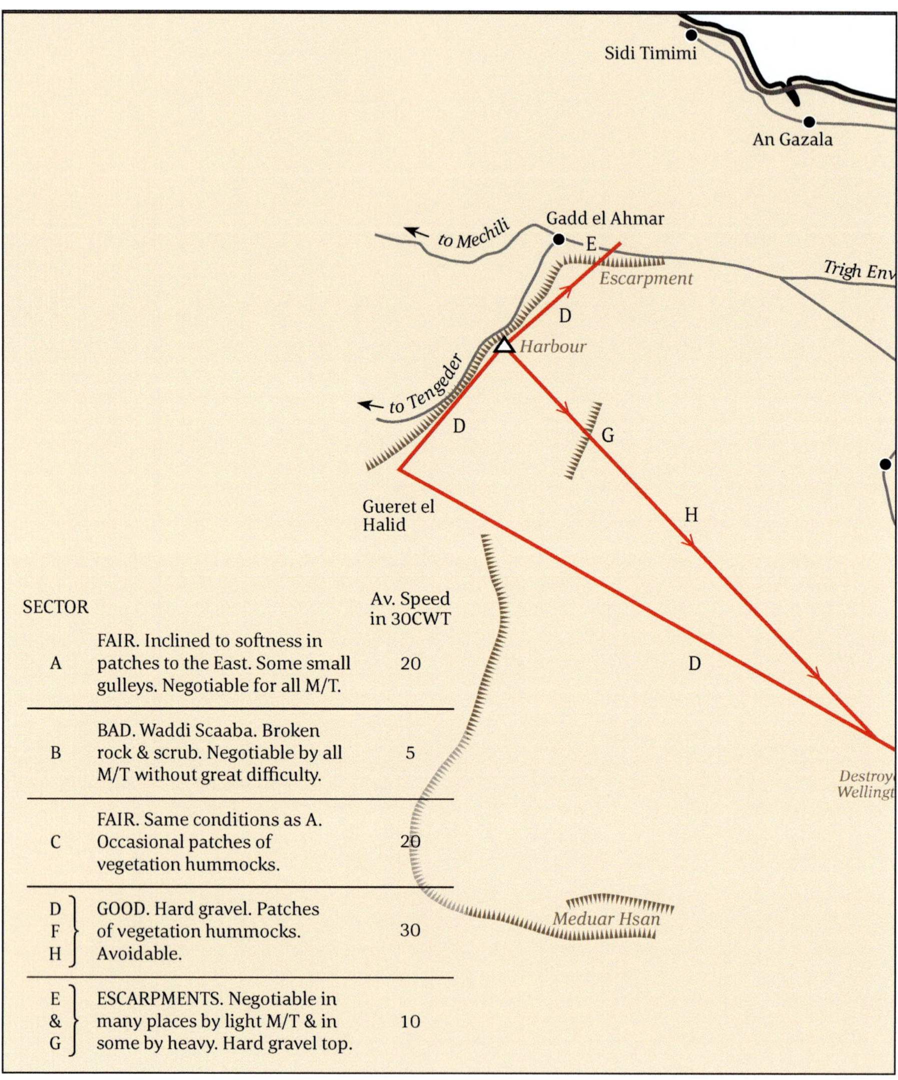

Fig. No 17. Sketch Map and Topographical Notes, Weshka-Timimi Route, R Patrol, 1-7 Oct. 1941 (TNA, WO 201/810).

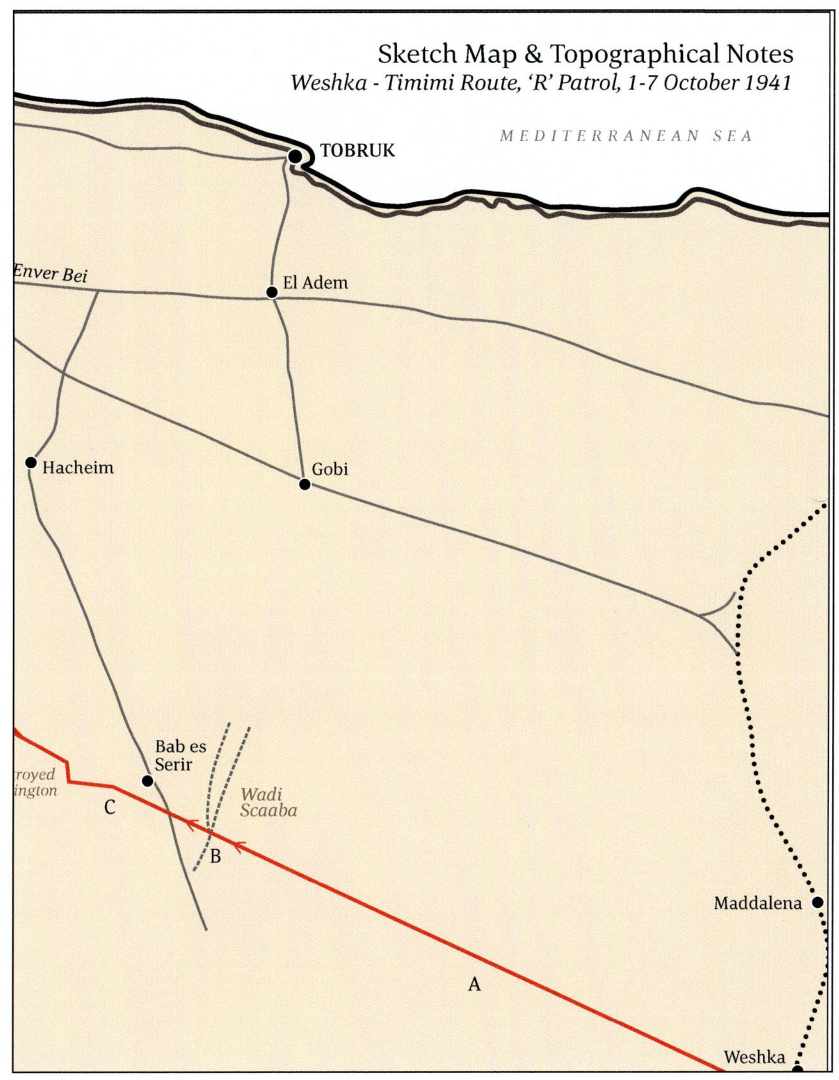

Sketch Map & Topographical Notes
Weshka - Timimi Route, 'R' Patrol, 1-7 October 1941
MEDITERRANEAN SEA
TOBRUK
Enver Bei
El Adem
Hacheim
Gobi
Bab es
Serir
Wadi
Scaaba
royed
ington
C
B
A
Maddalena
Weshka

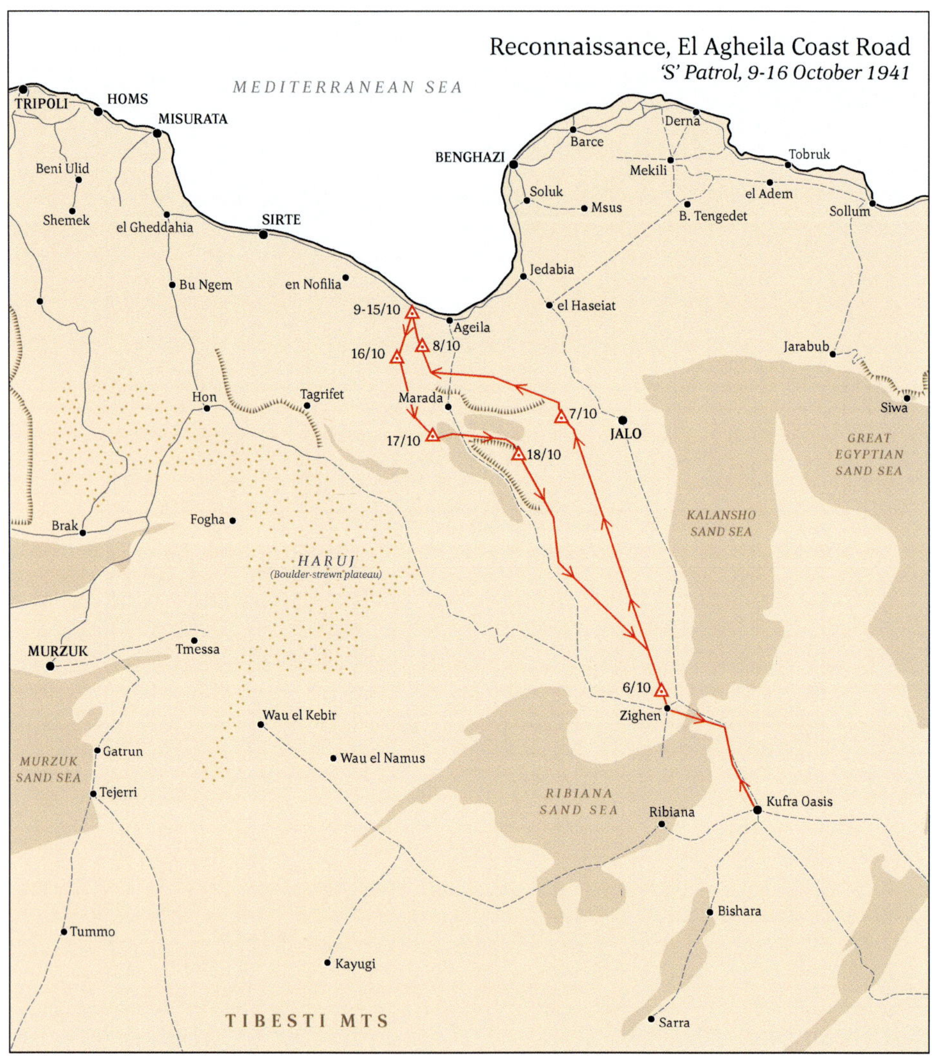

Fig. No 18. Reconnaissance, El Agheila coast road, S Patrol, 9-16 Oct. 1941 (TNA, WO 201/810).

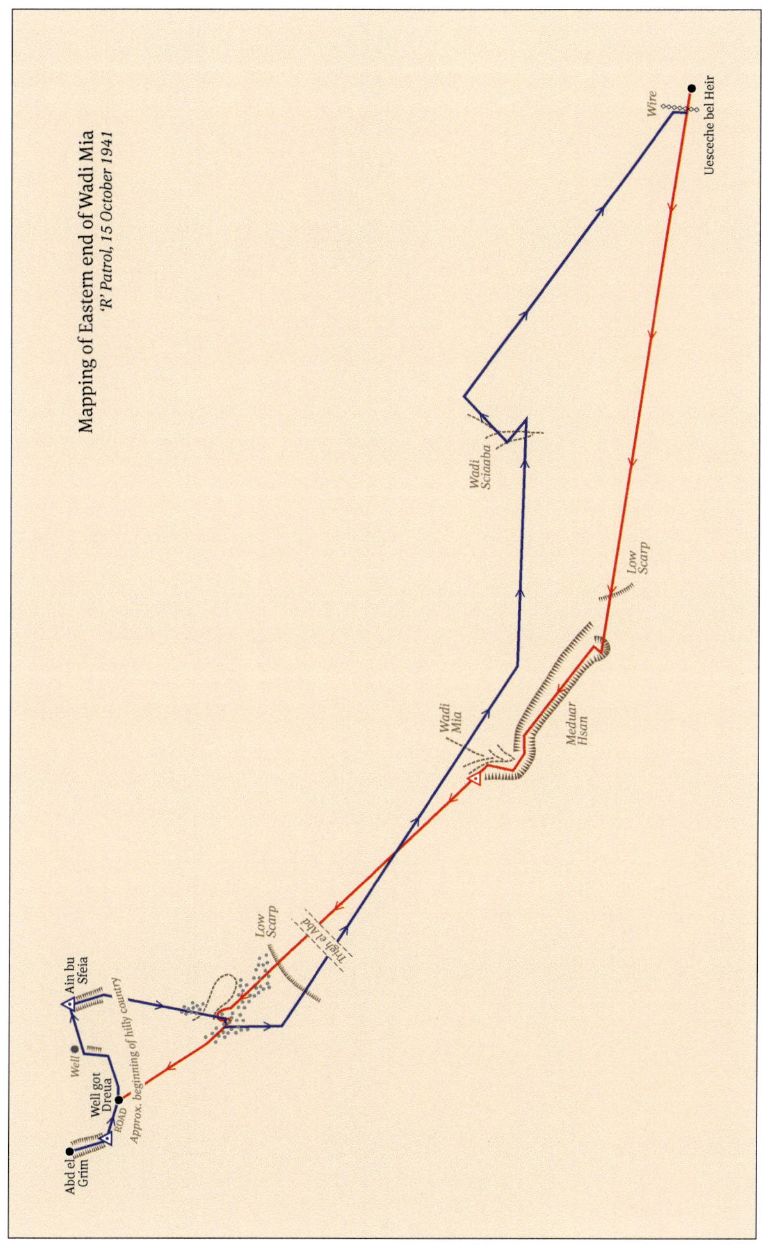

Fig. No 19. Mapping of Eastern end of Wadi Mia, R Patrol, 15 Oct. 1941 (TNA, WO 201/810).

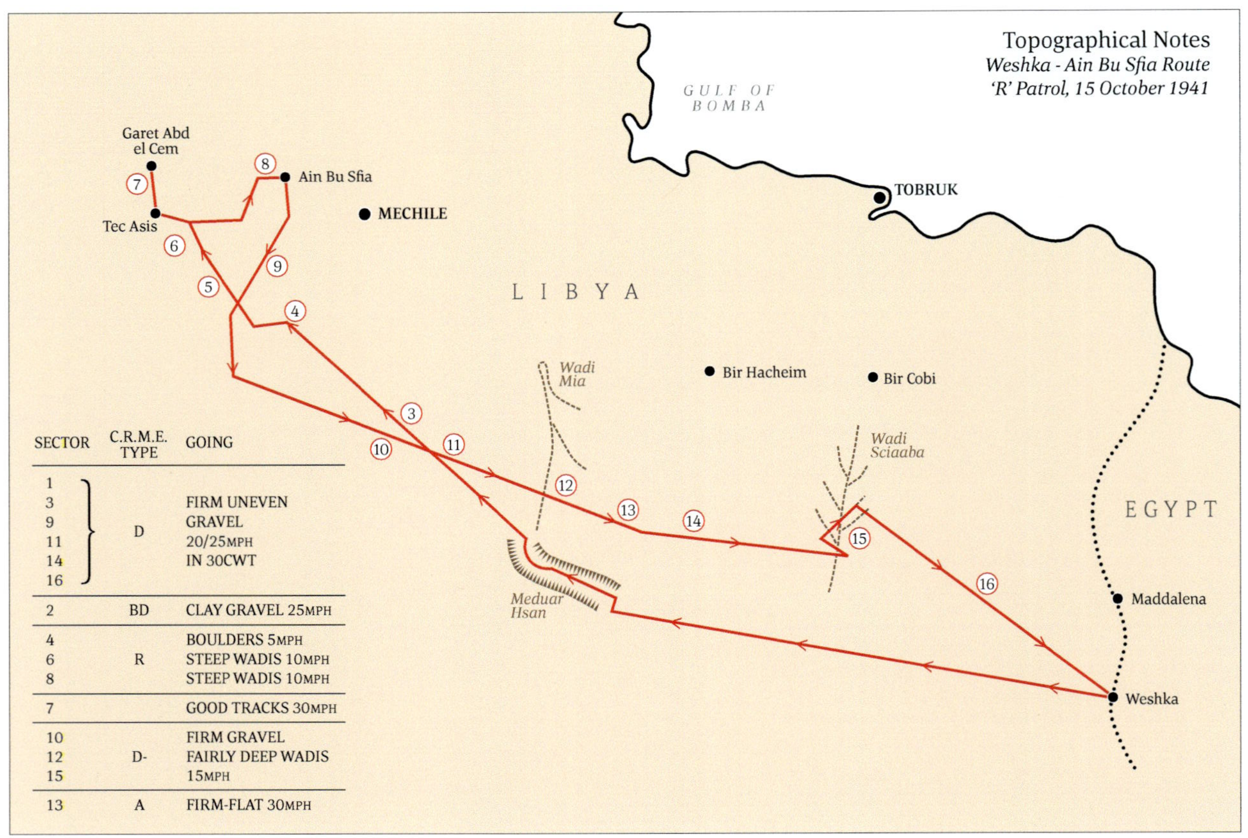

Fig. No 20. Topographical Notes, Weshka–Ain Bu Sfia Route, R Patrol, 15 Oct. 1941 (TNA, WO 201/810).

returning to Cairo with G and Y Patrols. Easonsmith left Siwa on August 29 for Jarabub with the task of finding out if the ground between Jarabub and Saunnu would present any serious obstacles for the movement of a large number of heavy, wheeled vehicles. Easonsmith went on a northwest course from Jarabub to Saunnu, looked over a disused Italian fort there, and then returned on a course which was about twenty miles south of the one he went out on.[3] The next operation was carried out by 2nd Lieutenant D.I. Ross of R Patrol who left Siwa with a small party on 16 September to obtain accurate positions of the aircraft landing sites, which Lance Corporal Hamilton had located on an earlier patrol, to plot Meduar Hsan, which was unmapped —although a month early in mid-August, R Patrol had been instructed to reconnoiter Meduar Hsan — and to recover a broken-down truck. Ross accomplished this task in five days and turned in a very detailed report giving the longitude and latitude of the aircraft landing grounds along with a map showing his route, the type of terrain crossed, and the configuration of Meduar Hsan.[4]

R Patrol at Siwa not only carried out missions to obtain geographical intelligence but also to place agents behind enemy lines. On 15 September Easonsmith departed from Siwa with two Arab agents and three trucks. The Arab agents were dropped west of Mechili, and Easonsmith waited outside of the town a day and a half until the agents returned. The patrol then set off for Siwa, which they reached on 19 September. Easonsmith had been directed to bring back to Siwa a broken-down truck, but the Italians found it first and had taken it away.[5] Easonsmith next took two Arab agents to a point between Timimi and Ain el Gazala, using two trucks; he waited four days for the return of the agents, and then took them back to Siwa,[6] which was reached on 7 October. On 13 October Easonsmith was off again for Cyrenaica with five trucks and orders to map various parts of Cyrenaica, pick up and send back to Siwa a British intelligence officer, and to obtain all possible information about Mechili. The mapping and picking up of the British intelligence officer were routine tasks; however Easonsmith also wanted to take a prisoner from Ain Bu Sfia to obtain intelligence about the place. He sent two trucks back to Siwa with the British intelligence officer and planned, with the remaining three trucks, to stop one or two enemy vehicles on the track leading out of Ain Bu Sfia. The plan was to hide two trucks off the track to cover Easonsmith's truck, which would block

---

3   TNA, WO/201/810, ff. 9-13.
4   TNA, WO/201/810, ff. 14-19.
5   TNA, WO/201/810, ff. 36-39.
6   TNA, WO/201/810, ff. 76-78.

the track and appear to be broken down. On the morning of 23 October the trap was set, but instead of stopping one or two vehicles, Easonsmith stopped sixteen trucks loaded with Italian troops. When the first enemy truck halted, Easonsmith walked up to the driver's door hiding a tommy gun behind his back; but just as his door was being opened, the driver of the enemy truck saw what was going on and jumped Easonsmith. In the ensuing struggle, the Italian got Easonsmith's weapon and attempted to run away, only to be killed by a grenade thrown by Easonsmith. Italians armed with rifles began jumping off their trucks, and the crews of the two R Patrol trucks which were hidden off the road opened fire. Easonsmith and some of his truck crewmen dragged two Italians out from under an enemy truck and threw them into theirs, and then all three R Patrol trucks retreated down the track as fast as they could. Two days later Easonsmith's patrol returned to Siwa.[7] The only reason why Easonsmith could take two prisoners out of a sixteen truck troop convoy without suffering any casualties was the totally unexpected nature of the operation and the great speed with which it was carried out.

In the middle of October, R Patrol was joined at Siwa by T Patrol, which had just finished being refitted at Cairo. On 16 October six trucks of T Patrol departed from Siwa under the command of Ballantyne with orders to take two Arab agents to a point near Agedabia, survey the region, and then pick up the two agents and bring them back to Siwa. The operation was a success and the patrol also captured an enemy salvage party found collecting spare parts from abandoned vehicles. On 1 November a patrol of four trucks made up of men drawn from both R and T Patrols was sent from Siwa for Bir Hachiem and Bir el Gubi to see if there was any enemy activity in that region. When the patrol was near Bir Hachiem it surprised and captured a five-man Italian motorcycle patrol. Four of the captured motorcycles were destroyed and the fifth, which had a radio mounted on it, was brought back to Siwa along with the prisoners.[8]

In the weeks before the *Crusader* counterattack, the operations of R Patrol and T Patrol in northern Cyrenaica provided British planners and commanders with a mass of geographical intelligence—information such as in which regions wheeled vehicles could operate—that could not be obtained by the use of aircraft. The units of the Long Range Desert Group based at Siwa also produced a great deal of intelligence on enemy activities and proved to be a very dependable means of putting agents into enemy territory and then safely bringing them back. Moreover, actions such as Easonsmith's ambushing a convoy to gain prisoners and the capture

---

7   TNA, WO/201/801, ff. 79-87.
8   TNA, WO/201/810, ff. 89-96.

of an enemy salvage party and a five-man motorcycle patrol must have made the enemy wonder what was happening behind their front lines.

While units of the Long Range Desert Group were conducting operations in northern Cyrenaica for the Western Desert Force, S Patrol based at Kufra was undertaking some extremely important missions for General Headquarters, Middle East. On 10 September Olivey of S Patrol was ordered to proceed north to the coast road west of El Agheila with four vehicles and to make a list of every type of vehicle that moved east or west on the coast road. He was to note such things as supply convoys, formed fighting units, time and date seen, direction of traffic, type and place, and in a column the number of armed escort vehicles, if any, accompanying supply convoys. This task had to be carried out in such a way that the enemy never knew that the patrol had taken place. Radio silence would be maintained during most of the mission. All paper, cigarette packets, cigarette ends, empty fuel cans and the like were to be buried. And there would be no fighting unless attacked.

Olivey's patrol left Zighen on 15 September and went north along the Kufra-El Agheila track, avoiding places such as Marada where there might be enemy troops. Unseen by the enemy, the patrol reached the coast road at a point twenty-eight miles west of El Agheila on 18 September. The trucks were hidden, and then for the next one hundred and sixty hours the coast road was watched with field glasses from a hundred foot high hill two and a half miles from the road; during the night the observation post was moved closer to the road. The biggest problem Olivey encountered was that he and his men did not have enough knowledge of enemy equipment to be able to note more than number and size of vehicles seen. Also, it was quickly seen that the existence of the patrol might become known to the enemy unless great care was taken. Two enemy vehicles broke down in sight of S Patrol's observation post, two convoys camped near them, and at one time when 2nd Lieutenant, L.H. Browne, was within three hundred yards of the road, a car suddenly stopped, two enemy soldiers got out and began hunting and shooting rabbits. On the evening of 25 September, Olivey withdrew from the coast road and headed back to Zighen and then on to Kufra.[9] When Olivey arrived at Kufra, Prendergast, his commanding officer, was given a list of every vehicle and the date and time it passed Olivey's observation post on the coast road.

On 5 October Holliman left Kufra with five trucks to set up another road watch west of El Agheila. Holliman's instructions were similar to those given to Olivey with two important exceptions. Holliman was directed to begin the road

---

9   TNA, WO/201/810, ff. 20-34.

watch on 9 October because "H.Q., M.E. expects important traffic to pass along the road from 8/10/41 onward."[10] Also, Holliman's instructions about what type of information was wanted on traffic on the coast road was very specific. Holliman's patrol traveled northward to the coast along the same route that Olivey had taken. The patrol watched the coast road from 9 to 16 October and made detailed notes on the numbers and types of vehicles that went along the road in both directions. The patrol used the same observation posts as Olivey, and another observation post was set up in "a shallow sand pit approximately 500 yards south of the road."[11] When Holliman's patrol returned to Kufra,[12] they had compiled a remarkably detailed list showing both numbers and types of vehicles going east and west on the coast road. The report also made a number of general observations:

> The majority of vehicles (Particularly those classified as medium) appeared to be new.
> Peak period of traffic passing observation point was between sunrise and 09.00 solar time daily.
> During the hours of darkness an average of only 8 vehicles passed the observation point. 75% of these were staff cars.
> Approximately 7/10 of the traffic was EASTBOUND. Heavy and medium lorries traveled at 20-20 M.P.H.[13]

This is the kind of information that intelligence officers dream about obtaining. It not only told them what went up and down the coast road to a given period of time but also they could use it to double-check other sources of information, such as <u>ultra</u> and agent reports. The two road watch missions conducted by S Patrol showed that units of the Long Range Desert Group were capable of crossing hundreds of miles of Libyan Desert, spending a number of days watching the coast road without being detected by the enemy, and finally producing large amounts of high-quality intelligence.

During the early autumn of 1941 the entire British command structure in the Middle East was changed. A new East African Command was set up to free the Commander-in-Chief, Middle East from East African problems.[14] British forces in the Middle East were divided into the 8th and 9th Armies. The 9th Army, under

---

10   TNA, WO/201/810, f. 41.

11   TNA, WO/201/810, f. 46.

12   TNA, WO/201/810, ff. 41-68.

13   TNA, WO/201/810, ff. 48.

14   I.S.O. Playfair, *The Mediterranean and the Middle East* (London: HMSO, 1956) vol. II, p. 316.

the command of General Sir Maitland Wilson comprised those forces in Palestine, Transjordan, and Syria. The 8th Army, under the command of General Sir Alan Cunningham, consisted of the forces in the Western Desert fighting the Germans and Italians.[15] On 21 September the whole of the Long Range Desert Group was placed under the command of the 8th Army, effective 1 October.[16] On 24 September Bagnold wrote a long letter and a memorandum to Prendergast explaining the new command arrangements and saying that Cunningham understood the role of the Long Range Desert Group and its limitations. Bagnold also told Prendergast that he must move himself, if not his headquarters, from Kufra to Siwa and spend some time at 8th Army Headquarters in order to learn how it worked and to gain the confidence of the commander of the army and of his staff. Prendergast was also to make arrangements to move all the units of the Long Range Desert Group out of Kufra in the near future to some place near the area where the 8th Army was operating.[17]

On 29 September at 8th Army Headquarters a meeting was held with Bagnold, Prendergast, and a number of 8th Army staff officers to decide the future role of the Long Range Desert Group. They defined the role of the Long Range Desert Group as follows:

(a) To obtain information as to enemy movements on certain tracks, and certain areas, and to watch his reactions to any offensive by us.

(b) Further information of the state of going in certain areas would also be required.

(c) At all times the L.R.D.G. should try and harass the enemy as far as possible, and in any way they liked provided they did not get too involved themselves. The Army Commander realized that the L.R.D.G. should not deliberately court trouble, and was in no way armoured. Targets for such action should where possible be P.O.L. dumps. Any available information of such Dumps would be given to L.R.D.G. by G.S.I.

(d) Any tactical information would be required as early as possible. During and just before offensive operations L.R.D.G. would be justified in taking

---

15   *Ibid*, vol. III, p. 1.
16   TNA, WO/201/810, f. 100.
17   TNA, WO/201/810, ff. 102-106.

more risks of being D/Fd than usual in order to send back up to date information.[18]

After returning to Kufra Prendergast discussed in some detail with Kennedy Shaw the role given to the Long Range Desert Group at the meeting on 29 September. Both Prendergast and Kennedy Shaw felt that the role assigned to the Long Range Desert Group was not offensive enough and that the unit should engage in the following activities:

(a) Topographical recce.

(b) Dropping agents.

(c) Traffic census.

(d) Traffic census linked by W/T to ground straffing aircraft.

(e) Laying ambushes on roads and shooting up convoys in order to encourage the enemy to escort them with amd. Cars withdrawn from the front.

(f) Approaching aerodromes on foot at night with the objective of damaging aircraft.

(g) Observing enemy reactions to our main advance.[19]

Prendergast's and Kennedy Shaw's thoughts on attacking airfields were very similar to those of Captain David Stirling, who was to found the Special Air Service and with whom they would closely collaborate. Prendergast and Kennedy Shaw wanted to train men of the Long Range Desert Group to attack aircraft on enemy airfields at night by placing time bombs under parked aircraft. Both men thought that attacks of this type should be undertaken in conjunction with major offensive operations by the 8th Army. They had reached the stage in this scheme where experiments in bomb making were going on at Kufra. The problem was that all they had in the way of explosives were anti-tank mines and Mills bombs, which are standard issue grenades. The general idea was to place an anti-tank mine with a

---

18   TNA, WO/201/810, ff. 109-110.
19   TNA, WO/201/810, f. 112.

Mills bomb attached to it under a parked aircraft. The Mills bomb would be made into a time bomb by "tying the handle down with tape, removing the pin, and soaking the tape in acid." This was a wild idea, but Prendergast thought it "would work satisfactorily if there is nothing better available."[20]

On 21 October Prendergast wrote a long private letter to Harding-Newman, who was on the staff of the 8th Army, asking him what he and other people at 8th Army headquarters thought about the idea of the Long Range Desert Group becoming more offensive in its operations.[21] Four days later Harding-Newman wrote a private letter back to Prendergast saying that he did not find much objection to most of Prendergast's ideas at 8th Army Headquarters but warning that "The aerodrome idea is all rather involved with other ventures possibly and no action on your part is required at the moment."[22] What Harding-Newman did not tell Prendergast was that Stirling was preparing a unit to carry out operations against enemy airfields in a way very similar to that proposed by Prendergast.

As the relationship of the Long Range Desert Group to the main British headquarters in the Middle East was being changed and defined, the make up and structure of the force itself was also being changed. One of the major problems confronting the Long Range Desert Group was the liability to keep the unit's vehicles in a state of good repair. Part of the problem was that most members of the group were not properly qualified to repair motor vehicles. Also, there was no one officer whose responsibility it was to see that vehicles were correctly repaired. Moreover, there was a shortage of spare parts. After Bagnold left the Long Range Desert Group and became a staff officer at General Headquarters, Middle East, he was able to arrange to have Captain T.W. Ashdown, Royal Army Ordnance Corps, attached to the Long Range Desert Group along with a number of Royal Army Ordnance Corps fitters and mechanics. These men under the command of Ashdown formed the Light Repair Section of the Long Range Desert Group. This addition to the Long Range Desert Group solved many of the problems encountered when getting vehicles repaired quickly and correctly.[23]

When the Long Range Desert Group was first set up and during the first patrols into Libya, the standard patrol consisted of one 15 cwt truck and ten 30 cwt trucks. During operations in northern Libya in 1941 it was found that this formation was too large for the tasks that the Long Range Desert Group was

20   TNA, WO/201/810, f. 113.
21   TNA, WO/201/810, ff. 112-115.
22   TNA, WO/201/810, ff. 116-121.
23   TNA, CAB/44/151, f. 71; WO/201/810, f. 2.

required to carry out. For instance, Easonsmith of R Patrol working out of Siwa sometimes used as few as two or three trucks. Also, the 15 cwt trucks were found to be unsuitable for the job and were being dropped. Towards the end of October 1941, the patrols of the Long Range Desert Group were reorganized. Each patrol was cut in half, doubling the number of patrols within the Long Range Desert Group. G Patrol became G1 and G2, S Patrol became S1 and S2, and so on. The change doubled the number of operations that the Long Range Desert Group could undertake at any given time, but it also doubled the number of radios, radio operators, and radio traffic that the Signal Section had to deal with.[24]

G1, G2, Y1, and Y2 Patrols arrived at Kufra on 21 October after being refitted at Cairo. S1 and S2 Patrols had just returned to Kufra from an operation and Prendergast thought it would take about a week to get the six patrols ready for further action.[25] G1, G2, Y1, and Y2 were sent from Kufra to Siwa and arrived there on 8 and 9 November, several days after Prendergast and Kennedy Shaw reached Siwa. The move to Siwa brought the Long Range Desert Group much closer to 8th Army Headquarters, a move Bagnold had earlier advised. By the beginning of the *Crusader* offensive, the entire Long Range Desert Group was based at Siwa with the exception of S1 Patrol and the Survey Unit. The group's headquarters was in the Rest House; a hospital and the quartermaster's stores were placed in empty buildings belonging to the Egyptian army, and the vehicle repair shops were in adjoining garages.[26]

While most of the Long Range Desert Group was establishing itself in Siwa, S1 and S2 Patrols were conducting operations. Before the decision was made to move the Long Range Desert Group to Siwa, it had been decided that S1 Patrol would undertake a raid into Tripolitania. When the decision was made to move to Siwa, S1 Patrol's orders were not changed. The plan called for S1 Patrol, in company with S2 Patrol, to proceed as far as Wadi Messiah. S2 Patrol would make a dump of fuel at this point and then return to Kufra, while S1 Patrol continued on into Tripolitania to attack enemy transport on the Hon-Misurata Road and then, if conditions were favorable, to attack traffic on the coast road before returning to Kufra. The two patrols left Kufra on 30 October, and at 1600 on 6 November S1 Patrol reached the Hon-Misurata Road at a point eighteen miles north of Bunjem where there was a small camp for locals who repaired the road. The locals were rounded up and kept in their camp while the trucks of S1 Patrol took up hidden

---

24   TNA, CAB/44/151, ff. 84-85; WO/201/810, f. 5.
25   TNA, WO/201/810, f. 115.
26   TNA, WO/201/811, ff. 3-4.

positions on the west side of the road; however, no traffic came down the road before nightfall. After dark the patrol moved within fifty yards of the road and built a barricade across it. At 0500 on 7 November an Italian truck carrying five Italians and seven locals stopped at the barricade and was captured by S1 Patrol. The captured truck was moved off the road and the seven locals were placed in the workers' camp. As it became light, the trucks of the patrol moved back into their ambush positions; but it began to rain lightly and the road turned to mud. Holliman, the commander of S1 Patrol, thought that there would not be much traffic on this road because of the mud and, therefore, he decided to attack the coast road that night. S1 Patrol proceeded northeast for some miles with the captured truck and natives and Italians, and then the truck was blown up and the native prisoners set free. S1 Patrol pushed on and at 1715 reached the coast road west of Sirte where they found a roadhouse, or truck stop, at which vehicles were seen to stop. It was decided to attack this roadhouse after dark and to destroy any enemy vehicles found there and at the same time to mine the coast road.

After dark two of S1 Patrol's trucks pulled up in front of the roadhouse, only to find the front door locked. Holliman then directed the mine laying party to join the raiding party. He then went himself to inspect a heavy truck with a trailer parked about fifty yards from the roadhouse and ordered some of his men to investigate the back of the roadhouse. When Holliman returned to the front of the roadhouse and asked his men what they could see in the house, he was told that a number of armed men were in the house. In fact, what had happened was that the men Holliman had sent around the back of the house had found an open door, entered the place, and were now conducting a room by room search for enemy troops. Holliman and his men in front of the house thought that those inside were enemy soldiers preparing to beat off an attack on the house by S1 Patrol. Holliman had the front door of the roadhouse broken down and then yelled in English, "Stop Stand Still." This command was not followed and half the raiding party opened fire on the other half. When the confusion ended, it was discovered that Lance Corporal Simpson had been shot in the shoulder. Holliman decided to break off the operation and return to Kufra, which was reached without incident.[27]

On 7 November S2 Patrol left Kufra with the mission of "planting" a fake map on the enemy. The map was one drawn up by the intelligence staff at 8th Army to show that the British were about to move against Jalo from the east. Browne, the commander of S2, did the actual "planting" at El Aseila on 9 November.[28] The patrol

---

27   TNA, WO/201/811, ff. 7-13.
28   TNA, WO/201/811, f. 4.

stopped at El Aseila, which is east of Jalo and nothing more than one palm tree and a water hole. At El Aseila a meal was cooked, and when an Arab was seen to be approaching, the patrol hurriedly departed, leaving some items behind, including the fake map. The map was left under an empty fuel can on a map board with a scale and a protractor, as if forgotten in the rush to leave.[29] The ruse was obviously successful, for two days after the capture of Jalo by the British, Kennedy Shaw saw all the details of the fake British map drawn in on the Italian commander's map of the region. After planting the fake map, S2 Patrol went to Siwa.[30]

The British attack on the Axis forces in Libya known as *Crusader* began on 18 November 1941.[31] Orders were issued at Siwa on 6 November to eight patrols of the Long Range Desert Group outlining their role in *Crusader*. T2 Patrol was to take Captain John Haselden, three other intelligence officers, and two Arab agents to a point near Mechili and, on the night of 17 November, to be in a position to observe as well as to report the movements of enemy traffic along the Benghazi-Mechili Road.[32] R1 Patrol was to leave Siwa and meet L Detachment of the Special Air Service Brigade.[33] Six other patrols—Y1, Y2, T1, G1, G2, and R2—were, by the evening of 17 November, to be in positions to observe and report the movements and types of vehicles along the major roads and tracks in northern Cyrenaica which Headquarters 8th Army thought the enemy would use when subjected to a major attack from Egypt. Each patrol was issued with thirty cases of fuel and food and water for three weeks. S1 and S2 patrols were to be held in reserve at Siwa.[34]

T1 Patrol left Siwa on 15 November and crossed into Libya at Weshka, and by 17 November reached Bir Belamed. On the afternoon of 18 November, the patrol was about sixteen miles southwest of Bir Hachiem, hiding from aircraft that kept flying over them. At 1630 a sentry saw lights moving towards T1's hiding place. It appeared to Ballantyne, the commander of the patrol, that an enemy patrol of armored vehicles was following T1's tracks. T1 Patrol moved out of its hiding place and separated into two groups. Two trucks remained with Ballantyne, while three others, including the one with the radio, went off with Sergeant I.H. McInnes. The two sections of T1 Patrol were chased for about ten miles before shaking off whoever was following them. Ballantyne and his two trucks went to Etla, where

---

29   TNA, WO/201/811, f. 17.

30   TNA, WO/201/811, ff. 4, 14-18.

31   Playfair, *The Mediterranean*, vol. III, p. 38.

32   TNA, WO/201/811, f. 21.

33   TNA, WO/201/811, f. 22.

34   TNA, WO/201/811, ff. 19-20.

T1 Patrol trucks were to meet if units of the patrol became separated. Not having a radio and not finding McInnes at Etla, Ballantyne pushed on to Siwa, arriving there on 19 November. Meanwhile, McInnes had arrived at Etla and radioed Siwa and been told to remain where he was. Ballantyne left again Siwa on the evening of 19 November and reached Etla at 0600 on 21 November. When he arrived at Etla, Ballantyne received orders to move his entire patrol northeast of Bir Hachiem, but when the patrol sighted several armored cars they decided to move off to the south. T1 Patrol sighted a lot of aircraft, but it did not see any vehicles; and on 23 November the patrol was ordered to return to Siwa, which it reached on 24 November.[35] T1 Patrol did not achieve much of anything on this mission.

On the same day that T1 patrol had returned to Siwa, the mission of the Long Range Desert Group patrols was changed by Headquarters 8th Army. Under the original order, the mission of the patrols was a passive one of watching roads and tracks and reporting the movement of enemy vehicles. But by 24 November the *Crusader* offensive had become bogged down with heavy fighting on the Egyptian-Libyan border between Axis and British forces; therefore, orders were issued to the patrols of the Long Range Desert Group to proceed to various points on the road net of Cyrenaica with the aim of conducting attacks on enemy supply vehicles—especially fuel trucks going east—and to harass the enemy in any way possible.[36]

In the meantime, G1 Patrol had left Siwa on 15 November and had headed north to watch Trigh el Abd near Bir ben Gania. Although the region is very flat, a good hiding place was found, and for the next seven days G1 watched the Trigh el Abd but saw nothing of interest. Then at 1500 on 24 November G1 Patrol was ordered to join G2 Patrol and to attack enemy traffic on the coast road between Agedabia and Benghazi. G1 Patrol passed within four miles of Msus and at 1230 was attacked by an Italian Ghiblis aircraft, which was driven away by gunfire. At 1600 G1 Patrol was again attacked, this time by a Junkers 87 dive bomber. In this attack, which lasted fifteen minutes, both machine-gun fire and bombs were used; nonetheless, the patrol sustained no casualties: "The method of evasion was to drive at high speed in all directions."[37] By the late afternoon of 28 November, G1 Patrol had reached the coast road near Beda Fomm but had still not met up with G2 Patrol. The patrol hid behind a small hill east of the road from the top of which the patrol commander, Captain A.M. Hay, saw that there was a rest house or truck stop on the coast road about four miles south with a number of vehicles parked

---

35   TNA, WO/201/811, ff. 26-27.
36   TNA, WO/201/811, f. 25.
37   TNA, WO/201/811, f. 46.

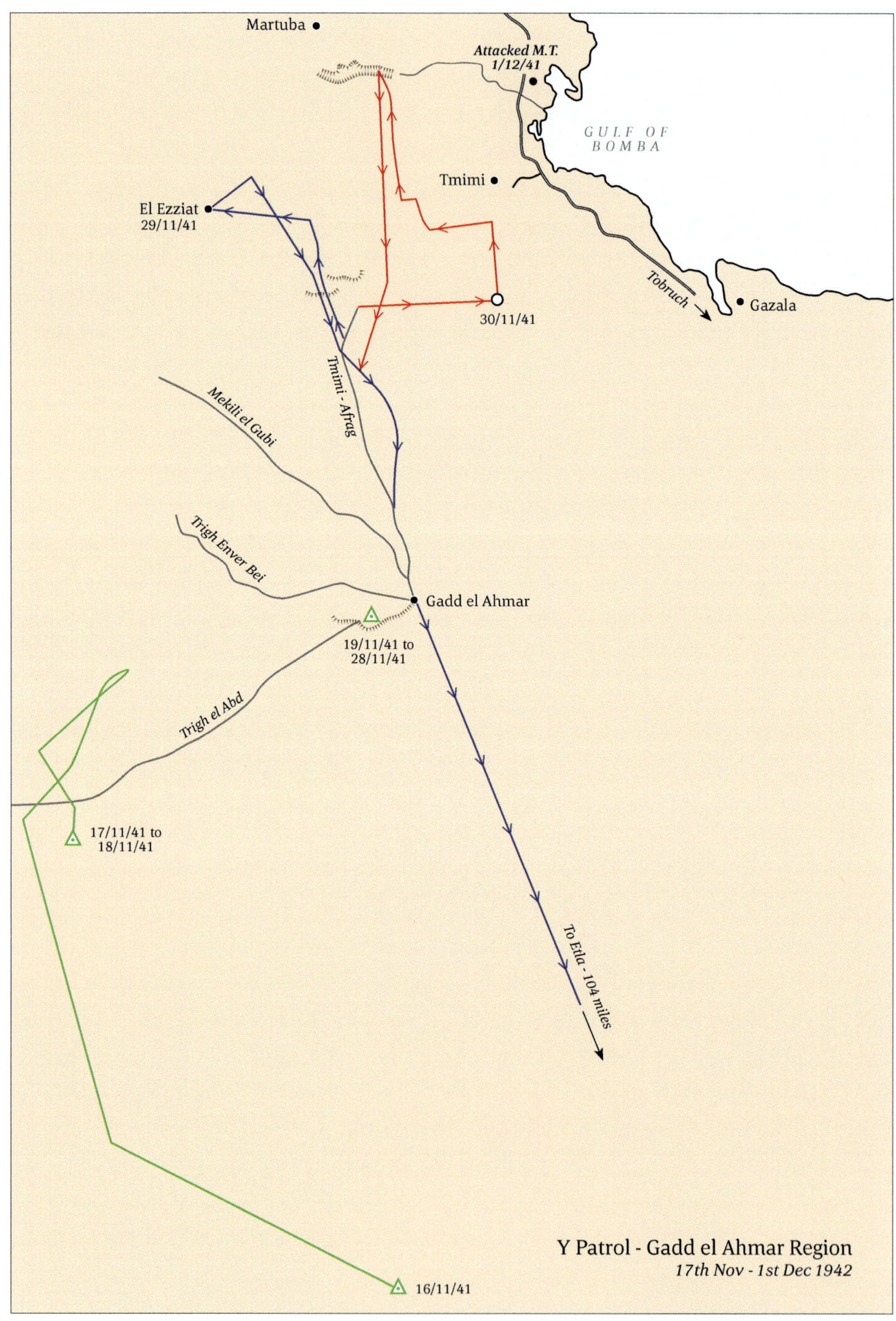

Fig. No 21. Road Sketch, Gadd el Ahmar region, Y2 Patrol, 17 Nov.-1 Dec. 1942 (TNA, WO 201/811).

around it. After sunset, G1 Patrol made its way to the coast road and headed south on the road at a speed of about twenty miles an hour towards the vehicles and the rest house. When G1 Patrol reached the rest house, the guardsmen began throwing grenades and firing machine-guns with armor piercing and incendiary rounds at the parked enemy vehicles. The enemy did not return the fire, and it was impossible to tell how much damage was done because it was dark and the action lasted only a few seconds. G1 Patrol then hid in a wadi, where it remained because of enemy aircraft until 1500 on 29 November. That night, G1 Patrol found a small hill about two hundred yards from the road behind which they parked their vehicles. Lewis guns were then taken from the trucks and set up on top of the hill. When a convoy of several empty tanker trucks passed the hill, Hay ordered that one of the largest trucks in this convoy be shot up. The Lewis guns opened fire, the truck ran off the road and almost turned over, and the truck's crew of two were killed. When the empty tanker was attacked, all traffic—going both north and south—was seen by the British to stop, turn around, and retreat. On 1 December G1 Patrol was ordered to return to Siwa, which they reached on 3 December.[38]

By 17 November, G2 Patrol had arrived at Maaten el Grara, where it was to observe the movement of enemy vehicles on the Trigh el Abd. However, there was no movement of vehicles on the Trigh el Abd, only a considerable number of enemy aircraft flying overhead. At dusk on 21 November G2 Patrol saw an explosion to the north and aircraft attacking with tracers the base of the explosion, from which smoke began to rise. Although he had orders to watch the Trigh el Abd and there were many enemy aircraft about, the next day Lieutenant J.A.L. Timpson went north with four trucks for about twenty miles in an unsuccessful attempt to find the site of the explosion. At 1420 a Fiat bomber, with engine trouble, flew over the top of the trucks at a height of about thirty feet and landed right in front of the British party. Timpson, who had orders not to fight unless attacked, attacked the aircraft with machine-gun fire at close range, killing two Italians and capturing three others. After all the maps and other papers had been removed from it, gasoline was poured over the aircraft. It was then set afire by tracer rounds and exploded within a few seconds. The three prisoners were taken to Landing Ground 125, which was a secret R.A.F. airfield north of the Libyan Sand Sea. The R.A.F. officer who was in command of Landing Ground 125 asked Timpson to take a message to the commander of E Force, which was attacking Jalo. Timpson decided to split G2 Patrol by sending two trucks back to Maaten el Grara to watch for enemy movement on the Trigh el Abd and to go with the other two trucks to

---

38   TNA, WO/201/811, ff. 45-48.

Jalo with the message for the commander of E Force; but when one of the trucks developed mechanical problems, Timpson decided to leave it at Landing Ground 125 and to go to Jalo with only one truck.[39] This decision violated the rule that one should never go anywhere in the desert with only one vehicle. Timpson either should have gone back to Maaten el Grara with three trucks or not gone anywhere until the broken-down truck was fixed. On 25 November Timpson's truck broke down about twenty miles north of Jalo and the guards officer had to walk to the oasis. Timpson now had two working trucks many miles to the north at Maaten el Grara, one broken-down truck at Landing Ground 125, and a disabled truck twenty miles north of Jalo. It was not until 6 December that all four trucks of G2 Patrol arrived back at Siwa.[40]

Under the command of Captain F.C. Simms, Y1 Patrol departed from Siwa on 15 November bound for Garet Meriem. Two days later on a plateau about a mile and a half southwest of Segnali, Y1 Patrol was machine-gunned for about ten minutes by three R.A.F. Beaufighters even though the patrol had displayed recognition signals. No casualties were suffered, but the truck with the radio on it was destroyed. Being attacked by Allied aircraft was one of the great dangers of using vehicles behind enemy lines. Recognition signals are hard for aircraft pilots to see, and most pilots assume that beyond a certain point on the front line all vehicles are enemy ones. With the loss of its radio truck, Y1 Patrol set off to find Patrol Y2 to radio Siwa for orders.[41]

Y2 Patrol, under the command of Captain David Lloyd Owen, was at Bir Hachiem when on November 17 at 1300 Simms arrived with two trucks to use Lloyd Owen's radio. Simms was ordered to return to Siwa with the two trucks and to pick up another radio truck; his other two trucks were to join Y2 Patrol, which was ordered to Gadd el Ahmar to await the return of Simms and to observe the movement of traffic at that crossroad. Y2 saw no enemy movement of Gadd el Ahmar, and on 26 November Simms returned with a radio truck. The next day both patrols set out in search of enemy vehicles to attack. For the next several days, both Y1 and Y2 Patrols scouted the road net between Mechili, Derna, Timimi, Ain el Gazala, and got to el Afrag looking for something to attack. It was not until 2 December that Y1 found and attacked an enemy motor pool, damaging some fifteen vehicles. During the fight Lance Corporal Carr, navigator for Y1 Patrol,

---

39   TNA, WO/201/811, f. 56.
40   TNA, WO/201/811, ff. 55-57.
41   TNA, WO/201/811, f. 50.

became separated from the main body and was listed as missing until he rejoined the unit at Siwa.[42]

On 29 November, Y2 Patrol captured a 15 cwt Ford truck along with three Italian and two Libyan soldiers. One of the Italians spoke some English and told Lloyd Owen that they belonged to the garrison of a small fort at El Ezzeiat and were on their way to Derna to pick up rations. Lloyd Owen decided to have a look at the fort and was guided there by the English-speaking Italian. Six hundred yards short of the fort Y2 Patrol dismounted from their trucks and advanced on the fort while the enemy opened fire with machine-guns and rifles. The machine-guns on the patrols trucks returned the fire as the rest of the patrol took cover in some ruined buildings. A Lewis gun was brought forward, but it was a standoff, for the attackers could not blast the enemy out of this "little *Beau Geste* fort" with small arms.[43] Lloyd Owen called a truce and tried to bluff the enemy into surrendering by telling the Italian commander that he had reinforcements coming with tanks and guns. When this did not work, both sides went back to shooting at each other with rifles and machine-guns, to no effect. The stalemate was broken when the British destroyed one of the Italian machine-guns with a rifle grenade and the seventeen Italian defenders surrendered. After destroying everything in the fort of any value, the patrol withdrew about thirty-five miles, hid in a wadi, and radioed Siwa for further instructions. When the instructions came, they read "Your orders were to operate offensively against transport in a certain area. Dispose of your prisoners and do what you were told."[44] It seemed to Lloyd Owen that he had only three alternatives: kill the prisoners; let them go free; or weaken the patrol by assigning men to guard them while the rest of Y2 Patrol went hunting for enemy transport to attack. That afternoon Lloyd Owen talked the problem over with his men. There were some who wanted to kill the prisoners, but nobody wanted simply to let them go free because they knew too much about Y2 Patrol and would make for the nearest Axis post and sound the alarm. And no one wanted to weaken the patrol guarding the prisoners. Finally, Lloyd Owen figured out a solution: take the prisoners to a point thirty miles south, give them some food and water, and leave them to walk eighty miles to the nearest known enemy outpost. This would give Y2 Patrol time to shoot up some enemy transport and be gone before the prisoners

---

42   TNA, WO/201/811, ff. 49-52. Lance Corporal Carr aided by Senussi Arabs hid near Ambar for fourteen days until he was picked up by the advancing 8th Army. TNA, WO/201/811, ff. 53-54.

43   David Lloyd Owen, *The Desert: My Dwelling Place* (London: Cassell, 1957), p. 122.

44   Lloyd Owen, *The Desert*, p. 129.

could reach an enemy post. In the late afternoon, the prisoners were taken into the desert and set free.[45]

After destroying the captured 15 cwt Fort truck Y2 Patrol moved north to a point eight miles south of the airfield at Timimi. The next morning it was discovered that the patrol was too close to the enemy, and they moved northwest and hid in a wadi. That day Y2 Patrol saw some two hundred enemy aircraft. At 1800 Lloyd Owen and twelve men in two trucks went to the Derna-Tobruk road. The two trucks were left with their drivers about three miles from the road, and Lloyd Owen and ten of his men went to the road on foot and set up an ambush. The road was banked and Lloyd Owen and his men lay on the road's banked edge. If Lloyd Owen saw a target he wanted to shoot, he would blow his whistle and his troopers would open fire. At 2115 six empty troop trucks passed going east, but Lloyd Owen did not think this target worth shooting up. Next, at 2200, a large truck and a car went by; and again Lloyd Owen held his fire. But at 2400 a large fuel truck came down the road. When it was alongside of Lloyd Owen, he blew his whistle and his men fired at the fuel truck at point blank range, but the vehicle kept going as if nothing had happened. Lloyd Owen later wrote, "We all assumed that the driver must have been deaf and the tanker armour-plated."[46] At 0045 a ten-ton truck came down the road and Lloyd Owen decided to attack because time was running out. The word was passed to attack the vehicle. When it was about fifteen yards away from Lloyd Owen's position, Trooper Titch Cave rolled a grenade out in front of the truck which exploded under it. Cave then ran up the embankment and threw two more grenades into the back of the vehicle. When two men jumped out of the rear of the truck, they were killed by gunfire. A third man got out of the vehicle and was also shot dead. When Lloyd Owen stopped his men firing, the truck was destroyed and two Italian officers and seven soldiers were dead. The next day was spent in hiding, and the patrol returned to Siwa on 3 December.[47]

In mid-November R2 Patrol had departed from Siwa to set up a road watch at Vadi el Mra near Meduar Hsan, but when Y1 Patrol lost its radio R2 was assigned the task of filling in the gap in the network of observation posts. This assignment resulted in R2 Patrol moving around the desert without seeing any enemy movement other than aircraft. On 25 November S2 Patrol joined R2 Patrol with the order that both patrols operate as a single unit under the command of Olivey of S2 Patrol. Olivey was ordered to attack traffic on the Barce-Maraua Road.

---

45   TNA, WO/201/811, f. 42; Lloyd Owen, *The Desert*, pp. 120-130.

46   Lloyd Owen, *The Desert*, p. 134.

47   TNA, WO/201/811, f. 43; Lloyd Owen, *The Desert*, pp. 132-135

At 1900 on 29 November the two patrols arrived at the Barce-Maraua Road. The overhead phone and telegraph wires were cut; then the two patrols moved eastward for several miles and an ambush was set. The six trucks were parked alongside the road with their tailgates facing the road and their machine-guns trained on it. At 2030 a truck heading west was ambushed. When the enemy vehicle was level with the rear of the first British truck, it was engaged with machine-gun fire and appeared to be put out of action; but when the vehicle stopped, enemy troops jumped out of the back firing rifles and submachine guns. Within seconds, however, those enemy troops who were not killed or wounded by the massed fire of R2 and S2 Patrols' automatic weapons fled into the desert in disorder. Another enemy vehicle was then seen coming down the road from the west. The British trucks pulled onto the road and proceeded east towards the enemy vehicle, which was shot up along with four more enemy vehicles that were encountered on the road; however, an enemy motorcyclist somehow managed to escape being shot and it was feared that he would reach Maraua within an hour and sound the alarm. Nevertheless, the British trucks pulled off the road where it cut through a small rise in the ground, machine-guns were taken off the trucks and mounted near the edge of the road, and from this position the British further attacked and destroyed two large trucks with trailers and one large fuel truck. At 2145, after again cutting the telephone and telegraph wires, the British moved off into open country and hid in a wadi. After the attacks on enemy transport on the Barce-Maraua Road, S2 Patrol was ordered to Jalo and R2 Patrol to Siwa.[48]

On 9 December orders were issued for four patrols to leave Siwa and renew the attack on enemy transportation in Cyrenaica.[49] Y2 Patrol was ordered to attack the Tobruk-Derna Road; but on 13 December, after leaving Siwa, Lloyd Owen was ordered to join G1 Patrol in an attack on the coast road between Benghazi and Agedabia because the 8th Army was overrunning northeast Cyrenaica. On 14 December G1 and Y2 Patrols met and their commanders, Hay and Lloyd Owen, decided that the two patrols should attack transport on the coast road at two different points that night. The two patrols then separated. Y2 Patrol reached the coast road at dusk and found that there was a considerable amount of traffic moving south. Lloyd Owen saw that most of the vehicles were formed into convoys which were armed with 20mm Breda guns and escorted by armored cars. Nevertheless, at 1920 Y2 Patrol attacked a ten-ton truck towing a trailer carrying one thousand gallons of fuel. The driver and his passenger were killed by gunfire, and the truck and trailer set on fire. Y2 Patrol then went north up the coast road attacking other

---

48   TNA, WO/201/811, f. 58-61.
49   TNA, WO/201/811, f. 73.

vehicles with gunfire. Before leaving the coast road, Y2 Patrol cut the telephone and telegraph lines. On 21 December Y2 Patrol returned to Siwa.[50]

After carrying out a number of attacks on the coast road south of the point where Y2 Patrol had attacked, G1 Patrol had the bad luck to run into a large group of enemy troops just after daylight on 16 December. Hay and ten guardsmen were captured, but two trucks and six guardsmen under the command of Sergeant H. Roebuck escaped.[51] G2 and Y1 Patrols' operations were called off because the 8th Army had overrun their objectives.[52] *Crusader* came to an end on 1 January 1942 when Rommel decided to withdraw from Cyrenaica to El Agheila.[53]

What effect did the operations of the Long Range Desert Group have on the outcome of the *Crusader* offensive? Before *Crusader* began the Long Range Desert Group provided the British with a great deal of intelligence from its reconnaissance operations in Libya. It also proved to be an effective organization for moving agents into and out of enemy-held regions. Once *Crusader* began the situation changed. The patrols of the Long Range Desert Group were used mainly to observe and to report the movement of enemy traffic along the road net of northern Cyrenaica. This mission was carried out under extremely difficult conditions, owing to the great numbers of enemy aircraft operating over northern Cyrenaica. In the face of these difficulties the results were negligible at best, for once in position there was almost no movement of enemy vehicles for the patrols to observe and report. Then on 24 November the passive observation of traffic ceased and the mission of the Long Range Desert Group changed to one of carrying out attacks on enemy transport throughout Cyrenaica.

At the time it was believed that the Long Range Desert Group's

"unexpected raids far behind the enemy's line, when reported to the enemy commanders with the inevitably gross exaggeration of the victims, caused them to be most anxious about the safety of their communications and to divert aircraft and vehicles which they could have employed much more usefully on the main front in order to counter the L.R.D.G.'s activities."[54]

However, the truth of this statement is questionable, for it was not until 14 December that the reports of the Long Range Desert Group mention that the

50   TNA, WO/201/811, ff. 85-87.
51   TNA, WO/201/811, ff. 77-78.
52   TNA, WO/201/811, ff. 71-72.
53   Playfair, *Mediterranean*, vol. III, p. 92.
54   TNA, WO/201/811, f. 72.

enemy used measures such as convoys and armored cars to protect vehicles on the coast road from attack by the patrols of the Long Range Desert Group. Moreover, in the period of the attacks on enemy transport in Cyrenaica, during *Crusader*, the enemy made no serious attempt to hunt down the patrols of the Long Range Desert Group. It is true that during *Crusader* the Long Range Desert Group's patrols did mount a number of very effective and spectacular attacks on enemy vehicles in Cyrenaica. These attacks were an attempt to force enemy commanders to divert resources from the main battle along the Egyptian-Libyan border to protect their supply lines in Cyrenaica. But a few score of enemy trucks destroyed or damaged by the attacks of the Long Range Desert Group simply passed over the head of a commander such as Rommel, who was engaged in fighting one of the biggest and most violent battles of the entire North African campaign. What did a few trucks matter when compared to the crucible which *Crusader* had become with masses of infantry, artillery, and tanks being destroyed each day? Maybe the full force of the Long Range Desert Group should have been used against the coast road west of Agheila and very deep in the enemy's rear. These attacks of the Long Range Desert Group would have been so far removed from *Crusader* that they might have goaded the Axis military authorities in Tripolitania to divert resources needed elsewhere into countering the Long Range Desert Group.

6

Who Dares Wins: The Special Air Service

"When you burst into a hut full of enemy soldiers you must remember the drill evolved for such occasions. Shoot the first person who makes a move, hostile or otherwise. His brain has recovered from the shock of seeing you there with a gun. He has started to think and is therefore dangerous. You must then shoot the person nearest to you, because he is in the best position to cause you embarrassment. Then deal with the rest as you think fit."
—*Lieutenant Colonel Robert Blair Mayne, D.S.O. (3 Bars)*, Légion d'honneur

The Special Air Service was conceived and organized by Lieutenant David Stirling of the Scots Guards. Stirling arrived in the Middle East in March of 1941 as a member of No. 8 Commando, which was made a part of a unit known as Layforce.[1] Layforce was originally organized to capture the Island of Rhodes, but when this operation was overtaken by events, part of Layforce was used to cover the evacuation of Crete and the conquest of Syria, while other units carried out seaborne raids, without much success, behind enemy lines in the Western Desert.

Just before Layforce was broken up in the late summer of 1941,[2] its commander gave permission for Stirling and seven other men to "experiment" with some parachutes that they had got their hands on. Stirling and the others then talked the pilot of an R.A.F. Valentia aircraft into helping them with their experiment. All eight men made a jump with the static lines of the parachutes secured to the legs or seats in the aircraft. Stirling came to earth on rocky ground, badly injuring his back, and ended up in the hospital for two months, during which time he rethought the whole concept of commando operations in the Middle East.

---

1   I.S.O. Playfair, *The Mediterranean and Middle East* (London: HMSO, 1956), vol. II, p. 40n.

2   James Ladd, *Commandos and Rangers of World War II* (New York: St. Martins, 1978), p. 120.

While in the hospital, Stirling came to the conclusion that commando operations in the Middle East were not being conducted correctly. Stirling himself had taken part in three unsuccessful raids on the North African coast. Each one of these operations had been carried out in the same way. A party of some two hundred officers and men were landed from either a destroyer or gunboats just after dark. In one case the operation could not be carried out because of bad weather, and in two other operations the element of surprise was lost and the naval vessels carrying the commandos were subjected to attack by enemy aircraft. Stirling thought that strategically the objective of these raids was sound, for

> the Enemy was exceedingly vulnerable to attack along the line of his coastal communications and on his various transport parks, aerodromes and other targets strung out along the coast, and the role of No. 8 Commando, which had attempted raids on these targets, was a most valuable one.[3]

The failure of No. 8 Commando's operations, according to Stirling was that they were planned on too large a scale, which "prejudiced surprise beyond all possible compensating advantage in respect of the defensive and aggressive striking power afforded." In addition, these raids required the use of naval forces "valuable out of all proportion to the maximum possible success of the raid."[4]

After the war Stirling wrote about the strategic and tactical assumptions upon which the operations of the Special Air Service were based. According to Stirling raiding operations against the enemy lines of communication in North Africa should be conducted by, in his words:

> a Unit based on the principle of the fullest exploitation of surprise and of making the minimum demands on man-power and equipment. I argued that the application of this principle would mean in effect the employment of a sub-unit of five men to cover a target previously requiring four troops of a Commando, i.e., about 200 men. I sought to prove that, if an aerodrome or transport park was the objective of an operation, then the destruction of 50 aircraft or units of transport was more easily accomplished by a sub-unit of five men than by a force of 200 men. I further concluded that 200 properly selected, trained and equipped men, organized into sub-units of five should

---

3   University of London, King's College Centre for Military Archives, McLeod Papers, Memorandum by Col. David Stirling, DSO, OBE, on the origins of the Special Air Service Regt., p. 2.

4   *Ibid*, p. 2.

be able to attack at least thirty different objectives at the same time on the same night as compared to only one objective using the Commando technique; and the only 25% success in the former was the equivalent to many times the maximum possible result in the latter.

The corollary of this was that a Unit operating on these principles would have to be so trained as to be capable of arriving on the scene of the operation by every practical method by land, sea or air; and that, furthermore, the facilities required for the lift must not be of a type valuable in tactical scale operation. If in any particular operation, a sub-unit was to be dropped by parachute, training must be such as to enable it to be dropped from any type of aircraft conveniently available without any modifications; if by sea, then the sub-unit must be transported either by Submarine or Caiques and trained in the use of folboats [British commercial name for a type of kayak]; if by land, the unit must be trained either to infiltrate on foot or be carried by the Long Range Desert Group.[5]

While Stirling was in the hospital he wrote a memorandum on his ideas of unconventional warfare with the objective of gaining permission to set up a unit to conduct raids against enemy lines of communication in North Africa. Stirling knew that memorandums written by lieutenants, if sent up the chain of command in the authorized manner, always got nowhere. But Stirling had the rare ability of being able to talk almost anybody into anything. In 1945, for example, he got David Lloyd Owen, against his better judgment, to agree to a bizarre and extremely risky parachute jump into Japan before the war in the Far East had ended.[6] Further, Stirling looked upon the chain of command of the British army as something to be dealt with in much the same way as the enemy—to be assaulted with the utmost boldness.

One morning in July 1941, after Stirling had been released from the hospital and while still on crutches, he set out to see the commanding general of all British land forces in the Middle East. When he arrived at the British army's Middle East Headquarters, Stirling found that the sentries at the door of the building would not let him in because he had neither a pass nor an appointment. Abandoning his crutches, Stirling pushed by the sentries when they were occupied checking passes; however, one of the sentries spotted Stirling just as he was entering the

---

5   *Ibid*, p. 2.
6   David Lloyd Owen Interview.

building and sounded the alarm. Stirling wanted to see the commander-in-chief, but he had to hide somewhere quickly because his unauthorized entry had already caused a huge commotion at the main door and military police surely would be sent to find him. Seeing a door with the sign "Adjutant-General" nearby, Stirling opened it and walked in. When Stirling entered the room he was confronted by a major sitting at a desk, and as Stirling attempted to explain what he wanted the expression of indignation on the major's face turned to one of absolute rage. The major remembered Stirling as having fallen asleep during a series of lectures he had given on tactics to the Scots Guards in 1939. Stirling quickly withdrew just as the major received a phone call informing him that a man wearing the uniform of a lieutenant in No. 8 Commando had entered the building without authorization.

Back out in the corridor, Stirling saw one of the sentries from the main door walking towards the office he had just left. Clearly he had to do something quickly, and he opened the first door he could find and walked in. This door was marked "D.C.G.S." and Stirling had no idea what the letters stood for, but upon entering the office he saw an officer he knew from photographs—Lieutenant General N.M. Ritchie, Deputy Chief General Staff, Middle East Forces. Stirling apologized for arriving in the general's office in such an unconventional manner and said that he had "vital business" to bring to the general's attention. Stirling then gave Ritchie a penciled memorandum on raiding.[7] The handwriting was poor and difficult to read, and it took Ritchie ten minutes to figure out what it meant. When Ritchie finished with the memorandum, he said, "I think this may be the sort of plan we are looking for. I will discuss it with the commander-in-chief and let you know our decision in the next day or so."[8]

Three days later Stirling was called to British Army Middle East Headquarters and informed by General Sir Claude Auchinleck, the Commander-in-chief, that he was now a captain and that all his requests were granted. Under the direct authority of the commander-in-chief, Stirling could recruit six officers and sixty non-commissioners and other ranks from what was left of Layforce and set up a training camp in the Suez Canal Zone to prepare for raids on major German airfields in North Africa on the eve of the *Crusader* offensive.[9]

It is easy to see why Stirling's scheme was accepted by Auchinleck and Ritchie. His plan was economical to an extreme. It called for using sixty-six men from

---

7   Virginia Cowles, *The Phantom Major; The Story of David Stirling and the S.A.S. Regiment* (London: Collins, 1958), p. 15.

8   *Ibid*, p. 15.

9   *Ibid*, pp. 13-15, 22-25.

Layforce, which was being disbanded and had not done much since the conquest of Syria, to attack five enemy airfields in the Ain el Gazala and Timimi region. Two days before the beginning of *Crusader* the R.A.F. would bomb Ain el Gazala and Timimi, and at the same time Stirling's force would parachute into the desert about twelve miles from their targets. The next day would be spent getting into position and observing the targets. On the following night five airfields would be attacked simultaneously.

> Each party was to carry a total of about 60 incendiary cum explosive bombs equipped with two hour, half hour, ten minute time pencils and also a twelve second time fuse. (Thus in the early stages of the raid a two hour time pencil was used, followed later on by the one hour and the half hour, thereby reducing the risk of the enemy removing the bombs after the warning given by the first explosion.)[10]

After the attacks on the airfields, the raiders would be picked up by the Long Range Desert Group at a prearranged point south of the Trigh el Abd.[11] This was the principle of economy of force carried out to the extreme; for even if only one airfield was wrecked on the eve of *Crusader*, it would be—in cold military calculation—worth the loss of Stirling's entire force.

Stirling's new unit was named L Detachment, Special Air Service Brigade. This name was chosen to assist Brigadier Dudley Clarke, who was in charge of deception operations, and wanted the enemy to think that there was a British airborne brigade in Egypt. Stirling encountered great difficulty in recruiting the men for his unit and in obtaining equipment, such as tents. The root cause of these difficulties was most likely the major in the Adjutant General's department who hated Stirling and whose office Stirling had entered when he was roaming around Middle East Headquarters obtaining permission to form the Special Air Service. Ritchie, not knowing the circumstances, he had actually assigned this major to assist Stirling in establishing the Special Air Service. In the end, in order to get the type of officers and men he wanted, Stirling had to go over the head of the Adjutant General's office and seek the aid of Ritchie. Stirling recruited the vast majority of the sixty-six officers and men that formed L Detachment, Special Air Service Brigade from what was left of Layforce and the remainder from the Scots Guards. All of these troops had been in combat, and the men from Layforce had

---

10   Stirling Memorandum, p. 3.
11   *Ibid*, p. 3.

also been extensively trained as commandos and had a lot of experience in night operations. According to Stirling, the men that he recruited into the Special Air Service from Layforce and the Scots Guards "were first class material."[12]

Two officers whom Stirling recruited at this time were to have a profound effect, second only to Stirling's, on Special Air Service operations. One of these officers was Lieutenant Jock Lewis, who was needed to think out all the problems that would be encountered when training the unit. Stirling said of Lewis that he "was the best training officer I have ever associated with or heard of in the War."[13] The other officer was Lieutenant Robert Blair Mayne, an Ulsterman known to most as Paddy, who would take command of the Special Air Service when Stirling was captured in 1943. Mayne was a large man of great strength who could move like a cat. Trained as a barrister at the Queens University in Belfast, while a student Mayne had won the Irish Universities' heavyweight boxing championship and then went on to play international rugby for Ireland and was considered one of the best forwards in the world. Mayne was usually very shy and gentle, except when confronting the enemy or when enraged or drunk. Mayne had already gained a measure of fame among the British army in the Middle East for knocking out, with one blow, his commanding officer, Lieutenant Colonel Geoffrey Keyes, in the course of a very heated argument over matters of military discipline. When Stirling recruited Mayne for the Special Air Service, the Ulsterman was under close arrest for assaulting his commanding officer. By the end of the war in Europe Mayne, who did not know what fear was, had with his own hands, caused more damage to the enemy than any other single individual on the Allied side.[14] When he joined the Special Air Service, Mayne found his true vocation—irregular operations behind enemy lines.[15]

For training, the Special Air Service was assigned to a camp near Kabrit on the shore of Great Bitter Lake in the Suez Canal Zone about a hundred miles from Cairo. When the Special Air Service troops arrived at their training camp in August, they found it consisted of only two little tents, one big tent, a few broken chairs, and one table. The major in the Adjutant General's office in Cairo most likely had a few friends in the Quartermaster's office. The Special Air Service solved their supply problems by sending a "raiding" party into the camp of the

---

12   *Ibid*, p. 4.

13   *Ibid*, p. 4.

14   David Lloyd Owen Interview.

15   Patrick Marrinan, *Colonel Paddy* (Dungannon, Ireland: The Ulster Press, 1968), pp. 7-23.

2nd New Zealand Division, which was away on maneuvers, and taking what was required to set up a proper training camp.[16]

The training at Kabrit of L Detachment, Special Air Service Brigade began early in August 1941. This allowed for about three months before the planned attacks, in support of the *Crusader* on the airfields near Ain el Gazala and Timimi, were to take place. Most of the men in the Special Air Service had seen combat and had been through the Commando School at Achnacarry in Scotland besides a number of similar type courses elsewhere in Britain and the Middle East. But the training under the direction of Lewis that the Special Air Service troops would be subjected to, at Kabrit, made commando training appear to be mere child's play. According to Stirling, Special Air Service training worked on the opposite set of principles from those employed by the commandos:

> A Commando unit, having been once selected from a batch of volunteers, were committed to those men and had to nurse them up to the required standard. "L" Detachment, on the other hand, had set a minimum standard to which all ranks had to attain and we had to be most firm in returning to their units those who were unable to reach that standard.[17]

From the beginning, the Special Air Service dispensed with certain commando traits, such as the idea that being in a tough unit meant that one always had to act tough, be more or less out of uniform, be noisy, and without standard military discipline whether it be in the barracks or on the streets of Cairo. When the unit was not in the field, Stirling "insisted on the Brigade of Guards standard of discipline and smartness of turnout."[18] Toughness was not to be used on the military police but to be saved for the enemy.

Every member of the Special Air Service had to be qualified to parachute out of an aircraft. There was no parachute training school in the Middle East, so Stirling and Lewis had to devise a parachute training course from nothing. The only two fatal training accidents in the Special Air Service occurred during parachute training. The ground part of the Special Air Service course consisted of such things as jumping off the back of a truck going thirty miles per hour, landing on one's feet, and then doing a forward roll. Next, movable platforms were built,

---

16   Marrinan, *Colonel*, p. 23.
17   Stirling Memorandum, p. 5.
18   *Ibid*, p. 5.

which the men had to jump off.[19] This type of training, which produced many wrenched backs and bruised knees, was just the preliminary ground practice before jumping out of an R.A.F. Bombay transport aircraft. Along with the parachute training, there was the usual training in weapons, map reading, and in demolitions, courses on handling small boats, as well as night raiding exercises in which troops were required to identify objects and fire weapons in the direction of a sound. And, as if these were not enough, there were endless hours of P.T. conducted under the direction of a sergeant major. Another aspect of Special Air Service training was forced marches of one hundred miles in the desert carrying full equipment. Stirling and Lewis both believed that if the Special Air Service was going to be effective, physical endurance and quick reflexes were much more important than the massed attacks the standard commando training was designed to teach.

The high point in the Special Air Service's infiltration training occurred as a result of an argument between Stirling and an R.A.F. group captain who maintained that Special Air Service troops could not get onto a well-guarded airfield without being detected. Stirling bet the group captain ten pounds that his men could get on and off the airfield at Heliopolis, which was the main military airfield at Cairo, without being seen. Stirling also told the R.A.F. officer that the raid would take place at the end of October. The plan for the "practice" raid on Heliopolis was simple. Four groups of ten men each would march across the ninety miles of desert between Kabrit and the airfield at night and hide during the day. When Heliopolis was reached, the four groups—independently of each other—would cut their way through the wire, place labels on aircraft then leave the airfield, go on foot to the army barracks at Abbassia, and be returned by motor transport to Kabrit.

At the end of October four parties of ten men each marched across the ninety miles of desert from Kabrit to Heliopolis during the night, and hid under camouflage cloth sacks during the day. Each man was issued with the usual army ration of bully beef and biscuits plus four canteens containing one pint of water each. The desert across which the march was made was totally flat and very hot during the day, and while crossing it nobody was seen. The hardest part of the whole operation was crossing the ninety miles of desert with only four pints of water. All four parties easily got onto the airfield. Mayne's group alone left forty-five labels on aircraft and then made their way, without being seen, to the barracks at Abbassia. The next morning the R.A.F. discovered labels on many aircraft, in some cases as many as four labels on one aircraft, plus a number of cuts in the fence surrounding the airfield. Apparently the R.A.F. had flown reconnaissance missions

---

19   *Ibid*, p. 4.

each day over the desert between Heliopolis and Kabrit but had seen nothing. Also, security had been increased at the gates to the airfield because it was thought that the Special Air Service might attempt to enter the airfield from the main road hidden in vehicles. Stirling got a ten pound cheque from the group captain, and the security forces at Heliopolis were bombarded with reprimands.[20]

If five airfields were going to be attacked and thirty or forty aircraft were to be destroyed on each airfield, the problem was that five to ten men could not carry enough explosives to do the job. If explosives alone were used, then only the airframes of the aircraft would be damaged, when the objective was to destroy the whole machine. If, however, the Special Air Service took both explosives and incendiaries, then the required number of bombs would be too heavy to carry. What Stirling and Lewis wanted was a bomb that would both explode and burn. The bomb experts were consulted, but to a man they said that the Special Air Service could have a bomb that would either explode or burn, but not one that could do both. Lewis decided that he would make a bomb that would both explode and burn. He set up a line of four-gallon oil drums with a pint of gasoline in each one. Each drum had a reinforced lid, and Lewis carried out his experiments by placing explosives on top of the oil drum. The objective was to find an explosive that would blow a hole through the reinforced lid and set the gasoline on fire. For several weeks the camp at Kabrit was subjected to endless explosions as Lewis tested various combinations of plastic, thermite, and gelignite. Finally, Lewis discovered a bomb that would explode and burn at the same time. He created his bomb by mixing rifle clearing oil with plastic and thermite until he got a sticky lump about the size of a baseball and weighing a little under a pound. This bomb was named the Lewis bomb and was used throughout the war by the Special Air Service for destroying aircraft on the ground.[21]

The Special Air Service's first operation was a total failure. The orders for the operations were issued on 10 November and called for the dropping by parachute of five parties of Special Air Service troops near Ain el Gazala and Timimi on the night of 16 November, two days before the beginning of *Crusader*. The objective was to destroy as many enemy aircraft as possible on the airfields near Ain el Gazala and Timimi. After the attacks on the airfields, the Special Air Service troops would then be met by R1 Patrol of the Long Range Desert Group.[22] Five R.A.F. Bombay transport aircraft of 216 Squadron were assigned to carry the Special Air Service

---

20   Cowles, *The Phantom Major*, pp. 29-31, 35-38; see also, Marrinan, *Colonel*, pp. 24-25.
21   *Ibid*, pp. 32-35.
22   TNA, WO/201/811, ff. 64-66.

troops from an airfield at Bagush to their drop zones near Ain el Gazala and Timimi.

On the night of 16 November, as the troops were eating a meal and preparing to embark on the aircraft, the weather forecast was not very favorable for parachute operations, and there was some talk of putting off the operation until the next night. But after consulting his officers, Stirling decided that the operation would take place. When the Bombays reached the area around Ain el Gazala and Timimi, the wind was blowing so strongly that the aircraft navigators could not even see the coast line because of the wind-borne dust. In Stirling's words, the navigators "had to take pot luck in their dead reckoning and as far as I know, no party was dropped within 10 miles of the selected DZs."[23] The troops in four aircraft jumped, and because of the high winds they were scattered all over the desert. Two men were known to have been killed on landing owing to the high winds, and only twenty-two officers and men, including Stirling, Lewis, and Mayne, made it to the rendezvous with R1 Patrol. The remaining forty Special Air Service troops just disappeared in the desert,[24] and one Bombay aircraft was shot down.[25]

---

23   Stirling Memorandum, p. 5.

24   *Ibid*, p. 5.

25   TNA, Air/27/1334, 16 Nov. 1941. The missing Bombay transport was piloted by Flying Officer Charles West. West, in an attempt to locate the drop zone, flew down through the clouds to a height of two hundred feet at which point the aircraft was hit by anti-aircraft fire. The instrument panel was mostly destroyed, the port engine was hit, and gasoline was leaking out of the wing tanks. The only undamaged instrument appeared to be the magnetic compass, and West used it to fly on what he thought was a due east course. But the aircraft was losing fuel and West was forced to land it in the desert, which he successfully did. When daylight came the next morning, the British airmen and troops in Bombay discovered that they had landed near the coast road which was full of enemy troops. It was discovered that the magnetic compass had a piece of shrapnel lodged near it and the aircraft, while appearing to be going east, had in fact been going in circles. West, with the Special Air Service troops still on board, took off in an attempt to reach the British stronghold at Tobruk. Flying low over the desert, with the enemy taking pot shots at the aircraft with anti-aircraft guns, machine guns, and rifles, West attempted to reach Tobruk but the aircraft was shot down by a German Me 109E fighter. Two members of the air crew were killed as was one member of the Special Air Service, and every other Briton on the aircraft was injured. West had a broken shoulder, broken ribs, a ruptured diaphragm, and a fractured skull. Nonetheless, he recovered from his injuries, escaped from a prison camp in Italy, and continued to fight the Germans with partisans in northern Italy. After the Bombay had been shot down, the Germans put out a propaganda story that it had been tricked into landing by an English-speaking German acting as a British air controller. Philip Warner, *The Special Air Service* (London: William Kimber, 1980), pp. 37-40. Even after the war was over, Stirling thought that the aircraft had been tricked by the Germans into thinking it was over British-held territory. Stirling Memorandum, p. 5.

The Special Air Service troops were ordered to meet R1 Patrol at the northern end of Uadi el Mra or at Garet Meriem after completing their mission.[26] R1 Patrol, under the command of Easonsmith, consisted of six Long Range Desert Group trucks, a Bedford truck belonging to another unit, and two other Bedfords manned by five members of the Special Air Service. It left Siwa on the morning of 17 November to meet the men of the Special Air Service who had parachuted into the desert the night before. On 19 November the trucks manned by the Special Air Service were hidden along with their crews at Uadi el Mra, and the R1 Patrol then went to Garet Meriem and hid to await the arrival of the Special Air Service troops. As R1 Patrol was proceeding to Garet Meriem it met Y2 Patrol, commanded by Lloyd Owen, which was on a different mission but also hiding in the same general area. During the next few days the twenty-two members of the Special Air Service who had not been killed or captured made contact with R1 and Y2 Patrols.[27] Stirling had lost forty soldiers out of a force of fifty-five men, six officers and the six man crew of the Bombay transport that had been shot down. Even if the remaining twenty-seven Special Air Service troops wanted to attack an enemy airfield they could not do it because they had lost all the fuses for setting off their bombs. After such a setback, a lesser man than Stirling would have given up. But Stirling, as soon as he realized the magnitude of the failure, set about figuring out where he had gone wrong and what lessons there were to be learned.

Just after the raid, Stirling and Lloyd Owen met for the first time and while still in the desert discussed all the events of the past few days. According to Lloyd Owen, Stirling was beginning to see that parachuting out of an aircraft was not necessarily the best way to get to a target. Stirling told Lloyd Owen that there were limitations imposed by the weather as well as the availability of aircraft. And in 1941 the techniques of jumping out of aircraft had not been developed to a stage where one could always land where one wanted. Lloyd Owen suggested to Stirling that the answer to his problem might be for the Long Range Desert Group to transport his men by vehicle to their targets and to pick them up after a raid and return them to base.[28] Many years later, David Lloyd Owen told the author:

I can remember very well talking to him and saying, look here, this business of parachuting, which I thought was crazy anyhow, is absolutely the wrong

---

26   TNA, WO/201/811, f. 22.

27   TNA, WO/201/811, ff. 28-29.

28   Cowles, *Phantom Major*, pp. 56-67; David Lloyd Owen, *Providence Their Guide* (London: Harrap, 1980), pp. 60-61.

way to go and do these operations. We can take you there. We can take you anywhere you like; just like a taxi. If you want to be set down outside of the Ritz Hotel, we will take you there, take you anywhere you like. And he didn't believe it, you see, because he had never worked with us. He didn't know. But the fact was that he accepted this. We drove him back after this operation and I suppose he was impressed.[29]

At midday on 22 November, R1 Patrol, which still had twenty-two Special Air Service troops with them, was ordered to return to base. That afternoon the patrol was attacked, first by an Italian Savoia 79 aircraft and then by a German Heinkel III, but suffered no casualties from either attack and dropped off Stirling and his men at Jarabub before returning to Siwa.[30]

Stirling knew that if the Special Air Service was to remain in being he had to mount some successful raids with the remaining twenty-seven men and four officers of his command. He also had to get the Special Air Service attached, for logistical purposes, to some unit, preferably one distant from any major headquarters.[31] Jalo was a perfect place for Stirling to use as a base. It was remote, being about one hundred and sixty miles SSE from Agedabia on the edge of the Great Sand Sea. In the meantime, a Squadron, consisting of S1, S2, T1, and T2 Patrols, of the Long Range Desert Group was ordered to make Jalo its base.[32] Moreover, Stirling had come to the conclusion that the best, and perhaps only, way to get to his targets was to make use of the Long Range Desert Group as a means of transport. Indeed, cooperation between SAS and LRDG would have spectacular results. For the combination of the ability of the Long Range Desert Group to cross the Libyan Desert at almost any point and the skill of the Special Air Service at raiding would produce an almost endless series of attacks on enemy airfields, transport, and supply dumps.

Stirling and Steele, the commander of A Squadron, quickly reached an agreement on how their respective forces should be deployed. Brigadier Reid, the commander of Jalo, had orders to attack northward from Jalo towards the Antelat-Agedabia region but was held up owing to a shortage of fuel. It was unlikely that he would be able to move until 22 December. Reid wanted Steele to take Stirling's men to the edge of the airfield at Agedabia in order that it could be attacked on the

29   David Lloyd Owen, Interview.
30   TNA, WO/201/811, f. 29.
31   Cowles, *Phantom Major*, pp. 48-51.*Ibid*, pp. 52-53.
32   *Ibid*, pp. 52-53; TNA, WO/201/811, ff. 35-36.

night of 21 December. Stirling put forth a much more far reaching plan which was agreed upon by both Reid and Steele. Stirling and Mayne would attack the airfields at Sirte and Tamet on the night of 14 December; Lewis would attack the airfield at El Agheila on the same night, and Lieutenant William Fraser would attack the airfield at Agedabia on the night of 21 December. Reid and Steele agreed not to mention the existence of the Special Air Service in their dispatches and to tell no one of the planned operations. It was Stirling's great fear that someone at 8th Army headquarters might figure out where the Special Air Service was and order the unit back to Kabrit for disbanding before it could mount some successful raids.[33]

On 8 December S1 left Jalo to attack the airfields at Sirte and Tamet. S1 Patrol had five trucks manned by ten men of the Long Range Desert Group under the command of Holliman and carried Stirling, Mayne, and eleven Special Air Service troops. The trip to the airfields was uneventful, although Holliman suspected that S1 Patrol had been located by an enemy radio direction finder because a number of enemy aircraft appeared to be hunting for the patrol. Late at night on 11 December Stirling and Sergeant Brough were dropped off near the airfield at Sirte. It was too late in the night to attack the airfield and Stirling decided to hide for two days and conduct his attack at the same time as Mayne attacked the airfield at Tamet. While making their way along the edge of the airfield at Sirte, which had a large number of aircraft on it, Stirling stepped on two Italian soldiers who were sleeping in a small hollow. One of the Italians let out a wild yell, and as Stirling and Brough made off into the desert, there was more yelling followed by gunfire. The next day the two Britons hid in the desert near the airfield and watched aircraft land and take off. But just before dark on 13 December, all the aircraft took off from the airfield and none returned. The only thing that Brough and Stirling could do was wait until 0045 in the morning of 15 December to be picked up as prearranged by Holliman on the coast road at a point west of Sirte.

After leaving Stirling and Brough near Sirte, S1 Patrol went to Wadi Tamet and hid during the daylight hours of 12 December. During 13 December the patrol moved closer to the airfield and the coast road. In the early evening of 14 December the patrol was divided. Mayne, with two trucks, was to attack the airfield at Tamet; and Holliman and the other three vehicles were to drive down the coast road towards Sirte and pick up Stirling and Brough. As Holliman drove east along the coast road, the steering gear on one of S1 Patrol's trucks broke and the vehicle veered off the road, crashed, and could not be repaired and so was destroyed. At 0045 on 15 December, just as Holliman met Stirling and Brough on the coast road,

---

33   Cowles, *Phantom Major*, pp. 55-57.

the night sky over Tamet was lit up by a series of explosions at the airfield. Before leaving the coast road and heading for the meeting point with Mayne's group, Stirling insisted that a number of mines be buried in potholes in the coast road. After waiting just off the coast road for about ten minutes, the British saw a large Italian truck hit one of the mines and explode in a sheet of flames. After driving the rest of the night, Holliman and Stirling arrived at the place where they were to meet Mayne's party.

Mayne and ten Special Air Service troops left the two Long Range Desert Group trucks with their crews a mile or so from the airfield outside of Tamet, and walking single file the eleven British raiders made their way unseen onto the airfield. The British could hear the sounds of a party coming from one building as they approached it. Then, as Mayne described it,

> I kicked open the door and stood there with my Colt 45, the others at my side with a tommy gun and another automatic. The Germans stared at us. We were a peculiar and frightening sight, bearded with long, unkempt hair. For what seemed an age we just stood there looking at each other in complete silence. I said: 'Good evening'. At that a young German arose and moved slowly backwards. I shot him, and as he fell, he knocked glasses to the ground from his table. I turned and fired at another six feet away. He was standing beside the wall as he sagged.
>
> Hawkins, a Londoner, opened up with his tommy gun…. The room was by now in pandemonium. So we left, throwing hand grenades to add to the confusion.[34]

Mayne left four men to continue battling the Germans, who were attempting to escape from the building and to fire small arms out of windows. The other seven Special Air Service troops planted bombs in two fuel dumps and then on the wings of parked German aircraft. The bombs were of the type invented by Lewis and were set off by thirty-minute time pencils. These time pencils had a spring with a striker held in place by a copper wire, a capsule of acid, and a detonator. When the capsule was broken, the acid would start burning through the copper wire, which took about thirty minutes. When the wire broke, the spring would force the striker to hit the detonator and the bomb would explode. The time between breaking the capsule filled with acid and the explosion depended upon the thickness of the wire.

---

34   Marrinan, *Colonel*, pp. 34-35.

Mayne's men quickly placed all their bombs on aircraft. As Mayne himself approached one aircraft, he saw that there was a light in the cockpit.

I thought someone was sitting there smoking. So I quietly moved round the rear of the plane and up to the cockpit. I clambered on to the wing and peered inside. Someone had neglected to switch off the panel lights, and the dashboard was softly illuminated. A sharp tug, then a heave, and I had ripped out the dashboard for a souvenir....[35]

There were two aircraft left untouched when Mayne's men ran out of bombs, so grenades were tossed into their cockpits. Mayne's force then withdrew from the airfield, picking up the four men covering the building, and headed for the Long Range Desert Group trucks out in the desert. The party had not gone more than a quarter of a mile when the explosions began at the airfield as bombs went off in dumps and on parked aircraft. Ever since the first attack on the building, there had been "spasmodic" gunfire in the airfield area, but with the beginning of the explosions, enemy guns of all types began firing into the air and out to sea. With the last of the explosions on the airfield, Mayne and his men withdrew to the Long Range Desert trucks and then the party drove for eighty miles across the desert to meet Stirling and Holliman. Finally, the unit returned to Jalo without incident.[36]

On 10 December T2 Patrol headed north from Jalo with five trucks, one Italian Lancia, fourteen men of the Long Range Desert Group commanded by 2nd Lieutenant C.S. Morris, and twelve Special Air Service troops commanded by Lewis. The group had been ordered to attack the airfield near El Agheila, the town of Marsa Brega, including traffic on the coast road, and to take a prisoner.[37] The original plan was to drop off the Special Air Service troops about twelve miles southeast of El Agheila. However, the only road through the marshes on the southwest side of El Agheila was found to have been mined by the Germans. Morris decided to double back and leave the Special Air Service group twelve miles southeast of El Agheila. This point was reached on 13 December. Here the Special Air Service troops set off on foot to attack the airfield, and Morris left two trucks and the Lancia with their crews while he and two other trucks set off north east for Marsa Brega. The next day Morris hid his two trucks about twelve miles from Marsa Brega. With each man carrying explosives and a mine, they walked

---

35   *Ibid*, p. 37.

36   *Ibid*, pp. 57-67; TNA, WO/201/811, ff. 91-91; Marrinan, *Colonel*, pp. 30-37.

37   TNA, WO/201/811, f. 93.

towards Marsa Brega. After a march of about twelve miles, however, the Long Range Desert Group troops found that they were cut off from Marsa Brega by an uncrossable marsh. Morris and his men had to turn around and walk back to their trucks, covering some twenty-four miles in all. Morris then returned with his two trucks to the place where he had hidden the other vehicles to await the return of Lewis and the Special Air Service troops from the airfield.

The Special Air Service party entered the airfield at El Agheila only to find that there were no aircraft or enemy troops there. They found and destroyed a truck loaded with munitions and blew down every other telegraph pole for a mile. Then Lewis and his men walked to the meeting place with T2 Patrol. While waiting for the return of Lewis and his men from the airfield, Morris did some scouting and came to the conclusion that because of the marshes the only way to get into Marsa Brega was to drive to it along the coast road. Morris also learned from locals that over two hundred vehicles per day passed both ways along the coast road between El Agheila and Marsa Brega.

So far neither Morris nor Lewis had achieved very much, so it was decided to attack Marsa Brega on the night of 16 December. All the British vehicles were driven that night to the coast road, where it was noted that the traffic was moving in convoys of about twelve vehicles each. Morris decided to form his own convoy. The Lancia, which did not have headlights and was manned by the Special Air Service, was the first vehicle in the British convoy. The headlight dimmers were removed from the five Long Range Desert Group trucks. Morris's truck, which had the brightest lights, was stationed just behind the Lancia "to dazzle any oncoming enemy."[38] The British convoy got on the coast road heading east towards Marsa Brega. The road was well paved but it was narrow so that oncoming traffic passed within a yard of the British vehicles. Morris counted forty-seven enemy vehicles going west. When the British column reached Marsa Brega a little after midnight, it stopped alongside a building to wait for two trucks which had fallen behind. While they waited, the British counted twenty-two enemy vehicles and about sixty troops in the place. Just as the two missing trucks arrived, the enemy discovered the British and began firing at them. The Special Air Service Troops in the Lancia jumped out, grabbed the nearest enemy soldier and threw him into a British vehicle, while the rest of the British party opened fire with automatic weapons and rifles and the Special Air Service men threw time bombs into enemy transport. The fighting between the British and the enemy was conducted at a range of about twenty paces. When it appeared

---

38   TNA, WO/201/811, f. 95.

that enemy reinforcements were arriving, Morris gave the order for the British vehicles to follow him as he led the way out of Marsa Brega, with his headlights on bright, heading along the coast road through the marshes towards Agedabia. To hinder pursuit, Corporal G.C. Garven stopped the last truck in the British column several times to place land mines on the road. T2 Patrol had to go some ten miles along a part of the coast road that was a causeway through the marshes before they could turn off the road into the desert. Seven explosions were heard along the coast road as enemy vehicles hit the mines laid by Garvin. Before leaving the coast road the Special Air Service attached time bombs to four more telegraph poles. T2 Patrol drove all night heading south, and before daylight they hid from enemy aircraft. The patrol returned to Jalo on 19 December. After making "careful enquiries", Morris estimated that about fifteen enemy troops were killed and several others wounded in the firefight at Marsa Brega, while the British had suffered no casualties.[39]

On 21 January S2 Patrol dropped off Fraser and three Special Air Service troops sixteen miles south of the airfield at Agedabia. S2 Patrol then went into hiding to await the return of the Special Air Service group.[40] Fraser and his men headed for the airfield on foot but found that they could go no more than two miles because of the lack of cover and the movement of enemy troops and vehicles. Fraser waited until dawn, when he and the others discovered that they were nearly surrounded by enemy troops digging in. The British party then withdrew several hundred yards to a fold in the ground where they hid while taking bearings on enemy defensive positions.

At 1830 Fraser's party headed once more towards the airfield walking between and around enemy positions, and at 2115 the four British soldiers entered the enemy airfield without being seen. Perhaps the most difficult part of the operation was finding the parked aircraft on the field because of the necessity of avoiding anti-aircraft gun sites and enemy sentries. At 0005 the Special Air Service force found the parked enemy aircraft and placed time bombs on thirty-seven aircraft and in a munitions dump. At 0030 the R.A.F. began a series of raids on Agedabia that lasted until daylight. The first time bomb went off at 0042, and in the confusion caused by the R.A.F. raids and the exploding time bombs, the four Special Air Service men left the airfield and met S2 Patrol, which then withdrew in a southerly direction. While going on to Jalo on 23 December, the patrol was attacked by machine-gun fire from an R.A.F. Blenheim and two members of the Long Range

---

39   TNA, WO/201/811, ff. 94-96.
40   TNA, WO/201/811, f. 99.

Desert Group were killed. The operation ended when S2 Patrol entered Jalo the next day.[41]

Within a week the Special Air Service, according to their count and with only twenty-seven men, had destroyed sixty-one aircraft, some thirty vehicles, and inflicted an unknown number of casualties on the enemy. On 23 December, when Fraser returned from Agedabia, he, Stirling, Mayne, and Lewis talked over their experiences to see what lessons could be learned from the four operations against enemy airfields and to plan future attacks. Everybody agreed that surprise was everything.[42] Mayne, for example, thought that the shooting at the beginning of his raid on the airfield at Tamet had been a tactical mistake. Shooting up the place should have come at the end of the raid. Lewis thought that the Italian Lancia was not worth the trouble and that the British vehicles would do the job just as well. Also, he felt he had not been bold enough during the raid on Marsa Brega. It was decided at this meeting to attack the airfields at Sirte, Tamet, Nofilia, and Marble Arch.

On 27 December S1 Patrol reached Wadi Tamet and dropped off Mayne and five Special Air Service troops about two miles from Tamet airfield. The plan was for Mayne's party to attack Tamet airfield at 0100, then return to the two S1 Patrol trucks waiting for them, and later meet the rest of the patrol out in the desert. Stirling, with five men, was going to attack the airfield at Sirte that same evening, also at 0100. Both Stirling and Mayne thought that staging a second attack against these two airfields so soon after the first attack would be the last thing that the enemy would expect. Mayne and his party made their way to the Tamet airfield, which took about two hours, and cut their way through the perimeter wire. The British raiders saw twenty-seven aircraft parked on the airfield. Without being seen or heard by the enemy, the Special Air Service party placed bombs with thirty-minute time pencil fuses in each aircraft. But just as a bomb was being placed in the twenty-seventh aircraft, there was a huge explosion as one of the time bombs went off ten minutes early. Mayne yelled to his men to make a run for it as Italian soldiers ran every which way yelling, "Avanti, Avanti."[43] Mayne and one of his men waited long enough to throw grenades at some Italians. The British escaped during the chaos caused by exploding bombs and Italian troops wildly firing small arms, reached their trucks in about twenty-

---

41   TNA, CAB/106/5, Report on operations at Agedabia 19-23/12/41 and Arae Philenorum, 25/12/41-11/1/42, by Lt. W. Fraser, Gordon Highlanders.

42   Cowles, *Phantom Major*, pp. 71-72.

43   *Ibid*, p. 78.

five minutes, and began to drive out into the desert some seventy miles to meet Stirling and the rest of S1 Patrol.[44]

After leaving Mayne's party at Wadi Tamet, Stirling and Holliman, the commander of S1 Patrol, agreed that the best way to get to the airfield at Sirte was to drive east along the coast road. When the patrol reached the coast road, however, it was discovered that a large German armored formation was moving east along the road, and the patrol had to wait until 0330 before it could get on the coast road. When the three trucks of S1 Patrol got on the road and drove east they passed German vehicles of all types parked alongside the road and saw hundreds of German soldiers camped there. Two miles from the Sirte airfield, the three British trucks pulled off the road and parked between a group of German armored cars and two German tank carriers.

Stirling and five Special Air Service troops headed for the airfield. It was 0400, and they had to be back at the trucks at 0500. When the British reached the wire that surrounded the airfield, they found it was so heavily patrolled that there was no way they could get through the wire without being discovered. Stirling and his men went to the coast road, hoping to find a way into the airfield from that direction. But the effort failed when the British were challenged by a German sentry, and Stirling's party returned to the trucks. As Stirling approached the trucks he forgot to say the password and one of the Long Range Desert Group sentries attempted to fire an Enfield rifle at him at pointblank range. The only thing that saved Stirling from instant death was that by some odd bit of luck the weapon did not have a round in the breech.

As the first signs of daylight were appearing in the eastern sky, Stirling suggested to Holliman that they drive along the coast road towards Tamet shooting up German camps and soft-skinned vehicles. Holliman had orders not to engage in such activities; nevertheless, he agreed to this course of action. When S1 Patrol saw twelve large German supply trucks parked just off the road, Stirling and his men went and placed time bombs in each vehicle but decided after planting them that this form of attack took too long. For the next twenty-five minutes, the three British trucks drove along the coast road at high speed, while their crews and the Special Air Service troops fired the Bofors gun, automatic weapons, and rifles and threw time bombs and grenades at German camps and vehicles. It was 0515 before S1 Patrol left the coast road and headed out into the desert to meet Mayne's party;

---

44   Marrinan, *Colonel*, p. 40.

and although attacked by an enemy fighter aircraft, which caused no damage, S1 Patrol returned to Jalo without incident.[45]

On 25 December T2 Patrol left Jalo with ten Special Air Service troops to attack the airfields at Marble Arch and Nofilia. Fraser and four men were dropped off about five to seven miles from the airfield at Marble Arch on 27 December. The next day, Lewis and four men were taken to a spot near the airfield at Nofilia. Then T2 Patrol went about ten miles into the desert and hid until it was time to pick up the Special Air Service raiding parties.[46] Lewis and his party marched across the desert to the airfield at Nofilia and spent some time observing the airfield to locate parked aircraft. As soon as it was dark, the five British soldiers entered the airfield without being seen and planted a bomb on one aircraft, but just as they were putting a bomb into a second aircraft, the bomb in the first one exploded. The thirty-minute time pencil fuse had malfunctioned. Lewis's men had to get off the airfield and just escaped being captured. The five British soldiers then made their way to the place in the desert where they were to meet T2 Patrol.[47]

T2 Patrol picked up Lewis and his men in the late afternoon of 30 January, and the next day the patrol proceeded towards Marble Arch to pick up Fraser's party. But at 1000 in a region of the desert where there was no cover, T2 Patrol was sighted by a Messerschmitt fighter aircraft, which attacked the British trucks at a height of about sixty feet with machine-gun fire. The trucks of the patrol dispersed as fast as they could, but there was no real cover and Lewis was killed during the second attack by the German fighter aircraft. The Messerschmitt attacked T2 Patrol until it apparently ran out of ammunition. Shortly after the Messerschmitt had left, a German reconnaissance aircraft and two Stuka dive bombers appeared. By this time the Long Range Desert Group trucks had been camouflaged as best they could, but this did not save them; for the German aircraft, using bombs, machine-guns, and 27mm cannon, systematically destroyed five out of the six British trucks. Then two more Stukas appeared and attempted, without success, to hunt down and kill the British truck crews. After dark Morris, the commander of T2 Patrol, searched the area. Lewis was the only known casualty, but ten men were missing.

---

45   TNA, CAB/44/151, ff. 119-120; Cowles, *Phantom Major*, pp. 74-78.

46   TNA, WO/201/811, f. 118.

47   Cowles, *Phantom Major*, pp. 79.

Morris loaded everybody he could find onto the remaining truck and returned to Jalo on 1 January 1942.[48]

Fraser's party, after reaching some high ground overlooking the airfield at Marble Arch, observed that it was used only as a refueling point. After three days, they decided to return to the meeting place with T2 Patrol and attack something else. At this point Fraser's party had only three days' rations. They waited for T2 Patrol for six days, not knowing that the Patrol had been destroyed and would never meet them. On 2 January 1942, Fraser decided to walk and fight his way back to the British lines—some two hundred miles to the east. On 3 January the group had reached a salt marsh about fifteen miles off Marble Arch. An attempt was made to distill water from the marsh, but it was a failure. Three men then went to the coast road and stopped an enemy truck at gun point and obtained three days' supply of water. For the next three days the group marched east and by the night of 6 January it had reached the edge of Wadi Faregh. During the night, however, a large body of Italian troops moved into the wadi and camped. Fraser found it impossible to move on the next day because of the large number of Italian troops in the area. On 8 January the group attacked an Italian truck and its crew. Water was drained out of the radiator and some food was also obtained. Next Fraser and his men moved to the coast road and stopped a truck and forced the driver to take them east along the road. At the point just east of Marsa Brega, the truck turned off the coast road and went seven miles due south where it got stuck in a salt marsh. Fraser decided to march on a course that was roughly ENE. For the next three days, the Special Air Service troops moved very slowly eastward past German-held positions; and on 11 January Fraser's party made contact with a patrol of the King's Dragoon Guards south of Agedabia.[49]

When Morris and what was left of T2 Patrol reached Jalo on January, Stirling learned that Lewis was dead and several of his men were missing and that Fraser's group had been abandoned near Marble Arch, two hundred miles behind enemy

---

48   TNA, WO/201/811, f. 119. The ten missing men were eight New Zealanders and one Englishman belonging to the Long Range Desert Group and one man from the Special Air Service. These ten men—with three gallons of water, nine biscuits, and a can of emergency chocolate ration between them—decided to walk to Augila, the nearest British post, which was about two hundred miles distant. The group set out across the desert, and on the second night they crossed the Marada-Agheila Road. On the third day the Special Air Service man dropped out and headed north saying he was going to steal a truck. The nine men belonging to the Long Range Desert Group kept on walking although suffering from lack of food, thirst, and the extreme cold at night. On 8 January 1942 the nine men reached Augila. W.B. Kennedy Shaw, *Long Range Desert Group* (London: Collins: 1945), pp. 130-135.

49   TNA, CAB/106/5, Report on operations at Agedabia 19-23/12/41 and Arae Philenorum, 25/12/41-11/1/42, by Lt. W. Fraser, Gordon Highlanders.

lines, with no way to get back to base except on foot. The Special Air Service was now reduced to two officers—Stirling and Mayne—and about ten or so other ranks. It was clear to Stirling that he needed to recruit more officers and men if he was to continue operations. Stirling knew that his raiding tactics had been a success, for with the support of the Long Range Desert Group a mere handful of men, that constituted the Special Air Service, had in a few weeks destroyed, by British count, ninety enemy aircraft, at least thirty (perhaps as many as fifty) enemy vehicles, and a number of dumps of various types. They had inflicted many more casualties on the enemy than either they themselves, or the patrols of the Long Range Desert Group that were involved in these operations, had suffered. But Stirling had also come to the conclusion that there were other, perhaps more important, targets than enemy aircraft and motor transport.

Stirling and Mayne flew back to Kabrit in the first week of January 1942 to rebuild the Special Air Service. The first thing Stirling did was to see General Auchinleck, the commander-in-chief, in Cairo. Auchinleck was impressed by the results of the Special Air Service operations, and he asked Stirling what he intended to do next. Stirling told him that he planned to enter the port of Buerat el Hsun in Tripolitania and blow up the ships in the harbour, destroy the fuel dumps there, and to wreck as many fuel tanker trucks as he could find. Stirling reasoned that modern armies need supplies and machines and that if these could be destroyed before they reached the enemy fighting forces in North Africa, it would make the task of the British forces that much easier. Stirling further reasoned that since *Crusader* had run its course, and the enemy had been cleared out of Cyrenaica, and the port of Benghazi was in British hands, a great part of the fuel required by the enemy forces would have to be landed through the port of Buerat el Hsun, about three hundred miles west of Agedabia. Stirling said that he intended to carry out this scheme with about a dozen men, but that he needed an officer from the Special Boat Section.[50] Stirling planned to attack Buerat el Hsun in the middle of January, which was the next moonless period. Auchinleck must have thought Stirling's scheme to be either mad, suicidal or both! But Stirling had shown great ability at destroying aircraft. So even if he did half of what he had said he would do, at the risk of losing only a dozen or so men, it would certainly be worth it. If Auchinleck gave his permission for the attack on Buerat el Hsun, Stirling could recruit an additional six officers and forty men; in the meantime, Stirling was promoted to the rank of major and Mayne was made a captain.[51]

---

50   The Special Boat Section was a small unit of Layforce trained to scout beaches and harbours.

51   Cowles, *Phantom Major*, pp. 86-88.

Stirling had great difficulty, as had been the case before, recruiting officers and men for the Special Air Service at the beginning of 1942. In part this was because the type of men he wanted were in short supply and in part because the Adjutant General's office was still placing all sorts of obstacles in his way; however, Stirling discovered fifty free French airborne troops at Alexandria and got permission to use them. It was soon apparent that these Free French troops were very good material for the Special Air Service. Stirling was also able to recruit Fitzroy Maclean into the Special Air Service. Maclean had got himself elected to the House of Commons as a way of escaping from the Foreign Office so that he could join the army. Maclean was one of the few British officers that Stirling could recruit at this time—in this case, officers in the Adjutant General's office knew better than to get entangled with a Member of Parliament. Another British officer recruited by Stirling was Captain William Cumper; R.E. Cumper had risen up from the ranks in the regular army and was considered the best explosives expert in the Middle East.

It was during this period that Stirling had still another fight with the Adjutant General's office. Stirling wanted Special Air Service to have its own badge. But the Adjutant General's office sent Stirling a letter stating that his unit was L Detachment and that detachments are not permitted to have their own badges. Stirling tore up the letter and had a badge designed anyway, for he was determined that the Special Air Service should have an identity of its own. The badge was light and dark blue in color with a winged dagger and the motto "Who Dares Wins." Stirling was able to secure approval for the badge from Auchinleck, and to this day it remains the badge of the Special Air Service.[52]

Before leaving for Jalo and mounting the attack on Buerat el Hsun, Stirling had a number of other problems to solve. Somebody had to train new members of the Special Air Service. Cumper could do the explosives part of the training, but with Lewis dead and Fraser missing Mayne was the only officer with experience in the field. With considerable ill grace, Mayne agreed to undertake the task. An agreement was reached with the R.A.F. not to bomb Buerat el Hsun at the time the Special Air Service planned to raid it. Another problem, which was never solved, was that the R.A.F. photo reconnaissance unit in Egypt could not locate the fuel storage dumps at Buerat el Hsun, which were thought to be underground. On 11 January Stirling returned by air to Jalo with eleven Special Air Service troops. Two days later Captain George Duncan and Corporal Barr of the Special Boat Section and Pilot Officer Derek Rawnsley and a flight sergeant, both of whom

---

52   Warner, *Special Air Service*, p. 51.

were in some kind of intelligence, arrived at Jalo to take part in the raid on Buerat el Hsun.[53]

Stirling's plan for the raid was simple to the extreme, in concept, but difficult to carry out. The plan called for a patrol of the Long Range Desert Group to transport Stirling's force, which consisted of thirteen members of the Special Air Service, two members of the Special Boat Section, and two members of the R.A.F., to a point near Buerat el Hsun. The two members of the Special Boat Section would go to the shore of the harbour at Buerat el Hsun, put together a collapsible Folboat, and then fix limpet mines to the sides of any ships in the harbour while the Special Air Service troops placed time bombs on any targets of value in and around Buerat el Hsun. After the mines and bombs had been placed, everybody would be transported back to Jalo by the Long Range Desert Group.

On 16 January 1942 G1 Patrol, commanded by A.D.N. Hunter, departed from Jalo with Stirling's men to raid the harbour at Buerat el Hsun. The going was difficult because the patrol could not pass westward through the gap between Marada and El Agheila, which was considered too dangerous, and had to pass south of Bir Zelten and then head northwest for Wadi Tamet. At the point where the patrol reached Wadi Tamet, the sides of the wadi were very steep, and it was with great difficulty that the patrol got its vehicles down into it.[54] The night before the patrol entered Wadi Tamet, radio silence was broken because Stirling wanted to find out if the R.A.F. photo reconnaissance unit had located the underground fuel dumps at Buerat el Hsun. Normally this would not be a problem, but the Long Range Desert Group thought that in this region the enemy had attempted to locate patrols with radio direction finders. This suspicion was confirmed the next morning; for just after the patrol had reached the bottom of Wadi Tamet, an Italian reconnaissance aircraft spotted the patrol. After the Italian aircraft had departed, all the vehicles were scattered and hidden in the bottom of the wadi. All that day enemy aircraft flew up and down Wadi Tamet looking for the patrol and bombing and strafing what they thought might be British vehicles. When the last of the enemy aircraft had departed in the late afternoon, it was discovered that the truck with the patrol's radio on it, along with its three-man crew had disappeared. They were never seen again. By 2030 the patrol had already left Wadi Tamet and had reached a point about sixty miles from Buerat el Hsun where the Long Range

---

53   Cowles, *Phantom Major*, pp. 86-93; Warner, *Special Air Service*, pp. 50-51.
54   TNA, WO/201/811, f. 152.

Desert Group planned to hide all but one of its vehicles; it would also serve as a main rendezvous.[55]

It was thought that Buerat el Hsun would be well guarded because of its importance to the enemy and because the Special Air Service had conducted two raids on Tamet and Sirte, which were in the same general region. It was for this reason that the Folboat would be assembled at the rendezvous, and then the whole raiding party and the assembled Folboat would be carried to a point near Buerat el Hsun in only one truck. At 2045 the one truck with twenty men, and all their equipment, as well as the assembled Folboat set out for Buerat el Hsun. While crossing twenty-five miles of desert before reaching a road that ran north to the coast road just west of Buerat el Hsun, the truck hit a cavity. The men in the back were thrown about every which way and the Folboat was smashed. Stirling quickly changed his plans—instead of attacking ships, Duncan and the two men would blow up the radio station outside of Buerat el Hsun. After passing a large and seemingly unoccupied fort, the truck turned onto the coast road and proceeded east to a point just a mile from Buerat el Hsun, where it drove off the road and stopped.

Duncan, Barr, and Corporal Rose of the Special Air Service set off on foot to destroy the radio station. Since it was 0005 and Duncan and his two men could not get to the radio station, blow it up, and return to the truck by 0200 which was the deadline set by Hunter for the raiders to return to the vehicle, Stirling and Duncan made arrangements for Duncan's party to be picked up the next night on the coast road. Next Stirling divided the Special Air Service troops into two groups of six and seven men each. One group would be led by Stirling and the other by Sergeant Major Pat Riley. There was to be no use of guns unless absolutely necessary, for stealth was essential for success. The fuses on the bombs would be set to go off at 0230.

The two groups walked to the harbour by two different routes, and when they reached it they found that there were no tankers or any other ships to attack so the Folboat would have been useless. Time bombs were placed in five different warehouses, on eighteen fully loaded 20-ton fuel tanker trucks, one anti-aircraft gun, and twelve general purpose trucks. By 0200 both parties were back at the Long Range Desert Group truck, which they drove past the fort heading south towards the rest of the patrol. At 0235, just as they turned off the road into the desert, time bombs began exploding at Buerat el Hsun.[56]

---

55   Cowles, *Phantom Major*, p. 96.
56   *Ibid*, pp. 98-104.

Stirling's group reached the rendezvous at 0500 and all the vehicles and men were hidden from enemy aircraft. All that morning aircraft remained overhead looking for the British, but by noon the enemy was forced to give up the hunt because of a sandstorm. By 2100 the sandstorm had ended and Stirling and several other men set out in a truck to return to Buerat el Hsun to pick up Duncan, Barr, and Rose. For the third time the Long Range Desert Group passed the fort, where there was still no sign of life, and Duncan's party was successfully picked up outside of Buerat el Hsun.

Duncan, Barr, and Rose had at first lost their way en route to the radio station and did not find it until after 0100. While entering the radio station, they upset an empty jerrycan and the noise caused two enemy soldiers to come out of a nearby building, but seeing nothing, they soon went back into the building. Using extreme caution so as not to alert the enemy again, it took until 0200 to set a charge of thirty pounds of T.N.T. with a two-hour fuse in the radio station. The three raiders then stole away, and when time bombs began exploding, they hid in a small cave until it was time to go to the place where they were to meet Stirling.

After picking up Duncan's party, the Long Range Desert Group truck turned around and went west along the coast road. Where the coast road meets the road that heads south into the desert the British saw a large fuel tanker truck that appeared to be abandoned parked along the edge of the road. Stirling could not resist this and blew it up. Then the British truck headed south down the road into the desert. But when they reached the fort, a telermine,[57] which did not go off, shot up into the air past the British vehicle and figures could be seen in the shadows on both sides of the road. Stirling yelled at the driver to swerve off the road, but the driver, whose name was Gibson, pushed the accelerator to the floor and the truck shot through the ambush in a hail of enemy small arms fire and exploding grenades. Several Italians were run down and the Special Air Service troops in the back of the truck fired automatic weapons at the enemy at point blank range. Luck was again with the British, for nobody was hurt and the truck escaped with a bullet in a tyre. Stirling returned to the rendezvous just before daylight; the vehicle was

---

57   There are four types of German anti-tank mines called telermines which were used extensively during World War Two. The mine that was run over near the fort by the Special Air Service was most likely either an anti-personal mine called a S-mine 35 or a S-mine 44. Both of these mines have propellant charges which go off on contact and make the mines jump up into the air before their main charges explode. Most likely the truck carrying the Special Air Service troops ran over one of these anti-personal mines setting off the propellant charge, but not the main charge in the mine. TM E 30-451, *Handbook on German Military Forces* (Washington, D.C.: War Department, 1945), pp. 71-72, 76-80.

then hidden, and the men again took cover for the daylight hours as enemy aircraft crossed over their position again and again looking for them.

That night G1 Patrol began the return trip to Jalo. The trip took five days. During the return trip, the group discussed the fact that the raid on Buerat el Hsun had been so easy and wondered why the place was not heavily defended. What they didn't know, because G1 Patrol had lost its radio set at Wadi Tamet, was that Rommel had counterattacked, regained Benghazi, and driven the British out of the most of Cyrenaica. It was not until 30 January, when one of the members of the patrol had managed to put together a radio that could pick up the B.B.C. news, that they learned of Rommel's counter-offensive. The next day, 31 January, G1 Patrol entered Jalo just before the British forces were about to pull out.[58]

The Special Air Service, supported by patrols of the Long Range Desert Group had, in a little over a month, raided behind enemy lines the airfields at Tamet and Agedabia and the towns of Marsa Brega and Buerat el Hsun. Ninety aircraft, at least sixty vehicles, five warehouses, and a radio station had been destroyed along with a number of fuel dumps and similar installations, and an unknown number of the enemy had been killed or wounded. The British forces involved in the operations had suffered very few casualties and had lost only a few trucks. Each one of these operations had been carried out by a very small number of men. The raid on Buerat el Hsun, for example, was carried out by four officers and twenty-five other ranks, including the crews of the Long Range Desert Group's trucks. There is no question that Stirling's tactics of using four or five men to wreck an airfield was carrying out the principle of economy of force to a point well beyond logic. Logical or not, in December of 1941 and January of 1942, Stirling showed that his raiding tactics worked when combined with the Long Range Desert Group's ability to cross the Libyan Desert at will.

Auchinleck and Ritchie, the two highest ranking British army officers in the theater, approved of Stirling's methods, otherwise they would never have permitted the formation of the Special Air Service. The Adjutant General's office in Cairo probably owing to a dislike of anything out of the ordinary, did not approve of Stirling or his activities and went to considerable lengths to place obstacles in his way. There was also an element in the British army in the Middle East that thought Stirling's admittedly irregular tactics to be in some respects "not cricket." Real soldiers fight battles and do not sneak around at night blowing things up and killing people. This type of thinking can be seen in various documents, such as an

---

58   TNA, CAB/44/151, ff. 124-125; WO/201/811, ff. 151-152; Cowles, *Phantom Major*, pp. 93-110; Michael Crichton-Stuart, *G Patrol* (London: William Kimber, 1958), pp. 121-123.

intelligence summary that refers to the Special Air Service as "thug columns" when describing the first raid on the airfield near Tamet.[59]

As for the enemy, it had apparently greatly overestimated the size of the forces involved in the Long Range Desert Group's and Special Air Service's raids behind their lines whilst at the same time it played down the damage caused by their action. For instance, Mayne's first raid on the airfield at Tamet was described by the Germans as "isolated demolitions."[60] The enemy's reaction to organized attacks on installations in its rear and assaults on its line of communication along the coast road, which began when the Long Range Desert Group was ordered on 24 November to attack enemy transport[61] and greatly increased in December of 1941 when the Special Air Service began working with the Long Range Desert Group, were in many respects not very effective. The enemy usually reacted to a major raid by sending aircraft, at the first daylight after the raid, to attempt to find the raiders, as they did after the raid on Buerat el Hsun. In most cases this was not very effective because the raiders would hide before the first aircraft had even left the ground. T2 Patrol being caught in the open and having its vehicles destroyed by enemy aircraft came about not by design but as a result of a chance sighting of the patrol by an enemy aircraft. Moreover, once enemy aircraft sighted the British, as they did G1 Patrol in Wadi Tamet, they responded by sending aircraft to attack the patrol instead of ground troops working in conjunction with aircraft.

In January 1942 the enemy, whether they be Italian or German, did not seem to realize that the only way to deal with the operations of the Long Range Desert Group and the Special Air Service was to organize a combined air and ground unit to go out into the desert, hunt down, and destroy the British raiders. By failing to do this, the enemy conceded to the British the deep desert and were forced into a classic military dilemma: they could either put up with the British attacks in their rear areas or they could attempt to guard everything of importance between Tripoli and their front lines, which would result in their being weak everywhere and strong nowhere.

Nothing was too far behind enemy lines or too deep in the desert to escape attack from the Long Range Desert Group and the Special Air Service. Also, no defense could protect an airfield or motor pool from an attack by men of the Special Air Service who operated in small groups and were skilled, determined,

---

59   TNA, WO/169/3803, G.H.W., M.E.F. Intelligence Summary No. 592.
60   TNA, WO/201/811, ff. 107-108.
61   TNA, CAB/44/151, f. 97.

and ruthless. Combining the Long Range Desert Group's techniques of penetrating the Libyan Desert with the seemingly "mad hatter" raiding tactics of the Special Air Service produced a new type of war in the Western Desert—mechanized irregular warfare.

A truck of the Long Range Desert Group near the western slopes of the Tibesti Mountains in the Free French Province of Chad, probably on the way to Free French outpost at Zouar. Photograph taken circa January 1941 by Trooper F Jopling. (Alexander Turnbull Library, Wellington, New Zealand)

Patrol of LRDG (Long Range Desert Group) on rough going terrain, Libya. Photograph taken in 1941 by an official photographer. (Alexander Turnbull Library, Wellington, New Zealand)

British Major P A Clayton of the Long Range Desert Group (L) conferring with Free French leader Lieutenant Colonel d'Ornano during the Fezzan Raid. Two junior Free French officers look on. Photograph taken at Kayugi in January 1941 by Trooper F Jopling. (Alexander Turnbull Library, Wellington, New Zealand)

Long Range Desert Group (LRDG) patrol halted in the desert on the edge of the Egyptian Sand Sea. Photograph taken in January 1941 by Trooper F Jopling. (Alexander Turnbull Library, Wellington, New Zealand)

Long Range Desert Group (LRDG) on patrol. The second truck was towed for more than a thousand miles over every conceivable type of desert country. Photograph taken on Fezzan Raid, January 1941 by Trooper F Jopling. (Alexander Turnbull Library, Wellington, New Zealand)

LRDG (Long Range Desert Group) truck bogged in soft sand. The angle of sand was greater than is apparent and it was necessary to offload the truck to release it. Photograph taken in Libya January 1941 by Trooper F Jopling. (Alexander Turnbull Library, Wellington, New Zealand)

Wheel tracks made in the sand by the Long Range Desert Group in the Libyan Desert. Taken circa 1941 by W B Kennedy Shaw. (Alexander Turnbull Library, Wellington, New Zealand)

Trucks of the Long Range Desert Group (LRDG) bogged in dune country on one of their patrols into Libya. Identified as G Patrol (British). Taken circa January 1941 by Trooper F Jopling (Alexander Turnbull Library, Wellington, New Zealand)

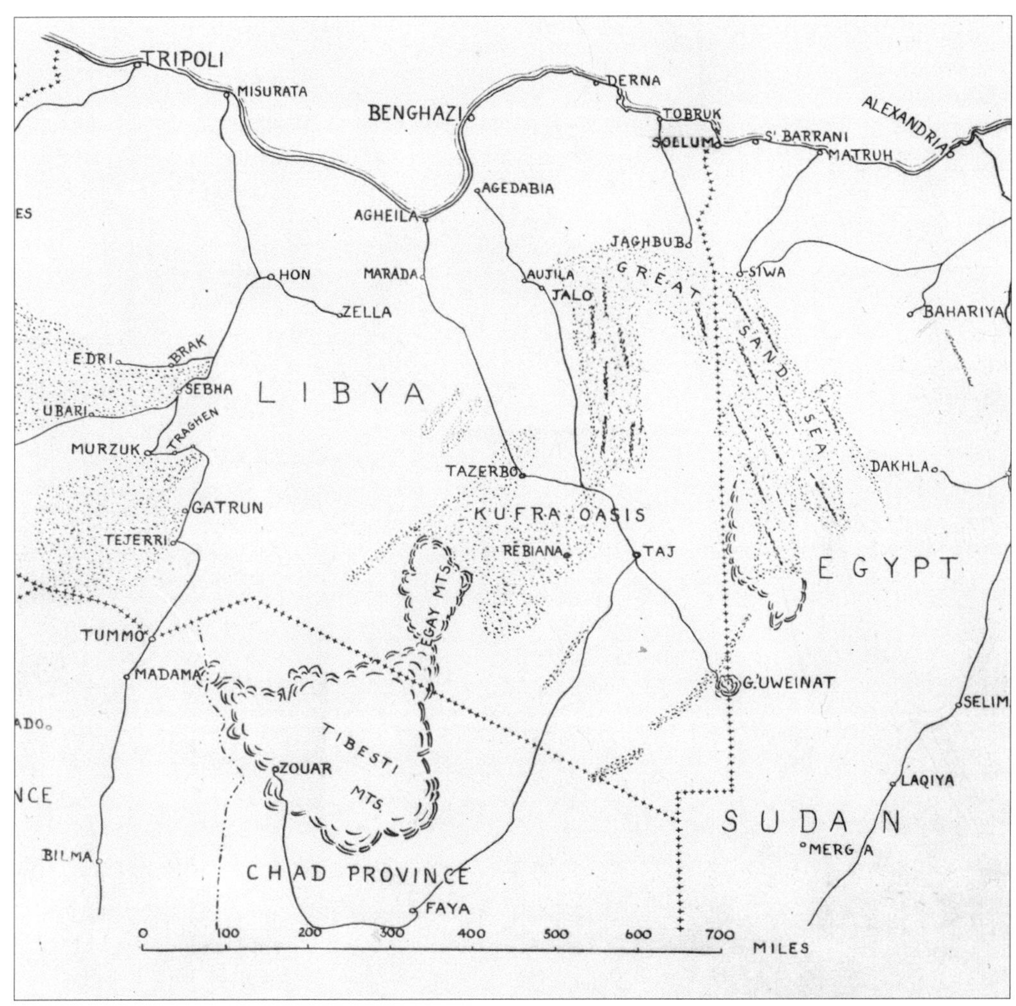

Original caption on file print reads: "The extent of the operations of the L.R.D.G (Long Range Desert Group) in which officers and men of the NZEF played a prominent part, may be judged from this map of Libya. The shaded area lying along the Egypto-Libyan border is the "Great Sand Sea" and the patrols were the first military force ever to cross it. Uweinat, on the border, Aujila in the north, Kufra in the south, and Musuk and Traghen in the sw, are the landmarks in the journeys of the NZ and British "desert raiders". They also went to the Free French province of Chad, south of Libya, and to the Sudan." Creator of map unidentified. Date of map unknown. (Alexander Turnbull Library, Wellington, New Zealand)

Long Range Desert Group (LRDG) patrol on the road between Murzuk and Traghen, during the Fezzan Raid. Photograph taken in January 1941 by Trooper F Jopling. (Alexander Turnbull Library, Wellington, New Zealand)

7

Going Off in All Directions

"It is just as legitimate to fight an enemy in the rear as in the front. The only
difference is in the danger."
—Col. John S. Mosby

At the end of 1941 the 8th Army had, after heavy fighting, forced the enemy out of Cyrenaica for the second time in the war. To many it appeared that it was only a matter of time before the campaign in the Western Desert would end with the British conquest of Tripolitania. Ritchie, in a letter to Leclerc in the Chad written on 26 December, told the Free French general, "It is my intention to operate against the enemy in TRIPOLITANIA as soon as the necessary forces can be adequately maintained."[1]

Several days earlier, Prendergast had been ordered by the 8th Army to "make preparation at once for your action in connection with the advance into TRIPOLITANIA." Specifically, the Long Range Desert Group was directed:

(i) To carry out offensive patrol as far as possible back behind the enemy lines and to act aggressively against enemy communications etc., in areas where such action is unlikely to be expected.

(ii) In the course of movement across TRIPOLITANIA, patrols will make note of topographical details that may be of assistance to the subsequent advance of other troops through the area.

---

1   TNA, WO/201/811, f. 104.

(iii) In addition, patrols will watch out for and report enemy movements and will indicate as soon as possible whether there are any signs of a position being prepared in the area of BUERAT.[2]

To carry these orders out, the coast road west of El Agheila to Buerat el Hsun was divided into four "target areas" and a region south of Tripoli was made a fifth "target area." Patrols G2, R1, T1, and Y2 were assigned to work in four out of five of these areas. Patrol Y1 was to be held at Jalo as a reserve.[3] A Squadron, in conjunction with the Special Air Service, was to carry out a separate set of raiding operations.

Lloyd Owen's Y2 Patrol with four trucks, one officer from the Indian Army, and fourteen other ranks left Jalo on 23 December for the target area in northwest Libya just south and west of Tripoli. Heading NNW, they encountered ground that was difficult to cross and it rained most of the time, which was not only uncomfortable but also made navigation extremely difficult because sun compasses could not be used. Also, because of a lack of preventive maintenance, the patrol's vehicles continually broke down. Nine days after leaving Jalo, having seen nothing except twelve trucks on the Marada-Bir Zelten track, Y2 Patrol arrived at the town of Scemech, which is due south of the coastal city of Homs. Lloyd Owen wanted to attack the fort at Scemech, but found the place unoccupied by the enemy. The next day, 6 January 1942, one of the patrol's trucks broke down and had to be destroyed because it could not be repaired.

At this time it was decided because of a shortage of fuel that the patrol had to return to Jalo. The shortage of fuel was caused in part by the difficult going which resulted in the trucks at times getting only one mile to the gallon, but the major reason for the shortage was leaking fuel cans. The patrol began the operation with thirty-five cases, each containing eight gallons of fuel, and lost fifteen cases of fuel because of leakage. The British army fuel containers were, in the words of Lloyd Owen, "incredibly flimsy";[4] and during the first years of the war in the desert the British forces lost thousands of gallons of fuel because of leaking containers.

After encountering more rain and further mechanical problems, Y2 Patrol and its three remaining trucks arrived back at Jalo on 12 January 1942. In sixteen days Y2 Patrol had travelled fifteen hundred miles over some extraordinarily difficult country which was largely unmapped and even more significantly had never before

---

2   TNA, WO/201/811, f. 106.
3   TNA, WO/201/811, ff. 115-117.
4   David Lloyd Owen, *The Desert My Dwelling Place* (London: Cassell, 1957), p. 160.

been crossed by a unit of the British armed forces. Although on the face of it Y2 Patrol's trip to Scemech did not appear to have achieved very much, the patrol did produce a huge amount of topographical information about Northern Tripolitania.[5]

In the last week of December 1941, G2 Patrol was sent to scout the Hon-Misurata region of Tripolitania; and on 7 and 8 January 1942, R1 and T1 Patrols respectively were dispatched to Tripolitania. The three patrols encountered very difficult ground, and a large number of enemy aircraft were seen which in some cases attacked the patrols without success. Several enemy vehicles were spotted and some were attacked. All three patrols had so many mechanical problems with their vehicles that it was becoming clear that the Long Range Desert Group's Ford trucks needed to be replaced by new vehicles.[6] At the end of 1941 the Long Range Desert Group withdrew completely from Kufra and made Jalo its headquarters. By 8 January the Heavy Section and Lazarus, with his survey group, had arrived at Jalo from Kufra. The Long Range Desert Group's headquarters and the Light Repair Section, both of which had been stationed at Siwa, arrived at Jalo on 10 January; for it was thought that Siwa was too far to the rear for the site of the Long Range Desert Group's headquarters and Light Repair Section.[7] By the middle of January 1942, the Long Range Desert Group had made Jalo its base for future operations in support of the 8th Army's forthcoming invasion of Tripolitania.

At 0800 on 21 January 1942, the Axis forces counterattacked. It was a bold stroke which took the British completely by surprise.[8] Ritchie thought at the end of *Crusader* that "the Germans have lost heavily, and the Italians are completely disorganized. It is not yet known if any remains of his armored forces have escaped into TRIPOLITANIA."[9] Rommel being able to take the 8th Army by surprise was a huge British intelligence failure. *Ultra* did not give a clue, or it was misread;[10] however, this surprise would never have occurred if the Long Range Desert Group had been ordered to maintain a road watch on the coast road some miles behind the enemy lines. By the end of January 1942, the British had been forced out of much of Cyrenaica.[11]

On 26 January the headquarters of the Long Range Desert Group was pulled back from Jalo to Ghetmir and then to Siwa, where it arrived on 31 January.

---

5   TNA, WO/201/811, ff. 139-141; Lloyd Owen, *The Desert*, pp. 149-160.

6   TNA, WO/201/811, ff. 142-150.

7   TNA, WO/201/811, f. 113.

8   I.S.O. Playfair, *The Mediterranean and Middle East* (London: HMSO, 1960), vol. III, p. 140.

9   TNA, WO/201/811, f. 104.

10   Cf., Ronald Lewin, *Ultra Goes to War* (New York: McGraw Hill, 1978), pp. 169-172.

11   Playfair, *The Mediterranean*, vol. III, pp. 151-154.

Shortly after the Long Range Desert Group's headquarters left Jalo, it was decided to abandon the place completely. Before leaving Jalo most of the Long Range Desert Group's stores which could not be moved to Siwa were hidden in a dump just inside the sand sea east of Ghetmir. Everything else of value at Jalo which was not removed was destroyed. The destruction was carried out by a patrol of the Long Range Desert Group which was left at Jalo to wait for G2 Patrol and for some Special Air Service troops to return from the raid on Buerat el Hsun before retreating to Siwa.

The greatest loss suffered by the Long Range Desert Group during the German offensive of January 1941 was the capture of Captain Richard Carr, the group's adjutant, along with fourteen other ranks and seven vehicles. Carr had left Jalo on January 24, without a radio, to bring back from Msus fuel for the Long Range Desert Group. Because he had no radio, it was impossible to warn Carr of the speed of the German advance and that the Germans had taken Msus. On 26 January Carr and his party were taken prisoners when they entered Msus thinking that it was still in British hands. However, later that same day when Carr and his men were being removed by the Germans from Msus, two British armored cars attacked the German column and in the resulting confusion seven Long Range Desert Group troops escaped captivity.[12]

After the withdrawal of the Long Range Desert Group from Jalo to Siwa, R1, S1, S2, T1, and T2 Patrols were sent to Cairo to be issued with new 30 cwt trucks. The 30 cwt Fords which had served the Long Range Desert Group well during the last year were totally worn out. When they were first put into service, the Ford trucks got an average of seven or eight miles per gallon of gasoline. This had now fallen to four or five miles per gallon. In fact, the Long Range Desert Group's Fords were to be replaced by new 30 cwt Chevrolets. The armament of each patrol was also being increased. In addition to personal arms, such as rifles, each patrol was to be armed with two .5 Vickers machine guns, three .303 Vickers "K" machine guns, and one .303 Vickers machine gun as well as five Lewis guns. Also, the 37mm Bofors gun which was issued to each patrol was replaced with one Italian 22mm Breda dual purpose cannon. The 22mm Breda cannon was adopted because it was thought, owing to its high rate of fire, to be a better anti-aircraft gun. The Heavy Section's White trucks were also replaced at this time by 10-ton Mack trucks. During this change of vehicles, the Long Range Desert Group always had at least two or more patrols in the field.[13]

---

12   TNA, WO/201/811, ff. 113-114.
13   TNA, WO/201/812, ff. 19.

In the weeks after the withdrawal from Jalo to Siwa, the Long Range Desert Group conducted several different kinds of operations. These operations, as had happened in the past and would happen again in the future, were tactically contradictory in nature. Missions such as road watches and transporting agents to and from various points behind enemy lines are best done in such a way as to attract as little attention as possible. On the other hand, transporting Special Air Service troops behind enemy lines to conduct raids was bound to attract the enemy's attention and result in his undertaking searches for the raiders, searches which might compromise some other activity of the Long Range Desert Group. This contradiction in the operations of the Long Range Desert Group was seen by many during the North African campaign, but the problem was never successfully resolved.

In February G2 Patrol was ordered to observe for four days and to record all the traffic passing in either direction on the Benghazi-Barce-Cirene road and the Benghazi-Barce-Maraua-El Faidia Road.[14] On 9 February G2 Patrol, under the command of Timpson, left Siwa with four trucks, Captain John Haselden,[15] sixteen other ranks, and three Senussi Arab guides. G2 Patrol headed northwest towards the Jebel Akhdar, and on 13 February hid its vehicles on high ground in a cleft at the upper reaches of a wadi which was located between the two roads that ran through the Jebel Akhdar. The patrol was then divided into three groups. The patrol sergeant, with three British soldiers and one Arab, would stay with the vehicles. Haselden, with four guardsmen and one Arab, would walk to the Benghazi-Barce-Cirene road and observe and record all movement on that road. And Timpson with six guardsmen and one Arab would do the same on the Benghazi-Barce-Maraua-El Faidia road. Both groups watched the two roads for four days beginning at midnight 14 February. Timpson's group had the most difficult task of the two because a number of Germans were hunting game in the region where the British party was observing the road. By 18 February both Haselden's and Timpson's groups had made their way back to where the vehicles were hidden.

When Timpson returned from road watch, he found that his four trucks had to carry forty-seven people back to Siwa. In the days since the trucks were hidden and the two groups had left to watch the road, British soldiers and Libyan soldiers in British Service who had been by-passed by the Germans began showing up at the patrol sergeant's camp or were brought there by friendly Arabs. One of these,

---

14   TNA, WO/201/812, f. 27.

15   Before the war, Haselden was a cotton merchant in Egypt, and during the war he was an intelligence officer who conducted many missions behind enemy lines in Cyrenaica. Haselden also was one of the very few Englishmen who could pass for an Arab.

Major J.T. Gibson of the 1st Battalion, Welch Regiment, who had been on the run in the Jebel Akhdar since 29 January, estimated that there were some two hundred British soldiers in northern Cyrenaica who were attempting to make their way back to the British lines with the aid of the Senussi Arabs. Somehow Timpson got all forty-seven British and Libyan soldiers into his four trucks, and G2 Patrol arrived back at Siwa about midday on 21 February.[16]

At the same time that Timpson and G2 Patrol were ordered to set up two road watches in Jebel Akhdar, Lloyd Owen and Y2 Patrol were ordered to discover if the enemy was making supply dumps east and northeast of Agedabia with the objective of advancing eastward towards Tobruk.[17] Lloyd Owen did not like this mission, for the region of the desert his patrol had to scout was very flat and there was no place to hide if there was any trouble. When he complained about the lack of cover, however, he was told that he could hide among the vehicles abandoned by the 1st Armoured Division when that formation had retreated eastward.

On 11 February Y2 Patrol left Siwa to search for enemy supply dumps. Shortly after they had set out, the latest intelligence from the 8th Army was dropped to the patrol by a Lysander aircraft. On 14 February Y2 Patrol discovered a large enemy camp, but because the ground was so flat, they could not get any closer than five miles. The next day, while heading toward Agedabia, the patrol came across a great mass of abandoned British vehicles of every known type, many of them in perfect working order. As Y2 Patrol passed through the abandoned British vehicles, Italian salvage parties were seen going through each vehicle. At one point Y2 Patrol went over a small ridge and almost ran into two enemy trucks going right across their path. The British patrol stopped dead and watched the enemy for what seemed like an eternity not knowing what they would do, but the enemy continued on their way. Y2 Patrol then moved off on a northeast course, and a little later Lloyd Owen discovered that his patrol was being followed by three enemy trucks. Y2 Patrol continued for fifteen or so miles before the three other trucks began to slow down and disappear in the distance. The next day southeast of Antelat Y2 Patrol continued to see enemy vehicles. There were several close calls when the patrol had to pass close to enemy vehicles that were moving not only along tracks but also across country. On 17 February Lloyd Owen decided to return to Siwa because there were so many enemy vehicles about that it seemed to him only a question of time before one of them discovered that Y2 Patrol was a British formation. On 19 February Y2 Patrol returned to Siwa and was ordered to Cairo to be issued

---

16   TNA, WO/201/812, ff. 2-17, 31-33, 59-67.
17   TNA, WO/201/812, ff. 28-29.

with new vehicles. Although Y2 Patrol did not learn much about the location of enemy dumps, it did discover that it was possible to drive around in the midst of enemy formations without being discovered to be British.[18] One of the reasons this was possible was that the Axis forces were using large numbers of captured Allied vehicles.

On 25 February S2 Patrol, under the command of Olivey, departed from Siwa to set up a road watch near Marble Arch, in the same place where the patrols of the Long Range Desert Group had set up an observation post, in order to observe traffic on the coast road, in September 1941. This new road watch was established to prevent the enemy from amassing men and material without British knowledge as was done before Rommel's counterattack of 21 January 1942. The road watch also served as a double check on *Ultra*. The Long Range Desert Group would maintain this new road watch for months on end. Every vehicle going either east or west on the coast road was recorded along with such details, if possible, as unit markings, state of repair, number of men carried, as well as kind and amount of cargo carried. The Intelligence people attached great importance to the movement of armored fighting vehicles, artillery pieces, and the like. In fact, it required three patrols to maintain the road watch. One patrol was positioned near Marble Arch watching the coast road, one patrol would be returning to base after completing a tour on the road watch, and one patrol would be proceeding to Marble Arch to relieve the patrol there. Two members of a patrol would man the observation post near the road for twenty-four hours, writing down the movements of enemy vehicles. When the twenty-four hours were up, the two men would be relieved by two others and they would return to the hiding place of the patrol and the information they had obtained would be sent to the headquarters of the Long Range Desert Group, by radio, for transmission to the 8th Army and the General Headquarters, Middle East, in Cairo.

The men of the Long Range Desert Group hated road watch duty because it was boring and sedentary work. It could also be very dangerous. The two men observing the road faced the almost constant danger of being discovered by the enemy or by Arabs. There were always repair gangs working on the road and at times enemy troops would leave the road for various purposes and pass alarmingly close to the Long Range Desert Group's observation posts. On 21 March, for example, an entire convoy stopped and made camp about one hundred and fifty yards from the two men who were watching the coast road, and they had to stay flat on their faces until they could escape under cover of darkness. On another

---

18   TNA, WO/201/812, ff. 68-69; Lloyd Owen, *The Desert*, pp. 169-175.

occasion a bus load of children drew up in front of the British observation post and the children played softball right in front of the two men watching the road. Danger and boredom aside, the road watch at Marble Arch nevertheless paid big dividends in terms of intelligence.[19]

Sometimes the intelligence departments in Cairo, or at the Headquarters of the 8th Army, required that traffic censuses or road watches be made on the two roads running east from Barce. For this purpose, on 25 February S1 Patrol, commanded by Holliman, with five trucks, Captain R. Melot (an intelligence officer), and seventeen other ranks left Siwa to set up a three-day road watch on the Barce-Cirene road and the Barce-Maraua road in the Jebel Akhdar. S1 Patrol proceeded northwest to Baltet el Zalagh where an Arab guide was picked up. At the southern edge of the Jebel Akhdar the patrol learned that there was so much enemy activity in the region that it would be impossible to conduct a traffic census on the Barce-Cirene road. Holliman, therefore, hid the patrol's vehicles in a wadi at the southern edge of the Jebel Akhdar while he, Melot, two other ranks, and the Arab guide made their way north on foot to the Barce-Maraua road, where a three-day road watch was conducted. When the party returned to the wadi where the patrol's vehicles were hidden, however, it was discovered that a cloud burst in the Jebel Akhdar had caused a flood in the wadi. The rushing water had smashed one of the trucks to bits against some rocks. Two other trucks had been "completely submerged and after driving them for 14 miles both clutches burnt out" and the vehicles had to be abandoned.[20] When S1 Patrol reached Siwa, it was discovered that, when removing kit and other gear from the two trucks with broken clutches, most of the notes taken during the road watch had been lost.[21]

Operations of the Long Range Desert Group and Special Air Service presented special problems in command and control because in most cases there was no way that a higher headquarters could know what was going on miles behind enemy lines. In fact, such operations were often to report conditions behind enemy lines. Because of their peculiar situation, the Long Range Desert Group and Special Air Service received operational instructions instead of direct orders. Whereas a direct order told where, when, and how an operation should be conducted, an operational instruction told a commander in general terms what was required and left the where and how up to him. The Long Range Desert Group received its orders from either the headquarters of the 8th Army or British Middle East Headquarters in Cairo,

---

19   Lloyd Owen Interview; TNA, WO/201/812, ff. 20, 84-87.
20   TNA, WO/201/812, f. 71.
21   TNA, WO/201/812, ff. 70-71, 82-83.

which were the two highest headquarters in the theater. Specialized units, such as the Long Range Desert Group and the Special Air Service, had to be commanded from the highest possible level in the theater in order that their operations could fit in with and aid strategy. No lesser headquarters than that of either the 8th Army or theater headquarters would, for instance, have the necessary strategic information to know which areas of the desert the Long Range Desert Group should map behind enemy lines for the future use of the British armed forces in North Africa. Nor could any lesser headquarters know when a series of attacks on enemy airfields by the Special Air Service would produce the greatest strategic benefits.[22]

The commander of the Long Range Desert Group received operational orders, directives, and the like from either the 8th Army or theater headquarters and these orders were then translated into operational instructions that were issued to patrols. The commander of a patrol was told in general terms what was required and sometimes the way in which a mission should be conducted. For example, on 15 March Holliman received the following instructions for S1 Patrol:

1. <u>TASKS</u>:

(a) Carry party of parachutists to area South of BARCE.

(b) Return them to SIWA on completion of their task.

(c) To salvage two trucks left by you on previous trip.

(d) To pass on to 2/Lt. Olivey, any information given you by Capt. Morris.

2. <u>METHOD</u>:

Leave SIWA 16 March and drop your passengers, arranging a rendezvous with them.

Return to point S 9468 or T 0575 and await arrival of Morris and Olivey.

While waiting, salvage the two trucks to the East.[23]

---

22   John W. Hacket, "The Employment of Special Forces", *Journal of the Royal United Service Institution* 97 (Feb, 1952), pp. 26-41.

23   TNA, WO/201/812, f. 281.

The commander of A Squadron, who issued this operational instruction to Holliman, could not be any more specific than this because Holliman was going to be operating in the Jebel Akhdar, which is well over three hundred miles from Siwa, and there was no way in which the conditions in the region of Barce could be known by anyone at Siwa until Holliman's patrol reached there. Moreover, conditions could change with such rapidity that the only possible form of directions that the patrols of the Long Range Desert Group could operate with were operational instructions, or some similar type of general orders, which gave the commander of each patrol the authority to change his methods of operating to fit the changing or unknown conditions under which he had to carry out a particular mission.[24] This method of command and control placed a great amount of responsibility on the individual patrol commanders, who for the most part were very young junior officers.

In the middle of March, which was a moonless period, the Long Range Desert Group took part in a number of Special Air Service and commando operations in northern Cyrenaica. These operations were part of a huge scheme thought up by Stirling. The commander of the Special Air Service had concluded from what little information he could obtain from Auchinleck's headquarters that the 8th Army was to hold the so-called Gazala line while the British amassed enough men and equipment to go on the offensive again. Stirling thought that the British were conducting the entire war in North Africa on the wrong set of principles, that the amassing of overpowering amounts of material and numbers of men to fight regular set piece battles was a mistake. Tactically and strategically, Stirling's thoughts ran to a radical extreme. To Stirling, if he had read their books and articles, the ideas and theories put forth by people such as B.H. Liddell-Hart and J.F.C. Fuller, on mechanized warfare, would be considered very conservative concepts

---

24   Lloyd Owen Interview:
DISTINCTION BETWEEN ORDERS AND INSTRUCTIONS
1002. <u>Orders</u>. An order required definite action to be taken to achieve an intention; the recipient must be in no doubt of the mission and the method of fulfilling it. It is issued when a commander has a degree of immediate control over the situation, and when execution by the method ordered is necessary for coordination; it should not, however, prejudice the use of initiative or local knowledge by a subordinate.
1003. <u>Instructions</u>. An instruction is issued to convey the intention of a commander; it may indicate his overall plan but leaves the detailed course of action for the subordinate commander. It is used when it is impracticable or imprudent to be specific; for example, when a subordinate is given an independent mission or when the timing or situation cannot be forecast. The particular form of instruction to a subordinate giving direction and guidance based on higher policy decisions is known as a directive.
Ministry of Defense, *Joint Service Staff Manual: Service Writing* (London: MOD., 1978), vol. I, p. 10-11.

of warfare indeed. Stirling believed that modern armies required fuel, machines, and places for people to fix machines. The enemy supply line in North Africa ran along one single road from Tripoli, through Benghazi, and then on to the front in eastern Cyrenaica. Therefore, according to Stirling's reasoning, if you attacked this very long enemy supply line hard enough with many small groups of specially trained men, the enemy would be given a stark choice: either lose to the raiders all the machines and fuel and other materials required for waging a modern war and thus be rendered incapable of fighting; or, guard everything along the coast road from Tripoli to the front lines, which would require so many troops that the enemy would not have the men at the front lines to fight a major battle. Stirling knew that he could not get the British army to adopt a scheme as radical as his, at this time, but he thought that he could educate, by example, the commanders of the British forces in North Africa about some of the advantages of waging war "Stirling style."

In support of the forthcoming 8th Army offensive, Stirling put together a scheme involving attacks on a number of airfields and Benghazi Harbour.[25] Attacks were to be conducted against the airfields at Barce, Slonta, Berca, and Benina. Fraser would attack the airfield at Barce, Lieutenant "Bobby" Dodds and his force would go to the one at Slonta, and Stirling and Mayne would attack the Berca and Benina airfields just outside Benghazi. After the attacks on the airfields at Berca and Benina, Stirling and Mayne would attack Benghazi Harbour.

On 16 March S1 Patrol, under the command of Holliman, left Siwa with seventeen other ranks and five special Air Service troops under the command of Fraser. Holliman was to carry out the operational instructions he had received on 15 March, and the Special Air Service troops were to attack the airfield at Barce. The patrol passed through the wire fence that marked the Egyptian-Libyan border, then went west-northwest, and arrived at Sidi Zamut at the south side of the Jebel Akhdar on 19 March. Holliman left three trucks with their crews under the command of Lance Corporal Eastwood hidden near Sidi Zamut. With the two remaining trucks and the Special Air Service party, Holliman headed north and dropped Fraser's group off near Barce. After Holliman had left Sidi Zamut for the Barce region, Lance Corporal Eastwood saw a number of enemy trucks and aircraft that were apparently hunting for the patrol. The British Lance Corporal decided to move south to a secondary rendezvous near Cheda bu Maun where there was good cover to hide the three trucks. The next day, Holliman arrived at Cheda bu Maun, having dropped off the Special Air Service troops. On 22 March Holliman sent two trucks off to salvage the two vehicles that had been lost during

---

25   Virginia Cowles, *The Phantom Major* (London: Collins, 1958), pp. 112-115.

the last patrol into the Jebel Akhdar. These two trucks were successfully repaired and driven a number of miles south into the desert and hidden, then the repair party returned to Cheda bu Maun.[26]

On 14 March Morris, the commander of T1 Patrol, had received orders to take six Special Air Service troops led by Lieutenant Dodds as near as possible to the airfield at Slonta and then to pick up twenty-seven commandos who were in the same area and bring them to Jarabub. Before leaving the region near the Jebel Akhdar, Morris was to meet with Holliman and inform S1 Patrol where it could meet the Special Air Service troops who were going to attack the airfield at Slonta.[27] T1 Patrol left Siwa on 16 March in company with S1 Patrol, and the two patrols parted company on 18 March.

On the night of 19 March, after some very difficult going, T1 Patrol met the group of commandos. The Arab guide who had brought the commandos out of the Jebel Akhdar agreed to lead the Special Air Service troops to the airfield at Slonta. At 0100 on 20 March the Special Air Service party started marching north. The plan was for Dodds's party to go north on foot in the remaining hours of darkness, hide during the daylight hours, and then complete the march to Slonta airfield the next night. An hour after Dodds's group left, Morris divided T1 Patrol into two groups because he thought that there was too much enemy activity to needlessly risk the safety of the whole patrol when it was not necessary. Second Lieutenant P.R. Freyberg was sent with three trucks to Jarabub and then on to Siwa. Morris then went in search of S1 Patrol at Cheda bu Maun. Morris and his three trucks reached the Cheda bu Maun region on the night of 20 March and began searching for S1 Patrol; but it appeared that the enemy was also searching the region, for they shot off Verey lights all around Morris, sometimes as close to the patrol as a thousand yards. At this point Morris decided to give up the search for S1 Patrol; he and his three trucks arrived back at Siwa on 23 March, after being chased by an enemy armored car that was escorting a truck along the Trigh el Abd.[28]

The operation to attack the airfields at Berca and Benina and then Benghazi Harbour began on 15 March. S2 Patrol, commanded by Olivey, left Siwa with Stirling and Mayne and six Special Air Service troops, six officers and men of the Special Boat Section, one intelligence officer, and two Libyan soldiers in British service. Stirling brought two vehicles of his own along: a Ford station wagon that was cut down and disguised to look like a German staff car and a real German

---

26   TNA, WO/201/812, ff. 282-283.

27   TNA, WO/201/812, f. 284.

28   TNA, WO/201/812, ff. 285-286.

staff car. Olivey's instructions were to take the Special Air Service and Special Boat Section parties as near as possible to the airfields at Berca and Benina, which were just outside of Benghazi. The patrol was then to set up a rendezvous east of Benghazi. After picking up Stirling's people, S2 Patrol was to proceed to meet with S1 Patrol and then to pick up Dodds's force at an agreed upon rendezvous before returning to Siwa.[29]

As S2 Patrol was proceeding towards the Benghazi area on 17 March, the Special Air Service's real German staff car hit an Italian thermos mine which exploded, damaging the vehicle and wounding Lieutenant David Sutherland and Sergeant Moss of the Special Boat Section. The German staff car was abandoned and the two wounded men were sent back to Siwa in a Long Range Desert Group truck. On 18 March the patrol had reached hilly ground with good cover near Garet El Genesc. The two Libyan soldiers were sent to scout the Berca and Benina airfields, and Stirling, Olivey, and Melot scouted the escarpment of the Jebel Akhdar east of Benghazi looking for a place to serve as a base. The next day the vehicles were moved into a hiding place with good cover near the escarpment of the Jebel Akhdar. For reasons that were never clear to the British, enemy aircraft were continuously bombing and machine-gunning a wadi several miles away. On 20 March Lance Corporal Ahmed Din of the 4/16th Punjab Regiment arrived in the patrol's camp. The lance corporal had been hiding out in the Jebel Akhdar for the last two months with the help of Arabs. That night Stirling, Mayne, and Lieutenant Gordon Alston attacked the airfields at Berca and Benina.[30]

The attacks on the airfields near Berca and Benina by the Special Air Service were not a complete success. Alston, whose target was the main airfield at Berca, could not find the place. Stirling, whose objective was the airfield at Benina, had to make two trips to the airfield. The first time he found it heavily defended and containing only dummy aircraft; however, he did destroy with time bombs a dump of aerial torpedoes. During the second raid on the airfield at Benina on the night of 26 March, and although the field was heavily guarded, Stirling got inside several hangars and destroyed five aircraft with Lewis bombs.[31] Mayne, with two men, managed to get onto and off Berca's satellite airfield undetected and destroyed with Lewis bombs fifteen enemy bombers. Mayne's party then got lost returning to

---

29   TNA, WO/201/812, ff. 287.
30   TNA, WO/201/812, ff. 288-289.
31   Cowles, *Phantom Major*, p. 120; TNA, WO/201/812, f. 22.

the British hide-out east of Benghazi, but with the help of some Arabs the group finally made it to the rendezvous.[32]

On the night of 25 March Stirling, Alston, Captain K. Allott, two corporals from the Special Boat Section, and Corporals Cooper and R.A. Seekings of the Special Air Service set out for Benghazi to attack shipping. Stirling knew from the two Libyan soldiers, who had scouted the road to Benghazi, that there were no roadblocks at the entrance to the city. The raiders drove down the road towards Benghazi in Stirling's fake German staff car followed by two trucks of the Long Range Desert Group. The two Long Range Desert Group trucks pulled off the road at Regima just outside Benghazi to await the return of Stirling's party. With headlights on, Stirling drove his Ford down the macadam road to Benghazi at seventy miles an hour. As the car neared Benghazi, Stirling slowed down and drove right through the middle of the city to the waterfront without anyone taking any notice.

Stirling knew that the harbour area would be guarded and wired off. The plan was to launch the Folboat outside of the fenced off area and to approach the shipping in the harbour from the seaweed side by going around the end of the wire fence. The car was left with the two Special Air Service corporals in a bombed out lot near the harbour, while Stirling and the Special Boat Section men with limpet mines and the disassembled Folboat went to the water's edge outside of the wired off harbour area. When Stirling's group reached the shore, they found the sea was too rough to use the Folboat. Nonetheless, Stirling told the Special Boat Section men to assemble the Folboat, for he could see the dim shapes of ships in the harbour and there was always a chance that the wind would drop. While the Folboat was being assembled, Alston kept watch and Stirling went off to make a reconnaissance of the Benghazi waterfront. Stirling spent about an hour walking through the streets of downtown Benghazi and discovered, among other things, that there was an unguarded entry into the fenced off section of the waterfront. When he returned to where he had left the Special Boat Section men, he found that the sea was much rougher than before. Moreover, the Folboat could not be assembled because it had been damaged when the German staff car hit the thermos mine several days earlier. Stirling agreed with the Special Boat Section men that there was nothing to be gained by continuing the mission, so the limpet mines and the damaged Folboat were taken back to Stirling's Ford, and the whole party drove out of Benghazi. They met the two Long Range Desert Group trucks at Regima at

---

32   Patrick Marrinan, *Colonel Paddy* (Dungannon, Ireland: The Ulster Press, 1968), pp. 50-51.

0400 and returned to the hideout at the edge of the Jebel Akhdar.[33] On the night of 27 March, S2 Patrol and attached members of the Special Air Service and the Special Boat Section withdrew from the Benghazi region. Two days later S2 Patrol met S1 Patrol at Cheda bu Maun, and S2 Patrol reached Siwa on 1 April.[34]

Fraser's party was able to get onto the airfield at Barce, but found only one aircraft and eight "repair wagons", all of which they destroyed with Lewis bombs. Then the party marched all the way across the Jebel Akhdar to Sidi Zamut, where they were met by Corporal Eastwood and Private Watson of the Long Range Desert Group. Eastwood and Watson led the party on foot to Cheda bu Maun, where S1 Patrol was hiding. While Fraser's party was being met at Sidi Zamut, Holliman, the commander of S1 Patrol, was making arrangements for some Arabs to hide Dodds's party, which had failed to get onto the airfield at Slonta, until 8 April when they would be picked up by another patrol of the Long Range Desert Group. S1 Patrol returned to Siwa on 1 April with the two trucks that had been lost on the last patrol because of the flood.[35] On 8 April Dodds's party was picked up by R2 Patrol, and the Special Air Service troops arrived back at Siwa two days later.[36]

The Special Air Service's operations in northern Cyrenaica had required the support in varying degrees of four Long Range Desert Group patrols; their losses were two men wounded by a thermos mine and one German staff car, while the enemy lost at least twenty-one aircraft and eight specialized vehicles. Stirling had shown that he could drive right into Benghazi at night, walk around the streets of the city, and then drive right back out again, which was no mean feat; however, he had failed, as he had at Buerat el Hsun, to destroy any shipping. Stirling returned to Kabrit determined to solve the boat problem and then to return to Benghazi and attack shipping.

On 7 April the Commander-in-Chief of the British army in the Middle East sent an official letter to the commander of the Long Range Desert Group expressing his "appreciation" for the conduct of the road watch and the other operations conducted by the Long Range Desert Group.[37] When the Special Air Service concluded its operations in the Jebel Akhdar at the end of March, the Long Range Desert Group continued to operate in the region and to maintain

---

33   Cowles, *Phamtom Major*, pp. 117-120; Philip Warner, *The Special Air Service* (London: William Kimber, 1980), pp. 52-53.
34   TNA, WO/201/812, f. 289.
35   Cowles, *Phantom Major*, p. 120; TNA, WO/201/812, f. 283.
36   TNA, WO/201/812, f. 22.
37   TNA, WO/201/813, f. 10.

the road watch at Marble Arch. Y2 Patrol departed from Siwa on 31 March with a group of twelve commandos and four Senussi guides, dropping them off near Ghedir bu Ascher and then picking them up five days later and returning to their base at Jarabub.[38] On 4 April R2 Patrol set out from Siwa on a mission similar to that of Y2 Patrol, except instead of hiding out waiting for the commandos to carry out their mission, R2 Patrol returned to Siwa carrying Dodds and six Special Air Service troops, six downed R.A.F. airmen, and two intelligence officers and their radio operator. Then R2 Patrol returned to the Jebel Akhdar and picked up the commandos and returned them to their base at Jarabub.[39] On 31 March G1 Patrol dropped off two of Haselden's Senussi agents near Jalo, and two days later picked them up and returned with them to Siwa on 5 April.[40] On 10 April Y1 Patrol, now under the command of Lloyd Owen, was ordered to the headquarters of the 8th Army. Upon arrival there, the patrol was made to sit around waiting for several days and then to spend a day driving three staff officers of the XXX Corps and an R.A.F. officer around the region south and southeast of Bir Tengeder; Y1 Patrol thought the entire operation was a waste of time.[41]

The Long Range Desert Group was running what amounted to a bus line from Siwa to various places behind the enemy lines in northern Cyrenaica; however, transport by the Long Range Desert Group at times could be very dangerous. For example, S2 Patrol, commanded by Olivey, had orders to carry two Arab agents as close as possible to Agedabia. For a good part of the time enemy aircraft were hunting the patrol; and in the early evening of 24 April, as the patrol sergeant attempted to approach the Hasieiat-Agedabia track with two trucks, he was met with a red Verey light followed by fifteen minutes of not very well-aimed 105mm artillery fire. After withdrawing from the artillery bombardment, the two Arab agents were let off and were told they would be picked up in seven days at an agreed upon point, but in fact they were never seen again by S2 Patrol.[42]

There were some operations into the Jebel Akhdar, which were routine to the point of being boring. For example, Hunter, in command of Y Patrol, after dropping off some commandos and intelligence agents to do a road watch in the Jebel Akhdar, had the task of observing and reporting enemy traffic moving between Mechili and Msus. But from 22 April, when the patrol left Siwa, until the

---

38   TNA, WO/201/812, ff. 290-292.
39   TNA, WO/201/812, ff. 293-294.
40   TNA, WO/201/812, ff. 297-299.
41   TNA, WO/201/812, ff. 300; Lloyd Owen, *The Desert*, p. 181.
42   TNA, WO/201/813, ff. 104-108.

patrol's return on 11 May, the men of Y2 Patrol saw not even a single new track in the desert.[43]

British operations behind enemy lines in Libya, in 1942, were nevertheless, becoming extremely complex. Patrols of the Long Range Desert Group were carrying out missions behind enemy lines; however, at the same time, groups of commandos, Libyan and British intelligence officers and agents, and the Special Air Service were also conducting operations of various types, equally, behind enemy lines; and at times, these operations conflicted with each other. As early as 24 February, the commander of the Long Range Desert Group pointed out to the 8th Army headquarters that the Marble Arch road watch could not be continued if Stirling put into effect a plan that he had, to systematically attack enemy transport on the coast road between El Agheila and Misurata.[44] On 9 March, 8th Army headquarters attempted to bring about a degree of coordination of the activities of various units and organizations operating behind enemy lines in Libya. It issued the following orders in the process dividing Libya up into several zones, that stated:

"The division of responsibility for sabotage operations will be as follows:

(a) Operations within the enemy's forward area will be undertaken by out forward troops under arrangements 13 Corps.

(b) Operations further West, between both excl the line MARTUBA-MEKILI and Benghazi, will be undertaken by Commandoes under orders HQ Eighth Army.

(c) Operations South and West of BENGHAZI inclusive will be undertaken by S.A.S. dets under orders HQ Eighth Army.

The L.R.D.G. will continue to be employed primarily on reconnaissance, and when necessary in guiding and collecting sabotage parties. L.R.D.G. activities will be closely coordinated with sabotage operations.

---

43   TNA, WO/201/813, ff. 109-112.
44   TNA, WO/201/812, ff. 304.

In addition, certain minor operations may be undertaken by G(R)[45] personnel. Notification of these operations, which are planned at G.H.Q., will be forwarded to those Comdrs concerned."[46]

It quickly became apparent that the 8th Army's directive of 9 March was not working and that the activities of British forces behind enemy lines had to be controlled and coordinated by one officer, and that this officer had to have a knowledge of and experience in operations behind enemy lines in Libya. On 23 April Lieutenant Colonel Guy Prendergast, the commander of the Long Range Desert Group, was placed in command of A and C Squadrons of the Middle East Commando, which were based at Jarabub, as well as of all intelligence officers, agents, and groups operating behind enemy lines including any other units or personnel who might in the future also be sent behind enemy lines in Libya. The selection of Prendergast for this task was logical, for he was a regular soldier, knew the desert, and had more experience in commanding operations behind enemy lines than any other officer in the British Army in the Middle East. Also, as commander of the Long Range Desert Group, Prendergast controlled the best means of transporting men and equipment into enemy-held regions of Libya.

Prendergast was directed to maintain the watch at Marble Arch and to set up and maintain an intelligence network in the Jebel Akhdar and to have, at any given time, at least two secret radio sets supporting this spy system. Prendergast was ordered as well to attack enemy motor transport west of longitude 17° and in the region west of longitude 20°30' and north of latitude 30°30'. These areas were chosen for attacking enemy vehicles because they were not in areas where road watches were being conducted. The main weight of these attacks was to be directed at fuel trucks, supply trucks, and tanks.[47] The road watches at Marble Arch and on the Msus-Mechili road were to be conducted by Long Range Desert Group patrols, while the two other road watches in the Jebel Akhdar were to be conducted by commandos. The commandos, however, were found to be ill-suited for this task. It was thought that because of a "lack of fieldcraft, and for other reasons, the Commandos were incapable of doing this work."[48] The task of organizing and running these two road watches was, therefore, turned over to Major Vladimir

---

45   G(R) is a unit of General Headquarters, Middle East which was responsible for certain types of clandestine raiding and escape and evasion activities in Libya.

46   TNA, WO/201/812, ff. 305-306.

47   TNA, WO/201/813, ff. 195-196.

48   TNA, WO/201/813, f. 6.

Peniakoff of the Libyan Arab Force, who was already working in the Jebel Akhdar as an intelligence officer.[49]

When A and C Squadrons of the Middle East Commando came under the command of Prendergast, they were in the process of being equipped with 15 cwt Chevrolet trucks; A Squadron had already received ten of them. It was thus decided to form two patrols, later to become three, of five vehicles each and organized along the lines of the Long Range Desert Group with an operational range of about two hundred and fifty miles. Along with the vehicle-carried patrols, three sabotage sections were formed to operate either on foot or to be carried to the target by vehicles. The training of these commandos was conducted by Steele, the commander of A Squadron of the Long Range Desert Group.[50]

During April and May, the tyres of the vehicles of the Long Range Desert Group kept blowing out. In one operation G2 Patrol had seven tyres damaged, mostly from blow-outs; and Y1 Patrol had fifteen blow-outs, which forced a mission to be called off altogether. All of the blown out tyres were made by Firestone, and obviously the Long Range Desert Group had received a defective shipment.[51] While the tyre problem was certainly frustrating, during the spring of 1942, the Long Range Desert Group had finally managed to solve a problem that had been plaguing it for some time: leaking gasoline containers. The thin-skinned and easily-damaged British containers were replaced by the standard issue German gasoline can, known as a jerrycan, which in time became standard issue in both the American and British armies. Leak-free gasoline containers were vital, given the large amounts of fuel required to carry out an average patrol. For instance, when G-2 Patrol, under the command of lieutenant hon. R.B. Gurdon, took a small intelligence unit from Siwa up into the Jebel Akhdar, at the end of April, each vehicle needed to be loaded with forty jerrycans of gasoline. On this mission G2 Patrol went eight hundred and eighty-nine miles and consumed, in all, five hundred and seventy-six gallons of gasoline at the average rate of 7.73 gallons per mile.[52]

On 6 May G1 Patrol, under the command of Timpson, was ordered to carry out attacks on enemy vehicles on the coast road near Sirte. In these attacks, Timpson was to attempt to throw time bombs into the backs of enemy vehicles in such a way as not to be seen by the enemy. The objective was to have enemy vehicles blow

---

49   TNA, WO/201/812, f. 6; Vladimir Peniakoff, *Private Army* (London: Jonathan Cape, 1950), pp. 71-188.

50   TNA, WO/201/813, ff. 113, 133-134.

51   TNA, WO/201/813, ff. 117, 136-137.

52   TNA, WO/201/813, ff. 113, 117.

up at various times and places without the enemy knowing the cause. If this did not work, Timpson was to attack enemy motor pools in much the same day as the Special Air Service attacked enemy aircraft on airfields. If this could not be done either, then Timpson was to "beat up" with gunfire enemy traffic and motor pools along the coast road as close to Sirte as possible.[53]

On 14 May G1 Patrol made its first attempt to throw time bombs into the backs of moving enemy trucks. At dusk, Timpson set out for the coast road with six other ranks, one truck, and twenty-five time bombs—each weighing about two pounds—in Italian haversacks. The truck was parked one hundred and fifty yards from the road in such a way that its guns could cover the road, and two guardsmen were stationed about fifty yards from the road and out of the field of fire of the truck's guns. A pile of stones and sand was then pushed into the road, blocking part of it. Five oil drums were placed in front of the pile of sand and rocks along with a sign saying "Achtung! Strassenbau". In addition, two red hurricane lamps were also placed.[54] The plan was for Timpson and a guardsman to place the bombs in the backs of the trucks when they slowed down due to the obstruction in the road. But for some reason the obstruction, instead of slowing down the enemy trucks, had the opposite effect – the enemy tended to increase speed when they saw it. Then G1 Patrol attempted to put a time bomb in the back of a truck by hiding behind one of the oil drums; but this did not work either. This was because the trucks came in groups and multiple headlights made the attacker clearly visible. Next, Timpson tried hiding beside the road and running up to passing trucks and attempting to throw an Italian haversack with a bomb in it into the back of a moving truck. The problem with this method was that there was no good cover near the road, an Italian haversack did not make a good missile, and the sides and tailgates of the trucks were higher than expected. At 0200 on 15 May, Timpson finally gave up attempting to place or throw time bombs into enemy trucks from the side of the road.

He did not give up however; instead Timpson turned to an even more harebrained scheme. One of the guardsmen was to sit on the front of the hood of a Long Range Desert Group truck which, with its headlights off, would chase an enemy truck down the coast road until the two trucks were close enough for the guardsman sitting on the hood to throw the haversack with the time bomb into the back of the enemy truck. Timpson actually attempted to place a time bomb in an enemy truck by this method and chased a truck down the coast road, only

---

53   TNA, WO/201/813, ff. 113-120.
54   TNA, WO/201/813, f. 121.

to have it apparently stop dead at the fake British road works! What Timpson did not know was that he was chasing two trucks instead of one. The second truck was disabled and was being towed by another; when the lead enemy truck, going at a considerable speed, swerved to pass by the British fake road works, the tow line broke and the first truck just continued on its way leaving the disabled truck behind. The two Italians in the disabled truck thought that the British were Germans. Timpson, not wanting to give up the element of surprise, explained in his "almost negligible Italian" that there was another Italian truck coming along the road and that he was in a great hurry to get to Sirte and could not tow the disabled Italian truck.[55] The British then continued to drive along the coast road looking for another place to throw time bombs into the backs of enemy trucks the next night. After going about five and a half miles, however, the rear tyre on the British truck had a blow out and there was no spare tyre. Timpson had the truck driven into the desert and hidden. The group then walked back to where the rest of G1 Patrol was hiding and had a truck sent off to repair the tyre on Timpson's truck.

The next day while G1 Patrol, with its trucks hidden and camouflaged in a wadi, was eating lunch, a sentry saw enemy troops approaching. Timpson gave the order to "stand to your guns," but it took about two minutes to get the camouflage nets off and begin firing at the enemy.[56] At first Timpson could not see the enemy or where their fire was coming from, but the gunfire appeared to come from two light machineguns and some rifles. Then the guards officer saw several Italian soldiers trying to work their way around the northwest side of the wadi. At this point Guardsman Matthews was killed. The British opened fire with their automatic weapons, but as soon as they did, "the enemy fire slackened. At times it almost dropped, and then burst out again."[57] Timpson, under the covering fire of his automatic weapons, was able to get G1 Patrol's trucks, in ones and twos, out of the wadi without being damaged or suffering any more casualties. Timpson thought that if the Italians had either pressed their attack home or managed to pin the British down with fire in the wadi until reinforcements arrived, it probably would have "been all up with us."[58]

G1 Patrol made off into the desert in a southeasterly direction for some sixty-five miles, expecting to be followed and attacked by aircraft, which did not happen. The patrol stopped and made camp at 1800. Timpson decided to hide for several

---

55   TNA, WO/201/813, ff. 124-5.
56   TNA, WO/201/813, f. 125.
57   *Ibid.*
58   TNA, WO/201/813, f. 126.

days and then to attack vehicles on the coast road with gunfire and explosives. The plan was to leave one truck with the medical orderly and "Guardsman Waiting, Guardsman Matthews's best friend, and much shaken by his death…" to form a rendezvous.[59] The two men left with the truck in the desert were told that if upon their return, the four trucks could not find the rendezvous because it was dark, Timpson would fire a white and green Verey light and they were to do the same.

On 22 May Timpson and the four trucks headed for the coast road, which was reached at 2000. The telegraph and telephone wires were cut. Four mines in pairs of two were laid in the road after holes in the surface were made with pick axes; two more mines were also laid on both sides of the road. At the first roadhouse, or truck stop, the British came to, the lead trucks opened fire

> on any vehicle and personnel we could see as we slowly passed by. The blaze of fire was tremendous, the first three trucks firing one Breda 12.7 (Tracer, incendiary, A.P. and H.E.), 2 Vickers. 303., 3 Vickers 'K'., 1 Double Browning, one single Browning and one Lewis; in fact there was too much tracer, for the rear trucks were blinded by the light of those ahead, and the multicoloured ricochet of tracer. Six large supply trucks were parked on both sides of the road, and into these we poured ammunition. Several enemy personnel were also fired at. One truck was left burning lightly, probably as a result of the 12.7 Incendiary.[60]

The first three British trucks stopped half a mile from the enemy truck stop and the telephone and telegraph wires were again cut while waiting for the fourth truck to appear. After about ten minutes of waiting the missing truck was heard, but not seen, moving through the desert off the road. The fourth and last truck in the British line, had mistaken "the ricocheting shots for heavy enemy fire, and had turned off the road, gone round the back of the Road House, throwing some time-bombs at some nearby enemy vehicles….".[61] The fourth truck then returned to the coast road at a point east of the three other British trucks and headed back to the rendezvous, thinking that Timpson and the other trucks had already withdrawn towards the meeting place. After an unsuccessful search for the missing fourth truck, Timpson also headed for the rendezvous. Later in the night, the British saw and heard mines and time bombs going off on the coast road.

---

59   TNA, WO/201/813, f. 127.
60   TNA, WO/201/813, f. 128.
61   *Ibid.*

Timpson and his three trucks made it back to the rendezvous early in the morning of 23 May, ahead of the fourth truck. As they approached the rendezvous, however, the medical orderly and Guardsman Waiting panicked and ran away into the desert because,

As they later explained, they thought [we] were the enemy for three reasons; firstly, we had only three trucks (G.4 arrived at 6:30 a.m.); secondly, we were a day overdue; and thirdly, they had apparently expected me to fire the Verey Lights, even in daylight.[62]

It took Timpson until the evening of 24 May to find Waiting and the medical orderly, for in two days the men had walked forty-two miles with only one fourth of a water bottle between them. The next day, with only thirty-two gallons of water remaining, G1 Patrol began the trip back to Siwa, which was reached on 28 May.[63]

When Stirling failed to achieve anything against shipping in Benghazi, he had returned to Kabrit determined to make another attack on Benghazi Harbour. This time nothing would be left to chance. Stirling was not going to be stopped by broken Folboats, as had been the case at Buerat El Hsun and Benghazi; nor was the next attack going to fail for want of proper training in the use of small boats. What started off as an attack on shipping in Benghazi Harbour was to end, however, as one of the most famous bits of high comedy in the whole war. Kennedy Shaw described the operation in a report as being "Gilbertian" in nature.[64]

Fitzroy Maclean was assigned the task of finding the right type of boat for the attack on ships in Benghazi Harbour. Stirling did not care what type of boat it was as long as it worked and could be transported by vehicle to Benghazi. After looking at a number of collapsible boats, Maclean remembered

an article of army equipment known as a Boat, reconnaissance (Royal Engineers), and with the help of Bill Cumper procured two of them. They were small and handy and made of black rubber and you inflated them by means of a small pair of bellows, which emitted a wheezing sound. Each held two men with their equipment.[65]

---

62   *Ibid.*
63   TNA, WO/201/813, ff. 121-132.
64   TNA, WO/201/813, f. 5.
65   Fitzroy Maclean, *Escape to Adventure* (Boston: Little Brown, 1950), p. 149.

These boats were successfully tested in the Great Bitter Lake, but Maclean and Stirling got into a disagreement over whether or not inflating the boats made too much noise. Stirling argued that the enemy would not be as alert as Maclean thought they would be. To prove his point, Stirling decided that a mock attack should be made on British shipping at Suez in much the same way that the Special Air Service had attacked the airfield at Heliopolis. One night Stirling, Maclean, and Corporals Cooper and Seekings drove into the city of Suez in an army truck. They parked the truck and walked, carrying the two boats and a number of disarmed limpet mines, to the edge of the water. While the boats were being inflated, the only person who showed any interest whatsoever was an anti-aircraft gunner who was told to "shove off." The four Special Air Service troops embarked in the boats and paddled to the nearest anchored merchant ships and placed a number of limpet mines on their hulls. Then they paddled back to shore, deflated the two boats, walked back to their truck, and drove back to Kabrit. The next morning Stirling telephoned the port authorities at Suez and asked them to give back the limpet mines. The reaction to this phone call is not difficult to imagine: the R.A.F. had been greatly embarrassed by Stirling's "raid" on Heliopolis; now it was the Royal Navy's turn![66]

Stirling wanted only six men to go on the second raid against shipping at Benghazi because that was all he could fit into his Ford station wagon. The six men would be Stirling, Maclean, Alston, and Corporals Cooper, Seekings, and Rose. Randolph Churchill, the son of the prime minister, had come out to the Middle East with No. 8 Commando and wanted to go along although he was not a member of the Special Air Service. Stirling had a policy of not taking people on operations who had not been through the Special Air Service training including the parachute course, but Churchill was the son of the prime minister and like his father had a silver tongue; moreover, on a lark Churchill had once parachuted out of an aircraft with Stirling. In the end, Stirling let Churchill tag along on the mission with the understanding that he would go only as far as the point where the Long Range Desert Group patrol would hide outside of Benghazi.[67]

On 14 May Gurdon, the commander of G2 Patrol, received instructions to take Stirling and his men to a point near Benghazi and to place an explosive charge under the Benghazi-Barce railway while Stirling was conducting his operation.[68] The next day G2 Patrol, with five trucks and Stirling's station wagon, left Siwa

---

66   Cowles, *Phantom Major*, pp. 123-124.
67   *Ibid*, p. 124.
68   TNA, WO/201/813, ff. 142-143.

for Benghazi. Although there was considerable air activity during the trip, by 20 May G2 Patrol had found a suitable hide-out near Benghazi. The morning and afternoon of 21 May were spent preparing for the attack that night on the shipping in Benghazi Harbour. During the course of these preparations, however, a detonator exploded by mistake, injuring a private of G2 Patrol and Corporal Seekings of the Special Air Service.[69] Seekings's wound, while not grave, was serious enough to prevent him from going on the raid. Randolph Churchill took Seekings's place.

At 1730 the group left the hide-out and headed for the road to Benghazi. Stirling's men were in his Ford station wagon, which had been painted and marked to look like a German staff car, and they were followed by two Long Range Desert Group trucks. At Regima, the two Long Range Desert Group trucks turned off the road to await the return of Stirling's group from Benghazi. While waiting for Stirling, Gurdon and three guardsmen placed a charge of forty pounds of dynamite, which would set off by means of "a pressure cap," under the tracks of the Benghazi-Barce railway. The two trucks continued to wait for Stirling until 0345 on 22 May, when Gurdon ordered that they return to the hide-out before daylight.

As Stirling's Ford turned onto the macadam road heading into Benghazi, the vehicle began to emit a high-pitched scream. The front wheels had been thrown out of line by all the cross-country driving and could not be fixed on the spot. Stirling drove very fast down the road, with headlights on bright and with the Ford making a sound similar to that of an American police car siren! Just outside of Benghazi they encountered an Italian roadblock. When the station wagon stopped, Maclean, who was fluent in Italian, picked up a large wrench from the floor of the vehicle with one hand and with the other beckoned the Italian sentry to come closer. Maclean then said in Italian, "Staff officers in a hurry."[70] What Maclean wanted to do was to get the sentry close enough to the Ford to do him in with the wrench, but the sentry was suspicious. Then Maclean heard a click in the back seat of the station wagon as the safety catch on a submachine gun was slid back. The sentry paused and then said that the car's headlights ought to be dimmed and opened the barrier and let the British through. Either the Italian sentry believed that they were indeed German staff officers, or he suspected that they were the enemy and knew when he heard the click of the safety catch on the submachine gun that he was to be the first man killed in a gunfight.

After getting through the roadblock, Stirling continued driving towards Benghazi with the car still making the screaming noise. As they neared Benghazi,

---

69   TNA, WO/210/813, f. 145.

70   Cowles, *Phantom Major*, p. 125

the British raiders passed a car with its headlights on going in the opposite direction. The car shot past, stopped, made a U turn, and began to follow the British vehicle. Stirling pushed the accelerator to the floor and went screeching into Benghazi as fast as the Ford would go. He turned into a side street, then into a bombed out lot and turned off the headlights, and the pursuing car flew past. Stirling's group suspected that the sentry at the road block knew that they were British and had phoned ahead telling of their approach, hence the car that followed them. Several minutes later the air raid sirens went off. Since the R.A.F. had been ordered not to attack Benghazi that night, the sounding of the sirens confirmed in the minds of the British that the enemy knew that they were inside Benghazi. Stirling thought that because the station wagon was so noisy that it would be best to escape on foot. A charge was placed in the station wagon with a thirty minute fuse.

The British raiders were in the Arab part of Benghazi, which had been heavily damaged by R.A.F. bombing. It seemed as if every other house had been hit as the British made their way over the rubble towards the waterfront. In a narrow street the British, carrying packs and submachine guns, came face to face with an Italian *carabinieri*. Maclean thought it would be best that he should start asking questions first. He asked why the sirens were going off, and the Italian replied, "oh, just another of those damned English air raids." Maclean then asked if it might be a warning that the British were going to raid the city with ground troops. The Italian laughed off such a suggestion. He assured that there was no need to be nervous about that, not with the British almost "back on the Egyptian frontier."[71] Maclean thanked the Italian for his information and the British went off down the street. As soon as they were out of sight of the *carabinieri*, however, there was a mad rush over the rubble back to the Ford station wagon to defuse the bomb in it. They made it just in time, for a minute or so after removing the detonator and throwing it away, the thing went off with a loud click.

The group still had to get to the harbour, which was about a mile away. The Ford could not be used because of the noise it made, so Churchill and Rose were left with the station wagon and ordered to find some place to hide it. Stirling, Maclean, Cooper, and Alston set off on foot for the harbour carrying a rubber boat, submachine guns, limpet mines, and time bombs. When they reached the wire fence around the harbour, they were seen by an Italian sentry. Maclean walked up to the sentry and explained that they had just been in a car accident and that all their gear was in their luggage and asked if the Italian could direct them to a hotel where they could spend the night. The Italian said that most of the hotels

---

71   *Ibid*, p. 126.

were bombed out but if they kept looking they might find something. After leaving the sentry, the four British soldiers went to the unguarded break in the fence that Stirling had found during his first trip to Benghazi. Moving around railway cars, cranes, and motor vehicles, the British made their way to the water's edge. Maclean and Cooper were given the task of inflating the boat while Stirling and Alston made a tour of the docks.

Maclean and Cooper set to work to inflate the rubber boat with the bellows, which made their usual squeaking sound and attracted the attention of the sentry on a nearby ship. The sentry yelled at the two British soldiers "*Qui va là?*" and Maclean yelled back "*Militari!*" But the sentry was still suspicious and asked what they were doing. Maclean yelled, "nothing to do with you," which seemed to satisfy the sentry.[72] No matter how much the two British soldiers pumped the bellows, however, the boat would not inflate, and Cooper and Maclean came to the conclusion that it had a hole in it.

Cooper and Maclean hid the damaged boat as best they could and went back to the station wagon to get the second boat. When they arrived, a small number of people mostly Arabs, were watching Churchill and Rose trying to back the Ford into a hole in the side of a bombed building. Maclean and Cooper got the second boat and returned to the water's edge, only to find that it would not inflate either. As Maclean and Cooper started to return to where the Ford was hidden, they met Stirling and Alston. The four British soldiers held a hurried council of war as the first signs of daylight appeared. It was decided to treat this expedition as another reconnaissance for a bigger and better raid, not to place time bombs on the docks, to pack everything up so as to leave no trace of their presence, and then to return to where the Ford was hidden. This meant that they would have to go back through the break in the fence and return to the water's edge and pack up the boats before going to where the Ford was hidden.

As Maclean went through the break in the fence for the fifth time that night, he encountered an African Ascari soldier from Italian Somaliland who pointed his rifle with a fixed bayonet on it at the pit of the Scottish officer's stomach. Maclean asked in an irritable tone what the Ascari soldier wanted. The soldier answered, "*Non parlare Italiano.*" Because Maclean believed "that in dealing with foreigners whose language one does not speak, it is best to shout," he began to wave his arms, yell, and bawl out the Ascari soldier for not being able to speak Italian.[73] After a few minutes of this treatment, the African soldier went away, and the four British

---

72   *Ibid,* p. 127.
73   *Ibid,* p. 128.

soldiers went down to the water's edge and packed up their boats, bombs and limpet mines.

As the British were making their way towards the unguarded break in the fence, Maclean noticed that two Italian sentries carrying rifles with fixed bayonets had fallen in behind them to make a party of six. The British could not shoot it out with the two Italians, nor could they go out through the unguarded break in the fence. Maclean decided the only thing to do "was to try somehow to brazen it out."[74] Following Maclean, the whole group marched up to the main gate, where Maclean demanded to see the sergeant of the guard. When the sergeant appeared, it was obvious to Maclean that he had been asleep. Maclean told the sergeant that he was a staff officer and that the sergeant was not doing his job because for all the sergeant knew the four of them might be British *saboteurs.* Maclean said that he would let him off this time, but the sergeant better set things right and also "do something about smartening up his men's appearance."[75] With that parting shot, Maclean walked out through the front gate followed by Stirling, Alston, and Cooper with their submachine guns, boats, bombs, and limpet mines, and all four in British uniform. It was nearly daylight when the four returned to where Churchill and Rose had hidden the Ford. The station wagon was parked in the ground floor of a partly demolished house. The six Britons decided to hide for the day in two rooms on the second story of the building in which the Ford was hidden.

They spent all day in the building, which turned out to be only several doors from a German headquarters. When it was dark, the commander of the Special Air Service, the son of the British Prime minister, a Member of the British Parliament, one other British officer, and two corporals, all in British uniforms, set off to tour downtown Benghazi. Then they got into the Ford station wagon, which was still screeching, and drove out of the city, through the roadblock, and to the hiding place of G2 Patrol, which was reached at 0900 on 23 May. Two days later the whole group reached Siwa.[76]

By the end of May the Long Range Desert Group found itself in the position of having become "universal aunts" to anybody who had "business in the desert behind the enemy lines."[77] Not only did the Long Range Desert Group have to administer and logistically support its own operations but also to support, and in many cases transport, an endless stream of commandos, intelligence agents,

---

74   *Ibid.*

75   *Ibid,* p. 129.

76   TNA, WO/201/813, ff. 144-146; Maclean, *Adventure*, pp. 157-168; Cowles, *Phantom Major*, pp. 125-131.

77   TNA, WO/201/813, f. 9.

Allied personnel, who either had evaded or escaped from the enemy, as well as an increasing number of Special Air Service troops. Most of the required fuel, rations, and munitions were brought to Siwa from Mersa Matruh by the Long Range Desert Group's Heavy Section. The Heavy Section, while bringing to Siwa all the supplies needed by the Long Range Desert Group and the units it was supporting logistically, was also able in the spring of 1942 to set up a line of "escape route dumps" which ran westward as far as Etla, and it was planned to extend this line of dumps as far west as Marble Arch.[78] Each dump contained food, water, and other stores for any men of the Long Range Desert Group who had to walk back to base, as T2 Patrol did in January of 1942.[79]

On 26 May Rommel attacked the 8th Army, and after several weeks of fighting he forced the British to withdraw eastward into Egypt.[80] One of the first reactions of 8th Army headquarters to the enemy offensive was to order the Long Range Desert Group to continue the road watches and to attack transport and other targets behind enemy lines. A Squadron, Middle East Commando was ordered to carry out a number of raids on enemy transports and supply dumps in the Jebel Akhdar.[81] This effort was undertaken by a force of eighteen vehicles and eighty-one men, and was a total failure. As soon as the commandos got into the Jebel Akhdar, they were attacked over and over again by enemy aircraft until all their vehicles had been destroyed.[82] These commandos simply did not have the required skills, training, nerve, or luck to work in the Jebel Akhdar.

With the failure of A Squadron, Middle East Commando to conduct raids on enemy lines of communications, the task was turned over to the Long Range Desert Group. On 13 June the Long Range Desert Group received orders from the 8th Army to attack enemy lines of communication in the Jebel Akhdar west of Timimi. That same day operational instructions were issued to G1 and R2 Patrols to carry out these orders.[83] R2 Patrol left Siwa on 13 June and three days later met G1 Patrol, which was conducting a road watch in the Jebel Akhdar. On the night of 18 June the two patrols set up an ambush on the Martuba-Giovanni Berta road. By 2000 the two patrols had hidden themselves about two hundred yards from each other south of the road. The first enemy vehicles to appear on the road were two Italian five-ton trucks, each towing a trailer carrying an M 13 tank.

78   TNA, WO/201/813, f. 8.

79   TNA, WO/201/813, ff. 8-9.

80   Playfair, *The Mediterranean*, vol. III, p. 223.

81   TNA, WO/201/813, ff. 198-199.

82   TNA, WO/201/814, ff. 86-89.

83   TNA, WO/201/814, ff. 111-112, 143.

Timpson, who was in command of G1 Patrol, let the first truck pass his position and withheld his fire until R2 Patrol, which was further down the road, opened fire on the first truck. Both trucks were destroyed by the massed fire of automatic weapons. After shooting up the second truck, G1 Patrol went down onto the road and found two dead Italian soldiers in the cab of their vehicle; two others inside of a tank were taken prisoners.

Timpson suspected that at least two more enemy soldiers had escaped north of the road. The tanks were destroyed with time bombs, at which point what Timpson called "a civil war" broke out when G1 and R1 patrols mistook each other for the enemy. Luckily no one hit anything, and the two patrols withdrew separately southward and hid during the daylight hours of 19 June, when they were ordered to return to Siwa.[84] The ambushing of two trucks with trailers carrying two tanks could scarcely have affected the German offensive against the 8th Army; nonetheless, almost every time either the British or the Germans mounted an offensive the 8th Army would order the Long Range Desert Group to attack the enemy's lines of communication.

At the time that Rommel went on the offensive in the Western Desert, Malta was running short of supplies. There was a direct relation between the fighting in the Western Desert and the ease with which a convoy could be run from the eastern Mediterranean to Malta. If the British held Cyrenaica, then R.A.F. aircraft could use airfields in that region to provide air support to the convoy over the greater part of its voyage to Malta. If, however, the British were pushed out of northern Cyrenaica, then enemy aircraft could use the same airfields to attack the convoy. With the German offensive in northwest Cyrenaica at the end of May, a convoy going west to Malta would be open to air attack not only from airfields in Libya but also from those on Crete in Greece, southern Italy, and Sicily. Nonetheless, the British intended to attempt to run a convoy from the eastern Mediterranean to Malta at the beginning of June despite the fact that the enemy controlled the airfields in Cyrenaica.[85] The British planned to reduce the enemy's ability to attack this convoy with aircraft by having the Special Air Service and the Special Boat Section attack a number of enemy airfields in North Africa and on Crete.

It is difficult to tell who formulated the plan for the attacks on the airfields on Crete and in North Africa in support of passing a convoy through to Malta. One authority states that as soon as Stirling returned to Cairo from Benghazi he was

---

84   TNA, WO/201/814, ff. 96-98, 144-145. For another example of this type of operation, see
        TNA, WO/201/814, ff. 136-139.
85   Playfair, *The Mediterranean*, vol. III, p. 299.

called to the office of the Director of Military Operations, where he was told that a convoy was going to be pushed through to Malta in June and asked what the Special Air Service could do to reduce the risks of enemy air attack; and that Stirling's response, the following day, was the scheme to attack a number of airfields in the Western Desert and on Crete.[86] However, the history of the Special Boat Service portrays the planning of the part of the operation that involved airfields on Crete to be almost an *ad hoc* affair.[87] And to add to the confusion, as to the origins of these plans, the Long Range Desert Group was issued an operational instruction by 8th Army headquarters dated 26 May—the day after Stirling reached Siwa from Benghazi—requesting that Prendergast be ready to provide the transport required for the raids to be made by the Special Air Service in the Western Desert in support of the Malta convoy.[88] In any event, no matter who thought up the scheme, it was planned that in Cyrenaica on the night of 13/14 June the Special Air Service would attack three airfields near Benghazi, three around Derna, and one at Barce.[89] On the same night, the Special Boat Section would attack airfields at Kastelli, Timbaki, and Maleme on Crete; while the Special Air Service was to attack the airfield at Heraklion, too, on the island. Stirling had become a collector of special raiding units and had been forming, unknown to the Special Boat Section, a unit for small boat operations within the Special Air Service and under the command of Captain Lord Jellicoe. Needless to say, the Special Boat Section was not very pleased about this, "but to oppose Stirling was like trying to stop a steam-roller with a banana."[90] All these raids were to be carried out by extremely small numbers of men with the objective of disrupting enemy air power in the eastern Mediterranean as much as possible in the middle of June.

To Stirling, the raids on airfields on Crete and in the Western Desert were straightforward operations, with the exception of the attack on the airfields near Derna. These airfields were very important, but the region was a staging point for German forces operating in the Western Desert and therefore full of enemy troops. The problem was one of getting the raiders into the region undiscovered. This was the same area where A Squadron, Middle East Commando had lost all its vehicles to enemy air attack. It was in the course of discussing the difficulties of this operation at General Headquarters, Middle East that Stirling first heard of a unit with a name as meaningless as L Detachment Special Air Service Brigade and

86   Cowles, *Phantom Major*, p. 136.
87   John Lodwick, *The Filibusters* (London: Methuen, 1947), pp. 17-18.
88   TNA, WO/201/813, f. 198.
89   Cowles, *Phantom Major*, pp. 137-138.
90   Lodwick, *Filibusters*, pp. 17-18.

with a mission even more dangerous than that of Stirling's own command. This unit was the Special Interrogation Group, and it was formed by Captain Herbert Buck of the Punjab Regiment. Buck, who spoke German fluently, had been captured near Ain el Gazala and then escaped. While making his way back to the British lines, he acquired a German army hat and badge and soon discovered that he could move through and into various German units with the greatest of ease. After reaching British lines, Buck got permission to set up a sabotage unit of anti-Nazi Germans consisting of one officer and twelve other ranks. Buck recruited an officer from the Scots Guards who spoke fluent German; the twelve other ranks were German Jews who came from Palestine. Each man knew the nature of his new assignment and that if he was captured he would be tortured and killed. In order to achieve greater authenticity, Buck had the intelligence people at General Headquarters, Middle East recruit two anti-Nazi German non-commissioned officers from among German prisoners of war. These two men had served in the French Foreign legion before the war and had been drafted into the German army and, after being "screened" by British intelligence, they were given to Buck. The Special Interrogation Group was cut off totally from the rest of the British army and was intensively trained in the arts of irregular warfare as if they were in the German army. The entire set-up was in fact German from beginning to end. The men of the Special Interrogation Group were also issued with German uniforms, weapons, equipment, and papers. By the end of May the Special Interrogation Group was ready for operations and Stirling was the first man to request their services.[91]

When Stirling and Buck met, the Special Air Service commander wanted the commander of the Special Interrogation Group to supply several German vehicles plus German appearing crews to carry Free French Special Air Service troops, who would be concealed in these vehicles, to the enemy airfields in the region of Derna. Both Buck and Lieutenant Augustine Jordan, who would command the Free French Special Air Service troops on this raid, agreed to Stirling's plan.[92] This plan, however, had three major flaws. First, it was complex and would require the coordination and cooperation of the Long Range Desert Group, the Free French Special Air Service troops, and the Special Interrogation Group. Second, neither the Free French Special Air Service troops nor the Special Air Service troops nor the Special Interrogation Group had conducted a raiding operation of this type

---

91   Cowles, *Phantom Major*, pp. 137-138.
92   *Ibid*, p. 139.

before. And third, the loyalty of the two German non-Jewish members of the Special Interrogation Group had not been tested in combat.

On 8 June R1 Patrol, with four 30 cwt trucks and accompanied by fifteen Free French Special Air Service troops and eleven members of the Special Interrogation Group in four German vehicles, left Siwa to raid three airfields in the region of Derna. The party travelled northwest across the desert for three days. On the morning of 11 June R1 Patrol, after parting from the four German vehicles near Baltet el Zalagh, went into hiding to await the return of the raiders at an agreed upon rendezvous.[93] The Special Interrogation Group and the Free French Special Air Service troops headed towards the three airfields in the region of Derna. The Free French soldiers were hidden in the back of the vehicles under tarpaulin covers, knapsacks, and supplies. Buck, dressed as a German private, drove one of the vehicles. Other members of the Special Interrogation Group either drove the other three vehicles, sat in the cab beside the driver, or were stationed on the roof of the cab serving as lookouts for enemy aircraft—all according to the way in which most Axis convoys were conducted. The movement towards the objective was slow because one of the trucks broke down and had to be towed; moreover no one knew the enemy password for the month of June, and they had to bluff their way past a number of enemy checkpoints. By noon of 13 June the raiders and their vehicles had reached a hiding place four miles from Derna.

After scouting two of the three airfields, it was decided to split the party up into several groups and attack the airfields on the night of 13 June. One truck would carry five Free French soldiers and three members of the Special interrogation Group to an airfield near Martuba, while another truck with a group of ten Free French and three members of the Special Interrogation Group would attack two airfields near Derna. Meanwhile, Buck and several of his men would conduct on their own an operation unrelated to the attacks on the airfields.

After dark, on 13 June, the two groups set off to attack the airfields. When the truck which was carrying the Free French troops on their way to attack the two airfields near Derna was within a hundred yards of the first airfield, the driver of the truck, whose name was Brückner and who was one of the two German non-commissioned officers recruited out of a British prisoner of war camp, stopped the vehicle, got out, and went towards the nearest building, which was a German guardhouse, muttering something about tools and overheated engines. Jordan, the commander of the Free French troops, was in the back of the truck and heard what he thought was a large number of men approaching the vehicle. He looked

---

93   TNA, WO/201/814, ff. 140-142.

out over the tailgate only to be pulled from the truck by a number of Germans. Brückner, the German driver of the truck, had betrayed the unit. As Jordan was being pulled from the truck, a German yelled, "All Frenchmen come out."[94] With this, a Free French Soldier stood up in the back of the truck and threw a grenade, which exploded in the middle of the group of Germans, who had captured Jordan; and in the confusion, the Free French officer escaped. As the Free French soldiers scrambled from the truck, one of them opened fire with a machine-gun that was mounted on the vehicle. One of the Special Interrogation Group soldiers, seeing that the situation was hopeless, threw, in a last act of desperation, a grenade into a pile of ammunition, which blew up destroying the truck. The Free French resisted until they were either killed, wounded, or captured. The only surviving Special Interrogation Group soldier to surrender was executed by the Germans.

Only one other Free French soldier, besides Jordan, escaped. His name was Corporal Bourmont, and he made for the rendezvous with the group, which had been sent to attack the airfield near Martuba. Bourmont linked up with this group; but the next morning they discovered that the meeting place had also been betrayed by Brückner, for it was surrounded by a company of German infantry. The Free French and the Special Interrogation Group soldiers, although heavily out-numbered and with no chance of escape, fought to the death. Aside from Brückner, only Jordan escaped death or capture. After escaping from the Germans Jordan made his way on foot to a rendezvous with Buck which Brückner appears not to have known about. The Free French officer and the British officer decided that they must march south as fast as possible and warn R1 Patrol that the whole operation had been betrayed, although Brückner most likely did not know the location of the hiding place of the Long Range Group Patrol. Buck, Jordan, and R1 Patrol returned to Siwa on 19 June.[95] Based on information obtained from captured German aircrew stationed at the airfields in the Derna region, a theory grew up among some of the British that Brückner had systematically betrayed the raid on the airfields even before the raiders had departed from Siwa.[96] Buck, however, shot down this idea by pointing out that Brückner had neither the knowledge nor the opportunity to betray the attack until he did so at the airfield near Derna.[97] The failure of the raid on the airfields near Derna on 13 June is a classic example of the dangers of using enemy prisoners of war in operations.

---

94   Cowles, *Phantom Major*, p. 144.
95   Cowles, *Phantom Major*, pp. 139-146; Warner, *Special Air Service*, p. 55.
96   TNA, WO/201/727, ff. 20-21.
97   TNA, WO/201/724, ff. 17-19.

Although the raid on the airfields near Derna on the night of 13 June was a failure, the Special Air Service raids at Berca, Benina, and Barce in Cyrenaica that same night met with varying degrees of success. On 11 June S1 Patrol, carrying four Free French Special Air Service Troops under the command of Lieutenant Jaquier, arrived at Cheda bu Maun on their way to attack the airfield at Barce. Two of the patrol's trucks were hidden here, and the other two trucks and the Free French troops went north into the Jebel Akhdar. By the morning of 12 June the party was hiding at the edge of the escarpment near the airfield at Barce, and on the night of 13 June the Free French Special Air Service troops attacked the airfield. The noise they made going through dry grass gave away the approach of the raiders before they could reach the heavily-guarded aircraft parked on the airfield; but during the gunfight with the Germans, Jaquier's men destroyed a bomb dump. When the Free French troops returned to where the two Long Range Desert Group trucks were hidden, they withdrew south to Cheda bu Maun, which was reached on 14 June. After attacking an Italian camp on 15 June, which failed because it was too heavily guarded, S1 Patrol headed back to Siwa, which they reached on 17 June.[98]

On 8 June G2 Patrol under the command of Gurdon left Siwa for the Benghazi region to attack the airfields at Benina and Berca and to blow up the Benghazi-Barce railroad. The force was comprised of twenty members of G2 Patrol and thirteen British and Free French Special Air Service troops carried in seven Long Range Desert Group trucks and Stirling's cut-down Ford station wagon. Just after the force had crossed the Trigh el Abd on 10 June, Stirling's Ford hit a thermos mine and had to be abandoned. A short time later one of the Long Range Desert Group trucks developed "a split brake-down", and it was sent back to Siwa along with another truck. The following day yet another truck hit a thermos mine and had to be abandoned.[99] With the remaining four trucks, the force pushed north and the Special Air Service troops were dropped off near Gasr el Gehesc and G2 Patrol went into hiding.[100]

After leaving G2 Patrol, the Special Air Service troops split into three groups. Stirling, with Corporals Cooper and Seekings, was to attack the airfield at Benina. Mayne, with Corporals Warburton, Bob Lilley, and Storey, was to attack the Berca satellite airfield. And a Free French group led by Captain André Zirnheld was going to assault the main airfield at Berca. After separately making their way on foot to the edge of the three airfields, the three groups of raiders hid throughout

---

98   TNA, WO/201/814, ff. 105-108.
99   TNA, WO/201/814, f. 101.
100   TNA, WO/201/814, ff. 99-101, 103.

the daylight hours of 13 June and then made their way onto the airfields after dark. The R.A.F. had been told not to attack the Benghazi region on 13 June, but at 2315 there was an air raid during which there was heavy anti-aircraft fire and "exceedingly bright flares were dropped." Gurdon, the commander of G2 Patrol, thought that "it was immediately obvious that the success of the whole enterprise had been jeopardized."[101] Nevertheless, Zirnheld and the Free French managed to get onto the main airfield at Berca, destroyed eleven aircraft, and fought a running battle with the airfield's guards, during which Sergeant Brouard was slightly wounded, before withdrawing into the desert and going to the rendezvous with G2 Patrol.[102]

At the Berca satellite airfield Mayne and the three corporals were on the landing ground when R.A.F. bombs began to explode all around them, enemy air raid sirens started going off, and fires and flares lighted up the whole area. The airfields in the Benghazi region had been raided by the Special Air Service so often that the Germans had to make a choice between grouping all their aircraft together in order to closely guard them from ground attack or spreading them out as a protection against air attack and placing two guards on each aircraft. At the Berca satellite field the Germans had the aircraft spread out and two guards on each machine. When the air raid stopped, the German guards discovered Mayne's group on the airfield and a firefight broke out during which the Special Air Service troops blew up a large fuel dump as they retreated into the desert. After the departure of the British, the German guards continued for some time to battle each other.

In the confusion of explosions and gunfire, Mayne and the three corporals lost their way leaving the airfield and ran into, one right after the other, two groups of Germans who were hunting them. During the course of evading these enemy troops, the four British soldiers entered, without knowing it, a large German camp and were hiding in it when daylight came. Mayne then decided to split into two groups of two men each. Corporals Lilley and Warburton hid in a large hedge behind a building that the Germans were using as a headquarters. Warburton lost his nerve and decided to make a run for it, but was gunned down within Lilley's hearing and never seen again. At this point Lilley decided the Germans would find him soon enough "and with this thought in my head I mercifully fell asleep."[103] When Lilley was awakened by German voices all around him, he decided he had to move. It was no use trying to crawl away unseen

---

101   TNA, WO/201/814, f. 102.
102   TNA, WO/201/814, f. 102; Cowles, *Phantom Major*, p. 152.
103   Cowles, *Phantom Major*, p. 153.

so I left all my kit and just stood up and walked. I walked through two miles of escarpment. Men were washing and shaving. Some were queueing up for food, others were cleaning their kit. No one bothered about me, but every minute of the journey I was expecting to be pulled up. However, I was wearing khaki shorts and shirt—and so were most of them—so I suppose I didn't look much different. I walked for a couple of miles beyond the escarpment until I reached the railway line that crosses the Benghazi plain.[104]

Lilley then walked along the road that runs parallel to the railroad and met an Italian soldier who attempted to arrest him. But the British corporal strangled the Italian and continued walking across the Benghazi plain to a Senussi camp ten miles away. It was there that Lilley met Mayne and Corporal Storey. The three British soldiers left the Senussi camp and began walking towards the escarpment where the meeting place with G2 Patrol was located. At dusk a German staff car stopped about fifty yards in front of the three men, who went to ground and prepared to fight it out; but after a time the Germans drove away and the three Britons continued walking towards the rendezvous, which was reached the next day.[105]

Stirling and Corporals Cooper and Seekings attacked the airfield at Benina, which was used by the Germans to repair aircraft. During the daylight hours of 13 June, the three British soldiers hid in the escarpment overlooking the airfield, and after dark they made their way onto the airfield. There were no guards and no wire at the point where Stirling and his two men entered the airfield during the R.A.F. bombing raid. After the British aircraft had left, the three British soldiers placed Lewis with one-hour fuses on the only two aircraft parked on the airfield. Stirling and the two corporals then made their way across the airfield to the repair hangars, which were guarded. Unseen by the sentries, the three Special Air Service troops entered three hangers and placed time bombs on three aircraft, a number of machines for repairing aircraft, and some thirty odd aircraft engines. In the course of the attack, Stirling, Cooper, and Seekings placed more than sixty time bombs on various aircraft, engines, and machines at Benina airfield. Before leaving the airfield, the three British soldiers went to the German guardhouse. With Cooper and Seekings covering him, the commander of the Special Air Service pushed open the door of the guardhouse to find about twenty Germans

104   *Ibid*, p. 154.
105   *Ibid*, pp. 152-155; Marrinan, *Colonel*, pp. 55-67.

inside the building. Sitting at a desk writing was a German officer who looked up when Stirling opened the door. Before the Germans could react, Stirling threw a grenade at the German officer and said in English, "Here catch." As Stirling closed the door, the German officer was seen to catch the grenade and then yell, "*Nein, nein.*"[106] Seconds later there was an explosion in the guardhouse, and then the time bombs began to explode. Stirling and the two corporals left the airfield and started walking towards the rendezvous with G2 Patrol, which was reached at 1200 the next day.

Several miles from the airfield at Benina, Stirling, Cooper, and Seekings looked back at the airfield, which was now a scene of total destruction with fires raging and secondary explosions still taking place. This raid confirmed in Stirling's mind the theory that a few highly trained soldiers could obtain great results by means of stealth and surprise. In fact, Stirling thought that he, Cooper, and Seekings had achieved at Benina airfield a higher degree of destruction of enemy material of all types than a conventional large-scale air bombardment could have done.[107]

On the night of 16 June Stirling suggested to Mayne that the Ulsterman might want to take a look at the destruction at Benina airfield. After looking at the airfield, Mayne said they ought to drive into Benghazi and shoot the place up. Stirling and Mayne were egging each other on as if they were engaged in a huge British public school prank, taking bigger and bigger risks in a situation which, by any standards, was already dangerous enough. They were many miles behind enemy lines, a number of airfields in the region had been attacked in the last few days with varying degrees of success, and now Stirling and Mayne wanted to drive into enemy-held Benghazi along the main road to attack targets within the city. Gurdon, the commander of G2 Patrol, must have thought that this was a mad scheme; nevertheless, and against standing orders, he lent Stirling two Long Range Desert Group trucks for the project, after making him swear to bring them back in one piece.

At 1745 on 16 June, the two loaned Long Range Desert Group trucks left the British hide-out in the escarpment east of Benghazi. One truck was driven by Mayne and contained Stirling, Corporals Cooper, Lilley, Seekings, and Storey, and a member of the Special Interrogation Group, named Karl Kahane. Kahane was a German Jew who had served for twenty years in the German Army before emigrating to Palestine in the 1930's, and he had a catholic knowledge of German military ways and argot. Stirling had borrowed Kahane from the

106   Cowles, *Phantom Major*, p. 150.
107   *Ibid*, pp. 146-151.

Special Interrogation Group for the purpose of bluffing past German road blocks in much the same way that Maclean had done with Italians in Benghazi. The second truck was commanded by Gurdon and manned by seven Long Range Desert Group troops. Shortly after leaving the escarpment, the two trucks parted company. Gurdon went off to mine the Benghazi-Barce railroad with fifty pounds of ammonal that was to be set off by a fifteen pound pressure fuse placed under a railroad tie. This operation was apparently successful, for the next day a huge explosion was heard by the British in the area where the mine had been placed.

The Special Air Service party drove down the main road towards Benghazi with Stirling assuring everybody that there was only a lightly-held Italian checkpoint between them and the city. But within yards of Benina airfield the British encountered a heavily-manned German roadblock. Seven British soldiers wearing British uniforms and riding in a British truck, within yards of an airfield, which they had attacked several nights before, were now confronted by a number of heavily-armed and very suspicious German soldiers. Kahane yelled and swore at a German non-commissioned officer as he approached the truck. The German non-commissioned officer demanded to know the June password, which the British did not know. Kahane answered by saying that they had been at the front for six weeks, gave the May password, and then began to yell that he could not be bothered with such things as keeping up with rear area passwords and did not have the time to argue with "blockheads."[108] But the German non-commissioned officer was not satisfied and continued to approach the British vehicle. When he was about three feet away from Mayne, the Ulsterman picked up the Colt pistol, which was in his lap, and cocked the weapon, which made a metallic click that was followed by several more clicks as the British made more weapons ready to fire. The German must have known that the men in the truck were not Germans or Italians but he also knew that if he made one wrong move he would be the first man on either side to be shot dead. To the German the choice was simple: death or let the British through the roadblock. After a second or two, the German ordered the barrier removed and waved the British truck through the roadblock. After passing through the German roadblock, Mayne drove the truck down the road towards Benghazi. But it was decided not to go into the city, for the British knew that the Germans would phone ahead giving warning of their approach. After going about four miles this suspicion was confirmed when the British encountered a number of Italian troops deployed on the road with their rifles pointing at the oncoming British truck. Driving the truck as fast as it would go, Mayne headed right for the

---

108   *Ibid*, p. 158.

Italians, who jumped off the road to escape being run down. For the next twenty minutes the British truck moved down the road while the Special Air Service troops attacked a fuel storage tank, enemy transport, a truck stop, and an enemy encampment with gunfire and short fused time bombs.

After turning off the road and heading across country towards the cover of Wadi Qattara, a German truck was seen attempting to reach the entrance of the wadi before the British did to cut off their escape. A mad race for the entrance of the wadi ensued, which Mayne won by a hair. They passed through the wadi and while moving across country to G2 Patrol's hiding place in the escarpment, Corporal Lilley suddenly yelled from the rear of the truck, "Hop it, quick. A fuse is burning!"[109] Without even stopping the vehicle, the seven Special Air troops bailed out, and a second or so later the truck blew up. After the loss of the truck, Stirling's party set off on foot for the rendezvous with G2 Patrol, which was reached on the afternoon of 18 June. On the return trip to Siwa, which was reached on 21 June, Stirling's Ford station wagon was recovered and repaired as was one of G2 Patrol's trucks that had been abandoned on the way out.[110]

Four airfields on the island of Crete were raided by the Special Air Service and the Special Boat Section at the same time as attacks were made by the Special Air Service on enemy airfields in northern Cyrenaica. Captain George Duncan with two other ranks of the Special Boat Section landed near Cape Trikala in Crete and attacked the airfield at Kastelli, destroying eight aircraft, six trucks, and thirteen dumps of various types. Another Special Boat Section party landed on Crete to attack the airfield at Timbaki, only to find the place abandoned. A third attack was to be carried out by the Special Boat Section on the airfield at Maleme, but the place was found to be too closely guarded and the operation was abandoned; however, eight New Zealanders who had been evading capture ever since the fall of Crete were brought off the island by the Special Boat Section raiding party. A Special Air Service group comprised of Jellicoe, Commandant Bergé, three French other ranks, and Lieutenant Costis, who was a Greek, attacked the airfield at Heraklion, which was a very difficult target. Twenty-one aircraft, four trucks, and a fuel dump were destroyed by the Special Air Service at Heraklion; but the four Free French soldiers, who were hiding while Jellicoe and Costis went into a village looking for an Allied agent, were betrayed and either killed or captured by

---

109   Some accounts say that it was Seekings or Cooper who gave the warning, but the two corporals have never said who gave the warning to bail out of the truck. Warner, *Special Air Service*, p. 57.

110   Cowles, *Phantom Major*, pp. 165-167; TNA, WO/201/814, ff. 102-103; Marrinan, *Colonel*, pp. 57-59.

the Germans. Several days later Jellicoe and Costis were picked up by the Royal Navy on the south coast of Crete.[111]

Stirling's June 1941 offensive against enemy airfields in Cyrenaica and Crete resulted in the destruction of forty-five aircraft, around fifteen supply dumps, thirty or so aircraft engines, three repair hangars and a number of vehicles. An unknown number of enemy troops were either killed or wounded during these raids, but at a cost of one British and eighteen Free French Special Air Service troops and five Special Interrogation Group troops who were either killed or captured. In terms of men killed and destruction of enemy material, Stirling was the victor. But the strategic objective of these raids was to assist the passing of a convoy from the eastern Mediterranean to Malta by systematically disrupting the enemy's air forces; however, of the seventeen ships in the convoy, not one reached Malta, mostly owing to attacks by enemy aircraft.[112]

During the first six months of 1942 there was bitter fighting between the 8th Army and the German and Italian forces in the Western Desert, but it was clear that neither the 8th Army nor General Headquarters, Middle East in Cairo had an overall scheme or plan for the employment of the Long Range Desert Group. In fact, none of the British commanders in the Middle East and the Western Desert, with the exception of Wavell, had any knowledge of or interest in irregular warfare or operations behind enemy lines. It appears that the Long Range Desert Group was employed on tasks because the unit existed and that Stirling was permitted to operate because of the great damage his unit inflicted on the enemy with no risk to the British. With the exception of the road watch at Marble Arch and of some of the operations with the Special Air Service, during the first half of 1942, the Long Range Desert Group did a multitude of tasks that in no way affected the outcome of the campaign. With the Long Range Desert Group the British had the means to go anywhere in the Libyan Desert. This great advantage was forfeited by using the Long Range Desert Group to carry agents into the Jebel Akhdar, to conduct watches on roads in Cyrenaica, which the enemy never used, and to ambush an enemy vehicle here and then another one there in the vain hope that this type of thing would slow Rommel down. Many British commanders did not see that while raids could and did inflict damage on the enemy, they very rarely, except by their cumulative effects, changed the strategic course of a campaign or a war. Many of the British never learned that wars cannot be won on the cheap.

---

111   Cowles, *Phantom Major*, pp. 162-165; Lodwick, *Filibusters*, pp. 18-21.

112   S.W. Roskill, *White Ensign: The British Navy at War, 1939-1945* (Annapolis, Md.: S. Naval Institute, 1966), p. 219.

Stirling believed that a modern army was totally dependent on machines, fuel, and a multitude of other items. His concept of attacking these targets, if it had been put into effect on a large scale, would have forced, through its cumulative effect, the enemy to fight on two fronts: one against the 8th Army and the other to protect his supply lines. By the end of June, the Special Air Service had proved that, with a very few specially-trained and well-led men, it could deal out some heavy blows indeed to the enemy. Not counting vehicles, buildings, or supply dumps, the Special Air Service had, in its short history, by the end of June 1942, destroyed, by their reckoning, a hundred and forty-three aircraft.[113] In the first six months of 1942 the Long Range Desert Group should have been employed solely on strategic reconnaissance missions, such as the road watch at Marble Arch.[114] In conjunction with an enlarged Special Air Service and possibly with the Free French in Chad, they could also have been sent to carry the war to the city limits of Tripoli, and beyond, to the border of Tunisia. In other words, during the first half of 1942, the Long Range Desert Group and the Special Air Service should have been used to hit hard and deep in the enemy's rear, especially at his supply lines in Tripolitania.

---

113   Cowles, *Phantom Major*, p. 166.

114   Information gathered by such missions was deemed to be "of the utmost value" to the leadership of the Eighth Army.

8

To El Alamein

"Battles are won by slaughter and maneuver. The greater the general, the more he contributes in maneuver, the less he demands in slaughter."
—*Winston Churchill, 1923*

21 June 1942, the day Stirling returned to Siwa after the raids on the Benghazi airfields, was a day of British defeat. The war in the Western Desert had again changed course. The Germans had captured Tobruk, and the 8th Army began to retreat into Egypt. This retreat ended with the British establishing a continuous line of unbreachable defenses from the Qattara Depression in the south running north to a little known railway station at El Alamein on the coast of the Mediterranean. Because of the Qattara Depression, this was the only position between Rommel's forces and the Nile where mechanized units could not force an abandonment simply by turning the enemy's southern flank. For months the armies of the Axis and the British Commonwealth and Empire fought a series of bloody battles of attrition, battles in which the Germans and the Italians were shattered. The fighting at El Alamein was different from any previous battles in the Western desert, for it was not a battle of maneuver but was rather similar to the great battles on the Western Front during the First World War.

The British withdrawal into Egypt in June of 1942 forced the Long Range Desert Group and the Special Air Service to leave Siwa. When the Long Range Desert Group departed from Siwa, it was decided to divide the unit into two groups. A squadron would be based at Kufra, and the rest of the unit would operate from northern Egypt. To carry out this new deployment, the movements of various patrols were complex. S2 Patrol, which was manning the road watch at Marble Arch, would be relieved by Y1 Patrol and then go to Kufra. R1 Patrol left Siwa on 28 June to relieve Y1 Patrol, which was then to follow S2 Patrol and go to Kufra.

R2 and T2 Patrols went directly south across the sand sea to Kufra by way of Cairo and Kharga. S1, G1, G2, and Y2 Patrols went to the coast of the Mediterranean behind the El Alamein line by way of Qara. T1 Patrol was sent to Cairo and then joined the headquarters unit of the Long Range Desert Group at Fayoum. Giving up the base at Siwa had many disadvantages. Siwa was well placed to mount patrols into northern Libya. Now, Long Range Desert Group patrols would either have to pass through the El Alamein line, which would shortly become impossible, or through the Qattara Depression, which was difficult and later it, too, would become impossible. This left only two routes into northern Libya: through the sand sea and desert south of the Qattara Depression, or from distant Kufra far to the south.[1]

On 21 July General Headquarters, Middle East ordered the Long Range Desert Group to end the road watch at Marble Arch. The reason for this action was that the enemy were now receiving most of their supplies through the ports of Benghazi and Tobruk, which were many miles east of Marble Arch. The road watch at Marble Arch had been maintained continuously for four and a half months with only one or two breaks of several hours each. Being continuous, the road watch had enabled the intelligence staff at General Headquarters, Middle East to figure out periods of enemy activity and inactivity and as well as a double check on *Ultra*.

The last patrol to carry out the road watch at Marble Arch was T2 under the command of Lieutenant J.E. Crisp. On 21 July Crisp received by radio orders to discontinue the road watch and to "Beat up" traffic on the coast road west of Nofilia.[2] The next night T2 Patrol set up an ambush on the coast road. Crisp, accompanied by one man, then went up the road from the ambush site some fifty yards to attempt to stop an approaching vehicle with fire from a submachine gun so as not to give away the ambush site. When the approaching vehicle neared Crisp, the British officer saw that it was preceded by a motorcyclist. Crisp shot the motorcyclist dead. The truck, which was towing a four-wheeled trailer attempted to stop but passed the point where T2 Patrol had orders to open fire on vehicles. The truck stopped when it was fired at by the T2 Patrol's automatic weapons; and when the shooting stopped Crisp found one Italian soldier had been killed, two others mortally wounded, and one soldier and a civilian had been slightly wounded. The two slightly wounded men were given first aid, the civilian was left on the coast road, and the soldier taken prisoner. The truck and the trailer blew up

---

1   TNA, WO/201/814, f. 3.
2   TNA, WO/201/813, f. 4.

after being set on fire. Because of a shortage of fuel, T2 Patrol headed for Kufra, which was reached on 27 July.[3]

The intelligence staff at General Headquarters, Middle East wanted the Long Range Desert Group to establish a road watch on the coast road east of Tobruk. On 20 July Lloyd Owen, the commander of Y1 Patrol, received operational instructions ordering him to go to the coast road east of Tobruk and, if possible, find a site for the road watch. If he could establish a road watch, Y1 Patrol would be relieved within ten days after setting it up. On 22 July Y1 Patrol left Kufra on the long trip north to the coast. By 26 July Y1 Patrol arrived at Etla, which is north of the Jalo-Jarabub track and where the Long Range Desert Group had hidden a fuel dump. After picking up additional fuel Y1 Patrol went northeast towards the coast road east of Tobruk, which they reached the next day.

The region was absolutely flat and there was no cover near the coast road in which to set up a road watch. Lloyd Owen hated the place and later wrote of it, "Everything seemed a little dead; almost petrified. The litter of battle remained in [the] area .... We sensed something quite evil in the atmosphere; the world around us had ceased to live."[4] The next day Y1 Patrol looked, without success, for a site for a road watch farther east, but again the desert provided no cover and it was strewn with the remains of war. Because of the lack of cover, it proved impossible to establish a road watch on the coast road east of Tobruk: for the point of a road watch is to be able to observe the enemy without being seen.

On 29 July Y1 Patrol received orders to search an area thirty-five miles south of Tobruk for the crew of a downed R.A.F. aircraft. The patrol did not find either the aircraft, or the crew, but it did find Private Ithar Khan of the 32nd Punjab Regiment, who had escaped from Tobruk. On 31 July Y1 Patrol was ordered to Fayoum. Lloyd Owen headed for Qara at the edge of the Qattara Depression and crossed that supposedly impassable region with almost no trouble. The only difficulty encountered was when four trucks began racing each other and got bogged down in a salt marsh that Lloyd Owen entered "for pure devilment because it looked so very flat."[5] In fact, Lloyd Owen found the going so good in the Qattara Depression that he thought he could outflank the El Alamein line by leading an armored brigade across it; however, no one would pay any attention to this suggestion. Y1 Patrol arrived at Fayoum on 4 August.[6]

---

3   TNA, WO/201/814, ff. 176-177, 212-213.

4   David Lloyd Owen, *The Desert My Dwelling Place* (London: Cassell, 1957), p. 217.

5   *Ibid*, p. 219.

6   *Ibid.*, pp. 216-220; TNA, WO/201/814, ff. 216-218.

During July and August the patrols of the Long Range Desert Group based at Kufra undertook for the most part long trips to the north carrying intelligence officers, agents, and the like to the Jebel Akhdar. These trips were extremely difficult and were carried out in the summer heat. For example, S2 Patrol commanded by Lieutenant Croucher left Kufra on 11 July for northern Cyrenaica. S2 Patrol's mission was to transport Melot and an Arab agent to the Jebel Akhdar and to pick up a Lieutenant Losco and two other men and return to Kufra. R2 Patrol's task was to pick up twenty men led by Peniakoff in the Jebel Akhdar and return with them to Kufra. On 16 July R2 and S2 Patrols parted company south of the Jebel Akhdar. R2 Patrol with four trucks, plus two more trucks from S2 Patrol, met Peniakoff and his people that same day at Wadi El Melem. At dusk on 17 July R2 Patrol began the trip back to Kufra carrying two British officers and two other ranks, one Libyan Arab Force officer and nineteen men, plus six Libyan civilians. R2 Patrol arrived back at Kufra on 21 July, having travelled fourteen hundred and fifty miles, consumed fifty jerrycans of fuel at an average rate of 6.4 gallons per mile, and endured fourteen blow-outs.[7] Olivey and S2 Patrol went with three trucks to meet Losco and his party, but they were not at the appointed rendezvous. On 18 July Melot and the Arab agent went off, without success, to look for the missing men. Finally, on 20 August Olivey found Losco by simply driving his trucks all over the region until Losco saw one of the vehicles and stopped it. After finding Losco, and his party of two, S2 Patrol returned to Kufra on 24 July. Olivey's only comment on the operation was: "*Condition of Troops*: - Very Desert tyred, and need a rest."[8]

In July the Indian Long Range Squadron arrived in Egypt from Syria. This squadron was a unit of the Indian Army which was similar to the Long Range Desert Group in organization, equipment and mission. Until the retreat by the 8th Army to El Alamein, the Indian Long Range Squadron had been a part of the 9th Army stationed in Syria. While the Indian Long Range Squadron did not have the extensive combat experience that the Long Range Desert Group had, a number of its officers and men had served with the Long Range Desert Group on operations in the Libyan Desert. From the time of the unit's arrival in Egypt until the defeat of the Axis forces at El Alamein, the mission of the Indian Long Range Squadron was to patrol the southwest approaches to Cairo and to give warning of, or prevent, any Axis forces attempting to reach the Nile valley by passing through the Qattara Depression or through the desert south of that area.[9] This was a boring

---

7   TNA, WO/201/814, ff. 206, 209-211.
8   TNA, WO/201/814, ff. 207-208.
9   TNA, WO/218/95, *passim*.

but necessary task because it was known that the Germans now had the capability to carry out long-range desert operations.

In the spring of 1942 the Germans at Jalo organized a unit called "Sonderkommando Almasy" with six small patrols for long-range desert work. Almasy, whose full name was Ladislaus Edouard de Almasy, had made a number of trips into the Egyptian desert before the war and was most likely the only Hungarian to have visited Uweinat. Working for the Germans, Almasy lead a party from Jalo across the desert to Asyut, and back, dropping off two German spies, who then made their way to Cairo, before being caught by the British. This is the only known operation undertaken by Almasy's unit; however, the threat was there and it had to be guarded against.[10] There was also a small chance that enemy units, other than Almasy's, might attempt to reach the Nile Valley, or Cairo, by passing south of the Qattara Depression. All of these threats had to be guarded against in the summer of 1942, and sending the Indian Long Range Squadron to Egypt freed the Long Range Desert Group from this task.

Those patrols of the Long Range Desert Group that were not based at Kufra during July and August were deployed in support of the Special Air Service, which was still conducting raids behind enemy lines. The role of the Long Range Desert Group patrols, when not actually conducting raids, was in fact to logistically support the Special Air Service, which had begun to obtain its own transport, and to provide skilled navigators as well as radio operators.[11]

As the Axis forces fought their way into Egypt, Stirling, after his return to Siwa from the raids on the Benghazi airfields, went to Cairo. Although the plan was to hold the enemy at the El Alamein line, when Stirling arrived in Cairo he found the place to be in absolute panic; official papers were being burned and everybody was preparing to depart. During a wild and confused week, working out of his brother's flat across the street from the British Embassy, Stirling seized the opportunity of the great panic to assemble a force of about a hundred Special Air Service troops, twenty three-ton trucks, and fifteen jeeps. These vehicles were quickly converted to desert use. American jeeps were new to the Western Desert and Stirling quickly saw that they were just what the Special Air Service needed. Jeeps had four-wheel drive; they were "fast, maneuverable, inconspicuous and uncomfortable…" and Stirling gave them great firepower.[12] Four Vickers K machine-guns in pairs were mounted on each jeep. These guns were designed for use in aircraft, could

---

10   W.B. Kennedy Shaw, *Long Range Desert Group* (London: Collins, 1945), pp. 168-172.

11   TNA, WO/201/814, f. 177.

12   Philip Warner, *The Special Air Service* (London: William Kimber, 1980), p. 59.

be electronically run, and had an average rate of fire of twelve hundred rounds per minute. Later Stirling greatly increased the firepower of these jeeps by mounting an American .50 Browning machine-gun on each vehicle. An aircraft parked on an airfield or a truck on the road taken under fire by one of the Special Air Service jeeps would be cut to bits in a matter of seconds. By acquiring trucks and jeeps, Stirling had made the Special Air Service, in essence, into a self-contained mobile force.[13]

The advance of the Axis forces towards El Alamein greatly weakened the morale of the British in Cairo, but it had a different effect on Stirling and the Special Air Service. Stirling used the crisis of the enemy's advance into Egypt not only to obtain more equipment, such as vehicles, but also to change his tactics. Ever since its conception, the main tactic of the Special Air Service had been to be carried to the target by the Long Range Desert Group and then to conduct, during the moonless period, a number of small-scale raids against targets of great value to the enemy, such as aircraft parked on airfields. Now Stirling intended to continuously maintain a base behind enemy lines and to subject the enemy to an endless series of small raids.[14] This concept, although on a much smaller scale, was very similar to Orde Wingate's second long-range penetration operation in Burma but with a major difference — unlike Wingate's Burma operation, Stirling's base moved around according to the demands of circumstances.

On 30 June operational instructions were issued to the commanders of G1 and Y2 Patrols to infiltrate through the El Alamein line and to attack enemy supply vehicles behind enemy lines.[15] Y2 Patrol, under the command of Hunter, successfully passed through the British and enemy positions on the El Alamein line with almost no problems, except for some ill-aimed artillery and machine-gun fire. Hunter planned to begin attacks on enemy vehicles on 3 July, but on that day he received orders by radio to proceed to Qaret Tartura and to await the arrival of G1 Patrol and the Special Air Service. G1 Patrol, commanded by Timpson, equally attempted to pass through the El Alamein positions at the same time as Y2 Patrol; however, it encountered such heavy fire from what appeared to be a British-held position so that Timpson decided to reach the enemy's rear area by crossing the Qattara Depression. Y2 Patrol crossed the depression by running west

---

13   Virginia Cowles, *The Phantom Major* (London: Collins, 1958), pp. 167-168; Warner, *Special Air Service* pp. 58-59.

14   University of London, King's College Centre For Military Archives, McLeod Papers, Memorandum by Colonel David Stirling, DSO, CBE, of the origins of the Special Air Service Regiment, pp. 6-7.

15   TNA, WO/201/814, ff. 186-187.

to Qara. Timpson also received a change in his orders and went to Qaret Tartura to meet the Special Air Service and G2 Patrol, which arrived on 6 July.[16] G2 Patrol and a number of Special Air Service vehicles had passed through the El Alamein positions without any problems. They then drove along the northern edge of the Qattara Depression, turned north, and arrived without incident at Qaret Tartura to meet G1 and Y2 Patrols.

Before Stirling left Cairo, Auchinleck's chief-of-staff had briefed him on the immediate British plans and intentions. This officer informed Stirling that the 8th Army was to go on the offensive during July with the objective of driving the enemy out of Egypt. In his operational report, Timpson stated,

> Major STIRLING was under the impression that the enemy was about to be forced to withdraw, in fact to be driven out of EGYPT, and his general plan was to attack enemy L.G.'s and communications first in the DABA and FUKA area, and to move our attacks gradually on objectives further West, as their aircraft were withdrawn westward. At the same time enemy communications were to be attacked, in order to precipitate a state of panic.[17]

What in fact happened during July along the El Alamein line was at best a series of limited British attacks that never came close to driving the enemy out of Egypt. Nobody informed Stirling, however, of the situation at El Alamein during July and there is no telling what his plan of operations would have been if he had any idea that a general British offensive would not take place for several months. As it was Stirling went ahead with his plan to carry out a series of raids on airfields at Fuka, Bagush, Sidi Barrani, and El Daba. During the morning of 7 July the Special Air Service troops were divided into three groups, each assigned to a Long Range Desert Group patrol. All three parties then departed from Qaret Tartura to move closer to their targets.[18]

Timpson, with G1 Patrol, had the mission of taking two parties of Special Air Service troops under the command of Captain Bernard Schott and Peter Warr to attack two airfields a few miles east of Sidi Barrani. G1 Patrol, with five Long Range Desert Group trucks and a Special Air Service three-ton truck and a jeep, headed northwest and that night dropped the two parties of Special Air Service troops off about four miles from their target. Two guardsmen were also left at a

---

16   TNA, WO/201/814, ff. 188, 190-191.
17   TNA, WO/201/814, f. 191.
18   Cowles, *Phantom Major*, p. 174.

watering point on the British-built water pipeline to see if the enemy was using it. Then Timpson went inland and hid his vehicle from enemy aircraft. The next night Timpson picked up the two men left at the watering point and Schott's troops but could not find Warr's party and before daylight had to move inland and again hide from searching enemy aircraft. For the next three nights G1 Patrol would hide during the day from aircraft and at night hunted for Warr's party. On the third night they finally found the missing Special Air Service troops. Both attacks on the airfields failed because the enemy only used them during the day, landing and unloading aircraft, which flew in from the west and then taking off again. The supplies brought in by these aircraft were removed from the airfields each day by the enemy.

While looking for Warr's group, Timpson received orders to attack enemy vehicles on the coast road. Operating near the coast where the two armies had fought back and forth was not very healthy. Every member of the patrol had desert sores that would not heal, and by the end of the patrol there were three cases of suspected dysentery, one of sand fly fever, and Patrol Sergeant Fraser had such a bad case of jaundice that he had to be evacuated to Cairo. When operating in the deep desert, patrols usually did not have this high rate of sickness because the region was clean; but along the coast road where there was the trash produced by two armies fighting back and forth over the same ground, the sickness rate in a patrol often would shoot up.[19] Timpson, not finding any enemy vehicles moving at night on the coast road between Sidi Barrani and Mersa Matruh, and with his men becoming sick, blew up the British water pipeline, which was found to be still working. He then returned, as ordered, to Fayoum, by way of Qara and the Qattara Depression, arriving at the Long Range Desert Group's headquarters on 21 July. G1 Patrol's trip was a difficult one because of health problems and enemy aircraft and did not accomplish much.[20]

At 0830 on 7 July G2 and Y2 Patrols with Stirling, Mayne, and a number of Special Air Service troops and vehicles left Qaret Tartura to attack enemy airfields and the coast road. After it was decided that Qaret Hiremas was to be the new rendezvous, Y2 Patrol with a party of Special Air Service troops parted company with the main body. Y2 Patrol headed for El Daba, to attack airfields there, while G2 Patrol with Stirling, Mayne, and other Special Air Service troops

---

19   For medical problems of the Long Range Desert Group, see Imperial War Museum, David Lloyd Owen's Collection of Long Range Desert Group Papers, 4/3 The Papers of Dr. R.P. Lawson.

20   TNA, WO/201/814, ff. 191-192; Michael Crichton-Stuart, *G Patrol* (London: William Kimber, 1958), pp. 158-159.

proceeded towards the escarpment overlooking Fuka. While driving towards Fuka, G2 Patrol and the Special Air Service saw a fast moving column of light armored vehicles. Nobody could figure out the nationality of this force because it appeared to be made up of a mixture of British and German vehicles. Stirling, however, was convinced that it was a British "Jock" column, which enraged him because it indicated that 8th Army and/or General Headquarters, Middle East had failed to coordinate their actions with his plans. A Jock column was a force made up of light armored vehicles whose task was to make rapid and deep penetrations into enemy rear areas, usually with the objective of drawing attention from some other part of the battlefield. If this force was indeed a Jock column, then the enemy in the Fuka region would be on their guard, making the work that night of G2 Patrol and the Special Air Service even more difficult.[21]

G2 Patrol and the Special Air Service party reached the escarpment overlooking Fuka at 2000, which gave G2 Patrol and the three Special Air Service groups, who were going to attack the airfields near that place, a few minutes to look over the region before dark. At this point the movements of the group became very complex because it split into six separate units all doing different tasks. The first to leave the escarpment were Stirling, Mayne, and nine other Special Air Service troops with Stirling's Ford station wagon, a jeep, and a three-ton truck. This group drove down to the coast road and then headed west towards the airfield at Bagush, which is eighteen miles from Fuka. The airfield at Bagush is just off the coast road, and about a mile east of it the three British vehicles pulled off the road and Mayne set off on foot with five men to attack the airfield with time bombs while Stirling with four men and three vehicles set up a block on the coast road. Stirling gave Mayne a half hour head start then he placed his vehicles in ambush positions just off the coast road and rolled several boulders into the middle of the road. The four British soldiers then waited for enemy vehicles to appear, but none did.

At 0135 an explosion at Bagush airfield was seen and heard by Stirling and his men at the roadblock, and over the next forty minutes there was a series of twenty-one explosions at the airfield. About an hour after the first explosion, Mayne's party joined Stirling at the roadblock. The Ulsterman was enraged because only twenty-two of his time bombs had exploded although he and his group had got onto and off the well-guarded airfield unseen and placed time bombs on forty aircraft. Later Mayne discovered that the fuses were wet because they had been placed in the Lewis bombs twenty-four hours before the operation instead of just before the attack, which was the usual method of arming bombs.

---

21   Cowles, *Phantom Major*, p. 175.

Stirling and Mayne concluded, from the lack of traffic on the coast road and the alertness of the guards at the airfield, that the column of armored vehicles that they had seen the afternoon before was in fact a British Jock column. After talking the situation over, Stirling and Mayne decided to attack the airfield at Bagush a second time that night. The truck with five troops was sent off to a point behind the airfield in the desert to be met later. Stirling drove his station wagon to the edge of the airfield followed by Mayne in the jeep. Both vehicles were armed with four twin Vickers K machine-guns. The plan was to drive around the perimeter of the airfield firing the eight machine-guns broadside into the remaining undestroyed aircraft. The four gunners were ordered to fire low and at the fuel tanks of the enemy aircraft.

The attack was over in five minutes. The two British vehicles drove onto the airfield, and the eight Vickers K machine-guns opened fire with a roar. By the light of burning aircraft, the two British vehicles drove around three sides of the airfield and shot up six clusters of aircraft. Each group of aircraft contained some machines that had been destroyed by time bombs and other that were undamaged. The enemy appeared to be taken completely by surprise, for there was no return fire until the British were leaving the airfield and heading out into the desert. This second attack on the airfield caused huge fires and explosions that were seen as far as eighteen miles away. By time bomb and gun, thirty-eight aircraft were destroyed that night at the airfield at Bagush, bringing the total number of enemy aircraft destroyed to date by the Special Air Service to one hundred and eighty.

After meeting the truck sent ahead earlier into the desert, the British drove south into the desert as fast as they could in an attempt to reach the escarpment and cover from air attack before daylight. But when daylight came, the three British vehicles were in an area of the desert which was flat and totally devoid of any cover. The escarpment could be seen with field glasses some fifteen miles ahead. There was nothing the British could do but drive there as quickly as possible and hope they were not caught by enemy aircraft. Within five miles of the escarpment, however, the truck had a blow-out, which took ten minutes to fix. Then, just as Mayne, who was in the lead in the jeep, neared the escarpment, three Italian aircraft appeared— one Ghiblis and two CR 24 fighters. The Ghiblis ineffectually attacked Stirling and his station wagon with bombs and gunfire when they were about half-a-mile from the escarpment, while the two fighter aircraft attacked and destroyed with gunfire the truck, which was some distance from Stirling and whose crew had already bailed out. Before the fighters could attack Stirling, he picked up the crew of the truck and made it to a small conical hill known as a "pimple." When the enemy aircraft banked and dove towards Stirling, he drove the station wagon around the other side of the small hill. Stirling effectively repeated this tactic four times, but he knew he could not keep it up. He therefore drove like mad towards three or four boulders that appeared to form a semi-circle at the top of the escarpment. The station wagon made it to the top of the escarpment before the two fighters could effectively attack it, but the vehicle then had to be abandoned because there was a drop of twenty feet between the top of the escarpment and the boulders. As Stirling and his men ran for cover, the station wagon was destroyed by the two enemy aircraft, which then flew away. The only vehicle left was the jeep, which Mayne had hidden in the mouth of a cave. After a breakfast of biscuits, chocolate, and whiskey followed by a nap, the group headed for the rendezvous, which was about thirty miles away.[22]

When Stirling and Mayne left the escarpment overlooking Fuka on the night of 7 July, G2 Patrol, with six trucks carrying a number of British and Free French Special Air Service troops, followed. Stirling and his group then headed for their target at Bagush, and G2 Patrol made for Fuka. As the patrol drove towards Fuka, four of the trucks, some of which had been malfunctioning all day, were sent to the rendezvous at Qaret Hiremas under the command of Sergeant Stocker, the patrol navigator. Gurdon, with two trucks carrying the Special Air Service troops, by-passed a motor pool and got around a minefield before dropping the Special Air Service troops off near two airfields at Fuka. The Special Air Service troops split into three groups: two groups under the command of Fraser and Jordan were to attack the main airfield, while a third party was to attack a satellite airfield. Jordan's group was challenged by an Italian sentry, but managed to get by him and to place time bombs with ten minute fuses on eight Messerschmitt Me 109F aircraft before the alarm was sounded. The enemy then started shooting off flares and firing automatic weapons every which way. Jordan's party was forced to withdraw, as was Fraser's unit which had also managed to get onto the airfield. When the flares were set off and gunfire was heard from the main Fuka airfield, the Special Air Service troops who were attacking the satellite airfield were also forced to withdraw because absolute pandemonium broke loose at both airfields, which were well defended.

As the Special Air Service raiders were making their way onto the airfields, Gurdon with his two trucks drove west to a point where the railroad crossed the coast road and then waited off the road. At 0130 Gurdon began heading east on the coast and attacked with gunfire and bombs a motor pool; the British estimated

---

22   *Ibid*, pp. 174-182; Patrick Marrinan, *Colonel Paddy* (Dungannon, Ireland: The Ulster Press, 1968), pp. 63-64.

that some thirty vehicles were destroyed there. Then a large tanker truck was destroyed by gunfire, and next an enemy camp was taken under fire. Throughout these attacks Gurdon encountered no opposition. After shooting up the camp, Gurdon headed out into the desert, picked up the three groups of Special Air Service troops and drove south until just before daylight, when the two trucks were hidden from enemy aircraft. Gurdon remained in hiding until the hottest part of the day, which was the most difficult time for aircraft to see things on the surface of the desert, then made his way to the rendezvous at Qaret Hiremas where he met Stirling's party and the four other trucks of G2 Patrol.[23]

Y2 Patrol, with four trucks, was to carry a part of French Special Air Service troops under the command of Jellicoe and Zirnheld to raid the airfields at El Daba. These orders were changed, however, when information was received that the airfields were not being used by the enemy. Y2 Patrol and the Special Air Service troops were ordered to attack traffic on the coast road between Fuka and Galal. After dark, Y2 Patrol set up an ambush on the coast road, but no vehicles appeared. Zirnheld was luckier. He and three Free French Special Air Service troops walked east down the coast road and discovered a truck and an aircraft tractor with a trailer parked on the side of the road. Three Germans were taken prisoner by Zirnheld's force and the vehicles were destroyed by short fused time bombs. Y2 Patrol then went to Qaret Hiremas without incident.[24]

Just before dark on 9 July, an Italian aircraft flew over the hide-out at Qaret Hiremas. Gunfire was exchanged between the aircraft and one of the Long Range Desert Group trucks, with no damage to either side; but as a result the whole group had to move to a new hide-out. On the night of 9/10 July they moved their base thirty miles east to an escarpment at Bir el Quseir that was about fifty feet high and several miles long and provided good cover from enemy aircraft. The group's only activity the following day was to throw a party.[25]

During the next two days Stirling wanted to mount five raids against three airfields near Fuka and two at El Daba. The attacks on the airfields at El Daba were undertaken because Stirling had learned from prisoners that, contrary to information received earlier, the airfields were in fact used by the enemy. Y2 Patrol, along with three groups of Special Air Service troops under the command of Mayne, Jordan, and Fraser, were sent to attack the three airfields near Fuka.

---

23   Cowles, *Phantom Major*, pp. 174, 183-184; Crichton-Stuart, *G Patrol*, pp. 156-157; TNA, CAB/44/151, f. 159; WO/201/814, ff. 179-180.

24   TNA, WO/201/814, f. 188; Cowles, *Phantom Major*, p. 184.

25   *Ibid*, p. 185.

Mayne's force got onto the airfield and destroyed fifteen aircraft with time bombs, and Jordan's men got another seven aircraft. However, when Fraser, with a jeep armed with two twin Vickers K machine-guns, attempted to shoot up another airfield near Fuka in much the same way as Stirling and Mayne had done at the Bagush airfield, the attack failed when the jeep was driven into a split trench. By the time the vehicle was freed from the trench, the enemy was alerted, flares were being set off, and automatic weapons were being fired in all directions.

After picking up the Special Air Service troops, Y2 Patrol was fired at while driving near the coast road by some infantry, who were driven away by the patrol's automatic weapons. Soon afterwards the patrol destroyed with gunfire three aircraft parked in a dispersal area of an airfield; but before more targets could be attacked, one truck fell into a hole and came to a sudden stop and the truck behind it crashed into it, smashing its radiator and damaging its engine. It took ten minutes to free the truck in the hole, and the one with the damaged engine had to be abandoned. Y2 Patrol then returned to Bir el Quseir. The next day Y2 Patrol was ordered to return to the Long Range Desert Group's headquarters.[26]

On 11 July at 1630 four G2 Patrol trucks under the command of Gurdon, along with a party of Special Air Service troops and a three-ton truck, left to attack the following night two airfields near El Daba. In the late afternoon of 12 July Gurdon's truck, which was leading the others, passed through a gap in a long sand dune and moved forward about four hundred yards into open ground and stopped. The guards officer then waved the second truck in the column, which was the navigator's truck to come alongside of his own vehicle so he could confer with the navigator. The other three trucks deployed under cover of the northern edge of the sand dune. At 1715 three Italian aircraft approached from the west. Gurdon waved to them, attempting to appear to be a friendly force, but one of them cleared his guns and began to bank and dive on the two British trucks in the open. Gurdon's truck would not start, and he ordered his driver and gunner to take cover. Gurdon got on board the navigator's truck, which then attempted to escape from the attacking aircraft by driving very fast and making "erratic swings."[27] But it was no use, for the attacking aircraft, only twenty feet off the ground and at a range of about eighty feet, fired all its guns directly into the truck. The navigator, Sergeant Stocker, was nicked and fell off the truck and hid under a bush. Just before the truck stopped, Gurdon was hit by one cannon round in the abdomen and a second in the right lung, and he also fell off. The truck's driver, Guardsman Murray, bailed

---

26   *Ibid*, pp. 191-192; TNA, WO/201/814, f. 189.
27   TNA, WO/201/814, f. 183.

out after being wounded in one leg and an arm. The aircraft made one more pass at the navigator's truck and set it on fire, but Gurdon's truck was not hit and the enemy aircraft flew off northward.

Gurdon was dying and Guardsman Murray was badly wounded. Both men were given morphia. Stocker and Lieutenant Martin, the commander of the Free French Special Air Service troops, now had to decide what to do next while the patrol's medical orderly did what he could for the two wounded men. There were several choices. They could take Gurdon and Murray north to the coast road and leave them where they would be found in the hope that the enemy would give them the medical aid necessary to save their lives. They could continue with the operation; or they could return to Bir el Quseir where there was a British medical officer. Choices of this type were among the most difficult for commanders of the Long Range Desert Group patrols. Each patrol had a medical orderly and every man knew first aid, but in Gurdon's case only a surgeon in a fully equipped hospital had a slim chance of saving his life. When consulted, Gurdon wanted the operation to go on; but Stocker and Martin ignored this order and decided to attempt to get Gurdon and Murray back to Bir el Quseir and the Special Air Service's medical officer. Although G2 Patrol's operation report, which was written by Stocker, does not say so, Stocker and Martin probably knew that Gurdon would die even if they reached Bir el Quseir. G2 Patrol drove all night for Bir el Quseir, but at 1200 on 13 July, four miles from Bir el Quseir, Lieutenant Hon. R.B. Gurdon died of his wounds and was buried in the desert. That afternoon the Special Air Service's doctor operated on Murray, and two days later G2 Patrol left for Fayoum, which was reached on 18 July and where Murray was sent to the Scottish General Hospital.[28]

On 7 July T1 Patrol, commanded by Captain N.P. Wilder, left Fayoum for Stirling's base at Bir el Quseir, which they reached on 12 July after crossing the Qattara Depression. The next day Stirling, Mayne, and a party of Special Air Service troops left Bir el Quseir to go to Cairo to pick up some badly needed supplies. The Special Air Service had been two weeks behind enemy lines without being resupplied, and eight vehicles had been put out of action. While Stirling was in Cairo, Wilder was in command of the British forces at Bir el Quseir. During this period, members of T1 Patrol carried out several unsuccessful road watches and sent vehicles to Qara to obtain water.

---

28   TNA, CAB/44/151, f. 159; WO/201/814, ff. 181-185; Crichton-Stuart, *G Patrol*, pp. 156-158.

While waiting for the return of Stirling from Cairo, the Special Air Service troops at Bir el Quseir were bored and had to continually fight off flies. The Special Air Service's medical officer, Malcolm James, thought that the flies were the result of an inability to put into effect proper hygiene measures, which was no doubt true. Another reason for the great number of flies at Bir el Quseir was that it was located in an area which had been fought over, and the ground was covered with the filth of two armies. James later wrote:

> My God! How we grew to hate those flies. And what a trial they became at sick parades, clustering round the desert sores, or the exudate that had seeped through the dressings and bandages. Sometimes you would see a man, waiting his turn, quite unaware of the black, rosette-shaped cluster of flies that had grouped round his sore, until, suddenly noticing their activity, he would slash at them in his fury and start the ulcer bleeding afresh. Yes, those sick parades were pretty grim. And the irritating tickling as the flies ran over your back, up your arms and round you lips and eyes, while you were bending over trying to adjust a dressing or tie a bandage. It is almost too nauseating to recall now, but it was so horribly true for us then.[29]

While at Bir el Quseir James also noticed that the men were having trouble keeping within the allotted water ration. He concluded that it was much more difficult for troops who were stationary and whose time was not occupied with either physical or mental exertion to maintain a self-regulated system of water rationing. Each man had his "water bottle" filled once a day and in addition received a "mug" of tea with each meal. James thought, "From the physiological standpoint of preserving a water balance, this was more than adequate; there was no cause to worry as long as you could urinate.[30] Yet,

> of course the whole thing was really psychological, and it was a case of resisting the temptation to drink. You knew the water would not quench your thirst, and yet the knowledge did not nullify the desire. It was a case of forcing yourself *not* to drink, and of making yourself realize that the water was not necessary. But it certainly was the devil sometimes, when you ran your tongue over your cracked lips; when your watch said it was only two o'clock in the afternoon; when the heat was fairly blanketing down

---

29   Malcolm James, *Born of the Desert* (London: Collins, 1945), p. 147.
30   *Ibid*, p. 143.

over you, and you knew there was worse to come; when you could see your water-bottle tucked away securely in the shade, and you must needs say to yourself, 'There's absolutely no use in having a drink now." You had to fight that dreadful desire to gulp at the water, to have one really good drink and not stint yourself. That was the battle which you were waging constantly throughout the long heat of the day.[31]

Finally, after what must have seemed ages to the men at Bir el Quseir, on 23 July Stirling returned from Cairo with twenty jeeps, each armed with two twin Vickers K machine-guns, and several trucks loaded with supplies.

When Stirling returned to Bir el Quseir he brought not only jeeps, machine guns, and supplies but also a new plan. This scheme called for an attack on the airfield at Sidi Haneish near Fuka with eighteen jeeps, each armed with two twin Vickers K machine guns, for a total of seventy-two guns. The plan was that just before reaching the perimeter of the airfield, the jeeps would be formed into a line abreast formation and at a given signal would open fire while rushing the defenses of the airfield. Then, when a green Verey light was fired, the jeeps were to form into two lines of seven jeeps each with four others forming an arrowhead formation at the head of the two columns. As this formation moved through the airfield, the jeeps forming the two lines would open fire with their guns in a broadside position at aircraft and other targets while three of the four jeeps making up the arrowhead formation would fire their guns ahead at the airfield defenses. The front jeep was the command jeep. After dark on the night of 25 July, T1 Patrol and eighteen Special Air Service jeeps went out into the desert and practiced this new form of attack until 0300. This scheme, unlike most of the other plans made by Stirling, did not depend on stealth and surprise but rather surprise and overwhelming firepower.

At 1800 on 26 July, T1 Patrol's five trucks and eighteen Special Air Service jeeps—each carrying three men, a driver, and two gunners—left Bir el Quseir to attack the two airfields near Fuka that night. The plan was for T1 Patrol to attack one airfield to draw the attention of the enemy while Stirling assaulted the airfield at Sidi Haneish with his jeeps. For a time the two groups of vehicles headed northeast together, then T1 Patrol split off from the Special Air Service jeeps and went onto a new course for the airfield it was going to attack. During the approach to the target, however, the patrol ran into a minefield and one truck was damaged beyond repair and time was lost finding a route around the mines. Because of the minefield, T1 Patrol's attack on the airfield was an hour later than

---

31   *Ibid*, pp. 144-145.

planned. From a position outside the airfield, T1 Patrol destroyed with gunfire fifteen enemy aircraft by their count.

At 0230 T1 Patrol withdrew fifty miles into the desert and planned to hide for a day. But at 0800 two flying enemy aircraft spotted the patrol and then landed in the desert about a mile north of the British hiding place. Wilder was 'suspicious'— why had the enemy landed?—and began walking towards the two aircraft. As he did so, an enemy ground patrol consisting of four trucks carrying infantry and two armed with 40mm guns was sighted by the British. A truck went to pick up Wilder, and the two enemy aircraft took off and flew low over the British vehicles, which opened fire on the aircraft and shot one of them down. Two of T1 Patrol's trucks had been hidden in a wadi a short distance from where Wilder had placed his other two trucks. The two trucks in the wadi made good their escape unseen by Wilder or the enemy and returned to Bir el Quseir. Wilder and the other two trucks fought a rear guard action with the six enemy trucks for several miles before the chase was given up. Wilder, not being able to find the other two trucks of his command and being low on supplies, decided to return to the Long Range Desert Group's headquarters at Fayoum, which he reached on 29 July.[32]

Stirling and his group drove for almost four hours across the desert towards their target at Sidi Haneish before the Special Air Service's Rhodesian navigator, who had been trained by the Long Range Desert Group, told Stirling to stop because the airfield was over the next rise.[33] The jeeps were put into a line abreast formation and the gunners in each vehicle checked their weapons and readied them for action. Then the formation moved forward, with about five yards between each vehicle, to the top of the rise, where they stopped dead in surprise. Before them, they saw the airfield completely lit up by floodlights—a remarkable sight in wartime. Stirling gave the signal to advance, and as the line of jeeps approached a runway an aircraft shot over them and landed a hundred yards in front of them. As the aircraft touched down, Stirling's gunners began to fire, which was the signal for the rest of the Vickers K machine-guns to open fire. Sixty-eight machine-guns poured red and white tracer bullets onto the airfield. The enemy quickly switched off the floodlights, and two minutes later Stirling fired a green Verey light and the jeeps then fell into a double line ahead formation and drove down between lines of parked aircraft with machine-guns firing. Aircraft started to burn, others exploded, and some simply fell apart under the weight of the machine-gun fire. The

---

32   TNA, WO/201/814, ff. 202-205; Cowles, *Phantom Major*, pp. 199-202.

33   On the Rhodesians and the L.R.D.G., see e.g., J. Pittaway & G. Fourié, *Long Range Desert Group Rhodesia* (Durban, S. Africa, 2002).

heat was so intense that some of the raiders had their eyebrows and hair singed. Then a mortar round landed between the two jeeps and a Breda gun began firing at the British. Stirling's jeep was hit by a splinter, which brought it to a stop and all the other jeeps followed suit. Stirling yelled at the gunners to put the Breda gun out of action, which was done in a few seconds. Then Stirling and his crew got into another jeep and the formation began to move again with its machine-guns blasting aircraft and buildings. As the jeeps were leaving the airfield, the British saw a man run up to the only undamaged aircraft and place a time bomb on it—it was Mayne, who then ran back to his jeep. At the cost of two jeeps and one man killed, the Special Air Service had wrecked an entire German airfield. According to the British count, forty aircraft had been destroyed, bringing the total number of enemy aircraft destroyed by the Special Air Service to two hundred and fifty-six.

After leaving the airfield, Stirling's orders were that the force split up into groups of three or four jeeps each and to proceed back to Bir el Quseir by different routes. The plan was to get as far away as possible from the airfield in the two and a half hours of remaining darkness, hide from enemy aircraft during the daylight hours, and then continue on to Bir el Quseir the next night. It was most important that they got west of the Bagush-Qara track into broken country. Only one group did not reach Bir el Quseir safely and that was the group of three jeeps manned by Free French Special Air Service troops. At daylight the three French jeeps were near the Siwa-Mersa Matruh track, which was bound to be searched by the enemy. The Frenchmen hid their jeeps and themselves under a cliff. Here they remained undetected until noon, when they were spotted by three Stukas that attacked them nine times with gunfire. Zirnheld was hit by two bullets and soon died of his wounds. He was buried near the Siwa-Mersa Matruh track and the grave was marked with a cross made out of wood from a packing case and inscribed, "Aspirant André Zirnheld. Died for France on 27th July 1942."[34]

Stirling had planned to remain behind enemy lines for several weeks conducting a series of raids every few days to keep the enemy under constant pressure, but the unit was in need of being resupplied. When Stirling was last in Cairo he had made arrangements with the R.A.F. for 216 Squadron to resupply the Special Air Service by air. Several days after the jeep raid on the airfield at Sidi Haneish, Stirling requested by radio that 216 Squadron fly in the needed supplies. The reply to this request was an order for the entire Special Air Service to return to Kabrit to take part in an important operation. Stirling sent back a protest saying that he flatly

---

34   Cowles, *Phantom Major*, pp. 203-215; Marrinan, *Colonel*, pp. 67-68.

refused to follow plans not of his own making, "under pain of court martial,"[35] and if people would leave him alone and give him the required supplies the Special Air Service would do great damage in the rear areas of the enemy's forces. Within an hour the answer to this message came back in the form of an order that the Special Air Service must return to Kabrit.[36] Enraged and very apprehensive, Stirling and the Special Air Service returned to Kabrit by way of the Qattara Depression.

When the Special Air service was ordered back to Kabrit from behind enemy lines in Libya, Stirling no doubt felt that 8th Army headquarters as well as General Headquarters, Middle East were not properly supporting the war behind enemy lines and did not understand the conduct of irregular or special operations. The failure of Auchinleck's chief of staff to correctly brief Stirling as to British intentions before most of the Special Air Service moved behind enemy lines, in the first days of July, and the encountering of a British Jock column before the raids on the airfields at Bagush and Fuka were to Stirling sure signs that something was wrong. When Stirling had gone to Cairo to get more jeeps and supplies in the middle of July, he and Prendergast had been given an operational instruction by 8th Army headquarters that outlined priorities of objects—such as tanks, aircraft, and the like—which were to be attacked as well as called for the establishment of a base for the Long Range Desert Group and the Special Air Service to be set up at Qara; however, Qara, because of the ease with which the enemy could attack it, was totally unsuitable for this purpose. The operational instruction in addition called for a number of roadblocks to be placed on the coast road for forty-eight hours at Salum, Halfaya, and Bagush. The one at Salum was to be held until a detachment of Royal Marines had been landed to take over this task.[37] Clearly, the Long Range Desert Group and Special Air Service were not designed for such types of operations. The Long Range Desert Group and the Special Air Service were two lightly armed specialized units that were incapable of blocking the coast road for a fixed period of time while fighting off enemy combat formations to do so. When the Deputy Director, Military Intelligence at General Headquarters, Middle East saw this 8th Army operational instruction, he shot the whole works down and declared most of it to be "virtually impossible."[38] What Stirling and Prendergast had to say about this operational instruction luckily has not been recorded for history. What is certain nevertheless is that the concepts put forth in this operational instruction

---

35   Cowles, *Phantom Major*, p. 221.
36   *Ibid.*, pp. 220-221.
37   TNA, WO/201/814, f. 283.
38   TNA, CAB/44/151, f. 161.

from 8th Army headquarters were contrary to everything Prendergast and Stirling thought about the conduct of operations behind enemy lines.

Most people, and especially staff officers, do not usually approve of anything that appears to be disorderly and irrational and which does not follow standard or known operational procedures. By the end of August 1942, there appears to have been some need seen by General Headquarters, Middle East to bring what it considered to be a degree of rationality to, or find "the best system of co-ordinating the enterprises of various organizations" that operated behind enemy lines in Libya. No doubt what troubled the staffs at 8th Army and General Headquarters, Middle East was that the Long Range Desert Group patrols, along with the Special Air Service, were attacking enemy airfields. By attacking airfields instead of tank-related targets, the Special Air Service was, apparently, not following priorities as set forth by various staffs. G(R), whose task it was to blow things up in the Jebel Akhdar, was also gathering intelligence, which was the mission of the Inter Service Liaison Department,[39] although this organization from time to time blew things up as well.

To bring order out of what appeared to be disorder in the British effort behind enemy lines, a meeting was held on 23 August at General Headquarters, Middle East. This meeting was chaired by Brigadier G.M.O. Davy, the Director of Military operations, and was attended by the commanding officers, or their representatives, of all the British groups working in Libya. Davy began the meeting by saying that the purpose of the conference was to "co-ordinate" British activities behind enemy lines. He saw two ways of doing this: place one office in command of all of these activities; or appoint a staff officer in General headquarters, Middle East to "co-ordinate the various operations." Prendergast responded

> that he would prefer to leave things as they are, but agreed that there should be a Staff Officer at GHQ, who would be responsible for planning and co-ordination. Units would continue to provide their own comns. He said that the role of LRDG and L Det SAS were closely connected with the question of control.[40]

Next, Davy defined the roles and missions of the Long Range Desert Group, the Special Air Service, G(R), and the Inter Service Liaison Department. The brigadier

---

39   The Inter Service Liaison Department was a secret organization run by the British to support resistance by the Arabs in northern Cyrenaica to Italian rule.

40   TNA, WO/201/814, f. 235.

stated that the Long Range Desert Group's mission was to transport people back and forth from various points behind enemy lines and long-range reconnaissance; attacking things was to be a "subsidiary role." The Special Air Service was to confine its activities to attacking and destroying things. "Recce was not part of their role." And G(R)

> Should not undertake recce tasks as such, as this is the work of I.S.L.D. Nevertheless, they gather much useful information incidentally, and should, of course, continue to report this.[41]

Prendergast, probably wanting to put as much distance as possible between himself and various headquarters and staffs, "recommended that the LRDG should move to Kufra."[42] Davy answered by saying that General Headquarters, Middle East had this under consideration along with the idea of placing the entire Long Range Desert Group under its direct command. The meeting ended with forty-four copies of its minutes being drawn up for distribution and signed by Davy.[43]

Six days later, under Davy's signature and in thirty copies, a directive was produced by General Headquarters, Middle East stating that a staff officer would be appointed "to deal with special forces."[44] The directive also contained a restatement of the roles of these forces as defined by Davy, placed the Long Range Desert Group under the command of General Headquarters, Middle East, and directed that the Long Range Desert Group could not conduct raids east of "AGHEILA-MARADA."[45] From an organizational point of view, this directive made things appear to be all very nice and neat on paper. But it did not solve the problem of the inability of the British high command in the Middle East to understand the use of special or irregular forces.

When Stirling was recalled from the desert to Cairo at the end of July, he was provided with conclusive proof that British commanders and planners did not understand the use of Special Forces and the tactics of raiding when he learned of the existence of what later would be known as *Bigamy*, *Agreement*, *Caravan*, and *Nicety*. What the planners at General Headquarters, Middle East intended to do was to commit the Long Range Desert Group and the Special Air Service to one of the most controversial and disastrous military operations in the entire campaign

---

41   TNA, WO/201/814, f. 236.
42   *Ibid.*
43   *Ibid.*
44   *Ibid.*
45   TNA, WO/201/814, f. 234.

in the Western Desert. This operation was in reality four separate operations of which three would be carried out on the night of 13 September and the fourth two days later. *Bigamy*, was a raid on Benghazi from the land, *Agreement* was a sea and land raid on Tobruk, *Caravan* was a land raid on Barce and its airfield, and *Nicety*, which would take place two days after the other three raids, was the capture of Jalo.[46] These four operations involved hundreds of troops, a number of large and small warships, several score of vehicles, as well as long-range bomber aircraft.

At this late date it is extremely difficult to figure out where the ideas for these operations came from, and why such risky and complex schemes were permitted to be carried into effect. The British official history of the war in the Middle East states:

> Plans to harry the enemy's lines of communication by raiding the shipping, harbour facilities, and fuel storage at Tobruk and Benghazi had been under consideration ever since the withdrawal from Cyrenaica. It was felt at Headquarters in Cairo that something of the sort ought to be done to play on the enemy's nerves and cause losses he could ill afford. Plans for a series of raids were sponsored by the three Commanders-in-chief and worked out by their staffs. Air chief Marshal Tedder did not like the operations because of the impossibility of providing fighter cover, but felt that he could not carry his dislike to the point of refusal. The 8th Army Commander had no part in making the plans or in carrying them out and, indeed, disliked the whole operation.[47]

The British history of the war at sea says:

> Early in August the Commander-in-Chief, Middle East, considered ways and means of relieving the pressure on the Army, and forcing Rommel to divert a proportion of his strength from the front near El Alamein. General Auchinleck had signaled from his headquarters in the desert that he considered 'any and every means' of accomplishing that purpose was justified. It was indeed a most anxious period for the Army. The plans discussed in Cairo included an attack from the sea on Tobruk.... On the 21st the three Commanders-in-Chief approved the plan finally presented to them.[48]

---

46   TNA, CAB/44/151, ff. 165-167.

47   I.S.O. Playfair, *The Mediterranean and Middle East* (London: HMSO, 1966), vol. IV, p. 20.

48   S.W. Roskill, *The War at Sea* (London: HMSO, 1956), vol. II, 309.

It was Auchinleck, the Commander-in-Chief, Middle East and at the same time commander of the 8th Army, who, in the beginning of August, set the planners working on different ways to attack the enemy's supply lines. On 4 August, Winston Churchill arrived in Cairo determined to find out what was wrong in the Western Desert and to get the 8th Army to go on the offensive. On 6 August, Churchill decided to relieve Auchinleck from command along with three other generals; and for the next six days Churchill ran amok, as only he was capable of doing, through the British military establishment in Egypt. By 10 August, when he left for Moscow, everybody knew that Churchill was only interested in attack, attack, and attack.

On 13 August, General Sir Harold Alexander assumed command of the British forces in the Middle East and General Sir Bernard Law Montgomery took over command of the 8th Army. On 17 August, Churchill returned to Egypt and did not leave until 23 August. Churchill's visit to Cairo after returning from Moscow was much like his visit to Egypt at the beginning of August. There were round after round of inspections, visits to troops in the field, meetings, talks, parties, and just plain confusion.[49] On 21 August, the plans for the raids in Libya were approved by the three commanders-in-chief of the British forces in the Middle East. Alexander, the new Commander-in-chief of the ground forces, had only been on the job for eight days. All the while Churchill was running around Egypt like an enraged bull talking of nothing but taking the offensive, and the new commander-in-chief was faced with a huge set of problems. Three raids into Libya were small change when compared to problems such as holding the El Alamein line, figuring out how to take the offensive against Rommel, and dealing with Churchill. Under these circumstances it is easy to see how a scheme such as *Bigamy, Agreement, Caravan,* and *Nicety* could and did get the approval of the British commanders-in-chief without too much thought, if any, being applied to the problem. Another partial explanation for this is possibly the fact that at a party, at the British embassy, during the Prime Minister's visit to Cairo, Stirling told Churchill about *Bigamy's* impending raid on Benghazi.[50] It is not known if this had any effect on the decision to carry out the operations, but it is known that Churchill would not be pleased at the calling off of any offensive operation in the Western Desert during August of 1942. What most likely happened was that under the pressure of time, and circumstances, the personalities included, ultimately produced approval for the

---

49   Winston S. Churchill, *The Second World War* (Boston: Houghton Mifflin, 1950), vol. IV, pp. 457-473, 503-524.

50   Cowles, *Phantom Major*, p. 231.

raids at the highest level of the British command structure in the Middle East, without too much thought being given to the possible consequences.

At a lower level in the British command structure, the circumstances surrounding the origins of, and the planning for, the raids are, at best, murky and confused. When Auchinleck's demand for a plan to attack the enemy's supply lines came out of the desert and reached the planners in Cairo, Benghazi and Tobruk seemed natural targets because the enemy was receiving the bulk of its supplies through these two ports. If Benghazi and Tobruk could be smashed, the advantages to the British would be huge. Further, for months Stirling had been advocating raiding the shipping at Benghazi. Stirling had also been saying, over and over again, that he was not getting enough support. However, during July, the Special Air Service had managed to set up a base in Libya, behind enemy lines, from which a number of successful raids had been conducted. It was an easy jump for the planners to think Benghazi would be a very good target: after all, Stirling, the expert on raiding, wanted to attack Benghazi. So what could be simpler than to give him men and equipment to attack it, and then capture Jalo, for Stirling to use as a base for further raids to keep up the pressure on the enemy. In 1982 David Lloyd Owen told the author that the Tobruk part of the plan grew out of a scheme that John Haselden had for blowing up the fuel dumps and setting free the English prisoners held in that city.[51] Again it was an easy jump for the planners: Tobruk was a worthwhile target and Haselden, the leading intelligence expert on Cyrenaica, wanted to attack it — so give him the men and a plan of attack. Then they would add to the enemy's confusion by attacking Barce and its airfield, too. So, in essence what happened was that the planners had taken bits and pieces of Stirling's and Haselden's ideas, which they did not really understand, and turned them into a crazy quilt of impossible plans.

The plans for the raids on Tobruk, Benghazi, Barce, and the capture of Jalo were ultimately extremely complex. Force B — commanded by Haselden and led by Y1 Patrol of the Long Range Desert Group — consisting of D Squadron, 1st Special Service Regiment plus attached gunners, signalers, and engineers would march north from Kufra to Tobruk. This force, pretending to be captured British prisoners guarded by Germans—in actuality members of the Special Interrogation Group— would enter Tobruk at dusk and capture the coastal guns on the eastern side of Tobruk at an inlet called Mersa Sciausc. As soon as this was done, Force C from Alexandria—consisting of D Company, 1st Argyll and Sutherland Highlanders, a detachment of machine gunners from the 1st Royal Northumberland Fusiliers,

---

51   David Lloyd Owen interview.

and attached gunners, signalers, engineers, and medical orderlies—would be landed from sixteen MTB's and two ML's at Mersa Sciausc. While all this was going on, a second landing place was to be marked on the coast north of Tobruk by men in Folboats from H.M. Submarine *Taku*. Force A — 11th Battalion, Royal Marines—would then be landed from H.M.S. *Sikh* and *Zulu* at the point marked by the men in Folboats. Then Forces B and C would move west towards the city, capturing anti-aircraft and coastal artillery as they advanced. In the meantime, the 11th Royal Marines would drive towards Tobruk from the north, over-running coastal artillery positions and the like as they advanced towards the city. The enemy's attention would be occupied during this time by a series of heavy bombing raids on Tobruk by the R.A.F.; and as soon as the harbour defenses had been taken out, H.M.S. *Sikh* and *Zulu* would enter Tobruk harbour and land demolition parties while the MTB's would destroy all the enemy shipping in Tobruk harbour. After everything of value was destroyed in Tobruk and the British prisoners there freed, some of the troops would board the ships and be carried to Alexandria while the rest, using captured vehicles, would move out into the desert and continue to conduct more raids. The raid on Tobruk would also have a distant covering force made up of an anti-aircraft cruiser H.M.S. *Coventry* and six Hunt class destroyers.

The raid on Benghazi was to be made by the Special Boat Section, Special Air Service, and S1 and S2 Patrols of the Long Range Desert Group. The size of the Special Air Service would be increased for this operation by one hundred and twenty men drawn from the 1st Special Service Regiment. The attention of the enemy was to be occupied, as at Tobruk, by Benghazi being bombed. The raid on Barce and its airfield was to be made by G1 and T1 Patrols of the Long Range Desert Group. The raid on Barce would be mounted from Fayoum and the one of Benghazi from Kufra. There was also to be a "demonstration" before Siwa by a motorized battalion of the Sudan Defense Force from Bahariya Oasis. To further confuse the enemy, the R.A.F. would drop dummy airborne troops on Siwa. Two days after the raids, another unit of the Sudan Defense Force from Kufra would attack and capture Jalo.[52]

The British investment in these raids was all out of proportion to what might possibly be gained. Large numbers of aircraft, scores of vehicles, hundreds of troops, one submarine, two Tribal class destroyers, six Hunt class destroyers, one anti-aircraft cruiser, sixteen MTS's, and two ML's were to be risked. It was possible that the British could lose all the vehicles, men, ships, and a large number of aircraft and

---

52   Playfair, *The Mediterranean*, vol. IV, pp. 20-21. On the Barce raid, see also, Brendan O'Carroll, *Barce Raid* (Wellington, NZ: Ngaio Press, 2002).

not gain their objective. Tactically, these raids are proof positive that the planners in General Headquarters Middle East knew nothing about special operations or raiding. The plan was too complex. Infiltrating troops into Tobruk combined with two amphibious landings, all of which had to take place at certain set times if the operation were to work, might look good on paper but was extremely difficult to carry out. An obvious question is what would happen to Haselden's Force B once it got inside of Tobruk if, because of maritime problems such as high seas, Forces A and C could not land troops? Another problem which Teder brought up, but to which nobody paid any attention, was what would be the fate of the British warships when the sun came up and the enemy's air force went into action? There were more questions of this type that could be asked concerning the plans for the raids on Tobruk and Benghazi, but they were never asked by the planners.

Most of the people who had to carry out the raids did not like the plan. Lloyd Owen, the commander of Y1 Patrol did not approve of what he knew about the operation. And before the raid, Haselden told Lloyd Owen that he "always felt that his plans for the Tobruk raid might have had a far better chance of success if so many others had not been involved."[53] Also, according to Lloyd Owen, Prendergast thought that the operation was "far too big, and involved too many people, to ensure essential security."[54] Most likely, Stirling had the greatest doubts, for the tactics of the Special Air Service were always based on principles of simplicity, smallness, flexibility, stealth, and doing the unexpected. Yet what Stirling was now being asked to do was to take a mass of vehicles, and one hundred and twenty men, many of whom had not been through Special Air Service training nor were they members of the Long Range Desert Group, north across hundreds of miles of desert and then carry out a commando style attack on Benghazi. Stirling felt that he was being drawn into an operation that was very different from previous Special Air Service operations and one in which he could not calculate the risks or the gains.[55] After the war, Stirling wrote, "I had become committed to this Benghazi operation before I fully understood its implications and it was a sharp lesson, which confirmed my previous views on the error of attacking strategic targets on a tactical scale.[56]

The British official history of the war in North Africa notes that these raids "relied greatly on surprise."[57] From the tactical point of view, surprise was going

<hr>

53   David Lloyd Owen, *Providence Their Guide* (London: Harrap, 1980), pp. 104-105.
54   *Ibid*, p. 105.
55   Cowles, *Phantom Major*, pp. 226-230.
56   Stirling, Memorandum, p. 7.
57   Playfair, *The Mediterranean*, vol. IV, p. 20.

to be hard to maintain, for both Haselden's and Stirling's operations were to be mounted from Cairo through Kufra, which meant that each force had to cross some seventeen hundred miles of desert and approach their targets all the while being unseen by the enemy. In the best of circumstances, this was going to be extremely difficult for Stirling, with almost a hundred vehicles, to achieve and he knew it. But surprise had already been lost, for there were too many people who knew too much and who talked too much. In the event, just about everybody who was going to take part in these raids knew that security for the operation had been compromised in Alexandria and Cairo and that the enemy must have some kind of foreknowledge of the raids. Fitzroy MacLean,[58] Stirling,[59] Peniakoff,[60] and Haselden, because Lloyd Owen told him,[61] all knew that because there had been a general breakdown in security procedures, the enemy had to know the raids were coming. Michael Crichton-Stuart has written, "it became apparent that there was a serious breach of security since the impending raids were the gossip of Cairo. Without the all important weapon of surprise the attacks were suicidal yet they were not cancelled."[62]

The raids on Benghazi and Tobruk were going to be carried out by people who did not approve of the plan moreover. These same people also knew that they probably had lost the element of surprise even before the operation had begun. Why, then, were not these raids called off? Because captains, majors, and lieutenant colonels cannot fight the entire command structure of a major theater of war. The planners at General Headquarters, Middle East, who knew little about special operations or raids, had produced the plan, which was then set in stone when the commanders-in-chief of the three services, without much question or thought, gave their approval to the scheme. The planning process was done backwards. What should have been done was that when the planners in Cairo received Auchinleck's request for a plan to disrupt enemy supply lines, they should have gone to people such Stirling, Prendergast, Haselden, and any other person who had conducted numerous special operations behind enemy lines, and should have told them what the problem was and asked for suggestions on how they could best help solve it. They should then have listened to the various plans put forth by these people and supported those schemes that appeared to have had the best chance of obtaining the required results. But, alas, it was not done this way. Instead, a huge unworkable

---

58   Fitzroy Maclean, *Escape to Adventure* (Boston: Little Brown, 1950), p. 171.

59   Cowles, *Phantom Major*, p. 233.

60   Viadimir Peniakoff, *Private Army* (London: Jonathan Cape, 1950), pp. 162-165.

61   Lloyd Owen, *Providence*, pp. 105-106.

62   Crichton-Stuart, *G Patrol*, pp. 161-162.

scheme was thought up by the planners and then various people and units were made to conform to it.

On 22 August Force B, under the command of Haselden, left Cairo for Kufra in seven three-ton trucks and headed south along the Nile. Before going eastward into the desert, Force B was joined by the Long Range Desert Group Patrol Y1 to guide it across the desert to Kufra, which was reached on 4 September. At 1700 hours on 5 September, after the operation had been explained to the men, Force B, led by Lloyd Owen's Y1 Patrol, which consisted of twenty other ranks and five 30 cwt trucks, began the eight hundred mile trek north to Tobruk. The next day the twelve British trucks crossed the sand sea and camped that night forty miles east of Zighen. They then proceeded rapidly north, passing well out of Jalo, to Etla, where gasoline and water were obtained from a secret Long Range Desert Group dump. By 1600 on 13 September, Y1 Patrol and Force B had reached El Duda just south of Tobruk without being sighted by the enemy. From this point on, Force B had to use stealth to reach and enter Tobruk.

At 1830 on 13 September, Y1 Patrol and Force B parted company. The plan was to hide several of Force B's trucks in the desert because they were not needed in the next part of the operation and could later be used by men evading the enemy in case something went wrong. The next step was for Haselden's eighty-three men to infiltrate into Tobruk in three trucks with German markings on them. The troops would appear to be recently captured British prisoners under German guard. All their arms and equipment were carried out of sight, and each truck was manned by three men in German uniforms and carrying German weapons. This ruse worked and Force B got into Tobruk undiscovered; and after light fighting, they successfully captured the enemy coastal defense guns covering the waters around Mersa Sciausc.

At this point, however, the whole operation fell apart. Only two MTB's, out of sixteen MTB's, and two ML's ever reached Mersa Sciausc and landed troops. When H.M.S. *Sikh* and *Zulu* arrived off the northern side of Tobruk's harbour at 0300, there was a fairly heavy sea running, which prevented the marking of the landing place because the Folboats could not be got off H.M. Submarine *Taku*. Nevertheless, a landing was attempted from the two destroyers with improvised landing craft that were totally unfit for this type of operation and especially so with a heavy sea running. Only some seventy marines reached the shore near Mengar el Auda, two miles west of the intended landing place. The marines who did not get ashore were either captured or killed as they attempted to fight their way into Tobruk. As the two destroyers were attempting the almost impossible task of putting more marines on shore, they were discovered by enemy coastal defenses. H.M.S. *Sikh*'s steering gear was destroyed by gunfire; and when H.M.S. *Zulu* attempted to take the damaged destroyer under tow, an enemy shell parted the towing wire. The commander of H.M.S. *Sikh*, who was the senior naval officer present, ordered H.M.S. *Zulu* to retreat and then scuttled his own ship. On shore the men of Haselden's Force B, without reinforcements, were either killed or captured as day came.[63] As soon as the sun was up, enemy aircraft began to take off from airfields in eastern Libya and attacked and destroyed H.M.S. *Coventry*, H.M.S. *Zulu*, three MTB's, and the two ML's. Of the two MTB's that actually entered Mersa Sciausc, one ran aground and the other one was destroyed. Eight Allied aircraft were also lost bombing Tobruk and Benghazi that night.

There is a bitter irony in the fact that the heavy bombing of Tobruk, intended as a diversion, instead made the German commander of that area suspicious; and just after Force B got into Tobruk, he put the two thousand German troops stationed in the region on alert. Because of "the great hazards of the plan,"[64] the sea conditions, poor landing craft, the inability of the MTB's and ML's to find Mersa Sciausc, no real knowledge of how to conduct amphibious landing operations, lack of air cover, as well as underestimating of the enemy, the British lost — they were either killed or captured — two hundred eighty officers and men of the Royal Navy, and three hundred Royal Marines; as for the army, it lost one hundred sixty men of all ranks. The great raid on Tobruk was in fact a total failure. The British official history of the war in North Africa says that there is no evidence to show that the enemy had any foreknowledge of the attack.[65]

Five minutes after Force B left Y1 Patrol and began to make its way into Tobruk, Lloyd Owen saw several enemy vehicles heading towards him. The British officer decided to attack and destroy these vehicles to prevent them from discovering Force B. The five trucks of Y1 Patrol spread out into a line abreast formation and drove very fast towards the enemy with the setting sun at their back. The enemy vehicles had stopped and did not suspect Y1 Patrol to be British, for a number of enemy troops had got out of their vehicles and were standing around as if waiting for the British to join them for 'a friendly chat."[66] The enemy did not learn of

---

63   Several officers and men escaped from Tobruk. They either were hidden by friendly Arabs in the Jebel Akhdar or walked several hundred miles east across the desert to the British lines in Egypt. TNA, WO/201/740, ff. 2-11; WO/218/97, Report by Lt. T.B. Langton, Irish Guards, on the raid on Tobruk, 22 Nov. 1942.

64   Playfair, *The Mediterranean*, vol. IV, p. 23.

65   TNA, WO/218/97, Report by Lt. T.B. Langton, Irish Guards, on the raid on Tobruk, 22 Nov. 1942; WO/201/740, ff. 2-11; WO/201/815, ff. 10-12; Playfair, *The Mediterranean*, vol. IV, pp. 21-23; Lloyd Owen, *Desert*, pp. 224-235; Lloyd Owen, *Providence*, pp. 106-107.

66   Lloyd Owen, *Desert*, p. 236.

their mistake until Y1 Patrol's automatic weapons opened fire on them at point blank range and killed all of them but one, who was taken prisoner.[67] The Italian prisoner told Lloyd Owen that his unit had just arrived at Tobruk that day, that the enemy was expecting trouble, and that the garrison of the city had been reinforced. The Italian also gave Lloyd Owen a great deal of other intelligence about enemy activities in Tobruk. Although Lloyd Owen had orders to attack enemy aircraft on various airfields around the city, the commander of Y1 Patrol decided to attempt to make radio contact with Force B to give it the information gained from the Italian prisoner.

For a considerable amount of time Y1 Patrol tried to make radio contact with Force B. Before Haselden had left Y1 Patrol, he told Lloyd Owen that after Force B got inside the Tobruk it would radio the patrol information about checkpoints and the like. But Y1 Patrol never did make radio contact with Force B, and finally Lloyd Owen decided to stop waiting for a Force B Radio transmission and continue his part of the operation. With some difficulty, Y1 Patrol got down the escarpment at Sidi Rezegh and headed for the Axis road, which was built by the enemy to by-pass Tobruk when the city was being held by the Australians in 1941. Before reaching the Axis road, the patrol passed a concrete pillbox, which exchanged fire with the British vehicles. After passing this pillbox, Lloyd Owen stopped the patrol and found that the truck with the radio on it was missing. The crew of the missing truck then appeared on foot, but according to Lloyd Owen "they could not give any very clear account of what happened."[68] Next Lloyd Owen, with a ten men patrol, went back on foot towards the pillbox and the missing truck but could not find either one in the darkness. Finally, after Lloyd Owen had fired his Verey pistol four times, the patrol located the pillbox and the missing truck. The pillbox was attacked, but there was no return fire, and the missing truck was found to have a flat tyre, which was changed.[69] When the missing truck rejoined the main body of the patrol, it proceeded to the Axis road. Once on the Axis road, the patrol went north towards the coast road and Tobruk. It was now well past 2300 hours. When Y1 Patrol reached the junction of the Axis and coast roads, Lloyd Owen expected to find a checkpoint or a roadblock. But when the British reached the junction, there was nothing except a steamroller and some barrels, so Y1 Patrol turned onto the coast road and drove down it past enemy camps and minefields to the outer defenses or perimeter around Tobruk, from which the sound of gunfire could be

---

67   TNA, WO/201/815, f. 12.
68   Lloyd Owen, *Desert*, p. 239.
69   TNA, WO/201/815, f. 13.

heard. Lloyd Owen decided to stop there and attempt again to gain radio contact with Force B.

Just as the patrol's radio operator was setting up his equipment, Lloyd Owen heard a vehicle coming out of Tobruk towards the patrol. The British officer yelled to his men to get their weapons, and then he ran into the middle of the road. When he had reached the middle of the road, Lloyd Owen saw a German staff car about fifty yards away, which was slowing down as it neared him. The commander of Y1 Patrol raised his weapon to fire at the car's driver, but his gun jammed. Perhaps thinking he was German or Italian, the enemy staff car stopped right in front of Lloyd Owen just as some of his men arrived. A German officer and three soldiers were captured, but in the confusion one of the soldiers escaped and most likely warned the enemy of the patrol's existence. For soon after searchlights began playing on the desert in front of Tobruk's defenses.[70] At this point, Lloyd Owen decided to wait for first light before entering Tobruk.

At 0530 Lloyd Owen decided to withdraw back to Sidi Rezegh. Things had obviously gone wrong in Tobruk. Radio contact could not be established with Force B, enemy coast artillery was still firing, and five trucks and twenty-one men could not win the battle for the British. Y1 Patrol withdrew down the coast and Axis roads the same way it had come in. At Sidi Rezegh the patrol attempted, without success, to contact both its headquarters and Force B by radio. Then the patrol moved into the desert about twenty miles, hid from enemy aircraft, and again attempted to make radio contact with Force B and its headquarters. At 1200 Y1 Patrol was informed by radio from its headquarters that the raid had failed. At 1730 Lloyd Owen decided to move southward to Etla to be in a position to aid any British service men who might escape from Tobruk southward into the desert.[71]

At the beginning of September Stirling went to Kufra to mount operation *Bigamy*. This was the name of the attack on Benghazi that Force X—the Special Air Service and attached units—were to carry out on the night of 13 September. The objective of this raid was to destroy the oil storage and docking facilities at Benghazi and any shipping that was found in the harbour. At the same time, the Long Range Desert Group's S1 and S2 Patrols were to attack the nearby airfield at Benina.[72] Stirling did not like the plan, for it was too big; and the planning, timing, and schedules were too rigid; in addition, a large part of the force had not been properly trained in the desert driving and raiding techniques. Moreover, Stirling

70   *Ibid.*

71   TNA, WO/201/815, ff. 12-14; Lloyd Owen, *Desert*, pp. 235-247.

72   TNA, CAB/44/151, f. 165.

believed that the security for the operation had not been very good. To top it all, there were also a number of obvious geographical problems with *Bigamy*. Stirling had to move, unseen by the enemy, over sixteen hundred miles from Kabrit to Kufra and then on to Benghazi with two tanks, seventeen three-ton trucks, forty-nine jeeps, and two hundred forty-four officers and men of the Special Air Service plus the six vehicles of S1 Patrol with their crews. Simply servicing this many vehicles was a huge problem in itself; however, there were other problems as well, most critically a lack of drivers skilled at desert driving among the Special Air Service troops.[73]

On 4 September the lead element of Force X under Mayne's command, left Kufra and headed north towards Benghazi. The next day the second party of Force X, under the command of Cumper, left Kufra for the north; and the third and last section of Force X left Kufra on 6 September under the command of Stirling. Each group was guided by Long Range Desert Group navigators supplied by S1 Patrol. Before the war, Bagnold and Clayton had proved that it was possible to cross the sand seas of Egypt and Libya with wheeled vehicles; and the Long Range Desert Group had done so many times during the war. But the Special Air Service drivers, who for the most part were untrained in desert driving, found the most difficult part of the trip north to be the crossing of the twenty-mile wide belt of sand sea between Kufra and Zighen. The two tanks lent to the Special Air Service to deal with roadblocks and the like found the sand sea in fact impossible to cross and had to be abandoned. The other vehicles of the Special Air Service got bogged down so often that they were lucky to average a mile an hour in the sand sea. After finally crossing the sand sea and giving Jalo a wide berth, Force X travelled north fairly quickly to the escarpment in the Jebel Akhdar near Benghazi. Mayne's advanced group arrived there on 9 September; Cumper's and Stirling's parties arrived on 11 September. Other than the sand sea, the only problem encountered was when a jeep ran over a thermos mine, killing a navy officer, severely wounding a Special Air Service non-commissioned officer, and destroying the jeep. Everybody in Force X agreed that they had not been sighted by enemy aircraft on their march north from Kufra to the Jebel Akhdar.[74]

When Mayne's party reached the escarpment in the Jebel Akhdar east of Benghazi, one of the first things they did was to get in touch with Melot, who had been operating in the area for some time. With the aid of some Arabs, Melot's hide-out was found in a nearby wadi. After talking over the operation

---

73   Cowles, *Phantom Major*, pp. 226-228, 232.
74   TNA, WO/201/735, f. 2.

with Melot and being told by the Intelligence officer of some suspicious enemy troop movements, Maclean, Mayne, and Melot concluded that, "it looked rather as though we were expected."[75] On 10 September Melot sent an agent, a private in the Libyan Arab Force, into Benghazi to obtain more intelligence. This agent returned from Benghazi to the British hide-out in the escarpment on the morning of 12 September. He told Melot and Maclean, in a mixture of Arabic and Italian, that there were more than five thousand Italian troops in and around Benghazi and that an additional seventy truckloads of Italian troops plus a German machine-gun battalion had arrived on 11 September. Most of the shipping had left Benghazi in the last few days, and the landward approaches to the city were covered by a double anti-tank ditch, minefields, pillboxes, and machine-gun nests.[76] And if this were not enough, the agent then went on to report that there was widespread talk in the bazaars of Benghazi that the city was going to be attacked on 14 September!

Maclean and Melot talked over the agent's report with Stirling, and it was generally agreed that it looked suspiciously like the enemy was expecting the attack on Benghazi. Stirling did not want to call off the operation, but he did want to change the timing of it. The new intelligence and the suggestion that the timing of the operation be changed was radioed back to General Headquarters, Middle East in Cairo.[77] Several hours later the answer came back that they were to disregard "bazaar gossip" and carry out the operation according to the original timetable.[78]

The plan of attack was simple. The main body would move off the escarpment at nightfall, go cross-country and take the roadblock by surprise, and then drive into Benghazi and start blowing things up. The attack on Benghazi would begin at 2330, and for two hours before the ground assault Benghazi was to be heavily bombed by enemy aircraft. While the Special Air Service was attacking Benghazi, S1 and S2 Patrols would attack the airfield at Benina. One known problem with this plan was that there was an Italian radio station in a small fort at the edge of the escarpment, which would most likely see the British as they headed for Benghazi and Benina. It was decided that Melot, two other officers, and ten men would attack and destroy the fort and radio.

Just after dark Melot's men rushed the Italian fort and, after a fight, captured it and destroyed the radio.[79] Five Italian soldiers were killed, three captured, and one got away. But Melot and Captain Christopher Baily of the Special Air Service

---

75   Maclean, *Escape*, p. 179.
76   TNA, WO/201/735, f. 3.
77   Marrinan, *Colonel*, p. 71.
78   Cowles, *Phantom Major*, p. 236.
79   *Ibid*, p. 238.

had been badly wounded. After the fort had been captured, the main force went down the escarpment, guided by Melot's Libyan Arab Force private. Melot was supposed to have guided the force, but because of his wounds the Arab had to take his place. The Arab did not know much about the eastern approaches to Benghazi, and he had no idea what type of ground a motor vehicle could not cross. The result was that the whole attacking force got lost, and it was not until 0430 that Stirling got his vehicles onto one of the roads leading into Benghazi from the east.[80] As the British raiding force drove toward Benghazi, it encountered a cantilever gate blocking the way. There was wire on both sides of the road, and Cumper discovered that there were minefields as well. After looking at the mines, Cumper went up to the gate, opened it, and said, "Let battle commence."[81] With these words, total pandemonium broke out, for the enemy began firing machine-guns, mortars, rifles, and several Breda guns. The Special Air Service had been ambushed. Because of the wire and mines, the British could not deploy their vehicles off the road. The first two jeeps in the column drove through the gate with their Vickers K machine-guns firing, only to burst into flames when incendiary bullets hit their gas tanks. The only thing left for Stirling's force to do was to stand and fight, using the combined firepower of many automatic weapons to beat down the enemy; indeed, it was by sheer volume of fire, that the Special Air Service finally forced the enemy to break off the engagement.

When the enemy fire began to fall off, Stirling decided to retreat. If the British had pushed on towards Benghazi, they would probably have encountered stronger resistance; for surprise had been lost with the fight at the cantilever gate and it would soon be daylight. The column turned around and the Special Air Service started back towards the escarpment. As it became light in the east, the force split up into small groups. Each of these small parties made a mad dash for the escarpment and cover from enemy aircraft, which could be seen taking off from nearby airfields. The Special Air Service lost five trucks and seven jeeps to enemy air attack before reaching the escarpment. Throughout the day, enemy aircraft bombed and machine-gunned suspected British hiding places in the escarpment. The next night small groups of Special Air Service troops, some with vehicles and some on foot, made their way through the Jebel Akhdar to the point assigned as the rendezvous. But in the course of the afternoon of 15 September, enemy aircraft discovered the Special Air Service rendezvous in the Jebel Akhdar and subjected the area to endless air attacks. At any given time during the remaining five hours of

---

80   TNA, WO/201/735, f. 13.
81   Cowles, *Phantom Major*, p. 237.

light there were at least fifteen enemy aircraft over the area bombing and machine-gunning anything that appeared to move or look like a vehicle. One enemy aircraft was shot down, but during that afternoon the Special Air Service lost three men who were killed, four men were wounded, and most of its vehicles.[82] During all the air attacks on the Special Air Service, Maclean and Mayne both wondered why the enemy did not mount an attack against them with ground forces and destroy the unit. This is a question which has not been satisfactorily answered to this day.

After dark on the night of 15 September, Stirling decided to split Force X into three groups. Mayne would command one party, the second group would be under Captain "Sandy" Scratchley, and the third and smallest would be under Stirling and remain in the Jebel Akhdar for several days to pick up any stragglers.[83] After taking a survey of all the food, provisions, and the vehicles that had escaped destruction it was decided that, if all unnecessary equipment was junked, it would be possible to make it to Jalo and link up with the Sudan Defense Force, which was supposed to be attacking Jalo. Food and water were the items in shortest supply, and Scratchley's party made up a ration table for the trip to Jalo consisting of one cup of water and a tablespoon of bully beef per man per day. Another problem was space on the remaining vehicles. Maclean's jeep had to carry eight men plus cargo, which was possible, since the Scots officer was, as was everybody else, travelling light for the air attacks had reduced his equipment to an automatic pistol, a prismatic compass, and a teaspoon. The Special Air Service's medical officer decided that the four wounded men should not attempt a trip of hundreds of miles through the desert. These four wounded men had to be turned over to the enemy for medical treatment if they were to have any chance of living—a most difficult decision. The next morning a British medical orderly in a jeep, flying a Red Cross and with two Italian prisoners, drove to the nearest enemy post and requested medical assistance for the four wounded British soldiers. The group of Stirling, which had stayed behind, saw the enemy picking up the four British wounded; however, some months later Maclean "heard" that they had died in the military hospital at Benghazi.

On the first night Scratchley's party drove very slowly to the southern edge of the Jebel Akhdar and went into hiding from enemy aircraft all through the daylight hours of 16 September. Both Scratchley's and Mayne's groups eventually made it to Jalo, although not without difficulty and some hardship. It is hard to relax with seven or eight men in a jeep, and when somebody did he would go to sleep and fall off. If it was the driver who fell asleep, as happened with Mayne's

---

82   TNA, WO/201/735, ff. 4-5.
83   Cowles, *Phantom Major*, p. 239.

driver, the vehicle would go out of control. During the trip to Jalo, Mayne had a brief altercation with two guards officers who suggested that he turn north and surrender. These two officers were thrown out of the Special Air Service when the unit returned to Egypt.

When the two Special Air Service Groups reached Jalo, they were in for another disappointment. The Sudan Defense Force, guided by the men of the Long Range Desert Group, had marched north from Kufra to attack Jalo only to find that the Italian garrison was alert and waiting for the attack. It was not going to be easy to throw the Italians out of Jalo. Before the arrival of the Special Air Service troops, the Sudan Defense Force had stormed Jalo once, only to be pushed back into the desert by the enemy. They were preparing to storm it a second time, but before the assault took place orders were received from Cairo calling the whole operation off. After staying for three days in the Jabel Akhdar, Stirling had picked up a dozen stragglers and then headed to Jalo and on to Kufra with the remains of the Special Air Service and the Sudan Defense Force.[84]

On the same night that the Special Air Service attempted to attack Benghazi, S1 and S2 Patrols of the Long Range Desert Group were supposed to attack the airfield at Benina.[85] After dark on 13 September, S1 and S2 Patrols followed the vehicles of the Special Air Service down the escarpment of the Jebel Akhdar. The two patrols were provided with an Arab guide who proved to be worse than useless. This so-called guide, according to Olivey, who commanded the operation, led the patrols "into impassable Wadi from which, after damaging two trucks, the Patrol had the greatest difficulty in getting out."[86] It was 0230 when S1 and S2 Patrols got out of the wadi. Olivey broke off the operation because there was not enough time left before daylight, in order to attack the airfield and get back into the Jebel Akhdar to hide from the enemy aircraft that were bound to be looking for the British.

While returning to their hiding place in the Jebel Akhdar, S1 and S2 Patrols came across a badly wounded Special Air Service officer. Before daylight Olivey had all the trucks out of sight except for two trucks belonging to S1 Patrol that were sent to the Special Air Service rendezvous in order to turn the wounded officer over to the Special Air Service's medical officer. But the two trucks did not make it back before daylight to the place where S1 and S2 Patrols were hiding.

---

84 TNA, CAB/44/151, ff. 165-166; WO/201/735, ff. 2-6; WO/201/815, ff. 6-7; Cowles, *Phantom Major*, pp. 232-239; Maclean, *Escape*, pp. 169-197; Marrinan, *Colonel*, pp. 70-79.

85 TNA, WO/201/815, f. 7.

86 TNA, WO/201/738, f. 5

About two miles from the hiding place, they were attacked by two enemy fighters. The crew bailed out of the vehicles as the aircraft were coming in to make the first attack and there were no casualties. One truck caught fire on the first attack of the aircraft, but the other truck with two radios and a theodolite on it was strafed for over an hour but did not catch fire. Later, both radios and the theodolite, all in working order, were salvaged from this much shot-at truck.[87]

After enemy aircraft had finished bombing and shooting up Special Air Service vehicles, during the afternoon of 15 September, S1 Patrol went to Cheda bu Maun with its four remaining trucks in the hope of locating the two patrols of the Long Range Desert Group that had attacked the airfield at Barce. The next morning S1 Patrol picked up four guardsmen who walked into their camp from Barce. On 17 September, S1 Patrol was ordered by radio to go to Landing Ground 125 and to wait there for the patrols that had attacked the airfield at Barce.[88] S2 Patrol remained in hiding in the Jebel Akhdar, during which time they also picked up eight stragglers belonging to the Special Air Service. On the afternoon of 16 September, Stirling released S2 Patrol from his command; and at 1800 the patrol left its hiding place. The following day it received orders by radio from B Squadron, Long Range Desert Group, to meet the party that had taken part in the attack on the airfield at Barce.[89]

Caravan, the raid on Barce and its airfield by two patrols of the Long Range Desert Group, took place on the night of 13 September. Unlike the other raids that night, it was not mounted from Kufra but rather from Fayoum in order to reduce the congestion of vehicles and men at Kufra, from which the attack on Jalo and the large raids on Benghazi and Tobruk were staged. By land there were only two routes to Barce from Fayoum: across the Qattara Depression to Qara and then northwest to the Jebel Akhdar; or across the Egyptian and Libyan Sand Seas and then north to the Jebel Akhdar and Barce. The route through the sand seas was the one used for *Caravan* because the enemy was thought to be at Qara. The distance the two patrols would have to travel was huge: Fayoum to Barce was 1,155 miles and Barce to Kufra was 675 miles, making up a total of 1,830 miles. The Long Range Desert Group's 30 cwt Chevrolets had a range of fifteen hundred miles, but jeeps could only do nine hundred miles. To extend the range of the jeeps, two 10-ton Mack trucks would accompany the force for the first two hundred miles and provide fuel for that part of the trip. When the force got through the

---

87   TNA, WO/201/815, f. 8.
88   TNA, WO/201/745, f. 14.
89   TNA, WO/201/815, ff. 7–9.

Egyptian Sand Sea, it would meet vehicles of the Heavy Section, which would have come three hundred and forty miles north from Kufra to Howard's Cairn, with additional fuel. The logistics alone of getting to and from Barce presented a considerable problem.

On 1 September at 0730, G1, S2, T1 Patrols, and a headquarters section left Fayoum for the Jebel Akhdar. S2 Patrol was to accompany the force that was going to raid Barce to a point south of the Jebel Akhdar, where it would then proceed to join Force X and Stirling to take part in the raid on the airfield at Benina. G1 and T1 Patrols and the headquarters section rode in twelve 30 cwt Chevrolet trucks and three jeeps; the vehicles were manned by five officers and forty-two other ranks including two members of the Libyan Arab Force. The force was commanded by Easonsmith, and it was also accompanied by Peniakoff and the Long Range Desert Group's medical officer, R.P. Lawson.

On 3 September the three Long Range Desert Group patrols reached the Egyptian Sand Sea. Despite the usual amount of mechanical problems and the digging out of bogged down vehicles, the force made good time crossing the sand sea. But on 6 September when the patrols were nearing the western edge of the sand sea, Timpson, the commander of G1 Patrol, drove a jeep too fast up the blind side of a razor back dune, and

> saw too late that the other side of the crest was an almost vertical drop of 30 to 40 feet. He tried to turn to avoid the drop, but the Jeep rolled over on its side and continued to roll to the bottom of the dune.[90]

Although he had facial injuries and a fractured skull, Timpson somehow got clear of the vehicle, but Guardsman Thomas Wann was pinned under the jeep with a broken back. Lawson "patched" up the two men as best he could and the three patrols left the sand sea and went to Big Cairn. By radio, arrangements were made for an R.A.F. Blenheim to fly to Big Cairn from Kufra to pick up Timpson and Wann. The two wounded men, Lawson, and S2 Patrol remained at Big Cairn, waiting for the Blenheim to fly in while the rest of the force went to Howard's Cairn to meet the Heavy Section and to pick up from it fifteen hundred gallons of fuel. Big Cairn was a five foot high pile of rocks on a low ridge just west of the western side of the Egyptian Sand Sea and was fairly easy for a patrol of the Long Range Desert Group to find, but not for the crew of the Blenheim sent to pick up Timpson and Wann; for the aircraft landed fifty miles from Big Cairn at a place in

---

90   TNA, WO/201/745, f. 13.

the middle of nowhere called Lazarus Landing Ground. The next day, guided by Browne of the Long Range Desert Group, the Blenheim finally found Big Cairn, and Timpson and Wann were flown to Cairo.

S2 Patrol then drove as fast as possible over the serir to Howard's Cairn to rejoin the other two patrols. The whole force then crossed the sand sea again, from south to north. Good time was made, but not enough to make up for the time lost because of the jeep accident. Easonsmith had wanted to arrive in the Barce region early enough for Peniakoff's two Libyan Arab Force soldiers to conduct a good reconnaissance of Barce. S2 Patrol left the other two patrols near Landing Ground 125 and proceeded to the Benghazi region to meet Stirling. Just south of the Jebel Akhdar, Easonsmith hid a truck at Bir el Gerrari with rations and enough fuel to reach Kufra and to serve as an emergency rendezvous.

On the morning of 13 September, G1 and T1 Patrols reached a point south of Barce. The vehicles were hidden from aircraft. Easonsmith and Peniakoff then took the two Libyan soldiers, who were not in uniform, as close as they could to Barce. The plan was that the two Arab soldiers would scout Barce and then return that night to the place where they had been let off and tell Easonsmith about Barce and its defenses. For the rest of the daylight hours of 13 September, the two patrols remained in hiding preparing for the raid. In general terms, the plan was for the two patrols to drive down the main road to Barce. T1 Patrol, commanded by Wilder, would attack the airfield; and G2 Patrol, now commanded by Sergeant Jack Dennis, and the headquarters group would shoot up Barce as a diversion to assist the attack on the airfield.

About 1600 enemy aircraft began searching, without success, the region where the two patrols were hiding. Easonsmith took this "to be a bad sign."[91] To make matters worse, the two Libyans who had been sent to scout Barce were never seen again. The aircraft delayed the start of the raid, but as soon as it was dark the whole force moved down a track to the main road to Barce. While driving towards Barce, a small police post was encountered. An Arab policeman came out of the building when the British vehicles pulled up in front of it. The British took a rifle away from the Arab, and he was then "popped" into the back of a truck to begin a new career as a "cookhouse scullion" for the Long Range Desert Group.[92] After capturing the Arab, Easonsmith called out 'Taala henna," which produced an Italian officer, who was shot. While stopping at the police post, one of G1 Patrol's trucks and one belonging to T1 Patrol smashed into each other, damaging their radiators and the

---

91   *Ibid.*
92   Lloyd Owen, *Providence*, pp. 107-108.

two trucks had to be left behind. As the two patrols drove away from the police post someone began to fire a machine gun at the British vehicles but did not hit anything. At Sidi Selim, several miles outside of Barce, T1 Patrol's radio truck was left with the medical officer.

When the two patrols were about five miles from Barce, Easonsmith made the following understatement: "it was obvious that we were expected as there was a light tank on each side of the road awaiting us."[93] But the headlights of the British trucks "blinded" the crews of the two tanks, who did not realize what was happening until they had grenades thrown at them and were shot at by machine-guns as the British raced by them. When the British reached the "main corner of the town" they stopped. Easonsmith sent Wilder's T1 Patrol to attack the airfield. G1 Patrol's radio truck was to remain at the corner with Peniakoff to stop anyone from getting into the city. The rest of G1 Patrol was sent off to attack the main barracks in Barce. Trooper Cranston was sent with a jeep and crew to find the enemy's motor pool in Barce and to destroy the vehicles in it. And Easonsmith went off in a jeep to find and attack the officer's quarters in Barce.[94]

At midnight T1 Patrol, consisting of four 30 cwt trucks and a jeep, entered the airfield through a side gate that Wilder had opened. Driving onto the airfield, the first Italians that the New Zealanders of T1 Patrol saw were subjected to machine-gun fire; next T1 Patrol's gunfire set fire to a fuel dump, destroyed a tanker truck, as well as a tanker trailer. By now the whole airfield was lit up by burning gasoline. Travelling in a line ahead formation, T1 Patrol headed for the aircraft parked on the airfield; and when the vehicles went by the Italian mess hall, the New Zealanders threw grenades into the windows of the building. Wilder thought that it appeared as though "the enemy was waiting for us, but they seemed to be very panicky and their fire was very wild and ultimately ineffective."[95] For the next hour, T1 Patrol drove slowly around the airfield destroying aircraft with machine-guns firing incendiary bullets. Those aircraft that did not catch fire had short fused time bombs placed on them by Corporal M. Craw, who from time to time would stop the truck he was driving in order to place a bomb on an undestroyed aircraft. By then it was complete pandemonium: the Italians were firing weapons in all directions, while the whole area was lit by burning gasoline and aircraft. T1 Patrol's vehicles continued driving slowly around the airfield with

93   TNA, WO/201/745, f. 13.
94   TNA, WO/201/745, f. 14.
95   Frank Jopling, *Bearded Brigands: The Diaries of Trooper Frank Jopling* (Wellington, New Zealand: Ngaio Press, 2002), p. 192.

the New Zealanders firing machine-guns and throwing grenades, and Craw's time bombs kept exploding. Wilder claimed later to have destroyed twenty aircraft and to have damaged another dozen; however, the figure was later increased to thirty-five aircraft destroyed.[96]

When T1 Patrol began to run out of machine-gun ammunition, Wilder, in the lead truck, left the airfield through the main gate into the town of Barce. Near the railroad station Wilder saw two light tanks firing up and down the street and blocking the patrol's route. Wilder drove his "30 cwt at full speed into the nearest tank to try to push it out of the day, and in doing so cannoned off it into the second tank. This had the desired effect of clearing a way through for the remainder of the patrol."[97] Then Wilder and Troopers D.S. Parker and H.R.T. Holland put grenades under the treads of the tanks and attempted to get another grenade into the turret of one of the tanks. Wilder and the two troopers then jumped into the back of the patrol's jeep; but Trooper P.J. Burke, the driver, lost control of the jeep and it ran up onto the curb and turned over. Parker and Wilder were rendered unconscious and Burke was injured. The crew of the following truck got the men out from under the overturned jeep and put them into their truck. Wilder and Parker soon came to with no apparent after-effect. The crew of the third truck put the two tanks out of action by throwing a grenade and a time bomb into the turret of the one and destroying the other with machine-gun fire and a time bomb. The driver of the third truck, Corporal K.E. Tippett, then took a wrong turn and drove into the town rubbish dump but regained the main road by smashing through a backyard. The last truck, driven by Craw, stopped at the two light tanks and then continued down the main road until he saw some enemy armored cars. Craw attempted to get away from them by going down a side street, but this did not work so he turned the truck around and attempted to make a run for it. Enemy gunfire set the truck on fire and it crashed into a concrete air raid shelter. When the truck hit the shelter Craw was thrown forward through the entrance of the structure and was then overpowered and captured by the Italians hiding in it. Trooper R.E. Hay was captured, too, as he was pulling Trooper K. Yealands, who was badly wounded, out of the truck. The fourth member of the truck's crew, Trooper T.A. Milburn, escaped from Barce, only to be captured later outside of the town.[98] In the town of Barce, T1 Patrol had lost six men, a jeep and two trucks.

---

96   TNA, WO/201/815, f. 18.

97   TNA, WO/201/745, f. 14.

98   Corporal Craw and Troopers Hay and Milburn successfully escaped from the enemy after one year of captivity. R.L. Kay, *The Long Range Desert Group in the Mediterranean* (Wellington, New Zealand: Department of Internal Affairs, 1950), p. 32.

At night, as T1 Patrol was heading for the airfield, G1 Patrol set off for the main barracks in Barce.[99] The patrol drove down the road and then stopped. Dennis and two guardsmen got out of their vehicles, within twenty-five yards of a group of Italian soldiers, and cut the telephone wires and then got back into the trucks and continued on their way. G1 Patrol passed the hospital in Barce and then was challenged by two Italian sentries. Dennis, who was driving the first truck, slowed down as if he was going to stop and then threw a four-second grenade at the two Italians, who were "seen to be blown down by the blast."[100] The patrol continued on to the main barracks where it was again challenged by two sentries who, according to Dennis were "dealt with in the same manner, eight or nine Italians were seen in a group on the steps of the main entrance, and five or six grenades were thrown (by men [Dennis] had detailed previously) amongst them."[101] At the same time G1 Patrol's gunners opened fire on the barracks. Hundreds of machine-gun rounds were fired through the windows of the building, and 20 mm shells from the patrol's Breda gun were shot through the front door. A sentry on a nearby ack-ack tower began firing on the British vehicles, but he was forced to stop by the massed fire of the patrol's automatic weapons which were immediately turned on him. Then Dennis ordered "cease fire." The Patrol Commander and five guardsmen jumped off their trucks and ran to the five foot high barracks wall. The guardsmen did not climb the wall because there were a number of armed Italians in slit trenches behind it. Dennis and the five guardsmen with him threw grenade after grenade into the doors and windows of the building until they ran out of missiles. The six British soldiers then got back into their vehicles, the barracks were given a parting blast of automatic weapons fire, and the patrol headed for the railroad station. Two tanks were encountered on the way to the railroad station, and G1 Patrol went down a side street in an attempt to get around them; but every time the patrol attempted to get back onto the main road it was met with fire from these two tanks. Dennis decided to break off the action and proceeded across the hospital grounds and some cultivated land to reach the main road, where he met Easonsmith.

While G1 Patrol had gone off to shoot up the barracks, Trooper Cranston and Easonsmith, each in a jeep armed with Vickers K machine-guns, went into Barce with the intention of causing as much trouble for the enemy as possible. Cranston and Easonsmith worked independently of each other, but their actions were similar in the way they drove around Barce throwing grenades at enemy

99   TNA, WO/201/739, f. 3.
100   TNA, WO/201/739, f. 10.
101   *Ibid.*

soldiers and shooting up buildings and vehicles. With grenades and submachine-gun fire, Easonsmith destroyed an enemy motor pool consisting of ten trucks, a tanker truck, and a fuel trailer before returning to G1 Patrol's radio truck, where Peniakoff was waiting.

An hour and a half or two hours after the attack had begun and with the night sky still lit up by the fires at the airfield and the sounds of gunfire being heard from every direction, the two remaining trucks of T1 Patrol arrived at the rendezvous at the edge of town followed quickly by Cranston and his jeep and G1 Patrol, which in the confusion had lost one truck, a jeep, and four guardsmen. The next task was to get away from Barce and hide the vehicles before daylight and the arrival of enemy aircraft. The plan was for the two patrols to leave Barce by the same route they had used to enter the town; but as the Long Range Desert Group vehicles were going down the road away from Barce, G1 Patrol's truck with the Breda gun on it went off the road and turned over. It was not until 0400 on 14 September that the vehicle was righted and back on the road. T1 Patrol's radio truck and the medical officer were picked up at Sidi Selim. Because the force now had only three jeeps and seven trucks, Easonsmith decided to pick up the two damaged trucks near the police post. After leaving the police post with the two trucks the Patrols met three Italian officers and about one hundred and fifty Arab troops armed with light machine-guns and rifles who were waiting in ambush on the side of a hill that the road passed. For some reason, however, the Italians had not blocked the road, and under cover of automatic weapons' fire the British vehicles got through the ambush with one truck damaged and three men wounded. About five miles past the ambush site, the two patrols left the road and hid from enemy aircraft in some woods.

Easonsmith decided to fix the three damaged trucks, which would have taken about two hours. But this scheme went by the wayside when mounted enemy Arab troops discovered the hiding place and the British force had to move to a new one. Everything that could possibly be removed from the damaged trucks was put into working vehicles and then time bombs were placed in the damaged trucks. While this was being done, about fifty enemy Arab troops attacked the patrols with small arms; two Italian fighter aircraft also appeared but then went away when they could not see the vehicles because of the trees. As soon as the aircraft had left, Easonsmith took a jeep armed with Vickers K machine-guns and, using folds in the ground as cover, worked his way around the flank of the enemy and drove back the enemy infantry about two miles by "appearing at unexpected places and firing

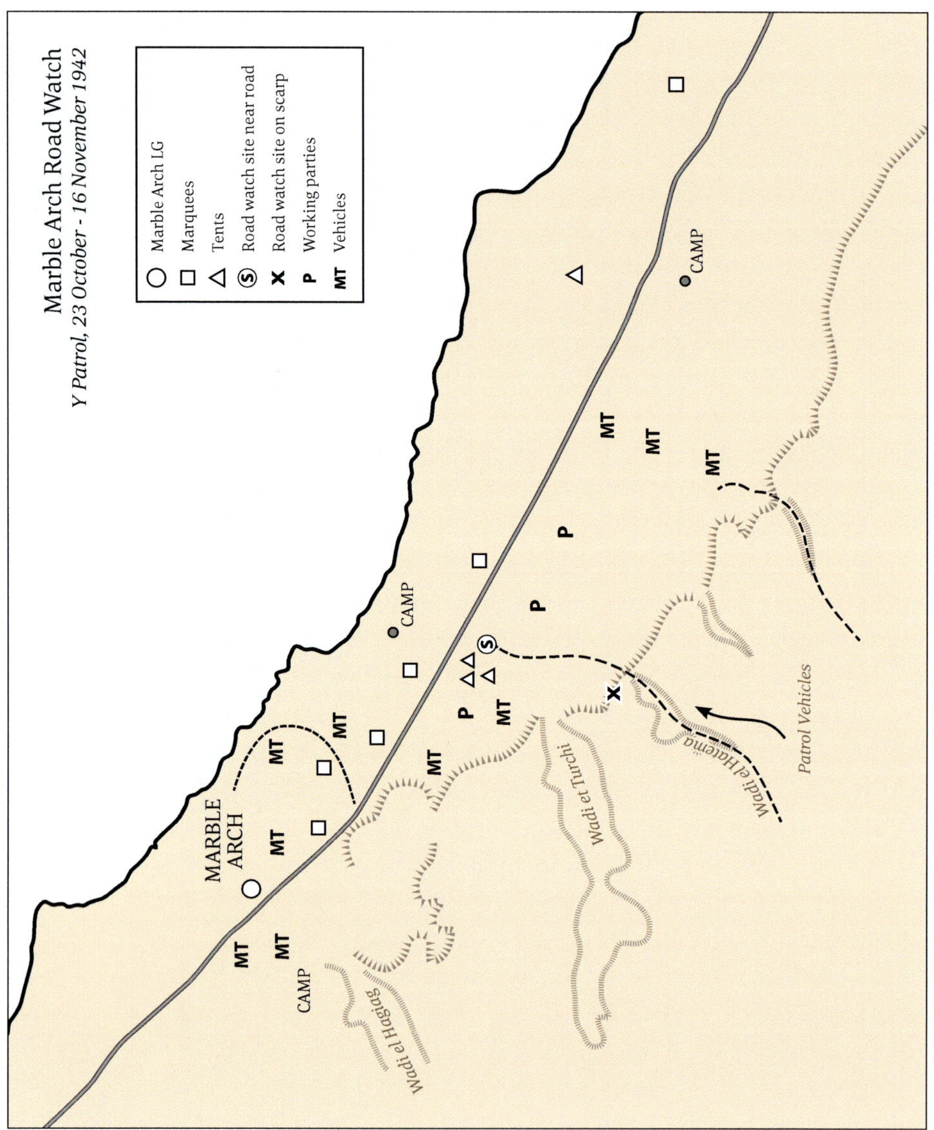

Fig. No 22. Marble Arch Road Watch, Y1 Patrol, 23 Oct.-16 Nov. 1942 (TNA, WO 201/815).

at them with the two guns."[102] When the enemy infantry had retreated, the two patrols, leaving three damaged trucks with time bombs in them, crossed about seven miles of difficult ground to a point where G1 Patrol's radio truck "stripped

---

102   TNA, WO/201/739, f. 7.

a rear axle pinion and was immovable on the top of a very bare hill."[103] The other vehicles were in the meantime hidden in some woods at the base of the hill. At that point, an enemy reconnaissance aircraft appeared and searched the region for about forty-five minutes. As soon as the enemy aircraft had left, however, the truck on top of the hill was pushed into a wadi and hidden.

For a short time it looked as if the two patrols might yet get away, but six enemy fighter aircraft appeared overhead just as the time bombs in the three abandoned trucks went off. These explosions occupied the attention of the enemy aircraft for a short time, but then the fighters began systematically to machine-gun places where vehicles could be hidden, and they very quickly discovered where the Long Range Desert Group's vehicles actually were. From 1030 until dark, enemy aircraft attacked the two patrols with bombs and gunfire. The men were well hidden and scattered, and luckily only Wilder and a guardsman were wounded. When it was dark and the enemy aircraft had finally left, only one truck and two jeeps remained in working condition. Also, there was very little water and food. Since, moreover, there was not enough transport to carry all of the men, Easonsmith divided the force into three groups. Ten men who realized that there would not be enough transport started walking south as soon as it was dark towards the place where Easonsmith had hidden a truck before the raid on Barce. Lawson, the medical officer, with a navigator and a fitter, was given one jeep with a bullet hole in its fuel tank and the sole remaining truck was used to carry the six wounded men; however, Lawson soon had to abandon the jeep because it was losing too much gasoline. So Lawson went south with the wounded towards Landing Ground 125 and Kufra.

The remaining fourteen men, with one jeep to carry their supplies and led by Easonsmith, also began walking south with Lawson's group. However, Easonsmith's walking group soon fell behind the medical officer's truck. Shortly after Lawson's group was out of sight, the jeep with Easonsmith's party broke down and it took two hours to fix it. After the jeep had been repaired and the group had, by then, been marching for about an hour, it was discovered that a medical orderly, Private Astle, was missing. Dennis and another man went back and attempted to find the missing man, but they failed to do so. It was thought that Astle had probably fallen asleep and nobody saw him drop out of the line of march.[104] The next day, 15 September, Easonsmith's group had a bad time; for there was almost no cover and enemy aircraft were out searching for the British and "a fair amount of time was

---

103   *Ibid.*
104   TNA, WO/201/739, f. 8.

spent lying in the dirt."That night, however, they came across some Arabs who sold them some lamb and enough milk for each man to have "a good drink."[105] The next day Easonsmith's group found a well with good water.[106] On the morning of 17 September, before daylight, Easonsmith's party heard vehicles they thought might be a Long Range Desert Group patrol. Two Verey lights were fired off, but the vehicles did not see the lights and continued on their way. Easonsmith followed these vehicles with the remaining jeep, and about two miles away he discovered S2 Patrol having breakfast. Easonsmith immediately radioed the Long Range Desert Group's headquarters to inform them about Lawson and the wounded men. Lloyd Owen and Y1 Patrol, which was hiding in the desert south of Tobruk, were ordered to go to Landing Ground 125 as quickly as possible and find Lawson's party. Lloyd Owen did not receive these orders until the afternoon of 17 September, but Y1 Patrol was only eighty-five miles from Landing Ground 125 and reached it that evening and met Lawson's party. The next day an R.A.F. Bombay transport aircraft of 216 Squadron flew into Landing Ground 125 and took the wounded to Kufra and then on to a hospital in Cairo. When Easonsmith's group met S2 Patrol they had walked about eighty miles across the desert. They "were very foot sore but there was no severe illness."[107] S2 Patrol and Easonsmith's men next went to the place where the truck had been hidden before the raid. When they arrived they found the truck along with a note from Lawson saying that he had taken some rations and was pushing on to Landing Ground 125. It was clear that the ten-man walking party, which had left before Easonsmith's and Lawson's groups, had not reached the hidden truck.

Early in the morning of 18 September, three of S1 Patrol's trucks with their crews and all of Easonsmith's men were sent to Landing Ground 125 and told to place themselves under Lloyd Owen's command and go with him to Kufra. Easonsmith, with his jeep and the three remaining S2 Patrol trucks, began searching for the missing men. On the morning of 19 September three of the missing men were found, and shortly after five more were discovered; but Trooper F.W. Jopling of T1 Patrol, who was slightly wounded, and Lance Corporal Gutheridge of G1 Patrol were still missing. The search was continued for the next two days, but no sign of the two missing men was found. Later it was learned that Jopling was captured

105   TNA, WO/201/815, f. 20.
106   TNA, WO/201/745, f. 15.
107   TNA, WO/201/815, f. 20.

on 23 September.[108] After calling off the search, Easonsmith and the three trucks of S2 Patrol went to Landing Ground 125 and met S1 Patrol, which had picked up four guardsmen who had also walked out of Barce. Just after the Long Range Desert Group vehicles left Landing Ground 125, the place was bombed by two unidentified aircraft.[109] The sand sea was crossed—north to south—in a day and on 23 September trucks of the Heavy Section with rations and fuel were met at Howard's Cairn. The whole party arrived at Kufra just in time to be subjected to an air attack, which wounded Lloyd Owen.

Caravan cost the Long Range Desert Group fourteen[110] men killed, captured or missing; plus two men were hurt when G1 Patrol's jeep overturned in the Egyptian Sand Sea, and six men were wounded in action. Fifteen out of seventeen vehicles were destroyed.[111] But aside from some material damage to the enemy, such as the destruction of aircraft at Barce, what did *Bigamy, Agreement, Caravan,* and *Nicety* achieve? According to the British official history of the war in North Africa:

> the results of the raids were on the whole disappointing. They led to a general overhaul of the defensive arrangements on the enemy's lines of communications and to a decision to reinforce Siwa, Jarabub, and Jalo. Three German replacement or draft-holding battalions were posted at Sollum [Salum], and for a short time the Pavia Division was kept at Matruh instead of moving forward. Finally, there was much talk of capturing Kufra, but nothing came of it.[112]

The cost in men, equipment, vehicles, and especially warships was too high a price to pay for what the official history blandly called "disappointing" results. Lloyd Owen is closer to the mark when he states that the effects of the raids "were virtually nil. In no way did they affect the main issue at Alamein…. This was the first time anything on such a scale had been attempted—and mercifully, it was also

---

108   Later in September Jopling escaped from the Italian camp where he had been held as a POW, only to be re-captured six weeks later, this time by the Germans, and sent to a POW camp in Germany. He escaped again, this time successfully. Jopling, *Bearded Brigands*, pp. 204-205.

109   TNA, WO/201/815, f. 21.

110   Guardsmen R. Duncalfe and P. McNobola escaped from Barce and hid in the Jebel Akhdar until the region was overrun by British forces. TNA, WO/201/815, f. 24.

111   TNA, WO/201/738, f. 5; WO/201/745, ff. 13-15, 22-25; WO/201/815, ff. 14-23; Kay, *Desert Group in Mediterranean*, pp. 7-10, 32; Peniakoff, *Private Army*, pp. 166-197; Crichton-Stuart, *G Patrol*, pp. 161-172; Lloyd Owen, *Providence*, pp. 107-114.

112   Playfair, *The Mediterranean*, vol. IV, p. 23.

the last."[113] The raids failed in part because of poor security. Far more important, however, was the fact that the raids were poorly planned by people who did not understand raiding and irregular warfare. As a result, the raids were too big and far too complex; moreover, the planners of these raids did not see nor acknowledge the need for flexibility in their plans. The planners of *Bigamy, Nicety, Caravan,* and *Agreement* did not understand, as did Stirling, the need for total flexibility or the principle that one should not risk the loss of more men and equipment in a raid than what could possibly be gained by the operation.

After the raids on Tobruk, Benghazi, and Barce and during the weeks before the British offensive at El Alamein, the Long Range Desert Group conducted a number of reconnaissance missions. On 10 October, for example, R1 Patrol was directed to take Squadron Leader Walker, R.A.F. north from Kufra to inspect the disused Italian airfields along the Zighen-Jalo track to see if they could be used by the British.[114] On 20 October S2 Patrol, commanded by Lieutenant J. Henry, left Kufra and went north to the region around El Agheila. It was the task of S1 Patrol to make a reconnaissance of the salt marshes, defenses, and terrain in the El Agheila-Marada region.[115] This task was very important; for both the 1940 and 1941 British offensive had stalled at El Agheila partly because of British logistical problems and partly because the salt marshes in the El Agheila region provide one of the few places between El Alamein and Tunisia where an army can anchor its southern flank.

On 26 October S2 Patrol reached the southern edge of the salt marshes and went into hiding in order to be able to make a detailed reconnaissance of the region by both foot and vehicle. S2 Patrol remained in the area until 1 November. During this time it was discovered that there was a twelve to fourteen foot wide anti-tank ditch running from the marshes northward to the coast road and beyond. Also, that the enemy had constructed a barbed wire fence along the east side of the El Agheila-Marada track, but that there were no minefields near the fence as had been reported. They also discovered a series of unoccupied stone sangars and machine-gun emplacements overlooking the marshes. While carrying out this reconnaissance, Henry found something that was all too common in the Western Desert at that time:

---

113   Lloyd Owen, *Providence*, p. 113.
114   TNA, WO/201/815, f. 58.
115   TNA, WO/201/815, f. 35.

[a] wrecked British Plane (Assumed to be a Beaufighter), twin engined, and the remains of two bodies (a Pilot-Officer and a Sergeant) at XA. 7840. Plane was in pieces, spread over 300 to 400 yards. Bodies had been mauled by Bird and Beast. Remains were buried. Remains of two unopened Parachutes were found.[116]

After completing the reconnaissance, S2 Patrol returned to Kufra at 0800 on 10 November.[117]

In the days before El Alamein, the Long Range Desert Group's patrols carried intelligence officers, agents, and supplies to the Jebel Akhdar from Kufra. On 15 October S1 Patrol left Kufra and carried north to a region of the Jebel Akhdar near Benghazi three intelligence officers, four Arab agents, and twelve hundred pounds of stores. It took ten days for S1 Patrol to carry out this mission and to return to Kufra.[118] Three days later, G2 Patrol was ordered to take seven intelligence officers and agents and their stores to the Jebel Akhdar and to look for possible "escapees" from the raid on Barce. G2 Patrol successfully carried out this task in seventeen days.[119] On 20 October Y1 Patrol, commanded by Lieutenant E.F. Spicer, was ordered to leave Kufra and to reinstate the road watch near Marble Arch. Ten days later Y1 Patrol began watching enemy traffic on the coast road.[120] Missions such as the road watch, secret reconnaissance behind enemy lines to determine geographical conditions, and the transporting of intelligence officers to places behind enemy lines were the type of missions that the Long Range Desert Group were best at.

When Stirling returned to Cairo from the Benghazi raid, he found that L Detachment of the Special Air Service Brigade had been made into the Special Air Service regiment. This meant that the *ad hoc* days when the unit was in some kind of military limbo were over. Stirling now needed men, for the Special Air Service had a strength of about only eighty men. Moreover, Stirling still believed that when the British would go on the offensive in the Western Desert, the role of the Special Air Service should be one of creating absolute havoc in the enemy's rear areas by means of an endless series of small raids. To put this scheme into effect, Stirling needed additional men. If they were to be ready to take part in the coming offensive, however, they had to be men who were already trained in and understood

116 TNA, WO/201/815, f. 37.
117 TNA, WO/201/815, f. 37.
118 TNA, WO/201/815, ff. 35-42.
119 TNA, WO/201/815, ff. 31-34.
120 TNA, WO/201/815, ff. 43-45.

war in the desert and who would only have to undergo Special Air Service training. Lieutenant Colonel J.W. Hackett, who was the staff officer appointed to oversee the raiding forces in the Middle East, agreed that Stirling's plan to attack the enemy rear areas to the greatest possible extent would be one of the best ways for the Special Air Service to assist the forthcoming British offensive. But when Hackett and Stirling went to the 8th Army Headquarters to obtain permission to recruit experienced men from the units of the 8th Army, its new commander, Montgomery, would not permit it. In fact, the exchange between Stirling and Montgomery came very close to an argument; but the general remained adamant. The only other sources of recruits for the Special Air Service were units stationed in such places as Palestine and Iraq or the Infantry Base Depot, which had mostly men newly arrived from Britain. Stirling decided to divide the Special Air Service into two Squadrons. One squadron, under the command of Mayne, would be made up of the experienced Special Air Service troops and would be sent at once behind enemy lines to begin operations as soon as possible. The other squadron would be made up of what men could be found in places such as the Infantry Base Depot, and Stirling would take them to Kabrit and train them.[121]

On 7 October Mayne left Kabrit with about eighty men and thirty-five trucks and jeeps and headed first for Kufra and then to Howard's Cairn inside the sand sea. Howard's Cairn would, until the British conquered northern Cyrenaica, serve as a forward base for the Special Air Service to stage attacks against enemy lines of communications and other targets. The Special Air Service, with its own vehicles and having mastered the Long Range Desert Group's methods of travelling across the desert, had the ability to cross the sand sea into northern Cyrenaica; while the enemy, even with aircraft, did not ever venture into the sand seas. This made Howard's Cairn an almost perfect base for Special Air Service operations whilst the enemy were at El Alamein.

Once the Special Air Service was established at Howard's Cairn, Mayne began operations against the enemy. Every day small groups of Special Air Service troops sortied from Howard's Cairn, crossing the sand sea, and attacking targets in the rear of the enemy's position at El Alamein. Vehicles on the coast road were shot up. The railway running along the Egyptian coast was attacked again and again from the base behind the sand sea. Mayne and his men, always in small parties, attacked any target they could reach. Once, the Special Air Service stormed a railroad station to destroy a train in it. In the days before the British El Alamein offensive, small groups of Special Air Service troops ran amok behind the German and Italian lines

---

121   Cowles, *Phantom Major*, pp. 243-248; Warner, *Special Air Service*, pp. 66-67.

at El Alamein. To the enemy it must have appeared as if these raiding parties were everywhere and had the ability to disappear into thin air.[122]

During the late summer and autumn of 1942 British planners and commanders in the Western Desert had demonstrated once again that they did not understand how to use the Long Range Desert Group and the Special Air Service. Before the big raids on Benghazi, Tobruk, and Barce, the Special Air Service, supported by the Long Range Desert Group, had destroyed by British count two hundred and fifty-six enemy aircraft; and if all the vehicles, supply dumps, and buildings that were destroyed by the Long Range Desert Group and the Special Air Service are added to the enemy aircraft destroyed, the material damage done to the enemy by these two small units was huge by any standard. The methods used by Prendergast and Stirling got results.[123] The Long Range Desert Group could go just about any place in the Western Desert; and by August 1942 Stirling and Mayne were very adept at conducting raids and destroying things. Whilst, the methods used at times were decidedly odd, nevertheless, Prendergast's and Stirling's units certainly got results. What the British planners should have done in the weeks before the El Alamein offensive was to reinforce success by giving Stirling more men and the time to train them and to use the R.A.F. to supply both the Long Range Desert Group and the Special Air Service. People such as Stirling, Prendergast, Mayne, Easonsmith, and Kennedy Shaw should have been asked by the planners in Cairo what measures would increase the effectiveness of the Long Range Desert Group and the Special Air Service and then plan accordingly.[124]

---

122   *Ibid.*, pp. 67-68; Cowles, *Phantom Major*, pp. 248-251; Marrinan, *Colonel*, pp. 82-90.

123   Alastair Timpson, *In Rommel's Backyard: a Memoir of the Long Range Desert Group* (Barnsley, S. Yorkshire: Leo Cooper, 2000), pp. 6-12.

124   Cowles, *Phantom Major*, p. 251.

9

To Tunisia and Victory

"Once the enemy has taken flight they can be pursued with no better weapons
than air-filled bladders. But if the officer you have ordered in pursuit prides
himself on the regularity of his formations and precautions of his march…there
is no use in having sent him. He must attack, push, and pursue without cease."
—*Maurice de Saxe, 1732*

According to the British official history of the war, the Battle of El Alamein ended at dawn on 4 November 1943. For twelve days, along the El Alamein line, the Axis and British Empire and Commonwealth armies had fought a battle of attrition in which Rommel's forces were smashed and forced to retreat westward as best they could.[1] Four days after the Battle of El Alamein, American and British forces landed in Morocco and Algeria, capturing most of the French Northwest Africa with little fighting.[2] Several days later the Long Range Desert Group's R2 Patrol manning the road watch at Marble Arch learned that the Axis forces were abandoning Cyrenaica. During the period between 30 October and 8 November, with Y1 Patrol manning the road watch, an average of less than a hundred enemy vehicles travelled up and down the coast road; but several days after the Battle of El Alamein enemy vehicles were moving westward at the rate of three thousand five hundred per day, and almost no traffic was going east.[3] It was obvious to the men of R2 Patrol, who were watching an endless line of enemy vehicles going west, having taken over from Y1 Patrol, that the Axis forces had been badly defeated at El Alamein.

---

1   I.S.O. Playfair, *Mediterranean and Middle East* (London: HMSO, 1966), vol. IV, p. 79.

2   George F. Howe, *North Africa: Seizing the Initiative in the West* (Washington, D.C.: Department of the Army, 1957), pp. 89-252.

3   TNA, WO/201/815, ff. 44, 99.

Having suffered defeat at El Alamein, and with the American and British forces, in the meanwhile, seizing French Northwest Africa, the Axis forces in Africa were caught in a strategic trap. Rommel's army was between the 8th Army advancing from the east along the coast of the Mediterranean and the Allied forces advancing on Tunisia and Libya from the west. For the Allies, the major strategic problem at this point was the following: could British and American forces in North Africa trap and destroy the Axis forces quickly, or would the campaign drag on for months with heavy fighting and large numbers of Allied casualties as a result? Yet if the 8th Army advanced westward fast enough, they could cut off the retreat of Rommel's forces and destroy them as General R.N. O'Connor had done to the Italians in 1941 at Beda Fomm at the end of the first British offensive of the North African campaign.

Now that the enemy was retreating out of Egypt westward, another question was what role would the Long Range Desert Group and the Special Air Service play in the campaign? On 22 September, well before the Battle of El Alamein, the mission of the Long Range Desert Group had been defined as one of long-range reconnaissance. The Long Range Desert Group was to watch enemy movements, supply routes and bases. The Long Range Desert Group had been further directed to attack targets far behind enemy lines, transport intelligence officers and agents to and from points behind enemy lines, and to provide navigational aid to other British units. Unless reassigned, the Long Range Desert Group was to be under the command and control of General Headquarters, Middle East. The Director of Military Operations would exercise command of the Long Range Desert Group through "a special branch", known as G (Raiding Forces) and headed by Hackett. It was further stipulated that, "NO other contact by the LRDG [was] permitted with the General Staff GHQ unless arranged by G (Raiding Forces)".[4] After the Battle of El Alamein, the Long Range Desert Group's main activities continued to be gaining topographical intelligence, long-range raiding, working with Leclerc's Free French forces, maintaining the road watch, and providing navigational aid to units of the 8th Army. The system of command and control, as it had been set forth on 22 September, was not working out as planned, however, and the patrols of the Long Range Desert Group were, at times, under the effective command of the 8th Army and Leclerc's headquarters as well as General Headquarters, Middle East.

One of the most difficult tasks of the Long Range Desert Group after the Battle of El Alamein became to maintain the road watch on the coastal road. On 15 November R2 Patrol was in fact forced to abandon the road watch at Marble

---

4   TNA, WO/201/815, ff. 262-264.

Arch because enemy aircraft were constantly overhead, and it appeared that the site of the road watch was going to be used by the enemy as a camp.[5] While R2 Patrol was being forced to give up the road watch at Marble Arch, G2 Patrol, under the command of Lieutenant H.K. Sweeting, was heading north from Kufra to relieve R2 Patrol. Because of the difficulties already encountered by R2 Patrol at Marble Arch, the Long Range Desert Group headquarters ordered by radio that G2 Patrol set up a new road watch to the west of Marble Arch between Merduma and Nofilia. However, because of the large number of enemy troops encamped along the coast road as well as the number of unfriendly Arabs in the region, it was not until 19 November before Sweeting had found a place suitable for establishing a road watch. To carry out the road watch effectively, G2 Patrol's trucks were hidden ten miles south of the coast road. Two trucks were used each night to relieve two men hiding at a point near the coast road where they were able to see and count enemy vehicles on that road. G2 Patrol maintained the road watch continuously until 11 PM on 27 November. At this time G2 Patrol had to quit the road watch because its radio was not working and Sweeting had come down with jaundice. G2 Patrol arrived back at Kufra on 7 December, four weeks after it had left—a period much longer than it had rations for. Because of his jaundice, Sweeting gave up command of G2 Patrol and was evacuated to Cairo.[6]

Due to the importance of the road watch and to the difficulties encountered by both G2 and R2 Patrols, the Long Range Desert Group sent two patrols north from Kufra by different routes to set up road watches at two different places on the coast road.[7] On 20 November G1 and T1 Patrols left Kufra and headed north by different routes to set up two road watches as well as to relieve G2 Patrol. Both patrols ran into trouble, however, before reaching the coast road. The enemy knew that the Long Range Desert Group and the Special Air Service were using Kufra as a base to mount operations against the coast road and had placed a number of mines in what was called "the Marada-Zella gap"; in addition, the enemy was also, for the first time, attempting to intercept units of the Long Range Desert Group and the Special Air Service with ground and air patrols in the Marada-Zella gap. Five days after leaving Kufra, the leading truck of T1 Patrol ran over a land mine which damaged the vehicle beyond repair and broke the left leg of Trooper P.J.

5   TNA, WO/201/815, ff. 204-205. TNA, WO/201/815, ff. 110-111, 114-115; Michael
     Crichton-Stuart, *G Patrol* (London: William Kimber, 1958), pp. 175-176.
6   TNA, WO/201/815, f. 99.
7   TNA, WO/201/815, f. 229.

Burke. Several days later, for reasons that are not known, T1 Patrol was recalled to Kufra.[8]

G1 Patrol's ordeal in setting up and maintaining a road watch shows how difficult this type of operation had become. On 20 November G1 Patrol, commanded by Timpson and consisting of one other officer and twenty other ranks, left Kufra in two jeeps and five 30 cwt trucks. The patrol's mission was to relieve G2 Patrol at the road watch near Nofilia. About 0900 on 25 November, near Tmed el Hofra in the Marada-Zella gap, G1 Patrol encountered two enemy patrols — one consisting of eight vehicles and the other of five. After a firefight with the two enemy patrols along the edge of the escarpment, Timpson broke free from the enemy and escaped northward with two trucks, one of which was the radio truck, one jeep plus Lieutenant Hon. Bernard Bruce and eight other ranks. The remainder of the patrol—eight guardsmen in three trucks and a jeep—were either killed or captured.

After what was left of G1 Patrol got clear of the enemy, Timpson hid for the rest of the day, about twenty miles from the site of the fight, expecting enemy aircraft to hunt him down. During the evening of 25 November, G1 Patrol continued north towards where G2 Patrol had set up the road watch. Because it had been cloudy with some rain for several days, G1 Patrol's navigator could not obtain a sun or star fix and the patrol was navigating by dead reckoning. Timpson had only a vague idea of the patrol's location, but on 27 November he "recognized the country";[9] however, it was not until dawn on 28 November that he located G2 Patrol's deserted campsite. In the darkness and rain, the two patrols had passed each other during the night! G1 Patrol thought that G2 Patrol had most likely moved the site of the road watch or had been driven away by the enemy. Timpson did not gain contact with headquarters until 29 November because of a failure of radio procedures, and he learned then that G2 Patrol was withdrawing to Kufra.

After learning of G2 Patrol's withdrawal, Timpson decided to set up a road watch because in essence his small group was the only unit of the Long Range Desert Group in a position to do so. Timpson made this decision knowing that he would encounter many difficulties. G1 Patrol had only one jeep, two trucks in poor mechanical condition, plus two officers and eight men. There was enough gasoline for only five hundred and fifty miles, water and food for twenty-four days, but no cigarettes. The patrol was constantly being overflown by aircraft landing and taking off from the nearby airfield at Merduma; and the Merduma-Nofilia track, which

---

8   TNA, WO/201/815, f. 141.
9   TNA, WO/201/815, ff. 137-146; Crichton-Stuart, *G Patrol*, pp. 176-188.

was used by the enemy, ran just south of the coast road. Nevertheless, Timpson set up a road watch at this point on the coast road. As soon as it was dark, Timpson and Guardsman Welsh were taken by jeep to a point thirteen miles south of the coast road on the Merduma-Nofilia track. From here Welsh and Timpson walked the thirteen miles to the coast road and began the watch. Timpson did not drive closer to the coast road because he did not want to leave any vehicle tracks crossing the Merduma-Nofilia track for the enemy to see. Timpson's plan was for the jeep to return to G1 Patrol's hide-out and for Bruce to find a hiding place for it and the two trucks; then at 0400 on 1 December the jeep with two guardsmen who were to relieve Timpson and Welsh would meet them at the same place where they had been dropped off on the Merduma-Nofilia track. This process was to be repeated every twenty-four hours. On paper this scheme appears to be simple, but in fact it was very difficult to carry out. The region was full of German camps, enemy vehicles were constantly moving about, off the coast road, and enemy aircraft were very active. Moreover, Bruce got a poisoned hand from a thorn, which forced his temperature up to 103½° before he recovered.

When moving between the patrol's hiding place and the site of the road watch, the men of G1 Patrol were constantly encountering enemy troops or camps. Two guardsmen who had the road watch duty on the night of 10 December simply disappeared. It was thought that they were captured when they entered an enemy camp by mistake. Timpson and Welsh, who had the last twenty-four hours of road watch duty on 13 December, carefully positioned themselves two hundred yards from the coast road between two German camps. This position, to the best of their knowledge, was the only place on the coast road in the area which was not occupied by the enemy. The Germans were so close that their voices could be heard, and the two guardsmen knew that the enemy had macaroni and goulash for lunch. That night Timpson and Welsh had the pleasure, along with the Germans, of being strafed by a British night fighter. The next day Timpson and Welsh withdrew to the south and met the rest of G1 Patrol along with 1 Patrol of the Indian Long Range Squadron at Denniff's Dump. G1 Patrol had maintained the road watch for fifteen days under conditions of great hardship and danger.[10]

It was obvious to the headquarters of the Long Range Desert Group that G1 Patrol was in no condition to maintain a road watch and that most likely it could not even return to Kufra without some assistance. On 27 November S1 Patrol was ordered to the coast from Kufra to set up a road watch on the coast road between El Agheila and Sirte. Lazarus, the patrol's commander, was also directed to find a

---

10   TNA, WO/201/815, ff. 147-148.

route to the coast which was west of Zella to avoid passing through the Marada-Zella gap.[11] Three days later, 1 Patrol of the Indian Long Range Squadron was directed to leave Kufra on 1 December and to go north to the coast road and set up a second road watch between Sirte and El Agheila. On 6 December, however, these orders were changed and 1 Indian Patrol was ordered to go to the assistance of G1 Patrol, which 1 Indian Patrol met on 13/14 December.[12]

In the meantime, Lazarus's S1 Patrol, consisting of sixteen other ranks in one jeep and four 30 cwt Trucks, had left Kufra on 28 November going north towards the coast, crossing an arm of the Rebiana Sand Sea, picking up additional fuel at a place known as Oliver's Dump, and crossing the Hon-Zella track west of Hon without being seen by the enemy. Before they reached the coast, however, it became known to the British that the enemy were pulling back further west; and by radio Lazarus was ordered to set up a road watch west of Gheddahia, which he did at 1700 on 13 December. S1 maintained this road watch until 20 December, when it was relieved by T2 Patrol. During the seven days that S1 Patrol conducted the road watch west of Gheddahia, it encountered a number of difficulties. On the evening of 14 November a unit of the Special Air Service shot up a number of enemy camps and vehicles along the coast road near the site of the road watch, which provoked searches of the region by enemy aircraft. There were no good hiding places near the coast road, and enemy convoys from time to time pulled off the road and enemy troops often would camp near the site of the road watch. Moreover, S1 Patrol was discovered by a number of Arabs who were not very friendly, and they had to be bought off with tea, money and sugar.[13] T2 Patrol, under the command of Captain R.A. Tinker managed to maintain the road watch west of Gheddahia for less than two days because of the large number of enemy troops in the region. On 22 December Tinker with two vehicles and nine other ranks went north to the vicinity of Sedada. While Tinker was away, three German armored cars overran the patrol's advanced base. They captured three trucks, including the one with the radio in it, and, apparently, six New Zealanders and two English soldiers, too.[14] The next day, with the approach of eight German armored cars, Tinker withdrew

---

11   TNA, WO/201/815, ff. 152-155.

12   TNA, WO/201/815, ff. 149-151.

13   Trooper J.L. Reid of the 2nd New Zealand Expeditionary Force walked across the desert for a week before being captured. He later escaped from the prison camp in Italy. Trooper E. Ellis, a New Zealander, and a British private, E.C. Sturrock, with no food and little water made their way back eastward to British lines. R.L. Kay, *The Long Range Desert Group in the Mediterranean* (Wellington, N.Z.: Department of Internal Affairs, 1950), pp. 10-11.

14   TNA, WO/201/815, f. 223.

with his remaining two vehicles; and on 29 December the road watch was ended by order of the 8th Army.[15]

The road watch on the coastal road was one of the Long Range Desert Group's greatest achievements during the North African campaign. On 14 December the Director of Military Intelligence at General Headquarters, Middle East wrote:

> LRDG road watch provides the only trained road traffic observers. Not only is the standard of accuracy and observation exceptionally high, but the patrols are familiar with the most recent illustration of enemy vehicles and weapons.
>
> During the periods of withdrawal or reinforcement of the enemy the LRDG road watch has provided and still provides an indispensable basis of certain facts on which calculation of enemy strength can be based. Without their reports we should frequently have been in doubt as to the enemy's intentions, when knowledge of them was all-important, and our estimate of enemy strength would have been far less accurate and would have been accepted with far less confidence.
>
> The road watch immediately in rear of the EL AGHEILA position has been of quite exceptional importance and the information which it has provided, in spite of interruptions due to a difficult and dangerous situation, has been invaluable. From the point of view of military intelligence and the risks and casualties which the patrols have accepted and are accepting have been more than justified.[16]

Unknown to most people at the time, the road watch on the coast road was a means of double-checking *Ultra* information. The importance of this cannot be overestimated, especially as, in many respects *Ultra* was the main source of intelligence for the Allies. However, at times, *Ultra* had also resulted in the British being surprised by Rommel, who did not always follow the directions of his superiors. But the Long Range Desert Group's ability to maintain an almost continuous watch on the coast road gave intelligence officers at both the 8th Army and General Headquarters, Middle East a very reliable means of knowing when

---

15   TNA, WO/201/771, Note on the Intelligence value of LRDG road watch, 14 December 1942.

16   TNA, WO/201/815, f. 223.

and what type of supplies and forces were actually being moved eastward by the enemy. This was so because the coast road was in fact the enemy's only supply line from Libyan ports to the front lines. The road watch also became a means of hiding the existence of *Ultra*, since information gained from *Ultra* could be cited as having come from the road watch. So the road watch acted not only as a way of checking information gained from *Ultra* but also as a means of hiding *Ultra* as a source of intelligence.

Besides the road watch, one of the other most important tasks of the Long Range Desert Group during the British advance westward across Libya towards Tunisia had become to provide, from time to time, patrols to guide units of the 8th Army in operations that required not only geographical knowledge but also skill at desert navigation. An operation of this type was the outflanking of the enemy's position at El Agheila in an attempt to cut off his rear guard at Nofilia. On 4 December R1 Patrol received operational instructions to leave Kufra at once and go north to Agedabia; in the meantime the patrol's commander, Browne, was to fly to 8th Army Headquarters for instructions and then rejoin his patrol.[17] On 12 December R1 Patrol, with Browne back in command, guided the 2nd New Zealand Division south into the desert. The plan was for the 2nd New Zealand Division, always guided by R1 Patrol, to march south, then west, and next northwest around El Agheila and the salt marshes through the open desert to the coast road at Wadi el Rigel, which was west of El Agheila.[18] If this movement was carried out quickly, the enemy forces that were holding the El Agheila position would be cut off by the 2nd New Zealand Division. But even if the flanking movement of the 2nd New Zealand Division was discovered by the enemy, they would be forced to quickly abandon their defensive position at El Agheila and retreat westward exactly to avoid being cut off by the New Zealanders.

The 2nd New Zealand Division, navigated by R1 Patrol and consisting of hundreds of vehicles, moved across the desert to outflank the enemy position at El Agheila.[19] On 12 and 13 December it rained and the movement of this mass of vehicles, men, and equipment in a southerly and then in a southwesterly direction towards Marada was not betrayed by huge columns of dust being thrown up by the division's vehicles, which might otherwise have been the case in dry weather

---

17   W.G. Stevens, *Bardia to Enfidaville* (Wellington, N.Z.: Department of Internal Affairs, 1962), pp. 225-230.

18   H.W. Wynter, *Special Forces in the Desert War, 1940-1943* (Richmond, Surrey: The National Archives, 2001), pp. 188, 190-192.

19   Mike Morgan, *Sting of the Scorpion* (Stroud, Gloucestershire: Sutton Publishing, 2000), pp. 69-71.

conditions. On 14 December, still guided by R1 Patrol, the 2nd New Zealand Division turned west and at about 1200 crossed the Marada-El Agheila track at El Halfa and then headed northwest; and on the morning of 15 December the leading elements of the division cut the coast road at Wadi el Rigel. But Rommel had been too quick; for the rear guard of the enemy's army had slipped by the New Zealanders in the early morning darkness.

On 16 December the 2nd New Zealand Division again attempted to cut off part of the retreating enemy forces. The New Zealanders, moving across the open desert in a wide flanking movement, by-passed Nofilia; and in the late afternoon of 17 December the lead element of the 2nd New Zealand Division fought their way onto the coast road at Wadi en Nizam some miles west of Nofilia just as the enemy's rear guard was withdrawing westward.[20] These two flanking movements, at the time called "left hooks," made across the desert by the 2nd New Zealand Division could not have been made without the navigational assistance of R1 Patrol. Although no large number of enemy troops was cut off and captured by these flanking movements, they did speed up the enemy's withdrawal westward from the defensive position at El Agheila.[21]

With the advance of the 8th Army as far west as Wadi en Nizam in Tripolitania, the main body of the British forces entered an area about which they had little geographical knowledge. R1 Patrol was split into three small groups and, with the addition of several British and South African officers and other ranks, was sent forward to scout the ground around Wadi Tamet, Chebir, and Wadi Zem Zem. Although both the Long Range Desert Group and the Special Air Service had conducted operations in this region, R1 Patrol was undertaking an extremely difficult and dangerous task. The first mishap occurred when the jeep in which Browne and a South African officer, Captain Le Rou, ran over a Teller mine near El Machina. Le Rou died of his wounds and Browne was brought back to Nofilia "suffering from severe shock and bruises and a broken collar bone…."[22] With the wounding of Browne, 2nd Lt. K.F. McLauchlan took command of R1 Patrol and continued to carry out topographical reconnaissance for the 8th Army. But on 27 December, near the Gheddahia-Bu Ngem track, the patrol was ambushed by two German armored cars. They lost the truck carrying the radio and a jeep, and the enemy

---

20   *Ibid.*, pp. 13-17; TNA, WO/201/815, ff. 235, 276-278.

21   TNA, WO/201/815, f. 235.

22   Captain Alexander and Lance Corporal H. Norton of the South African Armed Forces, along with Gunner Grimsey, Private Ineson, Trooper Hayes, and Sergeant Major Evans of the Long Range Desert Group.

captured six men;[23] however, the remainder of the patrol skillfully escaped from the ambush. When what was left of R1 Patrol returned to British lines, McLauchlan was able to brief the commander of the 2nd New Zealand Expeditionary Force, General Bernard Freyberg, on the geography west of Nofilia, and then R1 Patrol was returned to the command of the Long Range Desert Group.[24]

When the 2nd New Zealand Division outflanked the Axis defensive position at El Agheila and the 8th Army entered into Tripolitania, this was the signal for the Free French in the Chad to invade and conquer Fezzan in southwest Libya. As early as 22 September de Gaulle had ordered Leclerc to invade Fezzan and "then to debouch to captured Tripoli" as soon as the British had conquered Cyrenaica and entered Tripolitania.[25] On 19 November S2 Patrol, commanded by Lieutenant J. Henry and consisting of eighteen other ranks and six 30 cwt Trucks, was ordered to leave Kufra for Faya on 11 November to act as navigators for Leclerc's force and as a radio link between them and General Headquarters, Middle East via the Long Range Desert Group's headquarters at Kufra.[26] Two days later General Headquarters, Middle East issued to Prendergast "OPERATION INSTRUCTION NO. 151," calling for the Long Range Desert Group to provide the Free French in the Chad with "the fullest information possible regarding enemy dispositions and movements" and to attack the roads and tracks used to support the Italian forces in Fezzan.[27]

On 2 December S2 Patrol arrived at the Free French base at Zouar in the Tibesti Mountains of the Chad. Leclerc's objective was Tripoli, which was sixteen hundred miles north across the vast forbidding wilderness of the Libyan Desert. This was not going to be a raid, the objective of the Free French was to conquer Fezzan and join the 8th Army when it advanced westward into Tunisia. Leclerc's invasion of southwest Libya was mounted by a ragtag force of some 1,260 Free French and African troops from the middle of the wilds of the Chad into the unknown sands of the western Libyan Desert. It was the task of S2 Patrol to maintain a radio link with the main British forces in North Africa and to provide the desert navigational skills required by the Free French on their march north to the Mediterranean.

On 18 December S2 Patrol and the Free French advance guard began the march northward. Although Leclerc's campaign in Fezzan is one of the least known campaigns of the Second World War, it was one of the best conducted.

---

23   TNA, WO/201/815, ff. 234-237; Kay, *Long Range Desert Group in the Mediterranean*, p. 11.

24   Henry Maule, *Out of the Sand* (London: Odhams Books Ltd, 1966), p. 128.

25   TNA, WO/201/815, f. 127.

26   TNA, WO/201/815, ff. 272-273.

27   Maule, *Out of the Sand*, p. 140.

With a small motley force fighting a war of movement in an odd assortment of vehicles, the Free French, commanded by Leclerc, either bypassed or captured all the important Italian posts in Fezzan and on the Murzuk-Tripoli track. On 4 January 1943 the Italian fort at Oum el Araneb was captured by Leclerc's men. Next Sebha fell to the Free French. On 12 January the Cross of Lorraine was raised over Murzuk, and two days later Leclerc proclaimed: "in less than three weeks Fighting French forces have conquered the whole Fezzan territory."[28]

The biggest problem encountered by Leclerc's force in the march north into Fezzan was attacks by enemy aircraft. Before Leclerc's invasion of Fezzan, the Free French general had been told by the British that he could not expect to be aided by the R.A.F. because British fighter aircraft did not have the range to support his force and, further, because the British would not commit long-range strategic bombers to southern Libya. Nonetheless, Leclerc continued to wonder why he could not use S2 Patrol's radio to call upon British aircraft for assistance. Because they had no air support, during the first weeks of the Free French march north, the force was continuously attacked by enemy aircraft with the result that the Free French moved mostly at night. In the course of these air attacks the Free French credited S2 Patrol with shooting down an enemy aircraft, on 26 December, and setting a good example for the men of the Free French force on how to conduct one's self in the face of the enemy.[29]

Indeed, the Long Range Desert Group conducted a number of operations in support of the Free French invasion of Fezzan. On 11 December Y1 Patrol and 4 Indian Patrol were ordered to attack the airfield at Hon; however, owing to rain, lack of luck, and extremely bad going the operation was a failure.[30] R2 Patrol attempted to attack the airfield at Sebha, but this operation was also a failure because of rain, bad going, and mechanical failure.[31] On 6 December T1 Patrol, commanded by Wilder, left Kufra with orders to attack the Hon-Sebha track and the Esc Sciueref-Brach track. On 16 December T1 Patrol placed mines on the Hon-Sebha track and then moved on to the Esc Sciueref-Brach track, which was also successfully mined. After meeting Y2 Patrol, the two patrols destroyed a 10-ton Italian truck and took two prisoners. Y2 Patrol then returned to base with the prisoners while T1 Patrol again mined the track and shot up and destroyed two more Italian 10-ton trucks as well as took three more prisoners.[32] On the last day

---

28   TNA, WO/201/815, ff. 128-136

29   Maule, *Out of the Sand*, pp. 128-140.

30   TNA, WO/201/815, ff. 158-162.

31   TNA, WO/201/815, ff. 230-232.

32   TNA, WO/201/815, ff. 238-241.

of 1942, 2 Indian Patrol set off to attack traffic on the Mizda-Brach track; and on 6 January the patrol ambushed a column of about thirty truck and two armored vehicles. The enemy column was badly shot up before 2 Indian Patrol was forced to withdraw owing to heavy enemy return fire. On 12 January 1943, 2 Indian Patrol met an advance unit of Leclerc's Free French on the Brach-Esc Sciueref track and became the first unit of British forces in North Africa to encounter the Free French on their march north from the Chad.[33]

On 9 January 1943, 1 Indian Patrol, commanded by Lieutenant J.E. Cantlay, arrived at Oum el Araneb and relieved S2 Patrol from assisting the Free French force on their march north. On 15 January the advance guard of the Free French force, with 1 Indian Patrol navigating, left Oum el Araneb and continued to march north. By 24 February Leclerc had advanced north past Giado, southwest of Tripoli, while 1 Indian Patrol was relieved by a party of 8th Army radio operators and cipher personnel.[34] With the arrival of Leclerc's Free French force in the region of Tripoli, which had been captured by the 8th Army on 23 January, the Italian hold on Tripolitania was destroyed. For, as the Free French marched north out of Chad, the Italian forces between Fezzan and Tripoli were either killed, captured, or forced to flee northward into Tunisia or into the hands of the 8th Army. Perhaps Leclerc could have made the march north from the Chad to meet the 8th Army near Tripoli without the aid of the Long Range Desert Group, but certainly the assistance given the Free French by S2 Patrol and 1 Indian Patrol made the undertaking much easier for Leclerc and his men.[35]

The Long Range Desert Group carried out, in addition, a number of reconnaissance missions in Tripolitania in order to obtain the geographical knowledge required by the 8th Army for its advance westward to Tripoli.[36] On 28 December Y1 Patrol, having set out on a mission, commanded by Spicer with seventeen other ranks, four 30 cwt trucks and a jeep picked up additional fuel at Bir el Communia. And on 4 January Y1 Patrol crossed the Scemech-Beni Ulid track, where they saw several enemy vehicles. On 6 January, while scouting the area east of the Beni Ulid-Tarhuna track, Y1 Patrol encountered two Italian trucks that Spicer thought were "possibly a survey party." Spicer decided to attack the Italians and "wipe" them "out so that they could not inform the enemy of our whereabouts." As Y1 Patrol approached the two Italian vehicles, they drove off "at great speed

---

33   TNA, WO/201/815, ff. 192-193.
34   TNA, WO/169/14944, INDIAN 1 PATROL OP. REPORT, 5 March 1943.
35   Morgan, *Sting of the Scorpion*, p. 66.
36   TNA, WO/201/815, ff. 179-180.

northeastward."[37] The British took up the chase; however, it did not last long because the British were suddenly fired upon by a large number of enemy troops in a fortified position. The jeep was hit by 20 mm. Breda shell that luckily exploded in a roll of bedding, not hurting the two men in the vehicle. Spicer thought the patrol would soon be subjected to enemy air attack and made off westward into some hills and hid in a wadi for the rest of the day; however, no enemy aircraft appeared. The next day the patrol continued its reconnaissance.[38]

During the next ten days Y1 Patrol thoroughly reconnoitered the region east of the Beni Ulid-Tarhuna track. Then on 16 January the patrol received orders to meet R2 Patrol, which had lost two officers at Esc Sciueref. R2 Patrol had been ordered to meet Leclerc's Free French column at Esc Sciueref. When R2 Patrol approached Esc Sciueref on 15 January, a number of men were seen on a sand hill near the fort. R2 Patrol made the recognition signal, which was not answered. Then Captain J.R. Talbot, the patrol's commander, and Lieutenant Kinsman went forward on foot, thinking the men on the sand hill were locals.[39] Shortly after the two officers had disappeared from sight in a dead area between the fort and the patrol, the other members of R2 Patrol heard gunfire. Sergeant C. Waetford, who had been left in command, then went forward to investigate, but found no trace of the two officers. Waetford concluded that the enemy and not the Free French held Esc Sciueref. It was later learned that Leclerc's men had taken Esc Sciueref on 11 January and then continued on their march north, after which the enemy had reoccupied the place. The next day R2 Patrol met Y1 Patrol and Spicer ordered Waetford to return to base; and because of mechanical problems Y1 Patrol returned two days later.[40]

G2 Patrol, commanded by Bruce, with seventeen other ranks and Major J.D. Player of the 7th Armoured Division was given the task of scouting the region west of the Tauorga-Gheddahia road and as far north as Homs on the coast. G2 Patrol had six days at the beginning of January 1943 to explore an area a quarter of the size of Scotland. Bruce split G2 Patrol in half in order to gain as much geographical information about the region as possible and to do so as fast as possible. Player with one jeep and two trucks, covered the southern region between Sedada and Misurata; while Bruce, with two trucks, explored the area from Bu Talah northwards past Beni Ulid towards the coast near Homs. The two groups then met on 6 January at Bir bu Sofia and radioed all the geographical information

---

37   TNA, WO/201/815, f. 181.
38   TNA, WO/201/815, f. 182.
39   TNA, WO/201/815, f. 248.
40   TNA, CAB/44/151, ff. 192-193; WO/201/815, ff. 181-183, 245-249.

they had collected to headquarters. The next day Bruce's and Player's groups again separated and headed for Bir Cau by different routes. Bruce's group arrived at Bir Cau on 8 January, but Player's party did not appear. After waiting for two days, Bruce decided that he had to go with his group directly to 8th Army headquarters to provide that force with geographical intelligence and guides to aid the main British advance westward through the region he had just reconnoitered. After driving all day, Bruce's party managed to reach the headquarters of the 8th Army in the evening of 12 January. The next day Bruce was interviewed by Montgomery, who declared Bruce's information to be "Just what I wanted."[41] After leaving Montgomery, Bruce had to report to the commanders of the 7th Armoured and 2nd New Zealand Divisions. It was decided to attach a member of G2 Patrol to the 7th Armoured Division and one to the 2nd New Zealand Division to act as guides and navigators while Bruce himself would be with the 4th Light Armoured Brigade, which would be on the extreme left of the British advance.[42]

Just before the British offensive began, the missing half of G2 Patrol arrived at 8th Army headquarters but without Player and the patrol sergeant. Player's group failed to reach Bir Cau because they had encountered so many enemy troops that they were forced to go south and west into the desert before heading east towards the British lines. On 13 January near Bu Ngem, Player and the patrol sergeant were captured when they approached on foot two enemy armored cars which they thought to be British; the rest of the party then made their way to 8th Army headquarters.[43]

The geographical information obtained by Y1 and G2 Patrols, as well as data obtained by other patrols of the Long Range Desert Group, was extremely important to the 8th Army. Montgomery intended to attack the enemy at Buerat el Hsun with four divisions. His objective was to capture Tripoli and at the same time to attempt to cut off as many enemy troops as possible. The plan called for the 50th and 51st Divisions to attack northward along the coast road, while the 7th Armoured and 2nd New Zealand Divisions moved northwest across the desert directly to Tripoli. The attack began on 15 January. Guided by Bruce and two other men of G2 Patrol, the 7th Armoured and 2nd New Zealand divisions drove northwest into the desert. By 22 January the 7th Armoured Division was just east of El Azizia, and the 2nd New Zealand Division was closing in on Tripoli from the

---

41   Crichton-Stuart, *G Patrol*, p. 194.

42   TNA, WO/201/815, ff. 184-188; Crichton-Stuart, *G Patrol*, pp. 189-194.

43   Several days after his capture Player escaped, and after walking southeast for eleven days he entered British lines. *Ibid*, p. 195.

South. But once again Rommel was too fast for the British—he had withdrawn his forces eastward before the trap could be closed. Early in the morning of 23 January, British forces entered Tripoli without opposition.[44]

During the battle of El Alamein and its immediate aftermath, Stirling was at Kabrit training new members of the Special Air Service for future operations against the enemy's supply line along the coast road. After Rommel's defeat at El Alamein, it was obvious that the British would attempt to drive the enemy out of Libya into Tunisia and Stirling wanted the Special Air Service to play a major role in this offensive. After the new men had completed their training, they were to be formed into B Squadron, 1st Special Air Service Regiment; and most of the men of the Special Air Service who had survived the raid on Benghazi and were now at Kufra could be formed into A Squadron, 1st Special Air Service Regiment under the command of Mayne. Stirling's plan called for A and B Squadrons to attack the coast road along a four hundred mile front from El Agheila westward to Tripoli. A Squadron would conduct operations against the coast road between El Agheila and Buerat el Hsun, while the western section of the road would be attacked by B Squadron under the command of Major Vivian Street. A and B Squadrons were to be divided into sixteen sections consisting of three jeeps each manned by crews of two or three men. The sub sections were assigned a length of the coast road which they were to attack at least once every night. The targets of these raids were to be enemy vehicles and telephone lines. The objective of the Special Air Service's attacks was to force—by means of bombs, gunfire, and mines—the enemy to use the coast road only during the day, when its vehicles would be open to attack by Allied aircraft.[45]

Stirling's plan was, as usual, tactically radical and daring to an extreme. Montgomery approved Stirling's plan, even though he thought

The Boy Stirling is mad. Quite, quite mad. However in war there is often a place for mad people. Now take this scheme of his. Penetrating miles behind the enemy lines. Attacking the coastal road on a four hundred mile front. Who but the Boy Stirling could think up such a plan. Yet if it comes off I don't mind saying it could have a decisive effect, yes, a really decisive effect on my forthcoming offensive.[46]

---

44   Playfair, *The Mediterranean*, vol. IV, pp. 231-236.

45   Virginia Cowles, *The Phantom Major* (London: Collins, 1958), pp. 254-255, 268-269.

46   *Ibid*, p. 258.

The problem with Stirling's plan for attacking the coast road was that it did not work. While making the plan, Stirling apparently did not know that northeast Tripolitania was quite different from Cyrenaica. The locals were neither friendly to the British nor very hostile to the Italians; moreover, there were quite a few Italian settlers in the region, and the going at times was extremely difficult. There were other complications as well—most of the men of B Squadron were new members of the Special Air Service; and, finally, the enemy, as soon as the Special Air Service began to attack the coast road, made an effort to hunt down the attackers not only with aircraft but also with armored cars and infantry.

Stirling planned to begin the raids on the coast road about the same time as the 8th Army attacked the enemy position at El Agheila. Mayne and A Squadron were ordered north from Kufra to form an advanced base at Bir Zelten. B Squadron, formed almost entirely of men who had just completed their Special Air Service training, departed from Kabrit on 20 November for Bir Zelten. The force consisted of about ninety officers and other ranks in thirty jeeps and a dozen trucks. Each jeep carried two or three men plus two Vickers K machine-guns; twelve land mines, thirty-five gallons of fuel, forty gallons of water, and twenty days rations. There were the usual number of rifles and submachine-guns, along with personal kit. B Squadron went first to Agedabia by road and then headed south out into the desert and then southwest to Bir Zelten, which was reached on 29 November.

After explaining the nature of the operation to his men, Stirling and B Squadron left Bir Zelten and began the long and difficult trip to a hide-out near El Faschia which was to serve as an advanced base for raids on the coast road between Buerat el Hsun and Tripoli. B Squadron found the going extremely difficult and had to abandon several jeeps when their axles broke while crossing Wadi Tamet. Because of the rough terrain, it was not until 13 December that B Squadron was in position to carry out the planned raids on the coast road.[47]

A Squadron, under Mayne, carried out a few raids against the coast road between El Agheila and Buerat el Hsun before being overrun by the 8th Army. Within a few days, the 8th Army, after the 2nd New Zealand Division's sweep around the flank of the enemy positions at El Agheila and the attempt to cut off the retreating enemy at Nofilia, advanced west to a point just short of Buerat el Hsun. With the British advance westward, Stirling ordered A Squadron back to Kabrit to prepare to move to Lebanon for mountain warfare training.[48]

---

47   *Ibid*, pp. 256-258, 267.
48   *Ibid*, p. 279.

B Squadron began raiding the coast road west of Buerat el Hsun on 13 December. Stirling led one raiding party which shot up three enemy vehicles on the coast road, destroyed a mobile workshop and a motor pool, mined the road, cut the telephone lines, and swept an enemy headquarters with machine-gun fire. But Stirling could not remain with B Squadron because he had promised Hackett that he would return to base after B Squadron had arrived at its operational area. The problem was that Stirling now commanded a large force but continued to act as if he was in command of a small force. In the last year Stirling had become a collector of irregular forces in North Africa. In addition to the British and French troops which he had recruited himself for the 1st Special Air Service Regiment, Stirling had been given command of the Special Boat Section, the Greek Sacred Squadron and what was left of the Middle East Commando. All in all, a force of about eight hundred men. Also his brother, William Stirling, was raising in Britain a second Special Air Service Regiment which would arrive in North Africa soon. When Stirling left Kabrit for Libya with B Squadron, Hackett protested saying that Stirling had several hundred men undergoing training and that there were plans and decisions to be made which could not be done behind enemy lines. Stirling somewhat placated Hackett by leaving Jellicoe in charge of the training at Kabrit, stating that he must make the trip to Libya because almost all of the men of B Squadron had no experience at Special Air Service operations and therefore training must be conducted while the unit was *en route* to Libya, and promising that as soon as B Squadron began operations in Libya he would return to base.[49]

After Stirling left, B Squadron's assault on the coast road fell apart. Each sub section made one, two, or maybe three raids against the enemy before either being driven away or tracked down and killed or captured by the enemy. One of the problems was that almost none of the men in B Squadron, including its commander, Street, had any experience in this kind of operation. Another problem was the existence of enemy forces, often in close proximity, together with the combined use, by Rommel, of aircraft as well as ground troops to attack the SAS. Those few men who escaped from the enemy were mostly the few among B Squadron's ranks who had previous operational experience with the Special Air Service. For example, one of the few members of B Squadron to escape was Seekings, who was also the only member of Captain P. Hore-Ruthven's subsection to survive the operation. Seekings had been with the Special Air Service almost from the beginning and had vast experience at desert raiding and avoiding the enemy. But from Seekings's after-action report, on this operation, it seemed that almost every

---

49   *Ibid*, pp. 254-255, 269-270.

move that he made resulted in unwanted contact with the enemy. It was only by his skill at evading the enemy in the desert that Seekings avoided being captured or killed.[50]

Soon after B Squadron began to raid the coast road, enemy troops in conjunction with aircraft, started to hunt down the Special Air Service troops. On 24 December Rommel himself went into Wadi Zem Zem near El Faschia. He wrote:

> Soon we began to find the tracks of British vehicles, probably made by some of Stirling's people…who had been round there on the job of harassing our supply traffic. The tracks were comparatively new we kept a sharp look-out to see if we could catch "tommy"…Troops from my *Kampfstafffel* were also in the area. They had surprised some British Commandos the day before and captured maps marked with British store dumps and strong points. Now they were combing through the district also hoping to stumble on a "Tommy."[51]

Considering the circumstances it is no wonder that B Squadron had a hard time. To begin with, the force was not only made up mostly of inexperienced men, but through captured documents the enemy had learned the locations of some of B Squadron's hide-outs and dumps. In addition, the 8th Army's westward advance was stalled east of Buerat el Hsun, which gave the enemy the opportunity, and the troops, as well as the time to mount a proper hunt for the men of B Squadron. It is true that B Squadron did inflict a number of casualties on the enemy and caused him some concern about the security of his rear areas, but the price in British killed and captured was too high to pay for the results obtained. The destruction of B Squadron in December of 1942 was the greatest loss suffered by the Special Air Service since the unit's disastrous first raid on the night of 16/17 November 1941. Although the loss of B Squadron was in some respects due to bad luck, it was also the result of poor planning as well as attempting to do too much too quickly while at the same time employing too large a force to do it.[52]

It appears that Stirling did not give too much thought to the lessons that should have been learned from the failure of B Squadron's operations along the coast road west of Buerat el Hsun; for if he did, he did not apply these lessons to

---

50   TNA, WO/218/97, Patrol Report by Sgt. R.A. Seekings, B Sqn SAS Regiment.
51   B.H. Liddell-Hart, ed., *The Rommel Papers* (New York: Harcourt, Brace and Company, 1953), pp. 379-380.
52   Cowles, *Phantom Major*, pp. 267-281.

the next series of Special Air Service operations. On 3 January, after the capture of Tripoli, the 8th Army issued an operational instruction to Stirling for Special Air Service to begin operations, against enemy traffic on the coast road between Zuara, Gardane, Medenine, and Gabes. These operations were not to begin before 2 February.[53] The 8th Army might draw up operational instructions for the Special Air Service, but that did not necessarily mean that Stirling would follow them. In January 1943 Stirling planned to mount an attack on targets, just west of Tripoli, to send a party to watch German preparations for the defense of the Mareth line, and to have three French Special Air Service patrols, commanded by Jordan, attack enemy supply lines between Gabes and Sfax in Tunisia. At the same time a party commanded by Stirling would first attempt to "reconnoiter the territory in northern Tunisia"[54] and, then, it would aim to be the first force from the 8th Army to link up with the 1st British Army advancing into Tunisia from the West.

Stirling's wish for the Special Air Service to be the first unit of the 8th Army to gain contact with the British 1st Army was motivated more by army politics than by military objectives. When the 8th Army would have linked up with the American, British, and French forces in Tunisia, it would then just be one army among several—the real power would have rested in the headquarters of General Sir Harold Alexander, commander of the 18th Army Group, and with General Dwight D. Eisenhower, commander-in-chief of all Allied forces in North Africa. Stirling wanted to show the commanders of the Allied forces in Tunisia what the Special Air Service could do as well as to be the first unit commander from the 8th Army to get the ear of Alexander and Eisenhower; for he wanted to make the Special Air Service into a brigade size formation.[55]

Stirling might have thought out well the political side of this scheme but not the military part. For as the 8th Army closed in on Tripoli and southern Tunisia, the war would change. Gone would be the open flanks of the armies fighting in the Western Desert. Tunisia is a small mountainous place and not suitable for the type of operations which had been conducted in Egypt and Libya by the Long Range Desert Group and the Special Air Service. The last act of the war in Africa would not be a war of movement in the vast openness of the desert, but rather one in which the Allied armies would slowly crush the enemy, with its back to the sea, by means of set piece battles and massed firepower. Although it was possible in theory to get around the enemy's southern flank before the 8th Army entered Tunisia and

---

53   TNA, WO/201/815, ff. 281-282.
54   Cowles, *Phantom Major*, p. 282.
55   *Ibid*, pp. 282-283.

then to go west and north into Tunisia and gain contact with the British 1st Army, it would be a very difficult task. During the first half of January 1943, nobody in the 8th Army knew much about the geography of northwest Libya and southern Tunisia, for the Long Range Desert Group had just begun to explore the region. Nevertheless, there were some known geographical obstacles, such as, the Grand Erg Oriental sand sea and the Chott Djerid salt marsh to be dealt with; moreover, and adding to the difficulties, was the fact that nobody in the 8th Army knew anything about the Arabs in Tunisia.

At the beginning of 1943, Stirling began to implement his plan. He sent two patrols of the Special Air Service to attack enemy transport on the coast road west of Tripoli. Not much was accomplished by these two patrols because the terrain was difficult, the geography not very well known, and moreover, there were too many Arabs and enemy troops in the region. From the several after-action reports which were made by the men of the two patrols, it is clear that they should never have been sent into northwest Libya and southern Tunisia.[56] Stirling probably never read these reports, for if he had he might have changed his plans. There were only two routes that Stirling could have taken in Tunisia to meet the 1st British Army. One was to go north passing east of the Chott Djerid through the Gabes Gap passing between Gabes and Chott el Fedjadj; the other was to go west between Grand Erg Oriental and Chott Djerid and then north around the west end of Chott Djerid to Tozeur, as the Long Range Desert Group patrols would later do. Stirling chose the route through the Gabes Gap, probably because it was known and it was near the enemy supply lines that he wanted to attack. What Stirling planned to do was extremely risky, and in the rush of events the commander of the Special Air Service seems not to have thought out all the dangers involved.

On 10 January Stirling's group left Buerat el Hsun on the coast and went south and west across Tripolitania to Gadames at the edge of the Grand Erg Oriental sand sea and then north, crossing from time to time with great difficulty arms of this sand sea which ran from east to west, to a point just north of the northwest corner of the sand sea; there he met Jordan's and his party of French Special Air Service troops. Stirling decided that Jordan's party should go through the Gabes Gap that night and then Stirling's group would follow the next night. Jordan's party of nine jeeps encountered the enemy in the Gabes Gap, and the Frenchmen had to

---

56   TNA, WO/218/97, Report of Attack on Capt. Murphy's Patrol on 17.1.43; Report on Statement made by a British parachutist recaptured from the enemy in Tripolitania; Report on operations carried out by A Patrol of "B" Squadron 1 S.A.S. Regiment between 11 Jan. and 28 Jan. 1943; Report on operation carried out 18 Jan. by Capt. J.C. O'Sullivan and PCT 3711662 Higham, R. "B" Squadron 1 S.A.S. Regiment.

fight their way through. Then for the next few days Jordan's group placed mines in roads, blew up sections of a railway, and fought several skirmishes. But as soon as Jordan's French Special Air Service began operations north of the Gabes Gap, the enemy began hunting them down; and on 28 January they captured Jordan himself.

The day after Jordan's party fought its way through the Gabes Gap, Stirling headed north toward the Gabes Gap with five jeeps and fourteen men. Just before dark Stirling's group was spotted by two enemy reconnaissance aircraft. Although Stirling thought that the enemy knew that Jordan's French party had passed through the Gabes Gap the night before and his group had been seen by enemy aircraft, the commander of the Special Air Service decided to attempt to go through the gap that night. Driving all night, Stirling's party passed through the Gabes Gap without encountering any enemy forces and at first light the Gabes-Gafsa road was crossed. Twenty miles farther north of the road, Stirling decided to hide in a wadi during the day and to begin raiding that night. Everybody was very tyred, and after the vehicles had been hidden and camouflaged the whole party fell asleep in various individual hiding places in the wadi.

At about 1500 Captains Michael Saddler and Cooper, who were sleeping near the bottom of the wadi, were woken up by the sound of a large number of men entering the wadi. The two men sat up and saw two armed German soldiers looking at them. To their astonishment, the Germans motioned to them to lie down and be quiet, and then the enemy troops continued walking up the wadi. As soon as the enemy had left, Cooper, Sadler, and a French Special Air Service sergeant named Taxis who was hiding nearby, got to their feet and ran down the wadi and escaped capture. Stirling was captured when he awoke to see a German soldier standing over him with a side arm. Most of Stirling's party was also captured at this time in much the same way as their commander. Stirling later learned, much to his disgust, that the German who had captured him was the unit's dentist.[57] Stirling was not what the enemy would call "a good prisoner"; for the next night he escaped from the Germans only to be betrayed to the Italians, who recaptured him, by an Arab for eleven pounds of tea.[58] Stirling was sent to an Italian punishment camp for unruly prisoners of war near Gavi, Italy. Stirling escaped from this prison camp four times, but was recaptured each time. Finally, Stirling was sent to the famous Colditz Castle in Germany, where he remained for the rest of the war. Cooper, Sadler, and Taxis made good their escape and several days later, after walking west,

----

57   Cowles, *Phantom Major*, pp. 284-301.
58   *Ibid*, pp. 301-304.

entered the lines of the 1st British Army, as did seven other members of the Special Air Service that same day.[59]

The operations of the Special Air Service in January 1943 west of Tripoli were failures. They were not properly planned and were based upon the incorrect assumption that conditions in Tunisia would be similar to those of the Western Desert. In northwest Libya and southern Tunisia the Arabs were not pro-British. Moreover, there were too many enemy troops in southern Tunisia, and the region was too small to go riding around in jeeps in the same manner as was done in the Western Desert. The Long Range Desert Group foresaw these problems and conducted patrols only east of the Grand Erg Oriental and up to, but not through, the Gabes Gap. When the 8th Army moved into Tunisia, the Long Range Desert Group ended its operations in North Africa because it knew that Tunisia north of the Gabes Gap was not suitable for its kind of operations. Stirling, however, did not see the problems and dangers of conducting operations in Tunisia. There was as well the question of luck. The Special Air Service had always taken huge risks in North Africa and perhaps Stirling's luck simply ran out in Tunisia.

At the beginning of December 1942 a very small new raiding force, named No. 1 Demolition Squadron, or Popski's Private Army, arrived at Kufra. This unit consisted of twenty-two men, four jeeps, and three three-ton trucks; it was commanded by Major Vladimir Peniakoff, who was to be called Popski by the men of the Long Range Desert Group because they could not pronounce Peniakoff! He was a Belgian, of Russian origin, who had been educated in England and had lived a good part of his life in Egypt. When the fighting began in Egypt in 1940, Peniakoff wanted to join the British army and after becoming—according to some people in Cairo—a "confounded nuisance," this middle-aged Belgian was granted a lieutenant's commission in the British-officered Libyan Arab Force.

In March 1942 Peniakoff was conducting irregular operations in the Jebel Akhdar with Senussi Arabs. It was during these operations that Peniakoff came to know and admire the Long Range Desert Group. In August of 1942 Peniakoff was brought out of the Jebel Akhdar by the Long Range Desert Group, only to find when he reached Egypt that the Libyan Arab Force had been disbanded. It was then that Easonsmith requested that Peniakoff take part in the raid on Barce, where he was wounded. After leaving the hospital, Peniakoff asked Prendergast if he could join the Long Range Desert Group. Prendergast, however, would not permit this because he could see no useful role for Peniakoff in the Long Range Desert Group. Later on, and while looking for some employment in General

---

59   Liddell Hart, *Rommel-Papers*, p. 393.

Headquarters, Middle East, Peniakoff came across Hackett, who had become interested in a report the former had written about the conduct of irregular operations in the Jebel Akhdar. Hackett found Peniakoff "an interesting character from the first," and the two men came up with the idea of forming Popski's Private Army. The purpose of this force was to conduct irregular operations behind enemy lines in the Jebel Akhdar. Indeed, it was Hackett who, as a joke, officially requested that the name Popski's Private Army be tacked on the unit's original name of No. 1 Demolition Squadron. From then until the end of the war, the unit was known as Popski's Private Army. At first Hackett wanted Popski's Private Army to be a part of the Long Range Desert Group; however, Prendergast would not permit it. Instead Popski's Private Army was to be based with the Long Range Desert Group at Kufra for administrative reasons, but in all other ways it would act independently. By December, however, when Popski's Private Army arrived at Kufra to begin operations, the enemy had been driven out of the Jebel Akhdar. The unit should have been disbanded at this point, but Peniakoff was determined to fight and soon he and his army left Kufra heading northwest for the rear areas of the enemy in Tripolitania.[60]

Before the 8th Army entered Tripoli, on 23 January, units of the Long Range Desert Group, the Special Air Service, and Popski's Private Army were conducting operations west of that city across the border of Tunisia. At the time, the British had almost no detailed geographical knowledge of northwest Libya and southern Tunisia, other than that it was possible for the enemy to make a stand at the Mareth Line or at the Gabes Gap. The Mareth Line was a string of fortifications that had been built by the French before the war, just inside the border of Tunisia, and ran inland from the Mediterranean to the Matmata Hills. The Gabes Gap is a bottleneck of passable ground in Tunisia between the Mediterranean at Gabes and an arm of the Chott Djerid. Both of these positions could be defended easily, and the enemy could use them to block the 8th Army's advance into Tunisia as well as its attempt to link up with the Americans, who were attacking southern Tunisia from the west. If, however, a way could be found to outflank the Mareth Line, then there was a good possibility that the 8th Army could, in the confusion caused by outflanking the Mareth Line, rush the Gabes Gap, bust into southern Tunisia, and link up with the American II Corps, thereby trapping all the enemy forces in Africa in northern Tunisia.

---

60   TNA, WO/106/2332, Popski's Private Army; Vladimir Peniakoff, *Private Army* (London: Jonathan Cape Ltd, 1950), pp. 191-228; John Willett, *Popski: A Life of Vladimir Peniakoff* (London: MacGibbon & Kee, 1954), pp. 112-117.

On 6 January 1943 Easonsmith went to General Dwight D. Eisenhower's headquarters in Algiers to look into the possibility of establishing a base in Tunisia from which to mount operations by the Long Range Desert Group. Owing to the geography of most of Tunisia, however, it was decided that this would not be necessary. Nevertheless, Easonsmith was able to arrange for supplies of rations and fuel to be obtained by patrols of the Long Range Desert Group at Tozeur, which is just north of the western end of the Chott Djerid. Before returning to Libya, Easonsmith additionally obtained all available intelligence at Algiers concerning northwest Libya and southern Tunisia.[61] And on 14 January Eisenhower directed that a line running from Gabes along the northern edge of the Chott Djerid be, for the time being, "the general dividing line"[62] between operations of the Long Range Desert Group and patrols of the British 1st Army. At the same time the American general issued the Long Range Desert Group's recognition signals to all the forces under his command, operating in or near southern Tunisia, in order to prevent accidental fights between Allied units.[63] As the 8th Army's operations moved farther west, the location of the Long Range Desert Group was also moved. During the El Alamein fighting the Long Range Desert Group's headquarters was at Kufra; then, on 28 December, it was moved to Zella. On 16 January it was again moved, this time to Hon,[64] with the advanced operational headquarters being later located at El Azizia. Patrols going on operations there or returning from there would be based at El Azizia, while what Prendergast called "the 'bumph' part of the unit" would be kept at Hon.[65]

On 21 December 1942 the 8th Army ordered the Long Range Desert Group to send patrols for the purposes of topographical reconnaissance as far northwest as Gabes in Tunisia.[66] One of the first of these topographical reconnaissance was conducted by Y2 Patrol. On 1 January 1943 Hunter, the commander of the patrol, was issued with an operational instruction calling for the patrol to conduct a topographical reconnaissance of the area between 11° and 12° east longitude, northward from about thirty miles south of the Gebel Nefusa to the sea in northwest Libya and southeastern Tunisia.[67] This was the beginning of an effort by

61   TNA, WO/201/815, ff. 102, 291-297.
62   TNA, WO/201/771, f. 191-228; Allied Force HQ, 14 Jan., 1943.
63   TNA, WO/201/771, Allied Force Headquarters, Long Range Desert Group, 14 Jan. 1943.
64   TNA, WO/201/815, f. 102.
65   TNA, WO/201/771, L.R.D.G. Patrol State 23 Feb. 1943.
66   TNA, WO/201/815, ff. 279-280.
67   TNA, WO/201/815, f. 279, ff. 116-117.

the Long Range Desert Group to produce the geographical knowledge required by the 8th Army in its advance from Tripoli into southern Tunisia.

Y2 Patrol departed from Zella on 3 January, and by 10 January a base had been made on top of the escarpment that led down to the coastal region of northwest Libya and southeastern Tunisia, which was to be scouted. The next day Hunter sent two groups out from this base to make the reconnaissance. Two 30 cwt trucks under the command of Lance B. Springford were sent to make a "detailed" reconnaissance of the escarpment. Meanwhile, Hunter would attempt to make his way down the escarpment with two jeeps and scout the coastal region. This part of the operation was a failure, however. For Hunter's party could not get down the escarpment, and in the process, they lost a jeep when it turned over and "rolled down the cliff," so that the group "had to return to the base as it had aroused the curiosity of some Tripolitanian soldiers."[68] On 14 and 15 January, Hunter again looked without success for a route down the escarpment, and after meeting Springford's party, on 16 January, Y2 Patrol was attacked and forced to withdraw by enemy infantry who "presumably" had been hunting the British after discovering the wrecked jeep.[69] During this action one of Y2 Patrol's men was wounded in the thigh. Y2 Patrol was then ordered by radio to end the reconnaissance mission and was told to proceed eastward to a point on the Mizda-Esc Sciueref track.[70]

Of much greater importance than Y2 Patrol's reconnaissance mission was the one that had begun at the same time by T1 Patrol. Wilder, the commander of T1 Patrol, was given operational instructions on 1 January 1943 to conduct a topographical reconnaissance of a region of southern Tunisia which included the Matmata Hills and to obtain, among other things, "the information…required from the point of view of the advance of a force of all arms on a wide front."[71] This reconnaissance, moreover, had to be completed by 31 January.[72] T1 Patrol, consisting of two officers and fourteen other ranks, left Zella on 3 January and headed northwest. On 12 January T1 Patrol crossed into Tunisia, making the New Zealanders of the patrol the first troops of the 8th Army to enter that country. Two days later Wilder received instructions by radio to look for a pass through the Matmata Hills that could be used by regular army vehicles. Moving northward along the west side of the Matmata Hills, T1 Patrol found a pass through the hills west of Bir Amir. T1 Patrol did not go all the way through the pass because it was

---

68   TNA, WO/201/815, f. 169.
69   *Ibid.*
70   TNA, WO/201/815, ff. 168-169.
71   TNA, WO/201/815, f. 250.
72   TNA, WO/201/815, ff. 250-251.

running short of fuel and its vehicles were having mechanical problems. Instead, T1 Patrol headed eastward and arrived at Hon on 27 January.[73] The discovery of the pass through the Matmata Hills, later known to the men of the 8th Army as "Wilder's Gap,"[74] was to be of key importance to the success of the invasion of southern Tunisia by the 8th Army.

On 6 January S1 Patrol, commanded by Lazarus and accompanied by six members of Popski's Private Army, left Zella to make a topographical reconnaissance of the region of Tunisia between the Libyan border and the Grand Erg Oriental sand sea. But the mission was a failure, for the force was ambushed and shot up by the enemy while attempting to cross Wadi Zem Zem. On 20 January S1 Patrol, as ordered by headquarters, met T1 Patrol and other units of the Long Range Desert Group on the Midza-Brach track, where the men from Popski's Private Army were attached to T2 Patrol. S1 Patrol was then ordered to Hon.[75] T2 Patrol had operational instructions to guide two trucks belonging to Popski's Private Army to a place the location of which Tinker, the commander of the patrol, would be told later by radio. T2 Patrol was also to assist three three-ton trucks of the Heavy Section to make a dump on the Mizda-Esc Sciueref track and then to carry out a topographical reconnaissance of a region that they would be told of by radio at a later date.[76]

T2 Patrol and the vehicles it was guiding left Hon on 16 January for the Mizda-Esc Sciueref track. On 18 January T2 Patrol was ordered to go to a point on the Mizda-Brach track at latitude 29° 30' north and await the arrival of R2, S1, Y1, and Y2 Patrols and the rest of Popski's Private Army. The next day Tinker's patrol met R2, Y1, and Y2 Patrols at the appointed place along with a party of the Heavy Section. That afternoon Prendergast arrived in a WACO aircraft, and before returning to Hon ordered that R2 Patrol also go to Hon. The next day, 20 January, S1 Patrol and the rest of Popski's Private Army arrived at the meeting place and Prendergast again flew in from Hon. He ordered T2 Patrol, the party of Heavy Section, and Popski's Private Army to make a dump consisting of two hundred twenty-five jerrycans of benzene.[77] After establishing this dump, the Heavy Section party returned to Hon; while T2 Patrol and Popski's Private Army went northwest to Wilder's Dump at a point south south east of Nalut and met T1 Patrol, which was returning from Tunisia in order to receive some topographical

---

73   TNA, WO/201/815, ff. 252-255.

74   Morgan, *Sting of the Scorpion*, pp. 70-71.

75   TNA, WO/201/815, ff. 171-175.

76   TNA, WO/201/815, f. 256.

77   TNA, WO/201/815, f. 257.

information about that country from Wilder, the commander of T1 Patrol. T2 Patrol and Popski's Private Army next moved westward. On 24 January they crossed the Nalut-Gadames track, and the following day they entered Tunisia. That night Tinker received orders by radio to carry out a topographical reconnaissance west of the Matmata Hills and south of the line Matmata-Kebile. After crossing into Tunisia, T2 Patrol and Popski's Private Army turned north travelling with some difficulty along the edge of the Grand Erg Oriental sand sea. At first Tinker and Peniakoff thought of establishing their hide-out or base just inside the Grant Erg Oriental, but unlike the going in the sand seas of Egypt and Libya, this one in Tunisia was found to be impassable. On 26 January it was decided to set up a base or hide-out at the edge of the Grand Erg Oriental, at a hill called Qaret Ali.

Tinker's and Peniakoff's plan called for leaving six trucks and a jeep plus most of the men of both units at Qaret Ali while Peniakoff and Tinker in four jeeps carried out the reconnaissance mission farther to the north. The scouting party went north to Ksar Rhilane then split into two groups and went northeast to a hill overlooking the town of Matmata. That evening Peniakoff and Tinker approached Matmata close enough to get a good look into the place. The next day, 27 January, the British reconnaissance party of four jeeps scouted the area between Matmata and the Jebel Tebaga. If the Mareth Line was outflanked, it would be through the gap between Matmata and the Jebel Tebaga. The next day Peniakoff set out with two jeeps to return to the base at Qaret Ali and Tinker with two jeeps continued the reconnaissance moving westward to examine the Kebile-Matmata track, then southeast to Bir Soltane.[78] Tinker's party arrived at Ksar Rhilane on 30 January.

When Tinker arrived at Ksar Rhilane, he found men from both T2 Patrol and Popski's Private Army as well as two British and six French members of the Special Air Service Regiment. On 27 January the base at Qaret Ali had been attacked by German fighter aircraft and two members of T2 Patrol were wounded and all seven vehicles were destroyed. Peniakoff thought the location of the base had been betrayed by two Arabs in the pay of the enemy. There were now thirty-seven men and five jeeps at Ksar Rhilane. On the afternoon of 30 January Tinker, with three jeeps and eleven men including the two wounded men of T2 Patrol, left Ksar Rhilane for Sabria, which was thought to be held by the Free French. Peniakoff with twenty-five men, most of them on foot, and two jeeps to carry rations and the like would follow Tinker's tracks. As soon as Tinker found an Allied post, he would return with the necessary vehicles to pick up Peniakoff's party. Captain R.P. Yunnie of Popski's Private Army and Sergeant G.C. Garven of T2 Patrol would

---

78   TNA, WO/201/815, f. 258.

remain in hiding near Qaret Ali to warn S2 Patrol, which was proceeding towards Qaret Ali, about the dangers from the Arabs in the region.

When Tinker neared Sabria he found it was held by Germans and not the Free French.[79] Because of the shortage of fuel, Tinker then pushed on across the Chott Djerid, which was thought to be impassable, to Nefta and then to Tozeur, which was reached on 1 February. From Tozeur Tinker went on to Gafsa looking for a means to transmit by radio his topographical intelligence to the 8th Army and to obtain vehicles in order to go back and pick up Peniakoff's group in the desert. When Tinker found that he could not obtain vehicles in Gafsa nor make radio contact with the 8th Army from there, he went northwest to Tebessa in Algeria, where he was finally able to send a signal to the 8th Army as well as to obtain jeeps so as to go back and pick up Peniakoff's party. Tinker's small party was in fact the first unit of the 8th Army to make contact with the U.S. II Corps in Tunisia. In seven days Peniakoff's party had walked from Ksar Rhilane westward over a hundred miles to a point just short of the Algerian border when they were picked up, during the afternoon of 4 February, by Tinker, with jeeps he had obtained at Tebessa. On 6 February Yunnie and Garven arrived at Tozeur with Henry, the commander of S2 Patrol. The next day Tinker's and Peniakoff's commands moved to Tebessa, and then Tinker and a non-commissioned officer flew to Tripoli to brief the 8th Army on the topography of southern Tunisia.[80]

After reaching the U.S. II Corps in Tunisia, Peniakoff arranged for that force to give him the necessary vehicles, arms, rations, and equipment to enable him to conduct a few raids before the advance of the Allies into Tunisia made this type of activity impossible. There has been much misunderstanding in some quarters about Popski's Private Army during the North African campaign. Peniakoff is said to have inflicted a huge amount of damage on the enemy in North Africa.[81] But Peniakoff himself makes no such claim in his own book on the war.[82] At this late date it is impossible to know just how much Popski's Private Army hurt the enemy in Africa, but it is certainly nowhere near the exaggerated estimates of some people. The greatest achievement of Popski's Private Army in the North African campaign was not destruction inflicted upon the enemy but rather the

---

79   TNA, WO/201/815, f. 259.

80   TNA, WO/201/815, ff. 257-259; Peniakoff, *Private Army*, pp. 229-259; Kay, *Long Range Desert Group in the Mediterranean*, pp. 12, 21.

81   Eg., TNA, WO/106/2332, Popski's Private Army. This document, author unknown, claims that Popski's Private Army destroyed in North Africa 34 aircrafts, 6 armored fighting vehicles, 118 other vehicles, and 5,450,000 gasoline. Clearly this is impossible.

82   Peniakoff, *Private Army*, pp. 257-273.

topographical information it obtained along with T2 Patrol for use of the 8th Army in outflanking the Mareth Line.[83]

On 21 January Captain A.B. Rand, commanding 3 Indian Patrol, which consisted of eighteen other ranks in four 30 cwt trucks and two jeeps, left Hon with the mission of conducting a topographical reconnaissance of Tunisia west of 10° east longitude and the eastern edge of the Grand Erg Oriental sand sea between latitudes 32° and 33° north. 3 Indian Patrol travelled in a general northwest direction, and on 26 January the patrol crossed the Gadames-Nalut track and turned north towards Fort Le Boeuf; however, before reaching that place it established a hidden base from which to conduct the reconnaissance. Rand received orders by radio on 2 February to go north to investigate T2 Patrol's base at Qaret Ali because nothing had been heard from the New Zealanders for several days. When Rand reached T2 Patrol's base all that he found were the seven burned out vehicles belonging to T2 Patrol and Popski's Private Army. He did not encounter Yunnie and Garven, who were supposed to be hiding in the area. The Indian Army officer then returned to 3 Indian Patrol's base for the night. The next morning S2 Patrol encountered 3 Indian Patrol's base as the Long Range Desert Group patrol was moving north along the western edge of the Grand Erg Oriental sand sea. Again Rand returned to T2 Patrol's abandoned base near Ksar Rhilane and this time found two notes left by Yunnie and Garven warning of the dangers of Arabs telling the enemy the locations of British hide-outs. Next Rand's party left T2 Patrol's abandoned base "and continued on our job working from this base back to our own by stages."[84] Rand arrived back at 3 Indian Patrol's base on 5 February. The next day 4 Indian Patrol arrived with orders for 3 Indian Patrol to proceed immediately to Mizda, which was reached on 12 February. Rand then sent 3 Indian Patrol back to Hon while he was flown north to Tripoli to give topographical information to the 8th Army.[85]

On 25 January S2 Patrol left Hon with four 30 cwt trucks, three jeeps manned by one officer and sixteen other ranks, and a seven-man intelligence unit being carried as passengers. The operational instructions of Henry, the commander of S2 Patrol, called for the patrol to go to Tozeur, then drop the passengers off in Tunisia, make topographical reconnaissance of an area west of Tozeur, and to report "daily the 'going' encountered after crossing the NALUT-SINAUEN road."[86] S2 Patrol

---

83   Willett, *Popski*, pp. 116-117.
84   TNA, WO/201/815, f. 201.
85   TNA, WO/201/815, ff. 199-202.
86   TNA, WO/201/816, ff. 6-7.

crossed the Nalut-Sinauen road on 30 January. The next day, because of "the rough going," one of the patrol's trucks broke its steering column, which could not be fixed owing to the lack of spare parts. Henry went ahead with a jeep and two trucks to meet T2 Patrol at its base and to get from it the required spare parts. But when Henry arrived at T2 Patrol's base at Qaret Ali, all the Rhodesian officer found were the seven burnt out vehicles.[87] From the wrecked T2 Patrol's trucks, Henry's group salvaged the parts needed to repair S2 Patrol's truck and then returned to where the rest of S2 Patrol had been left. The next day the broken truck having been repaired, S2 Patrol headed north along the edge of the Grand Erg Oriental sand sea and met 3 Indian Patrol. After leaving 3 Indian Patrol, S2 Patrol went northwest across an arm of the Grand Erg Oriental sand sea, and on the north side of this sand sea they met Yunnie and Garven, who were walking towards Tozeur. On 5 February Henry went to Tozeur with Yunnie and Garven and two jeeps to pick up additional fuel and to return these two men to their units. The rest of S2 Patrol went to the southern edge of the Chott Djerid, which was then scouted on foot.

On 9 February the steering arm broke on another truck and the whole patrol went to Tozeur. The next day Henry, with a jeep and two 30 cwt trucks, one of which was carrying the patrol's radio, set out for Gafsa and Tebessa to see if the part needed to fix the truck could be obtained from the U.S. Army. About thirteen miles from Tozeur, the truck with the radio on it ran over a land mine and privates J.M.K. Higham and W.J. Stewart were wounded and the truck was badly damaged. Henry returned to Tozeur with the two wounded men, who were put into the French hospital there. The next morning Henry went to Gafsa and returned to Tozeur at 1600 with a U.S. Army ambulance, which took the two wounded men to an American military hospital.

On 11 February S2 Patrol left Tozeur to continue its mission, but six days later Henry received orders, on a radio belonging to the intelligence unit the patrol had carried into Tunisia, to end the mission. He was told to go to 8th Army headquarters and that the rest of the patrol should go to Hon. On 20 February, before the patrol could carry out these orders, the following incident occurred. The patrol's operational report, which was written by Lance Sergeant L. Calder-Potts, read thus:

---

87   J. Pittaway & G. Fourie, *L.R.D.G. Rhodesia. Rhodesians in the Long Range Desert Group* (Durban, South Africa, 2002).

We saw about 15 trucks which we took to be Free French. We were challenged by a Camel Corps that we took to be French, at Y.K. 4113. Signals were exchanged between O.C. Patrol and them. They were on top of a knoll and some on each side; we were in a basin about 1500 yards away; one of them came running down the knoll and O.C. Patrol went up in his Jeep to meet him. I was the last to come into the basin, the trucks were about 200 yards apart. The man came up to the Jeep and then ran back about 10 yards, waving one hand. I saw two puffs of dust next to him as he was running back. They then opened fire on the Jeep with one M.G. and rifles. I thought there was about 30 to 40 men and about 50 Camels. We uncovered our guns (we had come through a sand-storm the day before) and the only gun that worked was the 20mm BREDA. After the Breda had moved them from the top of the knoll and we had moved behind cover, it was decided that O.C. Party (Henry) and Pte. REZIN had been killed and that the enemy held the advantage so it would not pay to continue the fight.[88]

After the fight with the camel patrol, Calder-Potts took command of S2 Patrol and led it by way of Nalut to El Azizia. While at Nalut Calder-Potts learned from Henry, who had been found alive but mortally wounded by the French after the fighting and sent to the British at Nalut, that S2 Patrol had had a fight with a regular French colonial army patrol. Henry also told Calder-Potts that "he had fired two shots to warn[them] as he had taken the French to be Italians."[89] S2 Patrol had served with Leclerc's Free French force and the Free French general liked and respected Henry. When Leclerc learned of the fight between S2 Patrol and the French patrol, which was not a Free French unit but belonged to the French colonial army in Algeria, he sent for the commander of the French patrol. When the French officer arrived at Leclerc's headquarters, he was kept waiting for a long time. When at last the officer was seen by Leclerc, Leclerc looked at him with contempt and said before the junior officer could speak, "It has taken you a long time to start fighting—and now you do this. Not a very brilliant beginning was it? Good morning—and get out!"[90]

On 31 January Y2 Patrol, commanded by Spicer, left Hon to conduct a topographical reconnaissance of the escarpment near the Dehibat-Foum Tatahouine road and then to go northward as far as possible toward Matmata.

---

88   TNA, WO/201/816, f. 10.
89   TNA, WO/201/816, ff. 8-11.
90   Maule, *Out of Sand*, p. 145.

Lieutenant Bristowe of the 7th Armoured Division accompanied Y2 Patrol to see which areas were passable for armored fighting vehicles.[91] By 6 February Y2 Patrol had reached a point about four miles west of Wilder's Gap. In the next few days the patrol scouted Wilder's Gap and the region around Fort Le Boeuf. On 12 February Y2 Patrol, following orders received by radio, headed for Nalut, which was reached the next day. At Nalut Spicer was ordered to proceed as quickly as possible to the headquarters of the 2nd New Zealand Division where he and Bristowe made a map of the region the patrol had scouted and briefed General Bernard Freyberg, the commander of the New Zealand Corps, on Wilder's Gap.[92]

On 3 February Bruce set off from Hon with two jeeps, four 30 cwt trucks, eighteen other ranks of G Patrol, and Lieutenant P. Lee of the 7th Armoured Division on one of the longest trips ever made by the Long Range Desert Group. Bruce's operational instructions called for the patrol to make a topographical reconnaissance of the region between the Grand Erg Oriental and the Chott Djerid. The patrol went northwest, and on 8 February they camped inside of Tunisia. Bruce's patrol next went north along the eastern edge of the Grand Erg Oriental. Then, in order to reach the south side of the Chott Djerid but avoid Ksar Rhilane, which was now occupied by the enemy, Bruce decided to cut across the northeast corner of the Grand Erg Oriental. The terrain was extremely difficult, and it took the guardsmen three days to cross the sand sea. On the morning of 13 February, just as the patrol was breaking camp, it was attacked by a number of Arabs armed with French rifles. Several vehicles became bogged down, making it impossible for the guardsmen to withdraw, so they had to fight it out with the Arabs. For two hours the battle went on with the guardsmen firing machine-guns at Arabs seen moving around in some nearby bushes. If the Arabs had rushed the patrol, they might have by sheer weight of numbers overpowered the twenty British defenders. But the battle ended when the guardsmen got to their feet, advanced across the open ground, and drove the Arabs out of the bushes. The patrol next headed west along the south side of the Chott Djerid, passing the villages of Sabria and El Faouar and travelling some twenty-five miles before making camp for the night. Just as it was getting dark, however, the patrol was again attacked by Arabs, who in some cases managed to get within ten yards of the British vehicles. The battle lasted about an hour before the enemy was driven away by the massed firepower of the patrol's automatic weapons. Some seven thousand rounds of munitions were used

---

91   TNA, WO/216/816, ff. 12-13.
92   TNA, WO/201/816, ff. 14-15.

in the two battles against the Arabs. In the second attack, Guardsman Jennings was wounded in the chest and Guardsman Blaney was hit in the leg.

At dusk on 15 February G Patrol entered Tozeur, only to find that the Allied forces had left the place and the Germans were expected to appear at any moment. After re-supplying themselves with abandoned American rations and gasoline, the patrol headed towards El Oued—one hundred and twenty miles west—and just avoided getting caught up in the enemy offensive at Kasserine. Bruce's patrol entered Algeria and began passing units of the French army moving eastward. While passing a unit of the French Foreign Legion, there occurred what the historian of G Patrol has called "a classic Saharan meeting"[93] when Guardsman MacNabola met a *legionnaire* who had grown up two streets away from the guardsman's home in Dublin. The patrol did not stop for long at El Oued but pushed on to Touggourt, where Jennings and Blaney were placed in a French hospital. Bruce obtained from the French authorities at Touggourt permission to return to Libya by going around the western end of the Grand Erg Oriental by way of Fort Flatters and Gadames. But before making this trip, spare parts had to be obtained from Libya and Lee had to get to 8th Army headquarters with Bruce's and his own reports. Leaving most of the patrol's men at Touggourt, Bruce, Lee, and five men in three trucks drove two hundred and fifty miles north to Constantine. Upon reaching this city, Lee was flown to Tripoli, but Bruce had to wait six days for the spare truck parts to be flown in before returning to Touggourt and making the trip around the west side of the Grand Erg Oriental and then returning to Hon by way of Fort Flatters and Gadames. On 12 March G Patrol reached Hon, having completed a trip of 3,515 miles.[94]

On 24 January, 2 and 4 Indian Patrol were issued operational instructions to conduct a topographical reconnaissance of the region west of Wilder's Gap in Tunisia.[95] The next day 4 Indian Patrol left Hon and went northwest towards the base set up by 3 Indian Patrol south of Fort Le Boeuf in Tunisia. The patrol's progress was slow because of a number of mechanical problems, such as the burning out of a bearing on the truck which carried the patrol's radio. So it was not until 6 February that 4 Indian Patrol arrived at 3 Indian Patrol's base in Tunisia, although that same day 2 Indian Patrol arrived at the base, too. The commander of 2 Indian Patrol, Captain T.J.D. Birdwood, because of the mechanical problems 4 Indian Patrol had been having with its vehicles, decided to form from 2 and 4 Indian

---

93   Crichton-Stuart, *G Patrol*, p. 202.

94   TNA, WO/201/816, ff. 16-24; Crichton-Stuart, *G Patrol*, pp. 197-286.

95   TNA, WO/201/816, ff. 35-36.

Patrols a composite patrol which consisted of four jeeps and four 30 cwt trucks. One 30 cwt truck and seven other ranks were attached to 3 Indian Patrol, which was in the meantime returning to base. During the next four days, the composite Indian Patrol conducted a thorough topographical reconnaissance of the area of Wilder's Gap before being ordered, by radio, to return to Libya on 11 February.[96]

R2 Patrol, commanded by Lazarus, conducted the last topographical reconnaissance of southern Tunisia made by the Long Range Desert Group. R2 Patrol left Hon on 1 February and crossed into Tunisia just south of Bir Zar five days later. Three days later Lazarus was ordered by radio to go north along the edge of the Grand Erg Oriental to Ksar Rhilane, which had been abandoned by the enemy, to look for two members of the Special Air Service who were thought to be hiding in that place. But when Lazarus arrived at Ksar Rhilane he did not find any members of the Special Air Service and was told by Arabs that a French patrol had been there four days before. R2 Patrol next scouted an area west of Wilder's Gap, and on 11 February met Y2 Patrol, which was also on a reconnaissance mission. The next day R2 Patrol began the return trip and arrived at Hon on 20 February.[97] The topographical reconnaissance undertaken by the patrols of the Long Range Desert Group in northwest Libya and southern Tunisia were of great importance to the future operations of the 8th Army. The information supplied to the 8th Army on the topography of southern Tunisia enabled it to outflank the Mareth Line and smash through the Gabes Gap. It was then able to link up with the American II Corps, and by trapping the enemy in northern Tunisia to end the war in the Western Desert.

After the capture of Tripoli on 23 January, the 8th Army had been proceeding slowly, because of supply problems, towards the Mareth Line. On 25 February Leclerc's Free French force was at Ksar Rhilane, and about fifty miles to the northwest, units of the 7th Armoured and 51st Highland Divisions had already advanced beyond Medenine.[98] The next day units of the 8th Army had reached the Mareth Line, which was thought to be held by six enemy divisions. On 6 March, while the 8th Army was preparing to attack the Mareth Line, the Germans attempted a spoiling attack directed at Medenine but they were easily driven back with few losses to the 8th Army.[99]

---

96   TNA, WO/201/816, ff. 37-38-38A-39.

97   TNA, WO/201/816, ff. 25-28.

98   Playfair, *The Mediterranean*, vol. IV, pp. 316, 320.

99   *Ibid*, vol. IV, pp. 322-325.

On the night of 16/17 March the battle to force the Mareth Line began with frontal attacks on the enemy's positions by the 50th and 51st Divisions and the 201st Guards Brigade.[100] The next morning, north and west of the enemy's positions in southern Tunisia, the U.S. II Corps attacked eastward taking Gafsa; and by 23 March the Americans had advanced as far east as Maknessy, posing a threat to the enemy's north-south supply lines to the Mareth Line.[101] The New Zealand Corps was given the task of outflanking the Mareth Line to the west. This corps, consisting of 26,000 men, 151 tanks, and 287 guns, was to outflank the Mareth Line and force open the Gabes Gap. The last mission of the Long Range Desert Group in the North African campaign would be to navigate the New Zealand Corps on this flank march. Tinker and three men with two jeeps from T2 Patrol were assigned to act as navigators for the New Zealand Corps, which was assembled near Foum Tatahouine. On 5 March New Zealand engineers and provost parties led by the men of T2 Patrol began clearing, improving, and marking with the 2nd New Zealand Division's black diamond signs the road south from Foum Tatahouine to Bir Amir and the track westward from there through Wilder's Gap.

Beginning on 12 March, the men and vehicles of the New Zealand Corps led by Tinker's men from T2 Patrol began marching south from Foum Tatahouine and then west through Wilder's Gap to an assembly area some thirty-five miles southeast of Foum Tatahouine. On 19 March, during the night, the 8th Army mounted its first major assault on the Mareth Line; in the meantime, the New Zealand Corps, led by the party from T2 Patrol, began marching north towards the Gabes Gap and were in contact with the enemy by 21 March. The attack by the U.S. II Corps and the flanking march of the 2nd New Zealand Corps forced the enemy to move forces north and west from the Mareth Line. But five days later, reinforced by the 1st Armoured Division and heavily supported by tactical air power, the 2nd New Zealand Corps battled its way through the Gabes Gap forcing the enemy to withdraw from the Mareth Line; and on 29 March the New Zealanders entered Gabes.[102]

During the 8th Army's advance from El Alamein across Egypt and Libya, it was greatly assisted by the Long Range Desert Group. Throughout this phase of the campaign the Long Range Desert Group supplied the 8th Army with necessary

---

100   *Ibid*, vol. IV, pp. 334-335.

101   Howe, *Northwest Africa*, pp. 542-564.

102   Playfair, *The Mediterranean*, vol. IV, pp. 337-355; Kay, *Long Range Desert Group in the Mediterranean*, p. 22; Stevens, *Bardia to Enfidaville*, pp. 254-255

topographical information. Perhaps the best examples of this were the topographical reconnaissance made by the patrols of the Long Range Desert Group in southern Tunisia that enabled the 2nd New Zealand Corps to outflank the Mareth Line and bust through the Gabes Gap into central Tunisia. All the outflanking operations carried out by the 2nd New Zealand Division during the march of the 8th Army westward were made possible by the topographical information and navigators supplied by the Long Range Desert Group. Not all the operations during the march west from El Alamein were successful, however. During this period the Special Air Service raids on the coast road in Libya and Tunisia were among the worst failures in the entire history of the regiment. But the failures of the Special Air Service were more than offset by operations of the Long Range Desert Group, such as the road watch and assistance given to Leclerc's Free French force during the conquest of Fezzan and the march north from the Chad to Tripoli.

The capture of Gabes and the linking up of the 8th Army and the U.S. II Corps in Tunisia signaled the end of operations for the Long Range Desert Group in North Africa. The men and vehicles of the Long Range Desert Group were sent eastward along the coast road they knew so well to the Delta in Egypt. The men were rested, and the Long Range Desert Group then went to Lebanon to train for operations in the Aegean islands and the Balkans. The unit never again operated in the desert.[103]

---

103   TNA, WO 201/815, ff. 299-300, 303.

10

Conclusion

The Long Range Desert Group was perhaps the most effective of all the so-called "special forces" established by the Allies during the Second World War. At the urging of Major Ralph Bagnold, a noted desert explorer, the Long Range Desert Group was ordered into existence by Wavell when war broke out between the British and the Italians in June of 1940. Initially, the mission of the Long Range Desert Group was to discover what Italian military intentions and activities were in the deserts of southeastern Libya.

The Long Range Desert Group was organized very quickly, using at first New Zealand troops who were taught how to live, travel, and fight in the desert by several pre-war British explorers of the western desert. During the course of the Long Range Desert Group's operations in the deserts of both southern and northern Cyrenaica, the British soon established that the Italians were militarily ineffective and for the most part inactive south of the Trigh el Abd. And with the capture of Kufra by the Free French on 1 March 1941, the Italians generally conceded the interior of Cyrenaica to the Long Range Desert Group.

British commanders in North Africa had in the Long Range Desert Group a unit that could go almost anywhere in the Libyan deserts. This was spectacularly demonstrated by the four thousand mile raid to Fezzan made by the Long Range Desert Group in conjunction with the Free French at the end of 1941. But having a unit such as the Long Range Desert Group is one thing and knowing how to use it is quite another. A number of senior British commanders, such as General Philip Neame, never learned how to correctly employ the Long Range Desert Group.

It took, moreover, the British command in North Africa a long time to learn what the Long Range Desert Group could and could not do. Whenever the Long Range Desert Group was properly employed, its performance was extraordinary. In particular, the Long Range Desert Group showed great skill and effectiveness in long-range reconnaissance missions deep in the rear of the enemy's front line forces. Patrols of the Long Range Desert Group could cross huge areas of the desert very quickly, and for the most part undetected by the enemy; in addition, its communications systems enabled intelligence to be passed, again undetected by the enemy, with great speed to higher British headquarters. The road watch that was maintained by the Long Range Desert Group for weeks on end at Marble Arch was a textbook example of how to conduct an intelligence operation of that type. The topographical reconnaissance of northwest Libya and southern Tunisia that was conducted by the Long Range Desert Group was of key importance to the operations of the 8th Army. The mapping of the Libyan Desert that they carried out behind enemy lines in 1941 produced maps whose accuracy and value were recognized even by the Germans.[1] Equally important were the ability and exquisite skills of the men of the Long Range Desert Group, at the art of desert navigation, which enabled units of the 8th Army, such as the 2nd New Zealand Division, to outflank the enemy with wide-sweeping movement into the desert during the advance from El Alamein westward to Tunisia. The Long Range Desert Group provided as well the means to carry intelligence officers and their agents and supplies to almost any point behind enemy lines. As a result, during the North African campaign, the Long Range Desert Group in essence enabled the British to use the Egyptian and Libyan deserts almost as they wished. Whether or not British commanders in North Africa took full advantage of the opportunities thus given to them by the Long Range Desert Group is a question that is still being debated by historians.

During the Second World War, the British were obsessed with raids, as a tactic, to the point where raiding operations sometimes became an end in themselves. Even though its main function was reconnaissance, the Long Range Desert Group, because it operated behind enemy lines in North Africa, carried out many raids. Perhaps the most well-known ones are the four thousand mile raid into Fezzan and the raid by G1 and T1 Patrols on Barce. These two operations stand out because they were just the most spectacular raids conducted by the Long Range Desert Group; however, they were certainly not the only ones. At various times, which was usually whenever the 8th Army was in trouble, the Long Range Desert Group would be ordered to undertake raids against the enemy's supply lines. These raids routinely resulted in mines being laid on the coast road and a number of enemy vehicles being destroyed by gunfire and bombs. It is impossible to know what effect, if any, these operations had on the enemy except to say that a large number

---

1   Alfred Topp, "Desert Warfare: German Experience in World War II" (Historical Division, European Command, 1952) (Fort Leavenworth KS Combat Studies Institute, 1991), p. 3.

of enemy vehicles were destroyed and that traffic on the coast road was from time to time disrupted to varying degrees.

In 1941, when the Long Range Desert Group began working with the Special Air Service, the amount of material destruction dished out to the enemy by means of raids greatly increased. Stirling was a born commander of irregular raiding forces, and the men of the Special Air Service became very skilled in the art and techniques of raiding; and for most of the North Africa campaign, they were carried to their targets by Long Range Desert Group patrols. Towards the end of the campaign, the Special Air Service had mastered the Long Range Desert Group's methods of transport across the desert by motor vehicle and began obtaining their own jeeps and trucks. However, even with their own transport, the Special Air Service still on occasion operated with the Long Range Desert Group. Indeed, the combined operations of the Special Air Service and the Long Range Desert Group were particularly effective and deadly. The Special Air Service, supported by the Long Range Desert Group, succeeded in causing the enemy a huge amount of material damage in terms of casualties, destroyed buildings, vehicles, and supplies. The unit is credited by the British with destroying no less than three hundred enemy aircraft on the ground.[2] Exactly because of the great amount of destruction inflicted upon the enemy by Special Air Service raids, this unit did, ultimately, greatly aid the British in North Africa.

One of the missed opportunities of the operations of the Long Range Desert Group and the Special Air Service during the North African campaign was the failure to gain the direct support of the R.A.F. From time to time the R.A.F. flew out wounded men from behind enemy lines and provided aircraft to train Special Air Service troops in parachuting; however, this was the full extent of the R.A.F.'s support of the Long Range Desert Group during the North African campaign. The length and scope of operations conducted by both the Long Range Desert Group and the Special Air Service could have been greatly increased and enhanced if a systematic scheme had been worked out with the R.A.F. for these two units to be resupplied on a large scale behind enemy lines by aircraft, either landing at secret landing grounds, such as Landing Ground 125, or by having supplies dropped to them by parachute. Another way in which the R.A.F. could have cooperated with the Long Range Desert Group and Special Air Service, that would have greatly benefited the British effort in North Africa, would have been for R.A.F. aircraft to attack targets behind enemy lines once these had been found and marked by the Long Range Desert Group and the Special Air Service. An

---

2   TNA, WO/201/721, Brief History of "L" Det. S.A.S. Brigade & 1st S.A.S. Regiment.

effort of this type could have been rendered even more effective if a few men from the Long Range Desert Group and the Special Air Service had been trained to act as forward ground controllers for the attacking R.A.F. aircraft. Later in the war, the Long Range Desert Group carried out a number of operations in the Balkans, in conjunction with the R.A.F., with considerable success.[3]

One of the striking features of the operations of the Long Range Desert Group and the Special Air Service is the low number of casualties they suffered given the nature of their tasks. Equally striking is the lack of medical problems, such as sunstroke, among the personnel of both units. It is also surprising that one finds very little in the way of descriptions, or complaints, of day-to-day discomfort in operational reports or personal memoirs. Almost no mention is made of the problems of heat, diet, hygiene, lack of water, and sand, grit, and dust. Most of the medical problems of a non-combatant nature were encountered in regions near the coast that had been fought over by Axis and British forces.

No matter how much material damage the Long Range Desert Group and the Special Air Service inflicted upon the enemy by raids in his rear areas, they failed to force Rommel, a general of great single-mindedness, to divert major forces from the front lines to counter their operations. Rommel did not even know that there were two different enemy units operating in the rear areas of his forces. The German commander used the term "commando" when talking and writing about the Long Range Desert Group, the Special Air Service, and other British irregular forces operating behind Axis lines.[4] And if his published papers are anything to go on, Rommel did not give much thought to the operations of the Long Range Desert Group and the Special Air Service.[5] This was a grave oversight by Rommel; for if he had dealt with the Long Range Desert Group and the Special Air Service there would have been fewer unpleasant surprises for his men and operations would have been made much more difficult for the British.

The Long Range Desert Group and the Special Air Service gave the commanders of the British forces in North Africa a number of advantages that were not enjoyed by the enemy. They gave the British the ability to collect massive amount of intelligence from areas deep within the rear of the enemy front line positions, the navigational skills to guide large forces across the desert in outflanking operations, the means of transporting agents to points almost anywhere behind enemy lines,

---

3   Eg. David Lloyd Owen, *Providence Their Guide* (London: Harrap, 1980), p. 197.

4   B.H. Liddell-Hart, ed., *The Rommel Papers* (New York: Harcourt, Brace and Company, 1953), pp. 292n, 393.

5   Stirling's name is only mentioned two times in Rommel's published papers. *Ibid*, p. 540.

and the ability to mount wide-ranging raiding offensives.[6] However, given that the methods used by these units were in many respects radical and irregular—especially those of the Special Air Service—a number of British commanders never learned how to correctly use these two units. Nevertheless, the Long Range Desert Group and the Special Air Service, two very small units, rendered assistance to the British in North Africa beyond calculation and far out of proportion to their size.

6   Alastair Timpson, *In Rommel's Backyard: a Memoir of the Long Range Desert Group* (Barnsley, S. Yorkshire: Leo Cooper, 2000), pp. 6-12.

Bibliographic Essay

The best place to begin studying the use of wheeled vehicles for exploration and warfare in the Western Desert is John William Gordon's "Special Forces for Desert Warfare: British Improvisation, 1915-1943" (Duke University: unpublished Ph.D. dissertation, 1975), which covers the period from the beginning of the Senussi War to the end of the fighting in North Africa in World War II, and his *The Other Desert War: British Special Forces in North Africa, 1940-1943* (New York: Greenwood, 1987).

The Senussi and the Light Car Patrols are described in such books as E.E. Evans-Pritchard, *The Senussi of Cyrenaica* (Oxford: The Clarendon Press, 1954); S.C. Rolls, *Steel Chariots in the Desert* (London: Jonathan Cape, 1937); Geoffrey Inchbald, *Imperial Camel Corps* (London: Johnson, 1970); and George MacMunn and Cyril Falls, *History of the Great War: Military operations in Egypt and Palestine* (London: HMSO, 1928). But for a clear understanding of the Light Car Patrols one should consult two documents at the Royal Geographical Society: C.H. Williams, "Light Car Patrols in the Libyan Desert"; and John Bell, "Desert Reconnaissance by Motor-Car: Primarily a Handbook for Patrol-Officers in Western Egypt, 25 Jan. 1917."

For a better perspective of R.A. Bagnold's part in exploring the Western Desert, one should not only read his account of his expeditions in *Libyan Sands: Travel in a Dead World* (London: Hodder and Stoughton, 1942) but also his articles in the Royal Geographical Society's *Geographical Journal*. For example, R.A. Bagnold, "Journeys in the Libyan Desert 1929 and 1930," *Geographical Journal* 78 (July - Dec., 1931); "A Further Journey through the Libyan Desert," *Ibid.* 82 (Aug. - Sept., 1933); "An Expedition to the Gilf Kebir and Uweinat, 1938," *Ibid.* 93 (April, 1939) are all important and highly enlightening articles. One should also consult such works as Ahmed Hassanein Bey, "Through Kufra to Darfur," *Geographical Journal* 64 (Oct., 1924); Orde Wingate, "In Search of Zerzura," *Ibid.* 83 (April, 1934);

W.B. Kennedy Shaw, "An Expedition in the Southern Libyan Desert," *Ibid.* 87 (March, 1936); Michael H. Mason, *The Paradise of Fools* (London: Hodder and Stoughton, 1936); and G.W. Murray, *Dare Me to the Desert* (London: George Allen & Unwin, 1967).

There is a large amount of literature on the British use of mechanized forces in the Middle East during the inter-war years in various military professional journals and books. For the purpose of this study, I have used Bimbashi R.L. Scoones, "Ford Cars in the Libyan Desert," *The Royal Tank Corps Journal* 14 (Feb., 1933); Thomas I. Dun, *From Cairo to Siwa* (Cairo: privately printed, 1933); H.P. Drayson, "The War Office Experimental Convoy, 1933," *The Royal Engineers Journal* 48 (March, 1934); and his "A Brief Outline of the Supply and Transport Problems occasioned by the Operations in the North-West Libyan Desert, 1933-34," *Royal Army Service Corps Quarterly* 3 (Nov., 1935); John Bagot Glubb, *War in the Desert: An R.A.F. Frontier Campaign* (New York: Norton, 1961); and G. Surtees, "A Thousand Miles of Desert," *Journal of the Royal United Service Institution* 106 (Nov., 1961).

Any study of World War II in North Africa should begin with official histories. The British official history that covers the North African campaigns is I.S.O. Playfair, *The Mediterranean and Middle East* (London: HMSO, 1954-1960); and the U.S. Army's official history is George F. Howe, *Northwest Africa: Seizing the Initiative in the West* (Washington, D.C.: Department of the Army, 1957). After World War II, a German officer, Alfred Topp, wrote a staff study for the U.S. Army entitled "Desert Warfare: German Experience in World War II" (European Command, Historical Division, 1952) (Fort Leavenworth, KS: Combat Studies Institute, 1991). The governments of Australia, India, and New Zealand, respectively, have also produced extensive official histories dealing with various aspects of the war in North Africa.

In addition, there are a number of histories of the Long Range Desert Group in North Africa as well as accounts written by men who served in the unit. Among the better known histories and personal accounts are: W.B. Kennedy Shaw, *Long Range Desert Group: The Story of its Work in Libya, 1940-1943* (London: Collins, 1945); Eric Wilson, "Deep Penetration Patrols in the Libyan Desert," *Journal of the United Services Institution of India and Pakistan* 78 (Oct., 1948); R.L. Kay, *Long Range Desert Group in Libya, 1940-41* (Wellington: Department of Internal Affairs, 1949) and his *Long Range Desert Group in the Mediterranean* (Wellington: Department of Internal Affairs, 1950). David Lloyd Owen, *The Desert My Dwelling Place* (London; Cassell, 1957) and his *Providence Their Guide: A Personal Account of the Long Range Desert Group, 1940-1945* (London: Harrap, 1980); Timpson,

Alastair, *In Rommel's Backyard: A Memoir of the Range Desert Group* (Barnsley, South Yorkshire: Leo Cooper, 2000).

A number of people have written accounts of various aspects of the history of the Long Range Desert Group in North Africa. Michael Crichton-Stuart has written a history of one patrol in his *G Patrol* (London: William Kimber, 1958) as well as an account of the raid into Fezzan in "The Story of a Long Range Desert Patrol," *The Army Quarterly* 47 (Oct., 1943). On the cooperation of and support by the L.R.D.G. of Free French Forces' operations, particularly on the taking of Koufra, there are the following: Jean-Noël Vincent, "Koufra: 23 décembre 1940 – 1er mai 1941", *Revue historique des armeés*, Vol. 1 (1982); and Roger Ceccaldi, "Koufra. Souvenirs de l' Artilleur", *Revue historique des armeés*, Vol. 2 (1983). On desert navigation, W.B. Kennedy Shaw wrote "Desert Navigation: Some Experiences of the Long Range Desert Group," *Geographical Journal* 102 (Nov. – Dec., 1943); Bagnold produced an article entitled "Early Days of the Long Range Desert Group," *Ibid.* 105 (Jan.-June, 1945); and J.W. Wright wrote on mapping in conjunction with the Long Range Desert Group in "War-Time Exploration with the Sudan Defense Force in the Libyan Desert, 1941-1943," *Ibid.* 105 (March-April, 1945). Three volumes of the official history of the New Zealand armed forces touch on various aspects of the Long Range Desert Group: W.G. Stevens, *Official History of New Zealand in the Second World War, 1939-1945: Problems of the 2nd NZEF* (Wellington: Department of Internal Affairs, 1958); *Documents Relating to New Zealand's Participation in the Second World War* (Wellington, Department of Internal Affairs, 1949); and W.G. Stevens, *Bardia to Enfidaville* (Wellington, Department of Internal Affairs, 1962). In addition, there is Brendan O'Carroll, *Kiwi Scorpions: The Story of the New Zealanders in the Long Range Desert Group* (Honiton, Devon: Token Publishing, 2000); and his *Barce Raid: The Long Range Desert Group's Greatest Escapade* (Wellington, N.Z.: Ngaio Press, 2005) as well as Grower-Collins, Clive, "Raids, road watches, and reconnaissance: an analysis of the New Zealand contribution to the Long Range Desert Group in North Africa, 1940-1943" (unpublished MA thesis, Massey University, 1999). On the Rhodesians in the Long Range Desert Group, there is J. Pittaway and G. Fourie, *L.R.D.G. Rhodesia. Rhodesians in the Long Range Desert Group* (Durban, S. Africa: 2002).

The Long Range Desert Group was found by a group of scholars and soldiers. Probably no other unit in the British army had a commander who was not only a professional soldier but who was also able to write, as Bagnold did, a work of scholarship such as *The Physics of Blown Sand and Desert Dunes* (London: Chapman & Hall, 1973 reprint). The official records of the Long Range Desert Group for the

North African campaign in The National Archives reflect the scholarly background of men like Bagnold, Clayton, and Kennedy Shaw. As a result, for a unit of that size, the official records of the Long Range Desert Group are unusually complete and well ordered.

At the end of World War II, Brigadier H.W. Wynter wrote a very detailed staff history of the Long Range Desert Group during the North African campaign based on their official records. This staff history, which can be found at The National Archives, UK (formerly known as The Public Record Office), CAB/44/151, has now been published, as H.W. Wynter, *Special Forces in the Desert War, 1940-1943* (Richmond, Surrey: The National Archives, 2001). Of much greater value to the student of the Long Range Desert Group, however, are the documents to be found in TNA, WO/201/807-816. These documents, known as the Prendergast Papers, are all the operational reports of as well as the operational instructions issued to all the Long Range Desert Group patrols during the North African campaign plus a large number of other useful supporting documents. Summaries of each section of these documents can also be found in the above-mentioned series; these appear to have been written at the time by the intelligence officer of the Long Range Desert Group, W.B. Kennedy Shaw. Wynter's staff history and the Prendergast Papers together give the scholar an almost hour-by-hour account of the actions of the patrols of the Long Range Desert Group during the years 1940-1943. These two collections, although very complete, are not the only records of the Long Range Desert Group in the National Archives that throw light on the activities of the unit. Also of interest are WO/201/220, Reports on Long Range Desert Group vehicles, 1940-1941; WO/196/3803, G.H.Q., M.E.F., Intelligence Summary No. 592; WO/169/14944, Indian Long Range Squadron, Feb.-July 1943; WO/201/735, Reports on Operations at Benghazi, Sept. 1942; WO/201/740, Report on Tobruk raid, 13-14 Sept. 1942; WO/201/771, Eisenhower to Allied Forces, 14 Jan. 1943 and L.R.D.G. Patrol State, 23 Feb. 1943; WO/218/95, Order to Indian Long Range Squadron, 3 July 1943, and Operational Instructions Nos. 2, 6, 7 to patrols of the Indian Long Range Squadron.

Major General David Lloyd Owen's collection of Long Range Desert Group papers are located at the Imperial War Museum. Although the majority of these documents are about operations in the Balkans, there are therein, however, a number of documents of interest about the North African campaign, too. The author interviewed Major General Lloyd Owen at the Imperial War Museum, and the tape and a transcript of this interview are held by the Director, Combat Studies Institute, U.S. Army Command and General Staff College, Fort Leavenworth, Kansas.

The records of the Special Air Service for the North African campaign, unlike those of the Long Range Desert Group, are not very extensive or well ordered. Fortunately, however, the Prendergast Papers at The National Archives contain a great amount of information about the operations of the Special Air Service. Of particular interest are: AIR/27/1334, the log of 216 Squadron, which took the Special Air Service on its first raid; CAB/106/5, Report of Operations at Agedabia 19-23/12/41 and Arae Philenorum, 25/12/41-11/1/42, by Lt. W. Fraser, Gordon Highlanders; WO/201/721, Brief History of "L" Det. S.A.S. Brigade & 1st S.A.S. Regiment; WO/201/735, Report on operations—Benghazi—Sept. '42; WO/201/711,GHQMEF Operational Instruction No. 145; and WO/218/97, Reports on a number of Special Air Service operations, 1942-1943. One of the most important documents on the Special Air Service can be found in the Mcleod Papers, Centre for Military Archives, King's College, University of London. This is a memorandum by Col. David Stirling, DSO, OBE on the origins of the Special Air Service Regiment, 8 Nov. 1948.

There are a number of books about the Special Air Service and various aspects of the unit's operations. For this study the following books were consulted: Virginia Cowles, *The Phantom Major: The Story of David Stirling and the S.A.S. Regiment* (London: Collins, 1958); Malcolm James, *Born of the Desert* (London: Collins 1945); Patrick Marrinan, *Colonel Paddy* (Dungannon, Ireland: Ulster Press, 1968); Fitzroy Maclean, *Escape to Adventure* (Boston: Little, Brown and Co., 1950); John Lodwick, *The Filibusters: The Story of the Special Boat Service* (London: Methuen, 1947); Philip Warner, *The Special Air Service* (London: Kimber, 1980). There has not been very much written about Popski's Private Army in the Western Desert. There is the study in the National Archives, WO/206/2332, Popski's Private Army, No. 1 Demolition Sqdn. P.P.A. Historical Summary. There is as well Peniakoff's own book, namely Vladimir Peniakoff, *Popski's Private Army* (London, Jonathan Cape, 1950); and John Willett, *Popski: A Life of Vladimir Peniakoff* (London: MacGibbon & Kee, 1954).

Other published works that have been used in this study and that should be mentioned are: Henry Maule, *Out of the Sand: The Epic Story of General Leclerc and the Fighting Free French* (London: Odhams Books Ltd., 1966); B.H. Liddell-Hart, ed., *The Rommel Papers* (New York: Harcourt, Brace and Co., 1953); Chris Ellis, *Military Transport of World War II* (New York: Macmillan, 1975); Samuel Decalo, *Historical Dictionary of the Chad* (Metuchen, N.J.: Scarecrow Press, 1977); John Connell, *Wavell: Scholar and Soldier* (New York: Harcourt, Brace & World, 1964); Frank Jopling and Brendan O'Carroll, *Bearded Brigands: The Diaries of Trooper Frank Jopling* (Wellington, N.Z.: Ngaio Press, 2002). James Ladd, *Commandos and Rangers of World War II* (New York: St. Martin's, 1978); Ronald Lewin, *Ultra Goes to War* (New York: McGraw-Hill, 1978); John W. Hackett, "The Employment of Special Forces," *Journal of the Royal United Service Institution* 97 (Feb., 1952); Ministry of Defense, *Joint Service Staff Manual: Service Writing* (London: MOD, 1978); W.S. Churchill, *The Second World War* (Boston: Houghton Mifflin, 1948-1953); S.W. Roskill, *The War At Sea* (London: HMSO, 1954-1961); S.W. Roskill, *White Ensign; The British Navy at War, 1939-1945* (Annapolis, Md.: U.S. Naval Institute, 1966); TM 30-420, *Handbook on the Italian Military Forces* (Washington, D.C.: War Department, 1943); TM-E 30-451, *Handbook on the German Military Forces* (Washington, D.C.: War Department, 1945). Of course this is a selective rather than an exhaustive account of the secondary literature.

Bibliography

A. PRIMARY SOURCES

The National Archives, UK: London
AIR/27-1334
CAB/44/151
CAB/106/5
WO/201/220
WO/106/2128, 2332
WO/169/3803, 14944
WO/201/594
WO/201/711, 721, 724, 727, 728, 735, 738, 739, 740, 742, 745, 748, 752, 760, 771
WO/201/807-816
WO/218/89, 94, 95, 97
Map Room, MR 761 (3,6) and MHP 1095 (1-3)

The Royal Geographical Society, London
Ball, John, "Desert Reconnaissance by Motor-Car: Primarily a Handbook for
    Patrol-Officers in Western Egypt, 25 January, 1917".
Williams, C.H., "Light Car Patrols in the Libyan Desert" (?1918).

Imperial War Museum, London
David Lloyd Owen's Private Papers.

King's College, London University, Centre for Military Archives
McLeod's Private Papers.

B. ARTICLES, BOOKS, THESES

Bagnold, R.A., "Journeys in the Libyan Desert 1929 and 1930", *The Geographical Journal* 78 (July-Dec., 1931), pp. 13-39, 522-535.

Bagnold R.A., "A Further Journey through the Libyan Desert", *The Geographical Journal* 82 (Aug.-Sept., 1933), pp. 103-129, 211-235.

Bagnold, R.A., "An Expedition to the Gilf Kebir and Uweinat, 1938", *The Geographical Journal* 93 (April, 1939), pp. 281-313.

Bagnold, R.A., *Libyan Sands: Travel in a Dead World* (London: Hodder and Stoughton, 1942).

Bagnold, R.A., "Early Days of the Long Range Desert Group", *The Geographical Journal* 105 (Jan.- June, 1945), pp. 30-42.

Bagnold, R.A., *The Physics of Blown Sand and Desert Dunes* (London: Chapman & Hall, 1973).

Ceccaldi, Roger, "Koufra. Souvenirs de l' Artilleur", *Revue historique des armeés*, Vol. 2 (1983), pp. 40-49.

Churchill, W.S., *The Second World War* (Boston: Houghton Mifflin, 1948-1953).

Connell, John, *Wavell: Scholar and Soldier* (New York: Harcourt, Brace & World, 1964).

Cowles, Virginia, *The Phantom Major: The Story of David Stirling and the S.A.S. Regiment* (London: Collins, 1958).

Crichton-Stuart, Michael, "The Story of a Long Range Desert Patrol", *The Army Quarterly* 47/1 (Oct., 1943), pp. 70-80; 47/2 (Jan., 1944), pp. 197-210.

Crichton-Stuart, Michael, *G Patrol* (London: William Kimber, 1958).

Decalo, Samuel, *Historical Dictionary of the Chad* (Metuchen, N.J.: Scarecrow Press, 1977).

Drayson, H.P., "The War Office Experimental Convoy, 1933", *The Royal Engineers Journal* 48 (March, 1934), pp. 60-73.

Drayson, H.P., "A Brief outline of the Supply and Transport Problems Occasioned by the Operations in the North-West Libyan Desert, 1933-34", *The Royal Army Service Corps Journal* 3 (Nov., 1935), pp. 138-145.

Dun, Thomas I., *From Cairo to Siwa* (Cairo: privately printed, 1933).

El-Baz, Farouk, "Egypt's Desert of Promise", *The National Geographic* 161/2 (Feb., 1982), pp. 190-221.

Ellis, Chris, *Military Transport of World War II* (New York: Macmillan, 1975).

Evans-Pritchard, E.E., *The Sanusi of Cyrenaica* (Oxford: The Clarendon Press, 1954).

Funk & Wagnalls, *Funk & Wagnalls Hammond World Atlas* (New York: Funk & Wagnalls, 1875).

Glubb, John Bagot, *War in the Desert: An R.A.F. Frontier Campaign* (New York: Norton, 1961).

Gordon, John, Jr., "Special Forces for Desert Warfare: British Improvisation, 1915-1943" (unpublished Duke University, Ph.D. dissertation, 1974).

Gordon, John, Jr., *The Other Desert War: British Special Forces in North Africa, 1940-1943* (New York: Greenwood, 1987).

Gower-Collins, Clive, "Raids, Road Watches, and Reconnaissance: An Analysis of the New Zealand Contribution to the Long Range Desert Group in North Africa, 1940-1943" (unpublished Massey University MA thesis, 1999).

Hackett, John W., "The Employment of Special Forces", *The Journal of the Royal United Service Institution* 97 (Feb., 1952), pp. 26-41.

Hackett, John W., *Joint Service Staff Manual: Service Writing* (London: MOD, 1978).

Hassanein, A.M., Bey, "Through Kufra to Darfur", *The Geographical Journal* 64/4 (Oct. 1924), pp. 273-291.

Howe, George F., *Northwest Africa: Seizing the Initiative in the West* (Washington, D.C.: Department of the Army, 1957).

Inchbald, Geoffrey, *Imperial Camel Corps.* (London: Johnson, 1970).

James, Malcolm, *Born of the Desert* (London: Collins 1945).

Jenner, Robert and David List, *The Long Range Desert Group* (London: Osprey, 1983).

Jopling, Frank and Brendan O'Carroll, *Bearded Brigands: The Diaries of Trooper Frank Jopling* (Wellington, N.Z.: Ngaio Press, 2002).

Kay, R.L., *Long Range Desert Group in Libya, 1940-41* (Wellington: Department of Internal Affairs, 1949).

Kay, R.L., *Long Range Desert Group in the Mediterranean* (Wellington: Department of Internal Affairs, 1950).

Ladd, James, *Commandos and Rangers of World War II* (New York: St. Martin's, 1978).

Lewin, Ronald, *Ultra Goes to War* (New York: McGraw-Hill, 1978).

Liddell-Hart, B.H., ed., *The Rommel Papers* (New York: Harcourt, Brace and Co., 1953).

Lodwick, John, *The Filibusters: The Story of the Special Boat Service* (London: Methuen, 1947).

MacLean, Fitzroy, *Escape to Adventure* (Boston: Little, Brown and Co., 1950).

MacMunn, George and Falls, Cyril, *History of the Great War: Military Operations in Egypt and Palestine* (London: HMSO, 1928).

Malcolm, James, *Born of the Desert* (London: Collins, 1945).

Marrinan, Patrick, *Colonel Paddy* (Dungannon, Ireland: Ulster Press, 1968).

Mason, Michael H., *The Paradise of Fools* (London: Hodder and Stoughton, 1936).

Maule, Henry, *Out of the Sand: The Epic Story of General Leclerc and the Fighting Free French* (London: Odhams Books Ltd., 1966).

Morgan, Mike, *Sting of the Scorpion: The Inside Story of the Long Range Desert Group* (Stroud, Gloucestershire: Sutton, 2000).

Murray, G.W., *Dare Me to the Desert* (London: George Allen & Unwin, 1967).

O'Carroll, Brendan, *Kiwi Scorpions; The Story of the New Zealanders in the Long Range Desert Group* (Honiton, Devon: Token Publishing, 2000).

O'Carroll, Brendan, *Barce Raid: The Long Range Desert Group's Greatest Escapade* (Wellington, N.Z.: Ngaio Press, 2005).

Owen, David Lloyd, *The Desert My Dwelling Place* (London: Cassell, 1957).

Owen, David Lloyd, *Providence Their Guide: A Personal Account of the Long Range Desert Group, 1940-1945* (London: Harrap, 1980).

Peniakoff, Vladimir, *Popski's Private Army* (London: Jonathan Cape 1950).

Pittaway J. and G. Fourie, *L.R.D.G. Rhodesia. Rhodesians in the Long Range Desert Group* (Durban, S. Africa, 2002).

Playfair, I.S.O., *The Mediterranean and Middle East* (London: HMSO, 1954-66).

Rolls, S.C., *Steel Chariots in the Desert* (London: Jonathan Cape, 1937).

Roskill, S.W., *The War At Sea* (London: HMSO, 1954-1961).

Roskill, S.W., *White Ensign; The British Navy at War, 1939-1945* (Annapolis, Md.: U.S. Naval Institute, 1966).

Scoones, R.L., "Ford Cars in the Libyan Desert", *The Royal Tank Corps Journal* 14 (Feb., 1933), pp. 255-258.

Shaw, W.B. Kennedy, "An Expedition in the Southern Libyan Desert", *The Geographical Journal* 87 (March, 1936), pp. 193-221.

Shaw, W.B. Kennedy, "Desert Navigation: Some Experiences of the Long Range Desert Group", *The Geographical Journal* 102 (Nov.-Dec., 1943), pp. 253-258.

Shaw, W.B. Kennedy, *Long Range Desert Group: The Story of Its Work in Libya, 1940-1943* (London: Collins, 1945).

Stevens, W.G., *Documents Relating to New Zealand's Participation in the Second World War* (Wellington, Department of Internal Affairs, 1949).

Stevens, W.G., *Official History of New Zealand in the Second World War, 1939-1945: Problems of the 2nd NZEF* (Wellington: Department of Internal Affairs, 1958).

Stevens, W.G., *Bardia to Enfidaville* (Wellington, Department of Internal Affairs, 1962).

Surtees, G., "A Thousand Miles of Desert", *Journal of the Royal United Service Institution* 106 (Nov., 1961), pp. 510-516.

Timpson, Alastair, *In Rommel's Backyard: A Memoir of the Range Desert Group* (Barnsley, South Yorkshire: Leo Cooper, 2000).

TM 30-420, *Handbook on the Italian Military Forces* (Washington, D.C.: War Department, 1943).

TM-E 30-451, *Handbook on German Military Forces* (Washington, D.C.: War Department, 1945).

Topp, Alfred, "Desert Warfare: German Experience in World War II" (European Command, Historical Division, 1952), (Fort Leavenworth, KS: Combat Studies Institute, 1991).

Vincent, Jean-Noël, "Koufra: 23 décembre 1940 – 1er mai 1941", *Revue historique des armeés*, Vol. 1 (1982), pp. 4-19.

Warner, Philip, *The Special Air Service* (London: William Kimber, 1980).

Wavell, A.P., "The Army and the Prophets", *The Journal of the Royal United Service Institution* 75 (Nov., 1930), pp. 665-675.

Wavell, A.P., "The Higher Commander", *The Journal of the Royal United Service Institution* 81 (Feb., 1936), pp. 15-32.

Willet, John, *Popski: A Life of Vladimir Peniakoff* (London: MacGibbon & Kee, 1954).

Wilson, Eric, "Deep Penetration Patrols in the Libyan Desert", *Journal of the United Services Institution of India and Pakistan* 78 (Oct., 1948), pp. 395-401.

Wingate, Orde, "In Search of Zerzura", *The Geographical Journal* 83 (April, 1934), pp. 281-308.

Wright, J.W., "War-Time Exploration with the Sudan Defense Force in the Libyan Desert, 1941-1943", *The Geographical Journal* 105 (March-April, 1945), pp. 99-111.

Wynter, H.W., *Special Forces in the Desert War, 1940-1943* (Richmond, Surrey: Public Record Office, 2001).

Index

INDEX OF PEOPLE

INDEX OF PLACES

INDEX OF MILITARY UNITS

INDEX OF MISCELLANEOUS TERMS